THE WESTERN ALLIANCE

THE

European-American Relations Since 1945

WESTERN ALLIANCE

ALFRED GROSSER
Translated by Michael Shaw
With a Foreword by Stanley Hoffmann

VINTAGE BOOKS
A DIVISION OF RANDOM HOUSE
NEW YORK

First Vintage Books Edition, February 1982
English translation © 1980 by The Continuum Publishing
Corporation.
French edition: *Les Occidentaux. Les pays d'Europe et les Etat-Unis
depuis la guerre*, © 1978 Editions Fayard Paris.
German edition: *Das Bündnis. Die westeuropäischen Länder und
die USA seit dem Krieg*, © 1978 Carl Hanser Verlag München Wein.
All rights reserved under International and Pan-American Copy-
right Conventions. Published in the United States by Random
House, Inc., New York, and simultaneously in Canada by Random
House of Canada Limited, Toronto. Originally published by The
Continuum Publishing Corporation, New York, in 1980.

Library of Congress Cataloging in Publication Data
Grosser, Alfred, 1925-
The Western alliance.
Translation of: Les occidentaux.
Originally published: New York: Continuum, 1980.
Includes bibliographical references and index.
1. Europe—Politics and government—1945-
2. Europe—Foreign relations—United States.
3. United States—Foreign relations—Europe.
4. World politics—1945-
I. Title. [D1058.G7313 1982] 940.55 81-15977
ISBN 0-394-70815-6 AACR2

Manufactured in the United States of America

CONTENTS

FOREWORD

NO ELEMENT of American foreign policy since 1945 has been more important than the relationship between the United States and Western Europe. Ever since the Marshall Plan and the establishment of NATO, the transatlantic partnership has remained, despite all its troubles, an island of stability in a turbulent world. For the West Europeans, whether they see in the American alliance a protection or a factor of domination, it has been a determinant of their own foreign policies, and the United States has played—sometimes as a goad, sometimes as a foil—a major role in the slow but constant progress of West European unification as well.

And yet, despite a wealth of works dealing with separate episodes, and of symposia usually devoted to anxious assessments and worried warnings, no synthesis of U.S.–W. European relations had been written before Alfred Grosser's masterly study, which was published simultaneously in France and in Germany in 1978. A reader of this volume will soon understand both why such a gap existed for so long and why only someone like Alfred Grosser could fill it. The task requires, on the one hand, familiarity with strategic literature, with the data of international economic and monetary affairs, with intergovernmental relations, as well as with the transactions of multinational corporations or private bankers, with the attitudes of politicians, unions, churches, intellectuals, and the media, with the evolution of ideas, and with sudden cultural explosions. It demands, on the other hand, the ability to deal with nations as different as the United States, France, West Germany, Italy, and England. It was necessary to be neither too academic (or else many volumes would have been the outcome) nor too superficial. One had to impose a shape and to find a thread for a welter of events, trends, crises moving in all directions. Obviously, monographs and kaleidoscopic surveys are easier!

Alfred Grosser has now proven that the task could be accomplished. He was uniquely qualified to do so. He has been, for many years, France's leading analyst of postwar Germany, and his works on the Federal Republic are familiar to American readers. He is also a search-

ing and critical student of French foreign policy and politics—his book
(unfortunately not available in English) on the external policies of the
Fourth Republic remains the last word on the subject. As a scholar, as a
journalist and television commentator, as a participant in many conferences, he has written and spoken eloquently about Franco-German
relations (the spectacular improvement of which owe a great deal to
his own efforts since 1945) and also about European-American relations. His concerns with questions of method in social sciences research, and above all with the ethics of political action—subjects to
which he has devoted two books—also prepared him to deal with the
intricacies of writing so complex a study as well as with the controversies inseparable from the unfolding of an alliance that is, for its members, intimate, compelling, and uneven, and that brings together free
societies in which dissent is open and, at times, vociferous.

Alfred Grosser convincingly brings out both the profound changes
since 1945 (and turning points such as 1947 and 1973) and the continuities in the Alliance. His book is of particular importance for American readers. Many American authors (the most famous being Henry
Kissinger) have examined the transatlantic relationship from the viewpoint of the United States. Alfred Grosser, while reviewing American
policies and reactions, focuses on the West Europeans, and particularly on the French and the Germans—and on the persistent differences in these two nations' approaches to the United States. France,
with her determination to reverse the verdict of history in 1940, has
tried to follow a course that would be both as independent of the
United States as circumstances allowed, and aimed at increasing
French power abroad: hence not only the Gaullist attack on U.S. predominance, but also the Franco-American conflict over decolonization
and over German rearmament, under the Fourth Republic. West Germany, on the contrary, has treated the American alliance as essential
for the security of a divided country along the iron curtain, and as the
precondition for, indeed the matrix of, the Federal Republic's recovery of status and influence in world affairs. As Alfred Grosser shows,
this divergence has seriously limited the solidarity of West Europe and
its ability to reduce the weight of American domination (whose nature
he analyzes with the subtlety and fairness one can expect from a man
who is at his best in debunking intellectual clichés and fashions).

The truth of the matter is that U.S.-European relations cannot fail to
be troubled, for three sets of reasons. First, there is a fundamental
unevenness in the strategic situation. West Europe needs the American nuclear guarantee and the presence of American conventional
forces to deter Soviet military aggression, or Soviet political pressures
based on the preponderant might of the USSR. And while the West

Europeans emphasize deterrence—since actual defense, i.e., fighting a war, would mean their destruction—they know that the United States keeps oscillating between a reassuring (but not totally credible) emphasis on deterrence—i.e., treating West Europe as if it were really an extension of the U.S. territory—and advocacy of a strategy of conventional or even tactical nuclear defense, which they dread. Given their dependence on the United States for protection they themselves are bound to oscillate from the fear of being dragged by the United States into conflicts that may be deemed important for American interests but are not seen by the Europeans as their own causes (Vietnam, Israel), to the fear of being abandoned in the (unlikely) case of a U.S. return to isolation or the (more likely) case of U.S.-Soviet collusion or condominium, and to the fear of an American strategy that would not abandon the allies but "decouple" the "Eurostrategic balance" from the nuclear strategic balance between the superpowers.

Secondly, profound but more uneven interdependence in economic matters breed recurrent mutual dissatisfaction with the economic policies followed by the allies. Western Europe, whose share of foreign trade in the GNP is higher than in the United States, has proved to be most susceptible to American inflation and recessions, and of course to American monetary practices, given the role of the dollar in the world monetary system both before and after 1971. Just as the Europeans fear that both an aggressive and a passive America would be dangerous for their security, they resent both an overvalued dollar, whose exchange rate is preserved only by the more or less forcible absorption of a huge quantity of inflation-provoking dollars by the banks of their allies, and an undervalued dollar, which gives an unfair advantage to American exports. But Americans have become somewhat dependent on the state of their allies' economies: low growth rates in Western Europe are bad for U.S. exports and contribute to depressing the American economy, while huge West German trade surpluses are denounced as irresponsible. Both sides of the Atlantic are dependent on OPEC oil—but while this ought to be an incentive to cooperate, it has led to sometimes fierce competition for favors, and once again unevenness contributes to this: even though American imports of energy have risen spectacularly since 1973, the West Europeans' degree of dependence remains higher, and their capacity to absorb OPEC price increases much smaller.

Thirdly, each side keeps worrying about the domestic political performance of the other. And neither side understands very well the functioning of the other's political institutions. The Europeans fret about Imperial America when the "imperial Presidency" is unchecked, and about the decline of American leadership or the lack of

American resolve when the constitutional set of checks and balances recovers from the Congressional abdication characteristic of (hot or cold) war periods, and when the national consensus breaks down. The Americans find the complexities and rigidities of EEC decision-making exasperating, lament the flaws of weak parliamentary regimes (such as Italy's or the French Fourth Republic) and worry both about the presence of Communist parties (which not even prosperity can dislodge, despite simple-minded predictions made at the time one celebrated, here, the coming "end of ideology") and about the rise of Eurocommunism: phenomena whose own complexities, antecedents, contradictions, and prospects are most imperfectly understood on this side of the Atlantic.

And yet, as Alfred Grosser shows, the Alliance lasts, despite upheavals and uncertainties, for it rests on three pillars. There is the pillar of defense: while Europe could not protect its political independence and territorial integrity without America, all American administrations have acknowledged the vital American interest in a Western Europe that is neither Sovietized nor Finlandized. There is the economic pillar: with Japan, the United States and Western Europe are the core of the open, capitalist international economy, which all of them have a stake in preserving from the kinds of shocks that could lead to a return to protectionism or hostile monetary blocs. Finally, there is a pillar that is more political and cultural: not only is there a similarity of regimes—this, indeed, plus Japan, *is* the free world, an expression much abused when applied to petty tyrannies that happen to be America's clients in Latin America or Asia—but there are common values and traditions that bind Western Europe to a superpower whose population, institutions, and political thought are predominantly of European origin. A commonality of institutions and values means, in this instance, a double challenge. On the one hand, and especially at a time when many of what the sociologist Michel Crozier calls the traditional "social controls" that insured order, deference, or discipline are crumbling, and when the reliance on economic growth and Keynesian verities is faltering, all the members of the Alliance face serious tensions between their political institutions and their societies, unresolved problems of economic policy, a crisis of the welfare state, and occasional violence from determined ideological or ethnic minorities. On the other hand, their common values, as well as those nations' position as the leading capitalist industrial societies, and as countries with a colonial past, mean that both the United States and Western Europe will face, in the future, not only the continuing challenge of a Soviet Union whose military might keeps growing, but also that of developing countries which form the vast majority of the United Nations and whose demands, even if they are often presented in extreme ideological terms, cannot be brushed aside forever.

Neither with respect to East-West relations, nor insofar as energy, or other commodities, or the Arab-Israeli conflict, or the racial powder-keg in Southern Africa are concerned, is there perfect harmony between the United States and Western Europe, or within Western Europe, or between political forces within a given country. But these are the kinds of issues that *Les Occidentaux* (to use the French title of this book) will have to face together. The great merit of Alfred Grosser's work is to help us appreciate how far we have come, and understand better both the obstacles to harmony and the limits of discord.

STANLEY HOFFMANN

INTRODUCTION

AN EAST-WEST conference, a world monetary system, a nuclear umbrella, an energy problem, U.S. troops in Berlin, agricultural overproduction, linguistic penetration, scientific cooperation, anti-Communism, North-South conferences, the flow of information of all kinds . . . this motley inventory could be extended at will if one wished to indicate the multiform and massive presence of the United States in the most diverse spheres of European life and thought.

To see clear in this dense tangle of reciprocal relations, one must prune and order. One must also look back to see how these relations—whether between the United States and Europe as a whole, between the United States and individual European countries, or between sectors of the American economy and society and the corresponding sectors of one or several European countries—really came about.

In so doing, one encounters a number of difficulties. What individual and especially collective actors should one take an interest in? How does one grasp the changes and the constants in the periods which are most indispensable to an understanding of the present, the decades since the end of the Second World War?

What do the Western European countries mean to us? The borders themselves are arbitrary. Except where the Soviet Union, Poland, or Czechoslovakia plays a role in the relations between the United States and that part of Europe that concerns us here, we will leave aside what is commonly called Eastern Europe.

But Western Europe does not constitute a unity. It is no actor though it is true that it is no mere collocation of national political entities either. For on the one hand, transnational communities of an economic and psychological kind existed long before 1945. The ideological disputes that the crisis-ridden United States gave rise to in England and Germany around 1930 did not differ significantly from those in France. The slide toward the Left in the Europe of 1945 was almost general and also affected the image of the United States. Although the problem of decolonization presented itself neither in the same way nor at the xiv ───────────────────────────────────── INTRODUCTION

same time for Belgium, Great Britain, the Netherlands, and France, the policy of the American government nonetheless pursued similar aims in all four cases and they can therefore not be treated as separate and purely national matters. And doesn't the economic crisis which has been emerging since 1974 preoccupy all European countries, however widely their particular responses may vary?

But it is also true that Western Europe is more than a merely conceptual concatenation of individual countries, for it has lived through many forms of organized, institutionalized interdependence for the last thirty years. From the founding of the Organization for European Economic Cooperation in 1948 and of the European Payments Union in 1950 to the European Economic Community—which came into being in 1957, was enlarged in 1973, and temporarily even emerged as a single actor vis-à-vis the United States during the tariff negotiations in 1962—there existed and continues to exist (though one cannot say "increasingly") a configuration called "Europe" with special relations with its powerful partner on the far side of the Atlantic. And in the eyes of many American political and business leaders, but principally in the eyes of countries in Eastern Europe or in other regions of the world, all of which observe its development and its conduct toward the superpower American with hope or concern, Western Europe exists as a first step toward a unified whole.

It is clear nonetheless that the various Western European countries are also many independent entities and that it would not be admissible to treat them as a homogeneous complex. But neither can one give each of them the same weight or place. Some will be dealt with at greater length than others. The reader should know from the very beginning what order of rank has been established here and what the subjective and objective reasons for such a classification are.

At the head are two "superprivileged" countries, France and West Germany. It is pointless to try to hide the fact that the author's personal circumstances have something to do with this. As a Frenchman who wrote this book in French and has written others dealing with problems of French foreign and domestic policy under the Fourth and Fifth Republics, it is only natural that he should devote special attention to France. As someone who knows Germany and has specialized in German postwar history and is aware that this book will be published simultaneously in the two languages, he could not avoid also treating Germany at length.

But can he not claim in good faith that even a Peruvian or Japanese author would have had to accord primary importance to those same countries? During the last quarter-century, they have not only been the two centers of gravity in the history of Western Europe but also the two extreme instances of the various situations and forms of conduct in relations with the United States. General de Gaulle against Franklin D. Roosevelt and then against Harry S. Truman; Pierre Mendès-France against John Foster Dulles in the controversies over Indochina and the European Defense Community; the furious anti-Americanism at the time of the Suez and Algeria crises; the foreign policy of the Fifth Republic which is based on the idea of an independence that must be preserved or established vis-à-vis the big ally; the denunciation of American imperialism by a powerful Left: the most acute transatlantic antagonisms were and still are those between the French and the Americans.

The preponderant U.S. influence on a West Germany that had initially been reduced to the status of an object; the birth of the Federal Republic as the child of the Cold War and twin sister of the Atlantic Pact; a foreign policy based on the trust that was placed in the American leadership and the reciprocal trust that would have to be instilled in that leadership; the creation of an ideological community against the threat from the east as a more urgent priority than the restoration of national unity; the continuing desire never to neglect the transatlantic dimension of European problems; the acceptance of a limited political role combined with an ever increasing economic weight which produced, whether one wanted it or not, a political power which paradoxically became greater than that of those countries that were more concerned with their rank: all this certainly makes the Federal Republic an extreme case, the precise opposite of France, while both countries also constitute the core of a Europe about to be born.

Great Britain is also a privileged actor, though not at the same level. The author lived through the development of France and Germany as an observing participant and participating observer. He believes he knows the realities in both countries from personal experience. But although language presents no significant obstacle, his firsthand knowledge is superficial. And while he feels no need to apologize for his scholarship, it is also true that it lacks the thoroughness of his sustained familiarity with French and German documents.

Nor is Great Britain objectively as central to our subject as the two "super-privileged" countries discussed here. It is not therefore less important, however. With the support of an electorate that is very homogenous in this respect, the British leadership wanted for years to understand transatlantic relations as a game à trois in which Great Britain, in agreement with the United States but anxiously intent on its independence and together with a more or less cohesive Western Europe, was to occupy a special place.

A definition of Western Europe without Great Britain would be absurd, and in all spheres of European relations with the United States, the British are very much a presence. But we will discover that this presence has often been peripheral.

Although less privileged, Italy too is studied fairly systematically here. Initially less of a pure object than Germany but also a stake of lesser value and then a partner of lesser status, it is yet one of the great powers of Western Europe, a consequence both of its demographic and economic weight and of the foreign policy repercussions its internal conflicts give rise to. The author very much regrets having only a limited knowledge of the language and no very precise personal insight into Italian society and political life. But he has endeavored to enlarge his analytical resources by reading and by contacts with Italians.

The other countries appear only in those situations which especially concern them at a given moment or in a particular issue as, for example, the Netherlands and Belgium, which are mentioned with some regularity, while Greece is primarily referred to when it becomes the scene of a struggle in which the United States participates, as at the beginning of the period examined here. Portugal, on the other hand, makes an appearance only toward the end. The Scandinavian countries are mentioned only occasionally, and Switzerland and Austria more rarely still. Is it necessary to apologize for this? Does it have to be explained at this point? It should suffice if the reasons for this limited presentation are given wherever appropriate.

Why am I constantly using the term "countries"? Could one not more simply call them "states"? This would certainly be closer to current usage but could give rise to misunderstanding, for one might then believe that the actors in this game are only states as embodied in their governments, the governments being limited to decisions and conduct in the outside world.

But this is not sufficient for the author, although his ambition to investigate the nature of the relations between the states and governments over a more than thirty-year span may already appear excessive. Participants, actors, are also those forces which, whether organized or not, affect those who make or believe they make decisions on behalf of national entities. Since the subject of this book is not U.S. foreign policy, we will largely disregard the impact American domestic politics has had on it and will not spend much time examining the changes the foreign policy or domestic politics of European countries could produce in American domestic politics except when, as in the case of McCarthyism, for example, the development in the United States as triggered by events in Europe reacted back on European attitudes, either by the detour of U.S. foreign policy or, more directly, by the imitation effect the internal hardening in the United States produced in this or that European country.

But we will concern ourselves with the role the United States played either through its actions or its image in the domestic politics of Germany, France, and above all, Italy, for in Italian political life, foreign policy is perhaps more than elsewhere a mere weapon in internal conflicts.

To the greatest possible extent, we will try to avoid generalizations or simplifications as we discuss the national actors. At a given moment, "France" certainly means the government which legitimately and in the name of all the French addresses the outside world. It may even refer to a single individual if he sets the course, sees himself as the incarnation of the nation, and, what is more important, is judged such by the other participants. But at the same moment, France also means a given opposition party, a current of opinion, a union, an industry in direct contact with the government of the United States, one of its agencies, or an American entity of the same nature.

But do we have the right to deal now with one factor of the development, now with another, with one actor in the game of nations at one moment, and with another at a different time? Is it not rather our duty to select a particular kind of relationship, one specific element of the analysis, such as economic phenomena?

Certainly not. On the contrary, we will see how closely the various levels of reality are interdependent, indeed to what extent their significance can change at various times and in various situations. The entire last part of this book will demonstrate that in the early 1970s economics attained a status among explanatory factors which it certainly lacked before that time.

To consistently make economics the pervasive and fundamental explanatory factor is not scientific but an act of faith of which it can be said at the very least that it hardly does justice to the tragic realities of our century. Did Hitler's rise have economic causes? Certainly, but similar causes "produced" a Roosevelt, and that was surely not the same thing politically. And Hitler in power did not mean from the very beginning that the economic crisis and the support of industrialists would lead to the absolute will to war, let alone the "final solution" Auschwitz symbolizes.

But is it really necessary to discuss this act of faith at length, since today it is rejected even by those who once ardently affirmed it? And this rejection has already turned into the refusal to see the true role of economic power in the rise of political power: for the French Communist Party, for example, the Soviet Union continues to be an economic and social model while its political system is rejected as an historical accident or the product of a pre-revolutionary society.

Of course, a relatively simple theory of the relationship between economics and politics would be necessary if one wished to arrive at a well-ordered and systematic interpretation of reality. But we believe that such a theory cannot be had, especially as regards foreign policy. Not because the phenomena of domination and dependence are not realities but because so many dimensions of interpretation depend on evaluations the actors or analysts themselves make, or even on circumstances of time and place. The United States confronted with the temporarily seriously weakened Europe of 1947; the United States confronted with a Central America that lacks any sort of technical, administrative, or political resources: the inequality of economic power certainly does not always have identical consequences. Don't security and prosperity constitute positive compensations for imposed limitations on political action? And to what extent do those who imposed them see such limitations as measures that were *desired* rather than undergone?

But international economic power, it will be correctly objected, increasingly includes private enterprises with multinational subsidiaries. Their economic role can be analyzed, though the conclusions (and even the raw data) will vary considerably with the different authors of the countless books on this topic. But what about their political function—not in Guatemala but in Europe? And how does the large enterprise define itself as an actor in relation to the national state which is another? Marcel Dassault (or Friedrich Flick) as embodiments of capitalist power? Mirage jet fighters as the corresponding embodiment of the French state vis-à-vis the outside world? Both interpretations are certainly simultaneously true, but this simultaneity raises certain problems. That also applies, for example, to Péchiney as the excessively powerful giant enterprise and one of the damnable multinationals, and Péchiney as the firm which creates employment and earns foreign exchange, both of them essential because there are American competitors.

If one does not wish to see reality in a simplifying, dogmatic perspective, the principal difficulty is that the debate on the significance and nature of economic factors becomes itself part of the subject. For the disputes about relations with the United States which the French, Germans, and Italians have been carrying on for the last thirty years largely turn on the question of how the political consequences of an uncontested economic inequality are to be interpreted.

In particular, we will have to ask ourselves time and again: What is the true nature of the complex and shifting realities hidden in such terms as "power" and "domination"? The power of whom to make whom do what and when? Through what deliberately exerted compulsion? Through what unintentional influence? And what about the very real power of the weak over the strong, especially when the latter, in order to remain strong vis-à-vis a third, himself needs the support of the weak and must therefore support him?

Much depends on the view the actors themselves take of necessities, constraints, and dependences. In 1950, France needed American aid to continue the Indochina war. But this need and the constraints it created existed only because it was considered essential to maintain French rule in Hanoi. In 1956, Guy Mollet and Anthony Eden did not realize that the preservation of domestic prosperity in France and Great Britain was an imperative for them, while Nasser did not have to pay much attention to the misery of his fellahs, which was great in any case. They noticed too late that they were therefore much more dependent on the United States than was their enemy, that John Foster Dulles was consequently more interested in mollifying Nasser than in supporting them, his allies, of whom he was sure in any event. The German refusal to criticize American policy in Vietnam, on the other hand, derived from an underestimation of the necessity for the United States to defend the Federal Republic, come what may.

We touch upon a central problem of political analysis here. Two levels of reality must always be considered: there is the more or less material factor which can be detached and described, and there are the ideas the actors in the political game have of this factor and which are themselves an element whose consequences are often more important than the first. To understand French foreign policy and the attitudes of the great majority of the French toward the United States, it is more important to know what people in France imagined and still imagine about the Yalta Conference, however little that idea may have to do with the course that conference did in fact take. It is useful to study the conduct of the French Communist Party (PCF), but American policy toward France is always based on a certain conception of the PCF which assuredly does not invariably correspond to the reality such a study would uncover.

We therefore must include the convictions of the actors to the greatest possible extent, and that means the conviction of those in government, of the leading circles, and of that rather diffuse, almost undefinable force which is called public opinion. Politicians obviously do not believe everything they say, but it would be distorting reality to take them for pure cynics who are not caught up in reality themselves. They have acquired their view of things through individual or collective experience. Roosevelt saw Germany through the spectacles of a negative idea he had formed as a young man during a stay in that country. All the members of the French leadership class have passed through a kind of basic schooling which presents France as the center of the world and the axis of history. The United States is more than what is shown in American films that criticize that society. But the image millions of Europeans have of the United States and the foreign policy reactions this image gives rise to rest significantly on the content of such films.

Does this mean that we must investigate every conceivable nexus, from the biographies of countless ministers to the influence of pop music on the relations between states? There can be no question of that, of course. But it is important for both author and reader to always keep in mind this dimension of all rational analysis, particularly since both author and reader have their own system of ideas and convictions which they should be aware of.

The interpretations of reality by the actors themselves are important not only where they concern direct relations between Europeans and Americans. The idea Europeans have of third countries or of third continents may also play a significant role in their relations with the United States. The difference of opinion on transatlantic relations that has existed for the last thirty years between the majority of the French and the majority of the Germans has less to do with a difference of opinion about the United States than it does with two rather divergent conceptions of the nature of the Soviet Union. And we will see that the evolution of the Catholic Church introduced a significant change into our story when the Second Vatican Council analyzed world events and shifted the accent from the East-West to the North-South division. This modified not only the relative importance of Czechoslovakia and Chile but also the European image of the United States.

We have just given two examples, the first of which evokes constancy, the second change. To see constancy or to see change are two opposing temptations in the study of modes of conduct over time. Based on the observation that the countries treated remain identical throughout the entire period under consideration and that fundamental situations persist, one might make a kind of horizontal cut which is what sociologists and contemporary historians of remote eras do when they view societies and power relations as largely unchanging over many decades. Or one might proceed step by step and report the stages of an evolution, the development through a succession of events each one of which constitutes a break in continuity, and this is the more common method.

The difficulty which arises when one wishes to do justice to reality lies in the circumstance that both procedures must be combined. Discontinuity and continuity (in the twofold sense of constancy and seamless evolution) coexist side by side, especially because the breaks in the development are variously perceived by the actors and the observers. When the SPD initially came to power in Bonn in 1966 as a CDU partner in a coalition and sent its man into the Chancellor's office in 1969, people in Germany considered this an important turning point and a significant change in foreign policy as well. But I will show why I believe that decisive changes in German foreign policy occurred as early as 1961, and that continuity has been predominant since that time.

Secondly, they coexist because duration varies with the aspect of reality that is given priority. Socially experienced time is not the same in various kinds of phenomena. De Gaulle's return to power in 1958 and the transition from the Fourth to the Fifth Republic undoubtedly constituted a break in French political life and differed in more than one respect in their effects on Franco-American relations. The industrialization of France and its consequences for its foreign relations, on the other hand, occurred less suddenly, more slowly and continuously with high points both before and subsequent to 1958. And if one attempts to insert this date into the continuity of so significant a phenomenon as decolonization, it seems in retrospect a mere tremor amid the entire and certainly not unruffled development extending from the French Indochina action in 1945 to the withdrawal from Algeria in 1962.

The coexistence of continuity and discontinuity finally expresses itself in the intertwining of constancy and change. Compared to 1945, the world has profoundly changed, especially as regards the place continents other than Europe and North America occupy today. And where can one still find similarities between the destroyed, politically and economically nonexistent Germany of that time and today's two prosperous and respected German states? Yet the question whether the United States is or is not interested in the creation of an economically integrated Europe is not being raised in fundamentally different terms. And the cut across the heart of Europe and through Germany has since 1947 been a constant and essential element of global politics, particularly transatlantic relations.

The elements of permanence are so numerous that repetitions cannot be avoided. The United States refuses to admit that it engages in a policy of protective tariffs which is difficult to reconcile with its demand for liberalization by its allies. And this is an observation that applies validly to 1948, 1962, and 1978. Great Britain plays the trump called "the community of English-speaking peoples," and this is as true today as it was thirty or thirty-five years ago. In their relations with the United States, the French tend to compensate for a sense of economic inferiority by a feeling of politically weighty cultural superiority. This specific permanent feature has its origin in the time between the two world wars, or perhaps as far back as the nineteenth century. And finally, the dollar has been the decisive element in the economic life of the European countries since 1945 at least.

The temptation to assign a dominant place to elements of permanence and to dismiss changes as peripheral phenomena is therefore considerable. But this is a temptation not to be succumbed to, for otherwise the sin of anachronism becomes almost inevitable. The United States: the only true superpower in the Western world? This was undoubtedly already true in 1945 as regards all things that can be measured, but the political reality was different and the position of Great Britain was not as secondary as one might be tempted to assume in retrospect. Decolonization: the evident fundamental characteristic of the entire epoch? To make that assumption would be to overlook the large role the twofold image of an America that was both anti-colonialist and imperialist has played and continues to play in transatlantic relations.

One always writes for a specific public. But some publics are less homogeneous than others. Although children differ in terms of taste and milieu, a schoolbook always addresses itself to a specific age group in a specific country. A historian of antiquity writes to make better known a certain period about which his readers have more or less extensive theoretical knowledge but which none of them has lived through.

Our enterprise encounters two principal difficulties, one of which is common to all works of contemporary history: it can be assumed that some of the facts are known to those readers who attained political consciousness or at least were reading newspapers during the years considered here. But when I lecture on French or German foreign policy during the postwar era at the Paris Institute for Political Studies, I must always remind myself that my students were born in the late 1950s and attended elementary school when the Berlin Wall was built and the war in Algeria ended.

Must one therefore write as if even the older reader's knowledge were hardly any greater? The answer is largely *yes*. So often, we are dealing with partial knowledge and hazy recollection, and this not just among highly educated persons but even among experts in the social sciences. Too much is therefore better than too little. As best I can, I shall try to avoid allusions—though that is hardly possible in a book that does not want to be a report but a synthesis.

The second difficulty is more complex and perhaps even more difficult of solution, though also much more stimulating. As I write this, I know that my book will appear in France, in Germany, and in the United States. The problem here is similar to the one created by different age groups: How does one avoid boring one reader with information which another needs? De Gaulle and Pétain: in France, debate on this has become so extensive that even younger people can be presumed to know the facts. But what does even the educated German or American reader know about this matter unless he has a special interest in France? The Parliamentary Council which created the institutions of the German Federal Republic, its particular nature and mode of functioning are probably known to the German reader but they are certainly unfamiliar to his French or American counterpart. Here also, I shall try to avoid allusions, yet not provide an excessive amount of elementary information which would bore some of the readership.

But what is most important in a work of this kind is the basic orientation. The author certainly strives for objectivity, which means that he tries to sympathetically understand the human beings and trends of all countries and checks himself constantly as he selects his facts so that he may avoid making only those choices which his own unavoidable political and moral preferences dictate.

But he would also like to swim against the tide as he usually does, which means that he will present his reader with unfamiliar truths, that he will induce him to question a perspective which, in international relations, is usually determined by his respective nationality. But how does one proceed in the attempt to simultaneously make it clear to the French reader that his anti-Americanism ignores entire spheres of reality, to the American reader that French anti-Americanism has more than merely psychological causes, to the German reader that his ability to criticize the United States has been significantly eroded by the particular situation of his country?

There probably is no perfectly satisfactory answer, but the reader should know that the author did not experience these contradictory demands as an oppressive constraint but rather as an exceptionally stimulating challenge, the challenge to take full account of the legitimacy of all points of view, to dissect without wounding, to show the weaknesses here without nourishing self-satisfaction somewhere else.

We will thus attempt to tell a complicated story in simple words, to clearly analyze tangled situations, and to illuminate against a historical background an ensemble of relationships which weigh heavily on the fate of each German, each Frenchman, each Englishman, and perhaps each American.

In spite of serious inadequacies, this will force us to alternately play the role of sociologist, strategist, economist, and psychologist. But this does not disturb us excessively. If one waited for total competence before presenting a synthetic view, one would never get beyond that limited and piecemeal understanding of reality which is the spawning ground from which all incomprehension and all artificial antagonisms grow.

CONCERNING THE NOTES

The author would be pleased if his book reached two kinds of audience: first, the "large public" (even if in terms of numbers it should remain small) which takes an interest in the substance of the book but none in how it was written or what its ramifications might be. These readers should know that they have no obligation whatever to read the notes at the back. They contain neither additional information nor further explanations.

The notes are meant for a second public of students, teachers, and researchers to whom the author is obliged to show his sources and to justify his method. He may also have the ambition to help them in their work by opening paths or perhaps even new perspectives. They will also find there occasional critical comments on the listed works (instead of an exhaustive bibliography, which must always be controversial in so broad and many-sided a subject).

The works not mentioned were either intentionally omitted because the author considers them uninteresting or dated, or because he was ignorant enough to overlook them. He bears sole responsibility for that ignorance, for he found himself in the fortunate situation of having constant access to the library of the Fondation Nationale des Sciences Politiques in Paris, the richest, most complete French library for contemporary history and the social sciences. There is perhaps no other library in Europe so ready to acquire books from foreign countries—a fact that invalidates (if only partially) one of the themes of this study, which is that in France the realities of the outside world are ignored.

PART ONE

From One Alliance
to Another

1 NO YEAR ZERO

On May 8, 1945, the German surrender ends the war in Europe. The devastation is so considerable, the upheavals of all kinds so extensive that it is natural and legitimate to see this day as a turning point and the year of the Allied victory over Hitler's Germany as the beginning of a new era. Indeed, the break with the prewar period seems even more marked than in 1918. This time, Germany has ceased to exist as a sovereign state. France and Italy change their political systems. Instead of the distant rumbling of the October Revolution, there is the massive presence of Soviet power. Instead of a relative and vaguely sensed decline of Europe vis-a-vis the United States, we now see the spectacular rise of the American ally or adversary to the pinnacle of world power.

Yet one must guard against the temptation to view this particular moment of historical discontinuity as if it were a truly absolute break, as if, to use a term frequently applied to the extreme represented by Germany, 1945 were indeed "Year Zero." For in the relations to the United States and in other domains of reality, there exist at least two kinds of continuity which, if misunderstood, would not only falsify the view of developments directly following the war but of the entire subsequent evolution as well.

For one thing, the end of the war was far from being a kind of smooth transition from the military to the political. The interconnection of developments on various levels and in various regions of the world contradicts such an appealing simplification. The year 1945 was admittedly a time of reorientation in the relations between the United States and the USSR, but it did not represent a break in a development whose starting and terminal points are really 1941 and 1949. Profound upheavals in Italy's internal structure and international role set in in 1943. For Greece, 1945 seems almost secondary, since long before the German capitulation and for a long time thereafter, the civil war there first overlay and then replaced the external war. May 8, 1945, is a date of no particular consequence in the history of the political struggle General de Gaulle waged against his American ally, in which he fought for the recognition of his own representative role and for the international status of his country after the war. And in other parts of the world, as in Indonesia and Indochina, for example, the struggle of European countries to maintain or reëstablish their domination also began much earlier and did not end until after the German and even the Japanese surrender of September 2, 1945. There is the additional factor that a more or less distant past, especially the era between the two wars, was much more of an element during the period after the Second World War than it often seems, and this is equally relevant to an understanding of situations and attitudes.

THE WEIGHT OF THE PAST

It is even true for the beginnings, that is to say, the independence, of the United States, for, in retrospect, its meaning for the various countries with their own respective historical experience was by no means the same.

For the Americans, the victory over Great Britain was and continues to be that of a colony which emancipated itself from colonial rule. This gave rise to a feeling of anti-colonialist solidarity whose importance during the entire Second World War and postwar period will become apparent. But another, possibly exaggerated but significant interpretation is possible: confronted with the mother country, the colonists seceded after having first displaced the native inhabitants. George Washington's situation would then be comparable to General Salan's in his rebellion against de Gaulle rather than to Ahmed Ben Bella's or Colonel Boumedienne's: the Franco-American conflict over Algeria which erupted in 1955 was of course not based on this kind of comparison, but the foreshortened and analogy-creating perspective in which Americans see their past will play a role of some consequence.

For the French, the birth of the United States, in which they had a hand, has for the last two hundred years—and more especially since France's relative decline—been evocative of that flattering situation where power relationships are reversed. Celebrating the friendship between Lafayette and Washington is to one's liking, for it places the United States in the role of a debtor and thus allows for more sympathy than does mention of the Marshall Plan. We will discover that this has been a continuing aspect of French attitudes in the years since the Second World War. The American Declaration of Independence of July 4, 1776, proclaimed the rights and freedoms of individuals and nations. A violent revolution neither preceded nor followed it: the enemy was external. The French Declaration of the Rights of Man and Citizen of August 26, 1789, on the other hand, continued to be associated in people's minds with the storming of the Bastille and the revolutionary violence of the years thereafter. While the texts of the two declarations resemble each other in many respects, and although the later was influenced by the earlier, the differing contexts of their origin gave rise to frictions which are still very much with us.

In republican France, the Revolution has a positive meaning. Most Frenchmen of the twentieth century consider themselves the children of the France of that time, and thus heirs of the revolution which simultaneously gave birth to dictatorial rule and to freedom. The Russian October Revolution could more easily appear as the heir of the French Revolution—the attack on the Winter Palace being compared to the storming of the Bastille—than was the case in countries where the first stirrings of freedom invoked the American Constitution, for in them liberation was not or no longer associated with revolutionary violence. This is particularly true of republican Germany. I do not mean the Germany of the first half of the nineteenth century, which viewed the United States and revolutionary France as two equally stimulating models, but rather that of the first half of the twentieth century, to which revolution meant something which the Social Democrats fortunately managed to suppress in 1919. When, on the day before the decisive Reichstag vote on Hitler's Enabling Act on March 23, 1933, the great liberal newspaper *Vossische Zeitung* wanted to show how significant a break the proposed law constituted, it identified July 4, 1776, as the beginning of a civilization founded on freedom and equality. Alexis de Tocqueville was French; Karl Marx was German. But probably since 1917, a different conception of revolution has permitted Marxism to gain a firmer foothold in a France that invoked 1789, while in Germany it strengthened the idea of a democracy born of the spirit of 1776.

But one must guard against excessive simplification. In nineteenth-century Europe, the image of the United States was rich in contrasts and nowhere the same. Sometimes, this was due to the fact that one group or another changed its politics on this or that side of the Atlantic: one need only think of the shifting relations between the American and British Left since the middle of the last century.[1] But more frequently it was because, as early as the first half of the nineteenth century, stereotypes had come into existence which still prevail today: America the paradise, the democratic virtues of America, the rootlessness and lack of culture of America. And similarly, there is the two-sided image of economic reality: on the one hand, America is presented as the land where the "dollar is God," an expression we already encounter in Stendhal: "Money is the God of the United States, as 'gloire' is that of France." But "the moment we want to discover an example of the practical application of large discoveries that are so useful to the industrial progress and thus the well-being of nations, we are obliged to turn our attention to the United States of America."[2] Depending on milieu and conditions, one or the other view will prevail in France, Germany, or Great Britain.

Of course, the dimensions changed during and after the First World War when the United States first intervened militarily on the European continent and then played an important role in the political and financial arrangements of the postwar period. The ambiguities of the epoch already prefigured and put their stamp on those of America's second intervention and its consequences.

American soldiers, matériel, and credits contributed significantly to the victory. But the country had entered the war late. When American troops reached the front, France had already undergone three years of invasion and disturbingly severe losses. Wouldn't America's resources, increased rather than diminished by the war, necessarily confer the leadership role on the United States, now that the joint conflict was over?

But had it really been joint? Had the Allies fought for an identical cause? The irritating problem of war debts which recurred so persistently in so many speeches of American senators between 1919 and 1932, and still occasionally as late as the 1960s, was closely connected with this question. Not that anyone wished to revive the inverse precedent of the eighteenth century where after the War of Independence Congress had refused to settle the debts owed the king of France.[3] The question now was why the credits advanced should be laboriously repaid since after the common victory the creditor was reaping the benefits from the blood the English, and especially the French, had shed in such abundance. And if the comparison of money and blood were rejected, it simply meant that there had been no common cause, that the United States had waged the war in its own interest. In that case, the idea of gratitude for its intervention became meaningless. "What an injustice if now, after the money to clothe our soldiers has been lent us, we should be asked to repay the price plus interest for every single coat in which they died." Both in 1925 and in 1929, plans for the settlement of debts invariably provided occasion for sarcastic comments even when parliamentary majorities had agreed to whatever arrangements had been made.[4] And such parliamentary majorities did not always come about. One need only recall that Harriot's government was brought down in 1932 because it wanted to resume payments to the United States.

In spite of the homage paid Woodrow Wilson—especially by the parties on the Left, which saw the American President as the defender of right and freedom and the adversary of chauvinism and the spirit of revenge—the idea of a community in peace as there had been in war did not prevail. Yet embryonically at least, this idea had been realized during the conflict, particularly in regard to supplies and their transport by sea. A French-British-Italian body, the Inter-Allied Maritime Commission, had been formed in London. Its French member was Jean Monnet, a young man of twenty-nine. His activity was based on two elements, the first being the discovery of the "gigantic possibilities of common action"[5] when a few individuals can cooperate without having to bother too much with a cumbersome national administrative apparatus. And in a letter he sent his minister on November 2, 1918, he identified the second, which was a theory concerning the usefulness the principle of joint action had for the poorer partner: "The present organization has replaced the principle of the ownership of goods and means of transport by that of the satisfaction of recognized needs. But France has needs rather than anything else and would therefore find itself in the position of a beggar [after the war] ... when everybody once again insists on his freedom. But if things remain as they are, it will continue to find itself in the position of a partner who may lay claim to a satisfaction of his needs."[6]

As a matter of fact, common structures and their opportunities were hardly noticed at the time: transatlantic solidarity did nothing to mitigate the straits in which France found itself. It had been assumed in that country that the reparations of the vanquished would bring relief. But Germany was exhausted and in a state of chaos besides. How was it to be dealt with? Already during the peace-treaty negotiations, the American delegation had been unwilling to go along with the British and French proposals regarding the extent of the reparations to be demanded of Germany. The American delegate to the Paris Peace Conference, John Foster Dulles, thirty-one years old at the time, had wanted to avoid burdening Germany with moral guilt and leaving the amount of reparations payments unspecified.[7] During subsequent years, and in harmony with this stand, he proved an advocate of an overall solution which would put an end to the absurd game played by France, a country which had to be all the more demanding of Germany as it needed German funds to repay its own war debts to the United States.

The solution actually arrived at was even more absurd: the United States was to lend Germany money so that it might meet French demands and thus enable France in turn to fulfill its obligations to the United States. But since Germany did not pay much, and France even less, American credits were the only concrete element in this curious triangular arrangement. But these credits were not government credits. The significant turning point of 1924, when the great German inflation came to an end, was the massive intervention of banks: in no time at all, the American share of loans to Germany in October 1924 was underwritten by more than 1,100 banks. What concerned American bankers was to make the most favorable possible investments— and this at the insistence of British bankers, who were acting from political motives,[8] leading circles in England having recognized a little while earlier how extensively their impoverished country had become dependent on an America that had grown rich. The consequence was that they tried to make indirect use of American wealth.

Beginning in 1924, American banks and firms made massive investments in Germany, particularly in the iron and steel industries. Some of the men who would play leading roles in American foreign policy some twenty years later, particularly vis-à-vis a Germany that had again lost a war, entered into close relationships with German industrialists and were quite familiar with their view of things. It was then that Germany's economic development became dependent on American wealth. The fact that the world economic crisis of 1929 so promptly affected Germany can be explained by the withdrawal of short-term investments which were repatriated to the United States to cover losses incurred in the stock market crash. Transatlantic interdependence was there for all to see. But a variety of interpretations could be advanced for it.

As early as the 1920s, the idea of crisis had been at the center of European political and intellectual debate. The shock of the war had given rise to the conviction that beyond the bloody conflict between nations an entire civilization had failed. Because of its newly acquired power, Europeans had become more conscious of the United States, which—sometimes as model but more frequently as repellent example—also became part of the debate.

On the extreme Right, the theme of a "young" America, closer to the young Italian and German nations than to the old, "decadent" France and England, was discussed along with that of "plutocracy." It must not be forgotten that Italian Fascism and German National Socialism began their fight on two fronts: against "international" Marxism and against the no less international "big capitalism," and in this process American society became the perfect incarnation of the rule of capital manipulated by the few. The giant corporation and the department store emerged as the two dragons that had to be slain if the craftsmen, shop owners, and all the "little people" were to be saved whose traditional occupations constituted the lifeblood of a nation made up of "estates" not of antagonistic classes. And where were the large banks and big industry bigger than in the United States?

Quality versus quantity; individual expression versus the total loss of individuality: these were points of contact between the extreme Right and moderate conservatism. A kind of mass production that suppresses all individual development, a life rhythm exclusively directed toward a form of production that kills all joy in life and thought; barbarism in the name of a universal well-being wholly based on material goods: in the effort to denounce the American reality which was being experienced in Europe as the foretaste of a threatening future, this one theme was played in all its variations. A book like Georges Duhamel's *America the Menace,* a bestseller in France in 1930, presented a vision of America that confirmed the fears of the reader attached to what was lasting in French society. And if the epicenter of the storm felt in France lay on the other side of the Atlantic, one was all the more justified in denouncing social change, particularly since in so doing one was defending the culture of the weaker against the lack of culture of the stronger, a theme which had already been developed in an anti-American outburst of Thomas Mann's during the First World War[9] and which will recur like a leitmotif throughout this book.

After 1930, the crisis exacerbated the criticism, since now not even success could justify the castigated evils. An order was disintegrating or, more precisely, the economic and social order in which one had lived and still lived revealed itself as permanent disorder. A new order, different from the capitalist whose perfect model was seen in American society, would have to be found. In this new order, man and democratic rule were to be respected, which meant that the Fascist or Soviet model could not be adopted. Instead of the individual solely concerned with his own success, there would be the personality integrated in fraternal groups, for wasn't it true that the rule of money in America was also that of unbridled individualism?

To what extent such an image of America corresponded to American reality is not really consequential here. What is decisive is that, especially in France but also in Italy, it left a profound impression on men who would play a leading role in the political and intellectual life after 1945, particularly in Catholic circles but also among the most active advocates of European federalism. Americans will never truly understand the force which even after 1945 emanated from this current of the 1930s.

In 1931, the manifesto of the Ordre Nouveau movement was published in Paris. In it we read: "From liberal capitalism to state capitalism, no conformist, liberal or Marxist solution stands up to methodical analysis."[10] In that same year, the two leading lights of this small group brought out a very aggressive book, *The American Cancer,* in which they wrote among other things: "In Europe as in America, it is ultimately the goal of the United States to prevent the collapse of the myth of capitalist production. . . . Since that country leads the capitalist dance today, everything that gets in the way of its plans must be pushed aside, by corruption if possible, by violence, if necessary. . . . The second method of colonization consists in infiltrating Europe with the aid of American industries or corporations. For example: General Motors swallows Opel. . . ."[11]

In the following year, the journal *Esprit* presented the "Manifesto of Font-Remeu." It had been written by the same editorial team and described the situation in the spirit of Emmanuel Mounier, who was to run the journal until his death in 1950: "Excess production has caused unemployment and misery. . . . It is precisely the success of the capitalist economy that . . . preserves social injustice and exacerbates it by its anarchy. . . . At the other end of the world, capitalism has collapsed. But exploitation continues. Communism has shifted the practice of exploitation by the capitalist class to a leadership caste."[12] This twofold condemnation corresponded to the idea of a "third force" which issued in the conception of a Europe whose distance from America and the Soviet Union would be equally great.

Anti-capitalism was even more characteristic of the organized Left, particularly the British labor movement, which during the 1920s was ideologically much tougher than the German Social Democrats. Even during the time the powerful Communist parties in Germany and France saw the "social traitors" and the "social Fascists" as their primary enemy because the Stalin-dominated International had so ordered, the attraction of the Soviet model was greater in London than in Paris or Berlin. This period began in 1928, directly before the onset of the crisis.

It is true, however, that the anti-capitalism of the Labor Party had two peculiarities: it did not call for a revolution, and it had a more concrete idea of the United States. Which is not to say that a union leader such as Ernest Bevin succumbed to the charms of the American model during his visits on the other side of the Atlantic. When he came to Detroit in 1926, he wrote in his notebook: "A hard cruel city . . . No culture . . . No one talks to you except in dollars and mass production."[13] And formulations of this kind were advanced at that time by European visitors from all countries and of every political persuasion. Bevin did not see the United States schematically, however, but carefully compare the advantages and disadvantages of American union and employer practices with those of the British. In short, concrete experience and precise analysis were valued more highly than generalizing ideological conceptions. And British unionists, who had had to battle underemployment for decades, certainly did not see unemployment, the capital sin of capitalist society, as due to American influence.

A bare four years after the onset of the world economic crisis, its effects on attitudes toward the United States changed. In 1933, Weimar Germany became Hitler's Germany and Hoover's America became Roosevelt's. These two changes had a cumulative effect. In the face of National Socialism, the concept of democracy became prominent again: Germany was no longer a democracy, while the United States saw itself once more received in the family of free albeit capitalist countries. Besides, the New Deal seemed to demonstrate that the United States was capable of taking a new path, away from the liberalism of laissez-faire, i.e., from the law of the jungle, and toward a system of government where the state could intervene in the economy to create a new, more just order.

The tactic of the "popular front" to which the Communist parties began to adhere after 1934–35 aimed in the same direction. True, an internal class enemy still existed, but action in the outside world now demanded unity between the capitalist democracies and the fatherland of Socialism in the struggle against Fascism.

In spite of the feeble support the democracies gave the Spanish Republic which was being destroyed piece by piece by Franco's troops, in spite of the failure of the French Popular Front in 1937, and in spite of France's and Great Britain's capitulation to Hitler at Munich in 1938 and the absence of the Soviet Union, the Communists stuck to this line—at least until August 1939. The Nazi-Soviet Pact then caused a second turnabout: the imminent war was again seen as merely the conflict between two imperialist systems, the Fascist and the capitalist. Overnight, Roosevelt became the symbol of the dollar, the large banks, and exploitation, at least as long as harmony between Hitler and Stalin prevailed.

But the Communists no longer played a significant role. What seemed much more striking and odd in Great Britain and France after 1935 was the growing strength of American isolationism. If only President Roosevelt had managed to persuade the Congress and the American public that the certainty of a transatlantic solidarity would have deterred the belligerent Hitler! But both the French and the English discovered that without American guarantees they were not strong enough to talk the German dictator out of his war plans. A bare ten years later, this unforgotten experience was to play an important role in the creation of the Atlantic Alliance.

TWO ALLIES DURING THE WAR

When France and Great Britain declared war on Hitler after the German attack on Poland, they did not yet have America for an ally.

They did not even have American aid. Between 1935 and 1937, Congress passed four neutrality acts which forbade the shipment of arms to any warring country. And while other material could be sold, it was on the twofold condition that it be paid for in cash (within three months, at the latest) and that American ships not be used for its transport. On November 4, 1939, a fifth act was passed which, while lifting the embargo, retained the cash-and-carry demand.

In June 1940, after the collapse of France, Great Britain was facing a triumphant Hitler alone. How could its leadership and its citizens fail to derive the long-lived conviction from this challenge that their country had a very special role to play in the world, and one which differed quite clearly from that of the vanquished countries of the European continent? And when the United States first became England's partner and subsequently its ally, was it not perfectly legitimate to view this alliance as one between equals? When Roosevelt pushed his Lend-Lease Act through Congress in March 1941, which permitted him "to render, give and pass on all services and information which are destined for the defense of a country whose actions the President considers vital for the defense of the United States itself," Great Britain was saved from bankruptcy but continued alone in its struggle against Germany. Only the Japanese attack on Pearl Harbor in December had the indirect result of a declaration of war by the United States on Germany.

Practically speaking, the alliance started off as one between two men. Churchill had already been corresponding with Roosevelt when he joined Chamberlain's government in September 1939 as first Lord of the Admiralty. The relationship became closer when he became Prime Minister on May 10, 1940. Between this date and Roosevelt's death on April 12, 1945, the two men were to exchange more than 1,700 personal messages of often considerable length[14] and would meet on nine occasions, which they always used for extended private discussions. Sometimes this resulted in acrimonious debates, but they were always debates between equals. When Churchill yielded, and this was most often the case, it was not so much because Great Britain was less powerful but because of the respect and admiration he had for Roosevelt, and finally also because he felt compassion for the ill President. Other members of the wartime government, both Conservatives such as Anthony Eden and members of the Labour Party such as Clement Attlee, later reproached him for having given in too readily on more than one occasion.

The equality between the two warring nations was both real and artificial. Collaboration on all levels was close, yet did not result in the creation of joint bodies and institutions except in the military sphere.

Material and intellectual resources were combined, but American superiority in the former gave the British no inferiority complex, because they were persuaded that they could offset it through their superiority in the latter. Thus one of the participants in a discussion on economic and financial matters scribbled the following doggerel on a scrap of paper:[15]

> In Washington Lord Halifax
> once whispered to Lord Keynes:
> "It's true, *they* have the money bags,
> but we have all the brains."

Decisions especially were made jointly since there was the willingness to assume common responsibility. Whether it was a question of carrying out military operations, of becoming active politically or economically somewhere in Asia, Africa, or Europe, or of having to choose between the formula "a single goal: victory" and the determination of guidelines for the future, a process which had already begun during the war, the burden carried by Roosevelt and Churchill was enormous. And they carried it in the interest of all European countries under German occupation. Is one going to be surprised in retrospect that they were amazed at General de Gaulle's incomprehension when he reproached them for refusing to understand the significance of the problem of French legitimacy?

Nonetheless, as the war continued and expanded, the equality of status became increasingly less marked. It is true that Great Britain's power and influence remained considerable. The commander-in-chief in Southeast Asia was an Englishman, responsible, among other things, for Indochina and Indonesia during the Japanese retreat. Communications with resistance movements, especially in Yugoslavia and Greece, were primarily maintained by British services, and occasionally this resulted in joint political decisions of considerable scope.[16] But the fall of Singapore on February 15, 1942, made clear that the defense of Australia and New Zealand would now be assumed by the United States—nine years before the ANZUS defense pact, which excluded Great Britain. And as regards the atom bomb and currency problems, even the exclusion of third parties soon no longer sufficed to guarantee equality between the two partners.

On December 2, 1942, the team headed by Professor Enrico Fermi, an Italian physicist who had fled to the United States, achieved the first self-perpetuating nuclear chain reaction. This scientific success was the result of common efforts which had been carried on before the war in France, then in Great Britain, Canada, and the United States. To build the atom bomb, a Belgian raw material was needed. At the same time, German attempts to obtain this material were frustrated by Norwegian resistance fighters: in March 1942, British units of the Special Operations Executive, acting on information supplied by a Norwegian, destroyed the installations for the manufacture of heavy water near Vermork. Then, in February 1943, a Norwegian resistance group sank the ship transporting the entire German supply.

The French contribution had been considerable. Between 1934 and 1939, discoveries had been made by Irène and Frédéric Joliot-Curie and their associates Hans von Halban and Lew Kowarki.[17] After the defeat of France, von Halban, Kowarki, and other scientists who had been working there joined in the research being carried on in Great Britain and Canada. Nor was the French contribution solely theoretical: Frenchmen had made dangerous voyages across the Channel in which the entire supply of heavy water that had been produced in Norway by a French-Norwegian company and brought to France in March 1940 was safely taken to England.

The uranium which the teams of General L. R. Groves and Robert Oppenheimer needed for the manufacture of the atom bomb came from deposits in the Congo and had already been transferred to New York by the Belgian Union Minière in October 1940. In 1944, curious negotiations began in London with the Belgian government-in-exile.[18] They led to a provisional agreement which, after the liberation of Belgium, became definitive during December of that same year: beginning immediately, the Union Minière set aside its entire production for the United States, which paid a good price for it. When one compares the economic policies of France and Belgium in 1944–45, one must take account of the influx of dollars which enabled the Belgian government to vigorously intervene in public finances.

In spite of the active collaboration of foreign scientists such as the Dane Niels Bohr, who succeeded in leaving his occupied homeland in 1942, the building of the atom bomb became an increasingly and exclusively American and British effort, but the two sides had rather different ideas. For Roosevelt, it was important to achieve results quickly. In consequence, the Americans in charge began neglecting their British partners early in 1943 even as Churchill proposed to retain mutual responsibility. Finally, on August 19, 1943, Roosevelt and Churchill signed a secret agreement in Quebec which comprised five points regarding the so-called Tube Alloys Project (the code name for the atomic installation set up in England).

The first two points stipulated that "this agency" would never be used against either partner or against third parties without consent by both. The third point stated that the parties to the agreement could not pass any information about Tube Alloys to any third party except by mutual consent. The fifth decreed the establishment of a Combined Policy Committee in Washington which would define political goals and provide for a complete exchange of information and ideas. Only the fourth point abandoned the principle of equality: "In view of the heavy burden of production falling on the US . . . any post-war advantages of an industrial or commercial character shall be dealt with . . . on terms to be specified by the United States."[19]

Churchill had an additional reason for seeking an exclusive share in the atomic secret: after the war, possession of the atom bomb might turn out to be a political weapon of such magnitude that from the very beginning it should be at the exclusive disposition of the United States and Great Britain, and not be made available to the Soviets or—as Niels Bohr had wanted—some international organization. In early 1945, this desire was to affect both the USSR and de Gaulle adversely (see Chapter 2). But Churchill overestimated the influence of his country in the alliance with the United States. Two months after the destructive attack on Hiroshima on August 6, 1945, President Truman announced that the United States would retain its atomic monopoly both as concerned the dissemination of information and the manufacture of the bomb. With the signing of the McMahon Act on August 1, 1946, collaboration between American and British atomic scientists came to an end.

Collaboration in the area of monetary and trade policies fared similarly, although here decisive turning points are more difficult to establish. One might say, for example, that there was genuine continuity between the Atlantic Charter, which was signed by Roosevelt and Churchill on August 12, 1941, and the abandonment in the fall of 1950 of the charter project in favor of an international trade organization. Between these two dates, where the first expresses an agreement, the second a difference between the English and the Americans, we see a joint initiative in the Bretton Woods Conference of July 1944, which resulted in the creation of the International Monetary Fund and the International Bank for Reconstruction and Development. And in December 1945, the Anglo-American Financial Agreement, a document of considerable importance, was signed.[20]

But it can also be argued that Bretton Woods already marked the transition from the Anglo-American wartime alliance to the multilateral relationships of the postwar period which were unequal from the very beginning because they were dominated by the United States.

A third interpretation probably does more justice to other spheres of reality: the equality of the two allies was mere appearance from the very beginning. Great Britain's vulnerability was too great, and though obscured by the common struggle, it became abundantly clear when the United States brutally stopped the Lend-Lease Agreement on August 21, 1945, which triggered a devastating financial crisis in London.

At the center of the numerous bilateral negotiations during 1943 and 1944 were two men each of whom had worked out a plan for economic relations during the postwar period and published them in the spring of 1943. On the British side it was John Maynard Keynes, whose book *The Economic Consequences of the Peace* (1919) had decisively influenced international debate during the twenties, and whose *General Theory of Employment, Interest, and Money* (1936) undoubtedly ranks among the significant works of the twentieth century. On the American side it was Harry Dexter White. After a rapid rise during the 1930s in the U.S. Treasury Department, he had been assigned the task of working out an international monetary policy for the postwar era by Treasury Secretary Henry Morgenthau in December 1941.

The difference between the two plans and the personal conflicts of the two authors showed up in the Bretton Woods negotiations, where Harry Dexter White's theses finally prevailed. Yet the negotiators from the two countries had largely similar conceptions of the goals to be attained. The main difficulties did not originate with them but rather with the domestic politics of their respective countries, for the two could not negotiate in a purely technical, aseptic environment which would have enabled them to work out whatever solutions were most rational; instead, the negotiations came under the pressure of numerous demands and fears on the part of parliamentarians, parties, newspapers, and assorted interest groups.

The English worried that the interdependence of world trade and full employment as maintained by Keynes would not carry sufficient weight in practice if that practice were to be dominated by the American desire to give priority to the lifting of quantitative limits and the reduction of tariffs. The decline of the Liberal Party during the two world wars and the rise of the Labour Party had largely resulted from the experience of the connection between the free exchange of goods and unemployment, between the law of the market and social injustice. The Conservatives, for their part, were receptive to all protectionist demands from industry and agriculture which were based on the conviction that the abandonment of customs barriers meant their ruin. As the war drew toward its close, the rise of the Labour Party was accompanied by a problem which, more than thirty years later, still persists as the principal dilemma of the French Left: how to reconcile the aims of full employment and socialist change with the necessity of a liberal world economic system whose advantages and merits everyone recognizes. The continuing splits within the Labour Party relate to this question.

The Americans had altogether different worries. On the one hand, they were concerned with securing the freedom of international trade by abolishing quantitative limits and preferences. They considered nondiscriminatory customs duties to limit the import of certain kinds of foreign goods legitimate, particularly when they restricted import into the United States. "A great expansion in the volume of international trade after the war will be essential to the attainment of full and effective employment in the United States and elsewhere, to the preservation of private enterprise and to the success of an international security system to prevent future wars," a 1943 commission report states. But we also read: "International trade cannot be developed to an adequate extent unless excessive tariffs, quantitative restrictions on imports and exports, exchange controls, and other government devices to limit trade are substantially reduced or eliminated. Moreover, if this is not done, there may be a further strengthening of the tendency, already strong in many countries before the war, to eliminate private enterprise from international trade in favor of rigid control by the state."[21]

But wasn't it also true that monetary and trade problems would have to be closely tied to the question of Lend-Lease, especially when the latter was conceived as unilateral aid to the Allies and Great Britain in particular? The text of the Lend-Lease Act was in fact quite vague. Compensation to the United States for help it had provided could consist of "cash payments or compensation in the form of tangible or intangible assets or of direct or indirect payments provided the President of the United States considers them adequate." In the Mutual Aid Agreement which the United States and Great Britain signed on February 23, 1942, the definitive formulation, Article 7—in which both countries engage to combat discriminatory practices and to fight for liberalization—had been preceded by long and difficult negotiations. Did this not imply a significant concession by the British in "imperial preference" because they wanted the Lend-Lease Act acknowledged as a normal contribution by the Americans to common victory? The controversy "common sacrifice or repayable loan which one ally grants another" reminds one of the quarrel over war debts after the First World War. But it was not under this aspect that Churchill defended Article 7. In April 1944, he told the House of Commons that Roosevelt had assured him before he signed the agreement that "we were no more committed to the abolition of Imperial Preference than the American Government were committed to the abolition of their high protective tariffs."[22] The Americans presented matters quite differently, and the dispute was not resolved until December when a financial agreement concerning American loans to a Great Britain hard hit by the cancellation of the Lend-Lease Agreement was signed:

in the future, compensation for aid furnished during the war would no longer be demanded, but the economic goals to be worked toward now were the very ones specified in Article 7—affirmation of multilateral trade relations and abandonment of any preference shown the countries of the British Empire.

The question of the British Empire as a unit of trade rather than of currency arose time and again between the Allies during the war. Even before the war, many in the United States had maintained that import duties were an expression of a legitimate nationalism while preferences—which meant discrimination against third parties— represented imperialism. Criticisms of Great Britain were raised primarily because of the Ottawa Conference of 1932 which had established "imperial preference" in the form of preferential treatment for products from the dominions in exchange for corresponding obligations.

As expressed in the generous plans advanced in the eight points of the text, the Atlantic Charter of 1941 seemed to be the promise of a new world in the occupied countries: opposition to territorial changes which were not in accord with the freely expressed wish of the peoples concerned; respect for the right of all peoples to choose the form of government under which they lived; fullest collaboration between nations to secure better social and economic conditions. But in London, there was particular sensitivity to the ambiguity of Point 4; here, both countries pledged equal access by all nations to the raw materials needed for their economic development, but only "to the extent their existing obligations permitted." Did this mean a commitment to multilateral relationships or a chance to retain imperial preference? Tough negotiations had preceded this deliberately ambiguous compromise.

The American attitude—aversion to the British Empire and aversion to colonial empires—had at least two motives. To begin with, there were concrete material interests: the opening up of new markets and the abolition of private preserves. In conversation with the Dutch Foreign Minister von Kleffen in March 1942, the commercial adviser to the State Department told his guest "with vehemence that never again would the great American nation allow the British and the Dutch to dictate the prices at which it could buy its tin and its rubber."[23] The second motive was the moral anti-colonialism whose origin we have already referred to.

Roosevelt conducted himself with considerable circumspection toward his British ally, but the advice he gave on policies to be pursued in India was not kindly received by Churchill. In August 1939, Secretary of State Cordell Hull had proposed to the British ambassador that the two countries prepare a joint declaration on the future of the colonies. For two years, Washington and London considered a variety of projects, but in April 1944 it became apparent that the talks had ended in failure. And how, for that matter, could the future of the colonies be brought up without including the British Empire? Churchill certainly felt no inclination to allow anyone, including foreign powers and international organizations, to tamper with British sovereignty and responsibility. For the Dutch government-in-exile in London, the American attitude was naturally not the primary concern, though it might have recalled the 1920 conflict which had divided Washington and The Hague in the matter of Indonesian oil.[24] But in view of the new situation that had been created by the Japanese occupation of Sumatra and Java in February 1942, quick decisions had to be made. What policy should the Netherlands adopt, particularly toward the Indonesian nationalists, who were initially supported by the Japanese?

Much depended on one's judgment of the earlier situation. If, as a wartime prime minister wrote years later, "security, liberties, rights and a large measure of prosperity were being secured to some seventy million people of different races and varying development,"[25] American anti-colonialism, which was based on a criticism of despotic rule and exploitation, would be irrelevant. But if this was so, why did Queen Wilhelmina have to promise a wholly new future to the transatlantic regions in a solemn declaration on December 6, 1942?—a future which had initially envisaged the reconstruction of the Kingdom of the Netherlands to which these regions would belong, and subsequently the establishment of a Dutch Commonwealth every part of which would freely decide its own internal affairs.

In Indonesia, relations between the Japanese army of occupation and the Indonesian nationalists varied, for Japan wavered between a policy of annexation and one of support for Indonesian efforts to achieve autonomy. In view of the British and American advance throughout the Pacific in 1944, Indonesia was promised independence. But the slow process that the Japanese had initiated did not attain its goal. To avoid receiving their independence from an almost defeated occupying power, the Indonesian nationalists proclaimed independence on August 15, 1945, through their leader Sukarno, who had founded a nationalist party as far back as 1926 and been twice arrested by Dutch authorities.

Japan's surrender was signed on September 2. Since Indonesia lay in the theater of operations under British command, it was up to Lord Mountbatten to land troops to disarm the Japanese units. And the protracted conflict which now started between the Netherlands and the new rulers of their former colony—and which continued until sovereignty was transferred in December 1949 and even beyond, to August 1954 when the very loose Netherlands-Indonesian Union was dissolved—did not initially interest the United States directly.

But the United States could not remain indifferent. Should it support its wartime ally? That would have been a violation of the image of an America that advocated freedom for colonial peoples. But perhaps there was another reason for resisting the nationalists and for proclaiming solidarity with the Netherlands. On October 10, 1945, the Dutch ambassador in Washington called on Under Secretary of State Dean Acheson and informed him that the two leaders of the Indonesian independence movement had been in Moscow before the war and were, in his opinion, "Communist inspired" and that their movement "represented a foothold in a part of the Far East where it could cause a great deal of difficulty."[26] The Dutch attempt to harmonize American anti-colonialism and the idea of a defense against Communism ultimately succeeded less well than the French did later in the case of Indochina. Initially, by the way, the anti-Communist argument took a different form. On March 13, 1945, even before the defeat of Germany, General de Gaulle called in the American ambassador. According to the diplomat's report, he complained about the obstacles the United States was raising to the transport of a French expeditionary force to Indochina: "When Germany falls, they will be upon us. If the public here comes to realize that you are against us in Indo-China there will be terrific disappointment and nobody knows to what that will lead. We do not want to become Communist; we do not want to fall into the Russian orbit, but I hope that you do not push us into it."[27]

In Indochina, however, the situation was considerably more complicated than in Indonesia. After a lengthy period of complex relations between the Vichy-appointed Governor-General, Admiral Decoux, and the Japanese authorities, the latter had taken over the administration on March 9, 1945, and interned the French garrison. During the entire period, nationalist movements had emerged in Cochinchina, Cambodia, and Laos. In Tonkin, the Viet Minh criticized the French administration, though not without differentiating between the "French fascists that rule Indochina" and "democrats, anti-fascists and Gaullists." But when it became apparent that Free France would not give Indochina its freedom, a leaflet was distributed in June 1944 which read: "So this is the way the French who are fighting against German rule wish to maintain their own over other nations! We, as Indochinese communists, protest vigorously against the lack of logic of the committee of Algeria. . . . The Gaullists in Indochina hope that the intervention of allied forces will solve their problem for them. But the allies who proclaim themselves the liberators in Teheran do not have the right to force a yoke on other nations, even when that yoke is 'humanized' and 'mitigated' by de Gaulle's partisans."[28]

This coincided fairly closely with Roosevelt's thoughts during this period, for he had written to his Secretary of State on January 24, 1944: "I saw Halifax last week and told him quite frankly that it was perfectly true that I had, for over a year, expressed the opinion that Indo-China should not go back to France but that it should be administered by an international trusteeship. France has had the country—thirty million inhabitants—for nearly one hundred years, and the people are worse off than they were at the beginning. . . .I see no reason to play in with the British Foreign Office in this matter. The only reason they seem to oppose it is that they fear the effect it would have on their own possessions and those of the Dutch. . . . France has milked [Indo-China] for one hundred years. The people of Indo-China are entitled to something better than that."[29]

The United States as an ally that outmaneuvers an ally in the name of anti-colonialism; the United States as a power that intervenes in other regions of the globe and thus again exposes itself to the reproach of wishing to replace an old by a new rule; the United States as a democratic country that supports a national liberation movement and thus competes with the Soviet Union which is still its ally today but will presumably be its rival tomorrow: the ambiguities of the American position have certainly not been confined to Indochina and France.

THE CASE OF DE GAULLE

The wartime situation of France vis-à-vis the United States, on the other hand, was of a very special sort. France was the only major power that had been defeated by Nazi Germany, which meant that the question concerning its future as a major power arose at the very beginning. Besides, its political status during four long years had never been clear.

Certainly other countries had also wavered in their attitudes, particularly those that were neutral. Switzerland and Sweden never stopped compromising themselves with Germany until the Allies won decisive victories. Dean Acheson, who was charged with pressuring those two countries into suspending their shipments of weapons and iron ore to Germany, made this sarcastic comment: "Finally, in April 1945, the Swiss surrendered—only a month before General Jodl did."[30] Other countries had been torn between obedience toward a government-in-exile, submission to a national administration which invariably collaborated with the occupying power, and positive reaction to the appeal of a minority to make common cause with the Germans.

For them, however, there had at least been a government-in-exile whose legitimacy was uncontested, particularly when the head of state (the queen of the Netherlands, the king of Norway) also was in London, but even when the sovereign, like King Leopold III of Belgium, remained in his own country as a prisoner of war.[31] And when he went so far as to defy the occupying power and continued to run the country, as the king of Denmark did, he proved by his courageous and dignified attitude that he was on the side of the democrats in the fight against Nazism.

The situation of France had been different. A summary chronology suffices to show the dimensions of the problem. On June 17, 1940, Marshal Pétain, the head of the government since the day before, appeals for an end to the fighting. On June 18, General de Gaulle, Undersecretary for Defense in the government that has just resigned, calls on the French to continue fighting steadfastly. On June 21, the armistice with Germany is signed. The greater part of France is occupied. Only one region, approximately two-fifths of French territory, remains unoccupied and is administered by the regime which was formed in Vichy on July 9, 1940, after the parliament had resigned. On October 27, 1940, de Gaulle establishes a "Council for the Defense of the Empire" and on September 24, 1941, a "French National Committee." On November 11, 1942, after the Allies land in North Africa, the German army also occupies the south of France but permits Marshal Pétain to continue until August 1944 as the head of the French government in Vichy. After tedious negotiations, a "Committee of National Liberation" is set up in Algiers on June 3, 1943, which elects de Gaulle in November 1943 as the sole President and then constitutes itself on June 2, 1944, as the provisional government of the French Republic.

The dispute over legitimate representation created deep rifts among the French. But legitimacy is based not only on the readiness of the citizens to obey a recognized authority but also on diplomatic recognition by the outside world. When several parties compete for legitimacy, this recognition becomes a large stake for which the competitors fight bitterly, and they will readily make all relations to the other participants in the international game contingent on whether they are useful to them in this effort or not.[32]

General de Gaulle, who saw himself as a fighter for the sovereignty of his nation and the restoration of the state in a France that would be both liberated and returned to its former rank among the major powers, initially found himself in a straitened position. His temperament suggested and assessment confirmed that this obliged him to be intractable. "By acting as the unyielding champion of the nation and the state," he wrote later, "I found assent and even enthusiasm among the French and respect and consideration from foreigners. Those who took offense during this entire drama at my inflexibility refused to see that for me, who had to resist the countless pressures of my adversaries, the slightest docility would have led to utter ruin."[33] And he reports a conversation he had with Churchill in June 1942: "We came to talk about Roosevelt and his attitude toward me. 'Don't rush things,' said Churchill. 'Look at the way I yield and rise up again, turn and turn about.' 'You can,' I remarked, 'because you are seated on a solid state, an assembled nation, a united Empire, large armies. But I? Where are my resources? And yet I, as you know, am responsible for the interests and destiny of France. It is too heavy a burden, and I am too poor to be able to bow.'"[34] And in a telegram of August 1941 to the delegation of Free France in London: "Our greatness and our weakness lies solely in our inflexibility concerning the rights of France. We will need that inflexibility until we are on the far side of the Rhine."[35]

But since he was not directly involved in waging war against the common enemy, his inflexibility primarily affected his allies, particularly the most powerful among them, and it is only natural that this occasionally prompted interpretations which were not precisely well-meaning. To those who had to put up with his arrogance, "de Gaulle appeared less interested in the conduct of the war than concerned for his role afterwards."[36]

The Americans saw things altogether differently. Roosevelt pursued a twofold aim: victory over Germany, and the right of the French to choose their own government after that victory. If the presence of an American ambassador in Vichy was useful to protect North Africa from the Germans, for example, that presence would have to be continued as long as possible. If Admiral Darlan, the Vichy Prime Minister who was in Algiers at the time of the invasion on November 8, 1942, prevented the French forces from engaging the Allied troops, it was necessary to negotiate with him and to remind Churchill of the old Balkan proverb: "My children, in times of great danger, you may go with the devil until you have crossed the bridge."[37] "It must be remembered that hostilities in Morocco ceased by order of Darlan and not repeat not by full military conquest," Eisenhower telegraphed Washington on November 14.[38] At the same time, as of November 1941, the Lend-Lease Act was extended to all areas that fell under the control of Free France. And beginning in 1943, ten French divisions in North Africa were equipped with American arms.

Roosevelt's refusal to acknowledge General de Gaulle as the representative of France was based on his fear that he might be reproached for wanting to impose a head of government on the French, and one that was suspected of a dictatorial temperament at that. Even after the Allied invasion of Normandy, even after the arrival of the provisional government in Paris, Roosevelt stuck to this refusal, although Secretary of State Cordell Hull urged some immediate gesture on September 17, 1944, and stated specifically: "There is every indication that General de Gaulle has been accepted for the initial period as the national leader in liberated France. . . . Our present popularity in France is high. It will suffer if we delay recognition unduly."[39]

Asked by a journalist about his "reaction," de Gaulle said two days later: "The French government is pleased that it is to be called by its name."[40] Roosevelt's obstinacy was not just a result of his aversion to de Gaulle.[41] It also came from a surprising failure to understand the development France had undergone during the years of German occupation. He was unaware of the entire resistance ideology, which was based not just on the idea of the nation but perhaps to a much greater extent on the desire to create a French economy and society after the liberation which would differ substantially from the prewar period. The France of 1944—45 could not simply be the France of 1939 as if war and occupation had never been. The association between de Gaulle and the Conseil National de la Résistance that came about in 1943 symbolized for both sides the will toward a renewal, a will which, being neither acknowledged nor supported by the United States, could not but proceed without that country and in part even against it.

For his part, de Gaulle simplified and thus could write: "The United States brings to great affairs elementary feelings and a complicated policy."[42] He also saw things through a touchy sensibility and was—according to statements by the most Francophile of all English witnesses—"ever on the look-out for an insult"[43] from both Churchill and Roosevelt. But another actor in this drama, a man with an entirely different disposition, Jean Monnet, spoke of "illusions born of wounded pride in a memory that never forgot,"[44] in characterizing later relations with the United States.

Tensions between the United States and Free France continued almost during the entire war. The first conflict arose over Saint-Pierre and Miquelon, those French islands off the Canadian coast which de Gaulle claimed as part of Free France on December 24, 1941, without having first discussed this matter with the Allies and even though the United States had just concluded an agreement with Vichy by which the status quo of French possessions in the American hemisphere was retained. Other direct confrontations concerned the exercise of authority in more remote areas, as in New Caledonia in May 1942, for example, where de Gaulle gave expression to a principle he had just formulated in a public statement in London: "Fighting France intends to march with her allies under the express reservation that her allies also march with her."[45] In other words, the indispensable military subordination to a joint supreme command does not imply political subordination under the government of the United States.

The distinction did not harmonize with American plans concerning the campaign in North Africa. General Eisenhower fairly soon sided with de Gaulle and against President Roosevelt: it would be advisable, he said, to have a political authority represent France in Algiers and not to leave this merely to an administrative body under an all-powerful Allied Supreme Command.

But at its most profound—and not least in its psychological aftereffects—the conflict involved the mother country itself. For who would lead France after the Allied invasion? Who would command its advancing forces, and who would be in charge of the liberated areas? Beginning in 1942, the Allied Supreme Command began to prepare for the creation of a comprehensive machinery to reorganize and run the liberated or conquered territories so that military operations would be facilitated, local resources utilized, and the fundamental needs of the population (food supplies, sanitary installations, communications, etc.) be provided for. At thirty universities in Great Britain and the United States, thousands of area and language specialists were trained. Civil Affairs Departments or AMGOT (Allied Military Government of Occupied Territories) began functioning effectively in July 1943 in Sicily. But was the situation the same in Allied countries? Were the 1,552 specialists, four hundred of them officers, who were to go to France to play the same role there as they later would in Germany? The manuals printed for their use endeavored to be precise, yet in many passages they reproduced the worst clichés about the "happy-go-lucky, lazy" southerners or the "individualist Paris workers."[46] Were the Americans who used these manuals to exercise power themselves? Or were they going to act through the officials of the Vichy regime? And the designation AMGOT was an unfortunate choice: France was occupied by the Germans; was it going to be occupied by its allies in the future?

To some extent, the governments-in-exile had the same goals as de Gaulle. But with them, detailed agreements whose application created no particular difficulties were concluded.[47] For France, such an agreement (which actually comprised five memoranda) did not come into existence until the end of August 1944, i.e., almost three months after the Normandy invasion.

The harshest conflict erupted on June 4, two days before D-Day.

General de Gaulle heard about the imminent invasion, received the text of a speech he was to broadcast to his countrymen, and discovered that the paper money to be used by the British and Americans in France had already been printed. It was francs bearing the inscriptions "Printed in France" and "Liberté, Egalité, Fraternité."[48] After extremely violent disputes, he read a speech of his own in which he specifically called on the French to obey the instructions of the provisional government, and finally obtained the withdrawal of the "counterfeit money" and political priority for his representatives in the liberated areas. Thanks to the admirable undercover work of a resistance organization created by Michel Debré, they could everywhere be quickly put in place.

In practice, of course, the Supreme Headquarters Allied Expeditionary Forces (SHAEF) retained considerable authority in most of France until the provisional government was recognized. In large parts of the north, northeast, and southeast, it retained it until April 24, 1945, and in the entire east and the Alps even until July 14, 1945.[49] But something decisive had been attained, and that was the recognition of the legitimacy of administrative structures that both the resistance and Free France had created. Since that time, an entire generation of new leadership cadres has been convinced that this recognition was snatched from, or even imposed on, the Americans.

This belief was certainly not without foundation—although a comparison with other liberated countries does not furnish the slightest indication that AMGOT would have hampered the free development of national political life. But a second concession, which the Americans found much easier to make, was to have psychological consequences of considerably greater mythopoeic power: since General Eisenhower had allowed General Leclerc's armored division to be the first to enter Paris in August 1944, Parisians and other Frenchmen continue to believe that the capital was actually liberated by the joint action of the population and French troops, without American help, and perhaps even in spite of it, and this notion has been reinforced by the creation of later legends in books, films, and on television.

More serious differences of opinion both before and after the German capitulation and under both Truman and Roosevelt led to genuine conflict. Toward the end of April 1945, de Gaulle ordered General de Lattre de Tassigny to occupy Stuttgart and to remain there despite opposing orders from Eisenhower: de Gaulle wanted a pawn in order to obtain more acceptable borders for the French zone in Germany. And in June, in the Aosta Valley, an Italian border region which de Gaulle would have liked to see France annex, the French went so far as to threaten to open fire on American troops after the

French zone, which had been established by inter-Allied agreements, was deliberately enlarged. The indignation of President Truman, who ordered the immediate suspension of all weapon and ammunition shipments to the French army, is perfectly comprehensible and led to the failure of the French attempt.

But the incident which had the most severe psychological repercussions occurred a few months before, during the last German counteroffensive. When, during the first days of January 1945, Eisenhower threatened to stop supplies to the French First Army unless it obeyed him and de Gaulle reacted by threatening to interfere with the communications network of the American army in France, the fate of the population of Strasbourg was at stake: in order to straighten the front lines as the Germans advanced further northward, Eisenhower had ordered General de Lattre to evacuate Strasbourg and give the Germans the chance to reoccupy the city. As the highest-ranking politician, de Gaulle ordered a French general to resist the Allied commander-in-chief, and this tough reaction protected the population of the town from reprisals, which certainly would have been as severe as the enthusiasm with which they greeted their final liberation was intense.

Eisenhower's later comment on the matter went no further than this: "At first glance, de Gaulle's argument seemed to be based upon political consideration, founded more on emotions than on logic and common sense."[50] How could de Gaulle have failed to take such an affair as proof that even the most well-meaning of Allied commanders could not understand the chief concerns of a friendly nation? In other words, the existence of a common enemy could never justify a military integration which deprived the national political leadership of the possibility of pursuing a certain aim which it considered very important but that hardly appeared so from the perspective of the great, distant ally.

ITALY COMPLEX, GERMANY SIMPLE?

The conflict over Stuttgart concerned the question of zones of occupation in Germany, and the conflict over Aosta the politics of the victorious powers in Italy. It was no longer the problem of legitimacy but the position France—once more a normal nation-state—would take among the actors in the international game. During all of 1945, this struggle for rank was a fundamental aspect of the diplomatic disputes we will have to consider in the following chapter.

It is certainly true that the Franco-American conflict over legitimacy was artificially dramatized rather than truly dramatic, for after 1943 the Comité Français de Libération Nationale had been allowed to participate in countless international activities such as negotiations and agreements, and specifically on the consultative committee for Italian affairs and the Control Commission at the Allied Supreme Command in Italy. And this was an Italy whose legitimacy conflicts were much more complex and momentous and even involved bloody struggles. They were also much more closely connected with decisions taken by Great Britain and the United States.

What was Italy when Allied troops landed in Sicily on July 9, 1943? An enemy that was allied with Nazi Germany, that had entered the war against an already defeated France on June 19, 1940, that had invaded Greece in October 1940, and that had joined in the attack on Yugoslavia in April 1941. It had been an almost continuously defeated enemy which its ally constantly had had to succor, in the Balkans first, and then in North Africa.

But why had Italy been defeated? Because it was militarily incompetent or because the war was unpopular, the Germans being increasingly seen as oppressors, as responsible, both directly and indirectly, through Mussolini's regime, for the misery that had spread everywhere on the peninsula? The great strikes in northern Italy, which had already been significant in 1942 and taken on spectacular dimensions in March 1943, had also been political and social protests. And when eventual defeat of the Axis became apparent, anti-Fascist resistance had long been more than the work of a few. But Mussolini's overthrow on July 24, 1943, was not the work of the resistance. On the throne since 1900, Victor Emmanuel III had served Mussolini's dictatorship as a guarantor. At the insistence of the other dignitaries of the regime, he now had the Duce arrested and transferred power to Marshal Badoglio, the conqueror of Ethiopia in 1936 who had opposed Italy's entry into the war but had remained chief of staff until the Greek campaign had failed.

On September 3, 1943, the armistice with the Allies was signed. When it was proclaimed on September 8, the Germans reacted rapidly: they occupied Rome, and the king had to flee precipitately. An attack by British and American airborne troops could have seized the city and prevented the situation in which Italy found itself up to June 1944, i.e., the fateful division of the country into a kingdom in the south, a zone under direct German control in the middle, and a north where the tragedy continued with three actors: German divisions, Mussolini's militia (he had been freed by the Germans and created the Repubblica Sociale Italiana in Sala on Lake Garda), both in a bitter fight against increasingly numerous and increasingly better organized partisans.

In the south, the turnabout of the king became complete when Badoglio declared war on Germany on October 13, 1943. Italy was now fighting on the side of the Allies. It remained a defeated country nonetheless, for it had not only signed the "short" armistice of September 3 but also the "long" surrender document of September 29, 1943, which was a much more political instrument since among other things it contained the proviso that henceforth the Italian government would have to submit to the orders the "United Nations" had issued for the purpose of exterminating Fascism. These nations (at that time, the term "United Nations" did not refer to an organization but to the totality of countries fighting Germany and Japan) would be represented in Italy by a Control Commission serving under the Allied Supreme Command. Italy was thus a country which was both to fight Germany and to be punished as a former German ally: for a long time to come, this split reality was to burden relations between the Allies, and especially relations between Italy and the victorious powers, the United States in particular.

The United States had always been the power most favorably disposed toward Italy. One reason for this was the political weight of the millions of American citizens of Italian origin. Most of them longed to reestablish contacts with a country they also wanted to see effectively aided, once Fascism was overthrown. Italian-American committees of the most widely differing and occasionally even conflicting policies were founded, most often with the participation of Italian anti-Fascists who had fled to the United States and now wanted to return to participate in the rebuilding of their country. Besides, many American soldiers had found more or less distant relatives in Sicily and later on the peninsula. The films of Italian neorealism which were made directly after the war did not fail to include such scenes when they wished to show the varying but generally friendly reception of the G.I.'s.

But the connections made by American intelligence services were politically more significant. Practically nonexistent during the period between the two wars, they were reestablished through the efforts of the Office of the Coordinator of Information, which General William H. Donovan had set up in July 1941 at Roosevelt's request, and through the Office of Strategic Services (OSS), its offshoot, which had the twofold task of providing information and carrying out special missions. As long as they merely facilitated Allied military operations by supplying intelligence or provided resistance groups with parachuted weapons, the activities of the OSS and of the British SOE hardly created political problems. But was it always possible to clearly distinguish between services rendered to hasten victory and interventions designed to strengthen certain currents rather than others, or to set Italy on a specific course in preference to another?

Retrospectively, the activities of the OSS in Italy received two very different and one-sided evaluations. One of them ignored all political aspects, the other—an important component of the anti-Americanism of the extreme Left in Italy—later committed enormous anachronisms by presenting all efforts of the American intelligence services as if from the very beginning it had been their aim to cover Italy with an anti-Communist security network.[51] Thus the contacts between unions which Arthur Goldberg established from New York in 1943–44 because he wanted to make use of information provided by European unionists after their organizations had been dissolved by the occupying power certainly did not serve the same purposes as were pursued by American unionists with the help of the recently founded CIA when they attempted in 1947 to prevent unions in France and Italy from falling entirely under Communist control.

Yet even at that time, there was concern in America that the Communists might take power in Italy. In May 1944, for example, Robert Murphy, political adviser to SHAEF and the American member of the Control Commission, sent the Secretary of State a report prepared by the commission. After a detailed analysis of the rise of the Communist Party in a country "already ripe for that swing toward extremes which is the inevitable corollary of a shattered economy and the threat of inflation," he went on: "More than twenty years ago, a similar situation provoked the March on Rome and gave birth to fascism. We must make up our minds—and that quickly—whether or not we wish to see this second march developing into another 'ism.'"[52] The decision took the form of maximal aid to Italy in order to eliminate to the greatest possible extent the putative reason for any success of the Communist Party.

But the principal theme of the report was the moderate attitude of the Communists, which was seen as imposed by Moscow and as a danger for the future. And it is true that two weeks after recognizing Badoglio's government on March 14, 1944, Palmiro Togliatti, the leader of the Communist Party who had recently returned from Moscow, surprised the Americans and British by a dramatic step. Though a mere three months earlier, during an anti-Fascist congress in Bari, all parties of the Left had demanded the immediate abdication of the king and the transfer of the government to the Resistenza, Togliatti, like the Liberals, suddenly advocated that no decisions be made concerning institutional problems until after the end of the war.

The real motives for this attitude were certainly complex and have remained controversial.[53] Was it caution in the face of American dominance and the remoteness of Soviet troops? Recognition of the need for continuity in the united anti-Fascist policy which had been established in 1935 and reformulated between 1941 and 1943 (after the dissolution of the Comintern, to whose leadership Togliatti had belonged under the name Ercole)? The rejection of a violent revolution in a Marxism which had been shaped much more strongly by Gramsci than by Lenin? Whatever the reasons, the decision led to the formation of a government of all anti-Fascist parties and, on December 26, 1944, the recognition by the northern Italian resistance organization Comitato di Liberazione Nationale dell'Alta Italia of the government in Rome as the sole legitimate power. This committee was so powerful that as early as December 7 it could conclude a kind of agreement among equals with the Allies by which it transferred its power to them and was recognized in turn as the legitimate representative of northern Italy.

The ambiguity in the exercise of power continued for a long time. In the spring of 1944, the Allies were the de facto and de jure guardians of Italy. On September 26, Roosevelt and Churchill solemnly promised a new policy toward Italy which would entail a relaxation of controls. But up to the end of February 1945, the Allied Control Commission retained the right to veto legislation and the appointments of ministers and high officials. And in northern Italy, the Allied administration continued until January 1, 1946.

On October 26, 1944, the United States resumed diplomatic relations with Italy. Great Britain did not immediately follow. The constant quarrel between the two Allies as to how Italy should be treated finally left the co-belligerent in the situation of a defeated enemy, especially because the other countries agreed with Great Britain that Italy should be severely dealt with. This was especially true of Yugoslavia, which wanted to see the Trieste problem resolved in its favor. In terms of material recovery and its return to international status, Italy could thus count on no one but the United States.

It seemed that none of these problems would arise in Germany. While Italian forces had barely resisted the Allies when they landed in Sicily, German troops, including units of adolescents and old men, fought on to the bitter end, to the utterly absurd and perfectly senseless destruction of their country. While Italy had found itself in an ambiguous situation after September 1943, Germany was the absolute enemy whom unconditional surrender would reduce to the status of a mere object of international politics. An object, it might be added, that would have to be worked over and reshaped for some time before it could be reintroduced as a participant in the dialogue between nations. It was an object whose forms and structures had been defined and specified in countless models, both in Washington and during meetings of the victorious powers, the British and the Americans, or, after 1943, the Big Three.

It is true, however, that the third member of this alliance, the Soviet Union, had from the very beginning and even during the horrible invasion of its own country never been ready to entirely close the door on the German hope for dialogue, for it made a distinction between Hitler and the German people, while Roosevelt and Churchill refused to recognize the existence of a German opposition to Hitler. And yet there was not merely one but several opposition movements, each of which had its own conceptions concerning future relations with the outside world, and the German population as a whole was anything but a homogeneous mass with only one idea in its head: Hitler's superman ideology. But as defeat became a possibility, one feeling, fear of the Soviet Union, became dominant. In reaction to this fear, the expectation arose that Great Britian and especially the United States would be a positive force. "The English and the Americans will prevent Bolshevization"[54] was one of the "defeatist" slogans against which Goebbels began launching his tirades after February 1943. In spite of the aerial bombardments, in spite of the toughness shown by Roosevelt, in spite of the demand for unconditional surrender—a demand that thrust many still hesitant Germans back into Hitler's arms—the United States subsequently appeared increasingly as the only true Western and also humane power which could effectively counter the barbarism threatening from the East.

Anti-Communism and anti-Sovietism, either in combination or as distinct fundamental features of German political reality, are topics to which we will have to return repeatedly. Already at the time of Germany's collapse, the question of security against the Soviet Union emerged as a central theme in the "peace plan" which the resistance fighter Carl Goerdeler had worked out in the fall of 1943, before he paid with his life for his resistance a bare year later, when the attempt on Hitler on July 20, 1944, had failed. On May 1, 1945, on the morning after Hitler's suicide, Admiral Karl Dönitz, the successor-designate of the Führer, said on the radio: "Our leader, Adolf Hitler, is dead. . . . His commitment to the struggle against the Bolshevist floodtide was made on behalf of Europe and the entire civilized world. . . . The Anglo-Americans are therefore no longer continuing the war in the interest of their peoples but only in order to promote the spread of Bolshevism in Europe." In other words, their real interest is to confront the Soviet Union together with us.

Of course, this was neither the sole nor the most important topic of the political debates which were carried on before the total defeat in a seemingly monolithic Germany and in the émigré circles in London, Stockholm, and New York, discussions which were not unaffected by that intellectual and political ferment that seized all European countries when the tragedy of a war a belligerent Germany had deliberately provoked finally ended.

2 BEFORE THE RIFTS

THE war in Europe had ended with the total victory of that great alliance which had been produced by Hitler's attack on the Soviet Union and the Japanese attack on Pearl Harbor. The countries of Western Europe found themselves in situations which varied considerably and were yet quite similar. Common to all was poverty, but it was experienced differently by each, and all expected help from the one victor that had become richer. Their positions in international life seemed quite dissimilar, but what separated them disappeared when their situation was compared with those of the United States and the Soviet Union. Their internal ferment produced almost identical currents and ideas, but as a result of differing political traditions and presuppositions they took different directions, especially as regards their reaction to the gradual disintegration of yesterday's alliance.

GENERAL IMPOVERISHMENT AND THE HUNGER FOR DOLLARS

Who would deny that the war had brought heavy losses to all the countries involved? But could Germany, which had been devastated by massive bombing and a double invasion, really be compared with Great Britain, which had suffered only limited destruction? Or could even France, which had first undergone an exploitative occupation and then fought all those battles during the second half of 1944, be compared with Italy, which for almost two years had been wracked by various and protracted battles? The British order with its government intact and its political life unbroken was in fact the very opposite of the German chaos, a chaos which meant not only cities in ruins and millions of dead and missing but also large-scale migrations in a country where no authority any longer existed. And compared to the real famine in Germany, the few restrictions introduced in England during the war and retained in anticipation of a recovery hardly seemed to count.

Yet German productive capacity had not been destroyed as completely as it seemed, while French and English resources had been depleted more thoroughly than had been believed. Even in 1946, and right in the midst of evident misery,[1] German production already began to recover, while France, an agricultural country par excellence at the time, had to face the necessity of reintroducing bread rationing as early as December 1945. And gradually, a dismal reality began to dawn on the men governing Great Britain: the wealth of their country during the prewar period had been due less to its national production than to its international financial power. To finance the war effort, it had been necessary to increase external debts by $12 billion, and foreign assets of more than $5 billion had had to be converted into cash. During the 1920s, the trade deficit had been covered by surplus from "invisible" income (maritime freightage, foreign investments). During the 1930s, the situation had deteriorated. What would happen now?

"Everything depends on the extent the Americans are willing to cooperate," the British National Union of Manufacturers stated.[2] But the beginnings were not auspicious. As early as August 21, 1945, Truman ordered the suspension of all Lend-Lease operations and the cancellation of most outstanding contracts. This step proved catastrophic, a fact the President later admitted privately, though he disputes it in his memoirs.[3] The protracted and difficult Anglo-American negotiations finally led to the granting of the previously mentioned loan, but the amount, $3.75 billion, was too small and the conditions were such that the controversy which erupted in Great Britain sometimes turned into bitter criticism of the Americans.[4] The need for dollars was only very inadequately satisfied, and neither the domestic nor the external financial situation of Great Britain was put in order.

In a sense, defeated Germany found itself in a better position: the victorious powers who exercised supreme authority did not want anarchy and total misery which might so easily produce uncontrollable social unrest. Their policy of punishment, at least on the part of the United States, went hand in hand with aid, and gradually about $2 billion was placed first at the disposal of the American zone of occupation and then at that of the British-American "bi-zone." This was accomplished through the so-called GARIOA funds (Government and Relief in Occupied Areas). In principle, these sums were German debts which would be added to the reparations Germany would pay. In practice, and in the course of further political developments, they became a virtually unconditional subsidy, a fact which German government circles and newspapers do not often mention.

When the Allied Control Commission empowered the Roman government on August 1, 1945, to resume control of Italian foreign trade, it was in a catastrophic state. Its growth after 1946 was primarily due to imports, and the resulting deficits weighed the more heavily since freightage had to be paid in dollars. Industrial production, tourism, a merchant navy no longer existed. The United States intervened early. In 1946, it made up nearly four-fifths of the Italian deficit: $380 million through the United Nations Relief and Rehabilitation Administration (UNRRA), $98 million through the American Foreign Economic Administration, and $110 million in private assistance in the form of parcels and money orders, especially from Americans of Italian descent or from Italian immigrants.[5]

In the case of France, the Lend-Lease agreements concluded with the French committee in London in September 1942 and with the government in Algiers one year later were extended by new agreements which Jean Monnet had negotiated as the special delegate of his government on February 28, 1945. The cancellation of Lend-Lease led to an agreement in December which primarily took the form of a contract between the French government and the Export-Import Bank, which opened an account of $550 million which would be repayable within thirty years and was designed to pay for those orders which had not yet been firmly contracted for.

On the day the Consultative Assembly, the parliament of the time, agreed to ratify this agreement, it also ratified the Bretton Woods agreements, and the government devalued the franc since prices in France were significantly higher than abroad and exports almost impossible. The parliamentary debate proved that the ministers and parties were as aware of the significance of Bretton Woods—a policy of international cooperation, no structure of protective tariffs—as they were of the limits of the system. "All we can attain in 1946 is foreign exchange advances on the order of 112.5 million dollars, while we would have to come up with billions of dollars to make up for the deficit in our trade balance," the rapporteur of the financial commission, Christian Pineau, stated. "Our real problem is therefore to obtain credits from the United States in addition to the Bretton Woods agreements, for the United States will be the chief supplier of capital to Europe."[6]

Credits were all the more necessary because France was about to launch an ambitious project. On January 3, 1946, a general planning commission was established and entrusted with the creation of a capital investment and modernization program. When the governmental planning council met in March, General de Gaulle was no longer the head of government. He had resigned on January 20. But the High Commissioner he had appointed, Jean Monnet, made it clear in his report to the council that between 1946 and 1949 imports amounting to $11 billion would be needed. Then he sent the most highly re-spected French politician, the Socialist Léon Blum, who had been Prime Minister of the Popular Front government in 1936, to the United States. Blum had been deported to Buchenwald in 1943 and had recently returned from there with the prestige of a national leader.

After eleven weeks of negotiations, the agreements concluded between him and Byrnes were signed on May 28. They contained a memorandum concerning the final settlement of war debts and other demands amounting to $720 million which would be repayable within thirty-five years. In addition, there was a joint declaration of the two governments on trade policy which aimed at "abolishing the restrictions imposed on world trade," an agreement to open additional credits by the Export-Import Bank, and finally a special arrangement which made the import of American films into France considerably easier, and which was later vehemently criticized by the French press.

The American credits would not have been so urgently needed if French production could have availed itself of energy from foreign sources which would not have required dollars; in other words, access to German Ruhr coal as part of German reparations payments. But on this point, France ran into American resistance, for the United States had no intention of allowing occupied Germany to become totally impoverished, for then it would have to expend even larger amounts to keep it afloat. Did this mean that the defeated country would be granted special status at the expense of France, which was one of the victors. All countries were impoverished and exhausted. Was there going to be a repetition of what had happened after 1919 and was the recent enemy going to be favored above the ally?

GREAT BRITAIN AND FRANCE IN A GAME À QUATRE

The fate of the great defeated nation lay in the hands of the great victors, who had agreed in principle during the war to settle everything between them. At least as far as Germany was concerned, for with regard to southeastern Europe, Churchill had proposed to Stalin in October 1944 that countries such as Yugoslavia, Greece, and Rumania be subject only to the influence of the Soviet Union and Great Britain, though in varying degrees. Stalin had agreed to such shared influence, yet had never precisely defined what mechanisms would be used to bring such influence to bear, especially in those countries that were already occupied by Soviet troops.

But officially, problems concerning the organization of a future Europe were among the responsibilities of the European Advisory

Commission (EAC), which the three major powers had decided to establish in October 1943 and which convened 120 times in London between January 1944 and July 1945. Its task consisted primarily in drafting and working out a plan for the occupation of Germany, and its decisions had to be approved by the three governments.

By three governments, or by four? In November 1944, France was admitted to the commission. A month earlier, the Dumbarton Oaks Conference had taken place, in which the United States, the Soviet Union, Great Britain, and the new major power, China, had laid the groundwork for the future organization of the United Nations. France had not been invited, but in the executive organ—the Security Council—a seat was to be set aside for it. After numerous disputes between General de Gaulle and the other major powers had flared up in March, France did in fact become the fifth great power at the founding conference in San Francisco (April-June, 1945)—those five, in other words, who were "more equal than the others" in an organization based on the idea of the equality of all nations.

The permanent seat on the Security Council was a sign of power, for it carried the veto right, the decisions of the Five having to be unanimous. But it was not an expression of real power in Europe. How could such power be attained, considering that immediately after its liberation, France had been dependent on American aid for vital supplies to both its army and its civilian population?

For General de Gaulle, the answer lay primarily in Moscow: dealing on an equal footing with the Soviet Union, a nation that had the same status as the United States, could not fail to enhance and strengthen the position of France vis-à-vis the United States.

Already in 1943, the Soviet ambassador, F. I. Bogomolov (the same man that had represented his country in Vichy), had occupied a privileged position in Algiers where for the first time on April 4, 1944, two Communists had joined the French government, the Comité Français de Libération Nationale, whereas during the years 1936–37 the Communist Party had simply supported the Blum government without being part of it.

In October, General de Gaulle amnestied the secretary-general of the Communist Party, Maurice Thorez, who had fled to the Soviet Union and been found guilty of "desertion" five years earlier, after his party had been outlawed. Thorez returned from Moscow toward the end of November, a few days before de Gaulle's visit to Stalin.

This visit led to the signing on December 10, 1944, of a mutual aid and assistance pact which was essentially directed against Germany and would retain its validity up to and beyond victory, for "the high contracting parties commit themselves after the termination of the present war against Germany to jointly take all requisite measures to eliminate any new German threat and to prevent any initiative which might enable Germany to attempt another aggression." And Germany would have to accept a significant reduction of its territory, for according to de Gaulle's wishes, France would establish itself on the Rhine and attempt to gain Stalin's support in this, though this was by no means decided "since Washington and London had not yet taken a position."[7] For his part, de Gaulle agreed to Stalin's desire that Poland's western border run along the Oder and Neisse rivers and added: "It is our view that such a solution would preclude any understanding between Germany and Poland,"[8] an important idea as regards the future development of postwar relationships.

But the treaty also contained an Article 5 which sounded quite different: "The high contracting parties commit themselves not to enter into an alliance or to join any coalition directed against one of the partners to the treaty." What was at stake here was the answer de Gaulle would give to this question by Stalin: "What is a Western bloc?" In the short discussion following it, the United States was not mentioned by name. De Gaulle merely said in clarification: "England never called on us to form a bloc with it. Nor have we. In the interest of security, we wish to form a European bloc Moscow-Paris-London." As yet, there was no genuine "triangular relationship" since de Gaulle did not care to give a positive answer to Churchill's offer which had arrived in Moscow on December 6. "A pact," the General said to Ambassador Bogomolov, "represents not just an alliance for the duration of this war but one for an indeterminate period after the war. We are ready . . . to conclude such an alliance with you, first, because our interests do not conflict anywhere in the world but also because we are certain that your attitude toward postwar Germany coincides with ours. As regards England, however, those two presuppositions have not been met at this time." And to Stalin he said: "At this time, there is nothing at issue between France and the Soviet Union. But we have always quarreled with Great Britain and will always continue to." And indeed, less than half a year later, a bloody French-English conflict in Syria was only barely averted.

In spite of all this, it was Churchill and not Stalin who brought it about that France did become one of the Big Four that jointly governed a defeated Germany, though it is also true that Churchill did not insist that de Gaulle be invited to the conference that took place on February 4–11, 1945, at Yalta in the Crimea. Churchill nonetheless succeeded in obtaining Stalin's consent to the participation of France in the occupation of Germany, even though Stalin did not feel kindly toward France, which in his opinion had made an even smaller war effort than Poland, had not offered any significant resistance to the Germans, and had been more adequately represented by the Vichy regime than by de Gaulle. But finally Stalin agreed to a French occupation zone, provided that it be made up of parts of the zones set aside for Great Britain and the United States. Churchill was anxious to do everything in his power to keep the Soviet Union from becoming the single major power on the European continent, convinced as he was that the United States would withdraw from Europe shortly after victory had been won.

Roosevelt approved Churchill's position, though without giving him much support, while his Secretary of State recommended that all French wishes regarding equal participation in the occupation of Germany be complied with.[9] Above all, he was opposed to a wider application of the earlier British-Soviet agreement which had been renewed at Yalta; American policy proposed to be global in scope, the United Nations was to secure the peace, and the system of security zones had to be abolished.

No Soviet-American agreement of whatever description concerning an eventual establishment of a joint and simultaneously competing system of domination in Europe or any other part of the world was ever envisaged at Yalta. Yet *Yalta or the Partition of the World* not only became the title of a French bestseller[10] (though that title had no connection whatever with the contents of the book) but also the most enduring, most widespread, most deeply rooted myth of French political life. It does not matter that no document justifies such an interpretation: in France, Yalta remains the symbol of a world system run by the two superpowers. The quite different myth which arose in the United States during the Cold War, i.e., the idea of a seriously weakened, resigned, and naïve Roosevelt who capitulated to Stalin and betrayed American interests, was of significantly shorter duration.[11]

The effect the French myth had will be analyzed in Part III. Its starting point was that France had not been represented at the Yalta Conference and that Churchill's role was unknown. For this reason, Great Britain was all too quickly perceived as a kind of junior partner of the United States, and this led to another important concept in France, that of the "Anglo-Saxons." Being excluded was so severe a blow to General de Gaulle that he turned down a meeting with Roosevelt, who had stated at the end of the conference: "I profoundly regret to have to inform him [de Gaulle] that it is impossible for me at this moment to accept his kind invitation to come to Paris. But I must assume that Algiers will be an acceptable alternative. Should the general agree to meet me in Algiers. . . ." In his *Mémoires de guerre*, the

General writes: "If Roosevelt wanted to see de Gaulle for good reasons, why had he not permitted him to come to the Crimea? And then, how was the American President qualified to invite the French President to visit him in France? . . . How could I agree to be summoned to a point on the national territory by a foreign chief of state?"[12]

True, Roosevelt still mistrusted de Gaulle at that time. The French scientists who had collaborated on the atomic bomb project were scheduled to return home in December, and this caused him concern. He considered turning the atomic secret over to the Russians rather than wait until scientists with communist sympathies or de Gaulle himself did so. Churchill continued to insist on an Anglo-American atomic monopoly: "One thing I am sure, that there is nothing that de Gaulle would like better than to have plenty of T.A.* to punish Britain, and nothing he would like less than to arm Communist Russia with the secret."[13]

Yet what de Gaulle did achieve is astonishing: equal status, with the veto right in two decisive areas—the United Nations and occupied Germany—and this success marked the unmistakable return of France among the major powers. The final and undoubtedly painful snub France had to put up with was its exclusion from the Potsdam Conference (July 17 to August 2, 1945), where the Big Three agreed once again on the principles that would guide the four victorious powers in their joint administration of Germany. After that, the differences became so blurred that a joint administration of Germany with the assistance of German experts was vetoed by the French from the very beginning.

The Potsdam Conference was interrupted once: Churchill and Clement Attlee returned to Great Britain on July 26 for the elections. Attlee came back alone, as Prime Minister. Judging by the text of the election manifesto, the only change in course in international policy that could be expected from England was a greater openness toward the Soviet Union. The Conservatives had still distinguished between "our alliance with Soviet Russia" and "our close ties to the United States," while the Labour Party stated: "We must consolidate in peace the great war-time association of the British Commonwealth with the U.S.A. and the U.S.S.R. Let it not be forgotten that in the years leading up to the war the Tories were so scared of Russia that they missed the chance to establish a partnership which might well have prevented the war."[14]

In point of fact, the new British Foreign Minister, Ernest Bevin, proved considerably tougher in the negotiations with the Soviet

---

*Tube Alloys. See p. 14.

Union than his predecessor, Anthony Eden; indeed he showed himself to be just as tough as Churchill. Now, of course, it was no longer a question of the war effort against a common enemy, and the tensions which had first surfaced during the discussions of the Three in November 1943 in Teheran had already noticeably increased while Roosevelt had still been alive and become even more pronounced after his death—though it is not possible to determine with precision what intentions were pursued or where responsibilities lay.[15]

The heart of the problem was the question concerning the attitude and intentions of the Soviet Union. According to the statement Roosevelt, Stalin, and Churchill had made about a liberated Europe at Yalta, the liberated countries were to be put in the position of choosing their own democratic institutions. But the "friendly" governments whose installation in the states bordering on the Soviet Union Stalin demanded in the interest of the security of his country, especially in Poland and Rumania, all impressed observers as aligned regimes under Soviet domination. A few days before his death, Roosevelt wrote Churchill: "I have likewise been watching with anxiety and concern the development of Soviet attitude since the Crimean conference."[16]

This evolution took precisely the course Churchill had foreseen and feared in earlier years, and perhaps a policy nourished by such fears had even favored it. Since he was no longer in power, he felt freer to present the situation as he saw it to the public at large. On May 1945, when he was still Prime Minister, he sent a confidential telegram to President Truman in which he spoke of an "iron curtain" which had descended over the Soviet front. On March 5, 1946, in a speech at Fulton, Missouri, which created a considerable stir, he recurred more emphatically to this slogan: "An iron curtain has descended across the continent. . . . From what I have seen of our Russian friends and allies during the war, I am convinced that there is nothing they admire so much as strength, and there is nothing for which they have less respect than for weakness, especially military weakness. . . . If the population of the English-speaking Commonwealth be added to that of the United States . . . there will be no quivering, precarious balance of power to offer its temptation to ambition or adventure."[17]

In other words, resistance to the forward thrust of the Soviets justified new joint action by the British and Americans; Great Britain's status would not be maintained by its presence among the Great Five at the United Nations or as one of the Big Four in Germany, but by a special relationship with the United States; and as far as French politics was concerned, the place of France among the major powers was due primarily to the existence of an occupied Germany which furnished the pretext for a fictitious unity among the Big Four.

Actually, Great Britain stopped being the equal partner of the United States in the very year Churchill delivered his speech at Fulton. For different reasons than Churchill had had, the Labour Party submitted to restraints he also would have accepted and saw itself obliged to renounce responsibilities which until recently had been considered vital. England's economic and financial position was so strained that there was no possibility of avoiding transferring to the United States some of the burdens the country had borne so far: "America in Britain's place."[18] In 1946, this formula applied to at least two especially precarious areas: Greece and Germany.

Events in Greece in 1946 were the overture to the third act of a drama which had already begun during the war. In 1941, King George II had left his country after it had been overrun by German troops. Previously, Greece had been governed dictatorially by General John Metaxas but also maintained close relations with Great Britain. Two resistance movements had fought the German occupying power but also each other: the EAM with its military arm ELAS, whose leaders were mostly Communists; and the EDES, in which republicans and loyalists hostile to the dictatorship had united. From Cairo, the king, who enjoyed Churchill's support, intervened without political skill, while the American government was primarily anxious to stay out. The conflict between the rival resistance movements was settled in March 1944 by the establishment of a provisional national liberation committee and the twofold promise of the king that he would enlarge George Papandreou's government-in-exile and not return to his country until there had been a referendum. But a new element suddenly came into play when after the liberation of Greek territory, ELAS refused to let itself be disarmed and at the same time attacked British troops and Greek soldiers loyal to the monarchy that had landed with them.

The bloody "second round" was probably not based on a preconceived plan by the Greek Communists to seize power, and the civil war was not deliberately started by anyone.[19] But everyone was convinced that the intentions of the adversary were wholly evil. Churchill had justified participation in the war in the House of Commons: it was up to the Greek people, he said, whether they wanted to live under a monarchy or a republic, whether they preferred a government of the Right or the Left. But until they were in a position to do so, "we shall not hesitate to use the considerable British army now in Greece, and being reinforced, to see that law and order are maintained."[20]

In the eyes of the American press and the U.S. government, Great Britain's procedure was not justified. It was said that this was a quasi colonialist intervention, designed to perpetuate an influence in the name of exclusively British interests, that the king was a mere tool, that ELAS was anti-Fascist rather than Communist and the king a reactionary and no defender of democracy.

Even Churchill and Eden acknowledged that the Greek Communists had proceeded on their own and that Moscow had abstained from any and all intervention; indeed they even thanked Stalin for having observed the "division of spheres of influence" on which he had agreed with the British Prime Minister.[21] Churchill was interested in preventing any expansion of Soviet rule, even if this were accomplished through proxy, by a local Communist party. He also wished to preserve a conservative government in Greece. It seemed that this policy would succeed, for in January 1945 an armistice was concluded, and after much back and forth, elections under international supervision were held on March 31, 1946. A referendum on September 1 turned out favorable to the king, and on the twenty-seventh he returned to his country.

But at this moment, the United Nations was already debating new confrontations. A long guerrilla war had begun in which the fighters of the Communist KKE were supported by Bulgaria, Albania, and Yugoslavia, all of them "friendly" neighbors of the Soviet Union. And the government in Athens was no longer satisfied with British help, since Great Britain was in no position to meet its military and financial demands. Toward the end of 1946, the situation took a dramatic turn, and in February 1947 Attlee's government approached the United States with the request to take England's place in Greece.

This time, the American government decided to intervene. It gave the Greek government economic and military aid until the end of the "third round" in 1949. For the United States, Greece now was no longer a country which Great Britain wanted to continue to control but an important outpost in the struggle against an advancing Communism. To exorcise this danger, the United States was even prepared to support an authoritarian and repressive government (although the result here was not the same as in Indochina: since General Markos' partisans were finally crushed, Anglo-American relations concerning Greece became similar in many respects to what Franco-American relations over Vietnam were to become later).

In Germany, there was neither a bloody tragedy nor a complete substitution of American influence. In September 1944, at the Quebec Conference, Churchill had obtained Roosevelt's consent to Great Britain's occupation of the Ruhr, while the United States would content itself with occupying the less highly industrialized areas in central and southern Germany. But in a devastated country, it is much more difficult to supply bombed cities than rural areas. This drawback would have been minor if everyone had stuck to the fundamental decision made in Potsdam according to which Germany was to have been dealt with as an economic unit. But in practice, every occupation zone was administered individually.

In July 1946, an investigative commission estimated the cost to Great Britain for its zone for 1946–47 at more than £80 million. The only possible solution was fusion with the American zone, which would not only provide a better economic balance but also saddle the United States with a large share of the financial burden. The Anglo-American agreement, which set January 1, 1947, as the effective date for this unification, was signed on December 2, 1946. A jointly run organization, the JEIA (Joint Export-Import Agency), would be charged with the foreign trade of this "bi-zone." In principle, both military governors would have equal powers, and the two administrations continued to work separately, but from now on, British policy regarding Germany was firmly tied to that of the Americans, who tended to establish the course for both Allies.

GERMANY UNDER THE OCCUPYING POWERS

As the waning power of one of the great Allies became evident, the status of the defeated countries also changed. Actually, there was only one nation that had really lost the war in Western Europe, and that was Germany. The situation in Italy continued ambiguous. In the final Potsdam communiqué, Italy's contribution during the last phase of the war had been acknowledged, but already in late December 1945 the foreign ministers of the four major powers decided that the elaboration of a peace treaty was wholly the concern of the Big Four. Alcide de Gasperi, Prime Minister and Foreign Minister since December 10, protested the decision and its implicit failure to recognize the fact that Italy had fought on the side of the Allies. Protracted and complicated negotiations were needed until the treaty could be signed in Paris on February 10, 1947, when the treaties with Rumania, Bulgaria, Hungary, and Finland were also signed. Yet the text failed to put an end to one of the most complex and irritating problems of the postwar era, and that was the dispute between Italy and Yugoslavia over Trieste.[22]

The treaty was very harsh, and American support, which was limited out of consideration for the British, did not have the hoped-for result. Through the loss of all of its colonies (and the dissolution by French authorities of the Italian community in Tunis) and the disarming and demilitarizing of Italy, the country had shrunk and was now a small power no longer able to see to its own security, let alone engage in a new expansionist policy.

It was the United States which had facilitated Italy's admission to the IMF and the World Bank in October 1944. And the United States, more than anyone else, continued to provide material help to a country whose internal political development gave cause for persistent concern. An unbroken line runs from the agreement on economic cooperation signed on December 6, 1945, to the waiver of reparations payments in September 1946 to the American declaration in October of that year that Italy would be reimbursed for the expenses incurred by the American occupation. But the assistance granted in 1946 proved totally inadequate. On January 3, 1947, de Gasperi went to Washington where he hoped to get more. Theoretically, he went on behalf of the entire government, i.e., his second cabinet, in which there were still Communists and whose Foreign Minister was Pietro Nenni, a Socialist who advocated close collaboration with the Italian Communist Party.

Germany was thus the only truly vanquished nation—but did Germany exist at all in 1945? Almost one-quarter of the territory defined as "German" in the Treaty of Versailles had already been either partitioned off and become part of the USSR—like half of East Prussia—or, and this was the larger part, was placed under Polish administration, as millions were driven from their homes. The other three-quarters came under the administrative system that the European Consultative Commission had devised in London in September 1944. Through the Control Commission made up of the commanders-in-chief and with its seat in Berlin, the victorious powers would jointly exercise the highest authority and the former capital would be occupied by all four of them, each of the four sectors being administered by one, making Greater Berlin an enclave within the Soviet occupation zone. Each occupying power thus ran one area whose borders (except for the French zone) had been determined long before the German surrender.

Immediately after that surrender, it first had to be decided if the earlier agreement would really be implemented. The meeting of American and Soviet troops occurred along the Elbe River, i.e., far to the east of the line agreed to in London. Churchill urgently requested President Truman not to cede an inch of occupied territory to the Soviet Union, whose leadership, it seemed, had hardly expected that in any event. Truman resolved to stick to his obligation, provided the Russians kept to theirs. The American, British, and French troops moved into Berlin, which had been taken by the Red Army alone while the U.S. army evacuated an extensive area including Weimar, Jena, and Erfurt. This decision implied the right to existence of the three Western sectors of Berlin but also settled the fate of the population of the evacuated region, since the line agreed to in London represented a no less sharply defined and equally arbitrary partition as the lines the colonial powers had been wont to draw in nineteenth-century Africa or the borders which in sixteenth-century Europe decided the religious affiliation of the subjects and their progeny according to "cuius regio, eius religio."

The Control Commission never functioned very satisfactorily, and this was due both to the French veto and the Soviet attitude. Real power soon came to lie in the hands of the military commanders, though they did not exercise it as members of a joint control commission but as the absolute rulers in their respective zones. Each of them proceeded according to the instructions of *his* government and interpreted them according to *his* lights. In principle, the charter of the American zone was the harsh document JCS 1067 of the American Joint Chiefs of Staff, countless passages of which were reminiscent of the terrible "Morgenthau Plan" which Churchill and Roosevelt had initialed in Quebec in September 1944 but which had never been declared an element of official Anglo-American policy. Yet it was precisely this plan which was to feed German resentment for years: Germany had to be punished, its industry destroyed, its population treated as an enemy, which meant that it had to be excluded from public life or reeducated in authoritarian fashion.

In actual practice, however, such a plan could not be carried out when one felt responsible for a region and its population, when one tried to deal with the material concerns and the administrative chaos, and above all, when one represented a country which had not directly suffered under Nazism and did not demand that the resources of its zone of occupation be employed primarily for its own recovery, as was true of the USSR and France.

An occupation is first of all the physical presence of the occupying power. In this respect, the Americans did not initially succeed in promoting a positive image of the United States in Frankfurt, Nuremberg, Stuttgart, or Munich, for the American soldiers did not display the reserve of their British comrades. The euphoria of victory and the anxiety to be repatriated produced an astonishing laxness of discipline. In an order of the day in early 1946, General McNarney saw himself obliged to denounce the chief evils from which the army under his command suffered: extensive black market activity, absence without leave, automobile accidents, venereal disease, neglect of appearance. Discipline improved somewhat after 1946, but the black market became more widespread: it was too tempting to trade cigarettes for Leicas.

In principle, the Americans could have lived almost wholly apart from the Germans. Many public places were off limits; in a manner of speaking, the occupiers were to live in a sphere of their own. Every building in which Americans were housed had first to be evacuated by the Germans. Even a long time after the end of the occupation, a good many houses near the large I.G. Farben installation in Frankfurt had to remain virtually unoccupied because a few Americans lived there. And when the Federal Republic had been established and a large embassy had been built in Bad Godesberg, the architect bragged during a press conference that he had arranged everything in such fashion that the diplomats could live there, have their laundry done, and shop for groceries without ever having to come into contact with a single German.

In contrast, many Americans were seeing Germans, particularly young girls, even before the fraternization ban was lifted, and this led not only to a rise in the number of illegitimate births but to political consequences of some moment. The soldiers, who had never lived under an occupation and hardly knew any history, rebelled against the harsh policy of their government. It was inconceivable that Lisbeth's or Hanna's charming family could have had anything to do with the Nazi criminals! In this way, albeit in a different form, the views of officers such as General Patton or of administrators who had come from the private sector were adopted. Patton was relieved of his command in Bavaria because he had argued that the difference between a German Nazi and a German anti-Nazi was no greater than that between a Democratic or Republican American, and therefore resisted denazification with all his might. The businessmen in the administration could not see that bank director Müller had ever been anything other than a decent, apolitical official. But all these ideas, spontaneous rather than thought through, experienced rather than expressed, had a profound influence on the daily implementation of American policy.

The number of American administrators was not large (roughly 5,000 for a zone of 107,500 square kilometers with 17.1 million inhabitants toward the end of 1946, as compared to the British zone with 97,000 square kilometers and 22.3 million people and administered by 25,000 officials). On a local level, they controlled without actually governing. The higher positions—in the *Länder* or even at the top, i.e., in Frankfurt, where the commander-in-chief, General Lucius Clay, and his political adviser Robert Murphy had their headquarters—were initially staffed by experts who came from the Administration, the army, or the universities. After 1946, the number of industrialists and businessmen increased.

There is one aspect of German-American relations during the occupation which was significant and complex: the activity of Germans who had returned from the United States, where they had either lived as immigrants and waited for Hitler's fall to then return home, or had come to America to stay and had acquired citizenship. Among the émigrés, there were numerous well-known writers and intellectuals. They could not be considered a homogeneous group, since some had been favorably impressed by the United States, while others who had lived marginal existences on the other side of the Atlantic and experienced only the negative aspects of American society now spread the same derogatory clichés that characterize traditional European anti-Americanism. "A country in which we don't belong, that has nothing to give us, from which we have nothing to learn, and to which we have nothing to say. . . . A country without tradition, without culture . . ." Carl Zuckmayer said, for example. [23] The negative effects of a return from the United States also surfaced in the activities of some occupation officials, mostly Jewish émigrés or their sons who had become American citizens and now showed little readiness to understand the Germans after their defeat.

Numerous other officials or advisors, on the other hand, had an exceptionally positive influence, not only in the creation of new institutions but also in the reintegration of German intellectual life into the international stream. Some of the émigré professors who had built up or perhaps even founded departments of philosophy or sociology at American universities returned temporarily or permanently to German universities, either retaining their American or reassuming their German citizenship. Max Horkheimer, Theodor W. Adorno, Arnold Bergsträsser, Ernst Fränkel, Eric Voegelin—the list could easily be extended. Carl J. Friedrich, who had left Germany before Hitler's seizure of power and now worked as a respected advisor to the military government in all constitutional questions, undoubtedly occupied a special place. In 1949, he became one of the spiritual fathers of the *Grundgesetz* (basic law), exercised a mediating function between American and German political philosophy for three decades, and taught for many years at Harvard and Heidelberg. Yet his role was no more important than that of those politicians who returned from exile and sometimes exchanged their American for German citizenship. Perhaps the most remarkable among these was Max Brauer, who became the mayor of Hamburg in 1946.

As in the other zones of occupation, it was the occupying power, its administrative customs and ideology, that put its stamp on all of public life, and this was as true in local political structures as in recreational activities or the media, where the Americans, interested in impartial reporting, demanded that the editorial offices of all authorized German papers be staffed by representatives of every political persuasion, including members of the Communist Party. The Germans felt that the Americans and the other three occupying powers were jointly

responsible for whatever good or ill might come of the great Nuremberg war crimes trials. But the denazification program in the American
zone had its own special characteristics and pursued a complex and
contradictory policy, which was sometimes harsher but more frequently more lenient than procedures in the British and French
zones.[24]

Particular care was devoted to "re-education," the positive counterpart to denazification, a task the four occupying powers took so much
to heart that in June 1947 the Control Council devised a joint directive
concerning the "democratization" of the educational system in Germany.[25] In the American zone, this concern with schooling and youth
activities was often so paternalistic and even petty that the result stood
in inverse relation to the "democratization" intended. The strict instructions given the school administrators were not always complied
with, however, and as early as 1946 these authorities became increasingly autonomous.

Though merely an object of international politics and a country to
which the four major powers had denied all external and internal
sovereignty, occupied Germany nevertheless rapidly rose to become
a partner in the dialogue, or more precisely, it provided the occupying
powers with a variety of such partners, at first on the local level, then
on that of the *Länder*—which had come into existence in 1946 after
elections dominated by the Christian Democrats, the Social Democrats, and the Liberals—and finally at the parliamentary and governmental levels. The occupying powers occasionally intervened
quite dictatorially in both the choice of politicians and the running of
institutions. But the opposite occurred no less frequently. Close personal ties were created, as for example between the American colonel
William W. Dawson, an eminent jurist and administrative expert, and
Reinhold Maier, Minister-President of Würtemberg-Baden (as it was
still called at that time), a friendship that is described in moving language in Maier's memoirs.[26]

Above all, the selections made at that time by the American but also
by the British and French occupying powers became the cornerstone
of the political elite of the future German state. Many of the men they
had assigned to some office or given an important role in 1945 and
1946 continued on at a regional governmental level after the end of
the occupation or rose to leading positions in the central government.
The most spectacular case was undoubtedly that of Ludwig Erhard,
the Bavarian economist whom the occupation authorities called on to
reorganize industry in the Nuremberg—Fürth region. On October 3,
1945, Erhard, who belonged to no political party, became Economics
Minister in the second government of Bavaria. His economic thinking

was much closer to what prevailed in the United States than were the ideas that circulated in occupied Germany and most of the other European countries at that time.

THE SLIDE TO THE LEFT IN EUROPE AND ITS LIMITS

Differences in status did not prevent considerable similarities in ideological and political trends in the various European countries. The war had been waged in the name of democracy against Fascism, and it was therefore quite natural that in 1945 democracy in Germany as in France and Italy understood itself as anti-Fascist. Thanks to the military effort of the anti-Fascist powers, principally the United States and the USSR, freedom had been regained. The preamble of the French constitution of October 27, 1946, which was carried over into the constitution of the Fifth Republic of 1958, begins with these words: "After the victory of the free peoples, won over those regimes which sought to subject and degrade the human being . . ." All the victorious peoples were considered free, and those that had been defeated were victorious to the extent that the defeat was that of governments, not of nations.

Internally, anti-Fascism meant first of all the punishment and exclusion of indigenous Fascists and all accomplices of the National Socialist occupier. The severity and extent of the purges with all their injustices depended on the specific situation. They were especially marked in Norway and Belgium. But everywhere, many of those that were called to account had also engaged in anti-American and anti-Soviet propaganda. "That decadent race of Americans" had bombed Hitler's Europe. "How could one fail to see that their barbaric acts were a kind of sadistic revenge on those to whom the world owes its enlightenment and its art, and committed by those which could neither create nor invent anything?" a Fascist Paris newspaper had written in 1943.[27]

Such talk should really have discredited anti-Americanism, but it remained more virulent than anti-Sovietism—in part because through their extensive and effective participation in resistance movements, Communist parties had been able to make others forget the period from 1939 to 1941 when they had condemned Anglo-American imperialism more severely than the Fascist variety; and also because the social forces that had collaborated with the dictatorships were counterparts of those that ran American but not Soviet society. When the British occupation authorities arrested the industrialist Hugo Stinnes and thirty-nine members of the coal cartel in September 1945, when the Krupp family sat on the bench for the accused while the first German organizations General Eisenhower admitted as early as 1946 were unions, the powerful representatives of a specific social type were punished. Shortly after his return to liberated France, General de Gaulle received a group of entrepreneurs with the contemptuous greeting: "Gentlemen, I saw none of you in London," and then he added: "Well, at least you are not in prison."[28] But while it is true that they were not in prison, there was a decree which provided for the dissolution of employer organizations should their members be unable to give adequate proof of patriotism. Wasn't it a fact that the overwhelming majority of entrepreneurs had supported the Vichy regime?

In part because of the passive or active support it had given both the extreme Right in its own country and the occupying power, in part because of the economic and social system it stood for and defended, the Right had fallen into disrepute in 1945. The resistance movements had nowhere confined themselves to invoking the idea of the nation, and this was true whether we consider the charter of the Conseil National de la Résistance or the program laid down in June 1945 in Norway which was endorsed by all parties. Everywhere the view prevailed that a return to the chaotic economic conditions and the social injustice of the prewar period had to be avoided at all cost. The surprise at the victory of the Labour Party in the July 1945 British elections can be ascribed to the failure to recognize a profound transnational movement. Everywhere, in France, Denmark, Italy, Germany, and Belgium, a push toward the Left was taking place. To be "Left" meant to demand social change which would be brought about by having the national community take charge of the economy. To the extent socialism can be defined, the Europe of 1945–46 was certainly right to call itself socialist.

And this was all the truer since the disappearance of the parties of the Right caused many conservatives to vote for the least leftist party, a party which inspired the greatest confidence and made use of the then current vocabulary, and in Germany, Belgium, Italy, and France, that meant the Christian Democrats. The Italian Democrazia Cristiana (DC) and the French Mouvement Républicain Populaire (MRP) rejected the attitude of the Church under Fascism or toward the Vichy regime.[29] By their alliance with Socialist and Communist parties, they not only publicly confirmed that militant Catholics had fought Fascism but also rehabilitated in a sense those countless Catholics who had all too readily followed the general course of the episcopate. In Germany, the situation was not radically different.

The leftist course of the Christian-inspired parties made them reject capitalism in the name of justice but also condemn Marxism because it was based on materialism and explained society by the class struggle: "The CDU overcomes capitalism and Marxism" was the slogan in the party program which the Rhenish CDU adopted in Ahlen on February 3, 1947. The denunciation of monopolies, the refusal to equate political freedom and economic laissez-faire, the demand for a planned economy and participation of workers in the management of enterprises, were not peculiarities of this program but were found almost everywhere, especially in France in the documents and speeches of the MRP. The right to private property was not denied, but what was expressly and almost generally insisted on was the usefulness, indeed the necessity, of socialization in the name of a control of economic development, and traces of such demands could still be detected in the various constitutions when the ideological current had long been reversed. Article 43 of the Italian constitution of December 27, 1947, and Article 15 of the *Grundgesetz* of the German Federal Republic of May 23, 1949, expressed this with particular clarity.

During the years 1945—46, comprehensive socialization in a variety of forms was carried out in Great Britain, Italy, and France. In the Ruhr, a veto by the occupation authorities was required to prevent collectivization of the coal mines. At the same time, an effort was made to protect the individual against personal risk such as illness and old age. In Great Britain, France, and even more in the Scandinavian countries, encompassing social security systems were introduced. The push toward the Left which expressed itself in this fashion did not look for models beyond the Atlantic, for from the European perspective, ideology and reality in the United States continued to subscribe to a liberalism which appeared to guarantee the power of the stronger and the impotence of the weaker. America was not ignored by observers on the Left, but its image had a negative impact: the critique of America was part of the definition of what was *not* wanted. In this context, many literary phenomena seem extremely paradoxical: in the immediate postwar era, for example, France showed an exceptional preference for American novelists, and it may be that the influence of American literature had never been greater. Dos Passos, Faulkner, and Steinbeck enabled a man such as Jean-Paul Sartre to find models for the rejection of an existing social order.

The intellectual ferment occurred in the most diverse spheres of social life—the theater, public instruction, the Church, popular culture—and went beyond a merely parallel development in the various countries. Communications, especially between France and Germany, were quickly established. The first Franco-German meetings, which took place as early as 1945 and subsequently increased in scope, were dominated by this transnational ferment. The contacts between the editorial offices of two journals which were animated by an identical idea, *Esprit* and the *Frankfurter Hefte*, were typical of these relationships. What was common to their efforts to achieve spiritual renewal and change was their desire to open new paths while rejecting both the American and the Soviet models. The division of the world by the Cold War later doomed such a plan, and became the constraint to adapt to one or the other of these models.

The fact that the international situation and the intervention of the United States could be charged with failures which could be attributed primarily to social and political obstacles within each national society made the reaction all the livelier. And this was all the truer as two rather significant phenomena remained almost unnoticed. Wherever the problem of economic efficiency was concerned, the U.S. government went along with things in Europe that it would never have tolerated in the United States. In fact, the presupposition for aid was the demand for a rationally organized economy. Later it was said: "The Monnet plan worked while the plan proposed by the economic ministry in 1944 failed, and this was due to the fact that the former had a very concrete starting point which was to reassure the Americans on the use of the funds they would grant us according to the terms of the Blum-Byrnes agreements."[30] But the general appeal for control of economic development also went hand in hand with the desire to do away with the bureaucratic constraints which weighed on everyone. Wasn't the socialism of the resistance fighters simply the continuation of the planned economy of a Mussolini, a Hitler, the Vichy regime, indeed even of the Allied occupation authorities, who controlled food supplies by strict rationing? What if it was true that economic efficiency would be more adequately guaranteed by an economic liberalism of the American type, at least as the Europeans understood it?

Because its situation was unique in more than one respect, Germany was the country that reacted first and most strongly to the stimulus toward a neoliberal mode of thought which the American model provided. In part this was due to the occupation itself, in part to the fact that practitioners of a free economy were represented in the military government of the American zone. The *soziale Marktwirtschaft*, the social economics of Ludwig Erhard, did not entirely correspond to the American model but was markedly influenced by its advocates in occupied Germany.[31]

It is also true that liberalism could more quickly gain a foothold here because socialism was less closely tied to the ideology of resistance than in France and Italy. Quite incorrectly, it was believed that active opposition to Hitler had been largely and perhaps entirely embodied in the conspiracy of those men who had organized the unsuccessful attempt on Hitler's life on July 20, 1944. Its leaders had been conservatives. There was the additional circumstance that the resistance movement did not have the ideological significance it had elsewhere. The image of an ultimately treasonable opposition, treasonable because it had hastened the defeat of the fatherland, was never really destroyed, particularly since its intent to eliminate Hitler had helped not only a free democracy but also a dreaded Communism to achieve victory.

Yet the Communist Party in Germany (KPD) obtained quite remarkable results during regional elections in 1946 (though they were considerably less significant than those of 1932): 10.7 percent in Hessen, 14 percent in Nordrhein-Westfalen. In other Western European countries, comparable percentages represented a small increase in the Communist vote. In the Netherlands, the Communists had obtained a mere 3.4 percent of the vote in 1934, as compared to 25.7 percent for the Socialists. But in 1946, the figures were 10.5 percent and 28.1 percent, respectively. In Belgium, the 6 percent share of the Communists in 1936 increased to about 12 percent in February 1946, while the Socialists scored no gains (31 percent versus 32 percent). The threshold of 100,000 members was crossed toward the end of 1945. While the Communist Party was not in power in The Hague, it was part of the coalition in Brussels. Although the Danish Communist Party obtained 11 percent of the vote in October 1945, it was no longer represented in the government after that date. Because Great Britain has majority rule, the issue did not arise at the governmental level. The Communist Party certainly had no true power in the face of the Labour Party, and though its membership had almost tripled when compared to the rather insignificant number in 1939 (45,400 as compared to 17,700), its influence was already waning as compared to 1943, when admiration of the military operations of the Soviet Union had been at its height.

The situation of the Italian and French Communist parties was quite different. On June 2, 1946, the Italians did away with the monarchy by popular vote and elected the Constituent Assembly. While the Christian Democrats obtained 8 million votes (35.2 percent), the Communists with 4.4 million (19 percent) proved nearly as strong as the Socialists (20.7 percent). In France, the Communist Party even headed the list after the first national elections in October 1945 (26.2 percent as compared to 23.4 percent for the Socialists and 23.9 percent for the MRP). When the first Constituent Assembly of the Fourth Republic was to be elected for a five-year period in November 1946, the gap had even increased: 28.2 percent voted Communist and only 17.8 percent Socialist, while the MRP as the third member of the "three-party system" which had governed with de Gaulle attracted only 25.9 percent without him.

The two Communist parties were anxious to remain in the government and attempted to strengthen the alliance with the Socialists. On October 27, 1946, the Italian Communist Party could come to a united-action agreement with the Socialists, but the alliance proved too constricting for some of the Socialists. In January 1947, Giuseppe Saragat and his friends left Pietro Nenni's party and founded the Italian Social Democratic Party. In spite of the slide toward the Left in France in 1946 which resulted in Guy Mollet's becoming secretary-general, the Socialists under Léon Blum and Daniel Mayer were rather reserved toward the Communist Party and were really closer to Saragat than to Nenni. At the same time, the MRP took a less clearly anti-Communist direction than the Christian Democrats of Alcide de Gasperi. Yet it is undoubtedly true that the Italian Communist Party was much more moderate than its French counterpart, for when relations to the Christian Democrats had already become quite strained, it reconciled itself to the retention in the new Italian constitution of the Lateran Accords which the Vatican had concluded with Mussolini and which granted the Church numerous benefits. In France, on the other hand, it occurred to no one to question the separation of Church and state, which had become law in 1905.

In addition, the allure of the Italian Communist Party was quite different from that of the French. It is true that both created the impression of being organizations that were oriented toward youth and the future, responsible and creative, and thus they necessarily exercised a certain attraction for everyone who wished to rebuild the country on a new foundation—though that attraction was something foreigners, particularly Americans, could not understand. In May 1946, the French chief of protocol noted after a dinner at the Foreign Ministry: "Senator Vandenberg, who sat next to me, could not take his eyes off Maurice Thorez' beaming face: 'how can such a healthy man be a communist?' he kept repeating."[32] But the party (since the Second World War, "the party" in France has always referred to the Communist Party, whereas before the war it designated Edouard Herriot's liberal "Radical Party") also had a rougher, darker side which now fascinated many intellectuals. Stalin's toughness and revolutionary despotism were the forces that swept history along, and such a regime must not be seen with the same eyes as a reactionary tyranny. Although one of the leading young philosophers of the time, Maurice Merleau-Ponty, said at first, "It is impossible to be an anti-Communist and it is not possible to be a Communist," he went on: "A serious discussion of Communism must ... pose the problem ... on the ground of human relations. It will not brandish liberal principles in order to topple Communism; it will examine whether it is doing anything to resolve the problem rightly raised by Communism, namely, to establish among men relations that are human."[33]

In Germany, on the other hand, "liberal principles" were considered an indispensable, indeed the decisive antidote to the poison of National Socialism. And every new monolithism, every new suppression of freedoms, had to be rejected categorically even if it presented itself in the name of a social democracy to be created. For the Social Democrats in the British, American, and French zones and their head, Kurt Schumacher, who had survived Hitler's concentration camps as a cripple, the news from the Soviet zone in April 1946 was even more terrifying than for the Christian Democrats and the Liberals. While the only vote that could be taken by SPD members in the three Western sectors of Berlin showed that the party rank and file overwhelmingly opposed an alliance with the KPD, the SPD leaders in the Soviet zone convened an extraordinary party congress and pushed through the founding of the Sozialistische Einheitspartei Deutschlands (SED), in which the Communists, with the active support of the Soviet occupying power, set the tone.

For Kurt Schumacher, Communist control created an almost insurmountable dilemma. If he was to stand up to Soviet domination, was he not obliged to seek the support of the other occupying powers, specifically the United States? But he was also struggling against those powers, especially the Americans, in the effort to regain German sovereignty and recover unlimited fundamental freedoms which would no longer be subject to Allied control. His relations to General Lucius Clay were as bad as they could be, worse than General de Gaulle's relations to his American interlocutors had ever been. And there is nothing far-fetched about this comparison: Kurt Schumacher and Charles de Gaulle based their attitude on the same principle of intransigence because they had to compensate for their inadequacies and weaknesses. Like de Gaulle, Schumacher readily rejected the influence of the two superpowers even though he knew that support from one of them was indispensable. More indispensable than many Germans who dreamt of a "neutral" Germany that would keep out of all conflicts that might arise between yesterday's victors cared to admit.[34]

Wouldn't such support even increase as Germany moved toward the center of these conflicts? When Secretary of State James Byrnes stated in a speech in Stuttgart on September 6, 1946, that it "is not in the

interest of the German people or of world peace that Germany become
a partner or a pawn in the military struggle between East and West,"
he could hardly declare openly that it was precisely because of this
political struggle between the superpowers that he was promising the
Germans the end of the punitive period of occupation and a less
gloomy future.

But did a less gloomy future for the Germans also mean the onset of
dark times for the French? The Stuttgart speech touched off violent
reactions in France. Were the Americans going to give German aid
priority? If they underestimated the fears the French continued to feel
even though Germany had been defeated, they would provide considerable impetus to French anti-Americanism, particularly since
anti-German resentments fulfilled the same function in French
domestic politics as the Yalta myth. The alliance between the three
great parties for the rebuilding of France made sense only if the Big
Four were seen as united in their determination to keep Germany
under their tutelage and to confirm France's place among the great
nations.

In Great Britain, things took an entirely different course. The only
break the international development seemed to bring about was not
one between the various parties but one that divided the Labour Party.
England's desire to remain at the same level as the superpowers and
to act in concert with them was stressed more by the Conservatives
than by Labour Party members when the war ended.[35] When Churchill changed the tone he adopted toward the USSR in public, this did
not really affect his relations with Prime Minister Attlee and Ernest
Bevin. However, the left wing of the Labour Party, which was represented in the cabinet by Aneurin Bevan's strong personality, showed
its distinct displeasure. "Democratic Socialism, if it had any virility,
would have serious arguments to settle with the Americans no less
than with the Russians. Since the Americans were as aggressively
capitalist as the Russians were aggressively Communist, this conclusion could be deduced from first principles."[36]

In Great Britain, the conflict produced an opposition between the
practice of the Labour government and the ideology of the Labour
Left. In France and Italy, the dividing line gave the Communist parties a new place in political life and split the entire Left so profoundly
that its very existence seemed endangered. In Germany, the schisms
of 1947 divided the entire nation. Henceforth, all these rifts would be
reflected in relations with the United States.

3 MONEY AND ARMS

TIME does not always have the same value. Measurable duration is not the duration of experience, since density and intensity of experience can make a moment weigh more than an extended period. The two years from the spring of 1947 to the spring of 1949 were particularly dense and intensive. They saw such profound and enduring changes that one might be tempted to divide the postwar era into three periods: 1945–46, 1947–49, and post-1949. The partition of Europe, the partition of Germany, the new bases for relationships between the United States and the Western European countries, the paradoxes and difficulties which arose in West Germany and France from this double partition: all in all, the articulation during the longer period is not as distinct as the sudden break in 1945, but no later period would equal it in importance.

THE MAJOR TURNING POINTS OF 1947

One must not simplify excessively, of course. Earlier conditions persisted while new ones appeared on the horizon. Early in 1947, the old wartime alliance still produced significant manifestations in the governing coalitions in Rome and Paris. The first President of the Fourth Republic was elected on January 16. The result of the election was announced by Jacques Duclos, the first vice-president of the National Assembly and secretary of the French Communist Party. Vincent Auriol, who was elected president of the National Assembly, received the votes of the Socialists and Communists, the Popular Republicans having put up a candidate of their own. On January 28, the government was formed under the leadership of the Socialist Paul Ramadier. His deputies were a Popular Republican and Maurice Thorez, secretary-general of the Communist Party. For the first time, a Communist became Defense Minister, though it is true that alongside him were the War, Navy, and Air ministries which controlled him. And in Italy, the Communist Umberto Terracini was elected president of the Constituent Assembly on February 8.

But the coalition in France was already pregnant with conflict. Georges Bidault, who continued in the Foreign Ministry, which he had run since November 1944, told the American ambassador in confidence that he was convinced the Communists proposed "to eradicate Western civilization."[1] In Italy, the Vatican exerted strong pressure on the Christian Democrats to make them dissociate themselves from the Communists and their allies. In November 1946, Alcide de Gasperi had to resist an explicit demand to dissolve the coalition with the anticlerical parties.[2] And it seems that in January 1947, during a trip de Gasperi made to the United States, this demand of the Vatican was also emphatically raised by the Americans.[3]

Does this mean that the general orientation of the Western world had changed? In London, the left wing of the Labour Party had already stated in November that a decisive change was imminent, and had rebelled against the government (which its own party had formed) by introducing a motion in the House of Commons which called on it to revise its foreign policy, the aim being to create a "democratic and constructive alternative to an otherwise inevitable conflict between American capitalism and Soviet communism which would destroy all hope for world government."[4] In Paris, on the other hand, there seemed to be a willingness to abide by the formulation General de Gaulle had used before the Consultative Assembly in November 1944: "The fate of Germany is the central problem in the world." When General George C. Marshall, Secretary of State since January, was received by President Auriol on March 6, 1947, the conversation dealt exclusively with reparations, the danger to peace which would come from a centralized power in Germany, and the obligations the United States would have to take on in the interest of French security—a security which could only be guaranteed by "a peace signed by the Big Four."[5]

But at that time, Auriol's American interlocutor had altogether different worries. Two weeks earlier, the government in London had informed him that British aid to Greece and Turkey would end in one and a half months. Greece alone needed $280 million immediately and would require effective help for several years to come. The American government had to make a quick decision, and President Truman acted promptly: on March 12, he told Congress that he was determined to grant Greece and Turkey economic and military aid to keep these two countries from suffering the same fate as Poland, Bulgaria, and Rumania.

The situation of the other European countries seemed somewhat less dramatic. But Great Britain, France, and Italy were close to insolvency. The year 1947 brought financial collapse, total bankruptcy after a ten-year depression which had been followed by the worst war in history. A few credits would no longer suffice. Besides, the German economy for which responsibility had been assumed had to be preserved from collapse. And would that be possible without arousing anxiety and suspicion among Germany's erstwhile victims, especially France?

The fate of Germany and its four zones became the chief topic of the Conference of Foreign Ministers of the Big Four, which began in Moscow on March 10 and was to continue until April 25. In the course of a total of forty-four sessions, Bevin, Marshall, Bidault, and Molotov achieved no agreement. One of the points in dispute had enormous consequences, and this was the refusal of the Soviet Foreign Minister to accept the French position concerning the Saar region (which in December 1946 had been detached from the French zone and turned into a kind of French protectorate on the unilateral decision of the French government). As a consequence, Georges Bidault terminated his role as mediator between the Anglo-Americans and the Soviets. All later assessments agree that the Saar question was of enormous importance in the career of this French statesman.[6]

The failure of the conference did not take a dramatic form. At its end, a new meeting was agreed on. Yet the breakup of the wartime alliance was now an accomplished fact, and within a few weeks there were further rifts whose full import and scope did not immediately become clear. Toward the end of May, there were no longer any Communist ministers in Paris, Rome, or Brussels. On June 6, a conference of the minister-presidents of the German *Länder* took place in Munich. The five heads of government from the Soviet zone did not participate. After a dispute, they had refused to attend the conference and had left.

Outwardly, all these contentions arose for very different reasons. In Brussels, the Communist ministers resigned in March because of differences of opinion concerning domestic policies. In France, Ramadier's government collapsed because of social policy and the Indochina conflict. To avoid having to share responsibility for the increasingly bitter war against Ho Chi Minh, the Communist delegates abstained from a vote in February on military credits, though they did not break ranks with the government. Toward the end of April, the coalition members of the Communist Party did not go along with wage-policy measures because social unrest in the country made the party fear it might be outmaneuvered on the Left. Rather than announce the resignation of the entire government, Paul Ramadier, acting with the backing of President Auriol, availed himself of a possibility the new constitution gave him: on May 4, he dismissed the

Communist ministers. His Socialist party, the Section Française de l'Internationale Ouvrière (SFIO), approved the decision with a bare majority. In Italy, Alcide de Gasperi himself provoked a government crisis on May 13. On May 31, he formed his fourth cabinet, the first in which neither Communists nor Socialists were represented.

In Rome, the Communists had been outmaneuvered even more completely than in Paris. Was this done for the sake of American economic assistance? Immediately upon his return from Washington in May 1946, Léon Blum had stated that negotiations concerning American aid had contained "neither expressly nor implicitly, neither directly nor indirectly, any condition of whatever sort, be it civil, military, political or diplomatic in nature." But not only in Washington but also in Paris and Rome, it has been believed ever since that participation in the government by Communists was not reconcilable with the antagonism between the superpowers, and that this antagonism could and must hasten American aid.

The only politician to truly dramatize the end of the wartime alliance both at home and abroad was General de Gaulle. On April 7, he staged a spectacular political comeback by founding his Rassemblement du Peuple Français (RPF). "Our planet as it is today," he announced in a speech in Strasbourg, "shows two huge masses both of which are intent on expansion but are driven by wholly different internal forces and also by different ideological currents. Although one may hope that they will not become enemies, America and Russia are automatically rivals. . . . In view of our situation, the preservation of our independence becomes the most burning and decisive issue." Initially, de Gaulle merely alluded to the principal threat to this independence. Its preservation "presupposes that we remain what we are, Occidentals, loyal supporters of a particular view of man, of life, of law and international relations." In the following weeks, the tone became sharper, particularly toward the Communists. On July 27, de Gaulle stated:

During the liberation, I had believed along with the entire resistance movement that these "separatists" would have to be offered a chance to become part of the national community. The terrible events of the war had brought it about that many of those who believed the leaders of this foreign party were actively participating in the struggle against the enemies of France. The leaders themselves certainly did not take that decision until after Germany's attack on Soviet Russia. . . . And now we have reached this point: on our soil, in our midst, men have vowed to give unconditional obedience to the orders of a foreign regime which is run by the leaders of a Slavic power. They have made it their aim to create a dictatorship here, just as their likes have already succeeded in doing elsewhere with the support of that power.

Actually, neither the French nor the Italian Communist Party was at that time resolved to wage an all-out struggle. But both parties seemed a serious threat, even militarily. On June 18, the American ambassador to Italy reported to his government that he had heard the Communists were about to take their arms out of hiding and organize an elite unit of 10,000 men which would serve as shock troops in an uprising in northern Italy.[7] On September 24, a memorandum of the Policy Planning Staff of the State Department examined in detail how to counter the threat to American interests which Communist seizure of power in northern Italy would pose.[8] Shortly after the signing of the peace treaty, which provided for the almost total disarmament of Italy, this fear gave rise to the first military contacts between Americans and Italians, and they were soon followed by an ongoing collaboration between the U.S. army and Italian forces.[9]

The Munich rift did not raise fear of violence in Germany, particularly because the Soviet occupation zone already formed part of a territory which was becoming increasingly subject to the Soviet Union. But now the restrictive economic policy would have to be ended in a way which would be acceptable to those European countries that had been harmed by Nazi Germany. On July 11, the instructions JCS 1779 to General Clay replaced the American document JCS 1067. The new directive stated that for an orderly and thriving Europe, the economic contribution of a productive and stable Germany was indispensable. The next day, the representatives of sixteen countries accepted American aid in Paris and declared: "The German economy must be integrated into the European economy in such a way that it contributes to a general improvement in the standard of living."

This statement marked the first stage on that road which had been sketched by General Marshall in his famous speech at Harvard on June 5, 1947—a speech which was immediately understood as an event of major scope. Marshall had not put forward a "plan" in the real sense of that word, and he had nothing to propose. But by simultaneously addressing his own countrymen and the European countries, he made two decisive gestures which were directed to both. For one thing, he put an end to the business spirit of 1945–46, which had found its clearest expression in the American loan to Great Britain, and proposed comprehensive free aid which could not fail to sound seductive to the Europeans. But in order to prove to the Americans that his effort aimed at both multilateralism and efficiency, he made it clear that aid would only be granted on the basis of joint demands by

Europeans, which prompted the various countries to act in concert and to even create European organizations (though this went counter to Great Britain's wish to maintain a special and privileged relationship with the United States).

Like any historical decision, the Marshall Plan had a variety of reasons and aims,[10] many of which had already been clearly indicated in Marshall's Harvard address: Europe had to be kept from sliding into hunger and chaos; trade relations, which had become difficult due to large balance-of-payments deficits, had to be opened up again; and Europe thus had to be given the chance to become a dependable global partner once more. Beyond the goals proclaimed was the concern that countries such as France and Italy might easily fall into the hands of the Communists if they were abandoned to their economic chaos. Or into those of that future dictator which de Gaulle as the founder of the RPF threatened to become, as the U.S. ambassador in Paris had hinted on May 12: "If the Communists won, Soviet penetration of Western Europe, Africa, the Mediterranean and the Middle East would be greatly facilitated, and our position in our zone of occupation of Germany rendered precarious if not untenable. If de Gaulle won, France would be headed into a new and unknown adventure which by the nature of the forces generated in such a struggle would make the practice in France of democracy as we understand it difficult if not impossible for some time to come."[11]

Quite in contrast to the widely held view expressed in the European debate on the plan, the search for markets for a future American overproduction was not a consideration for Marshall. But after the failure of the foreign ministers' conference in Moscow, the necessity to act quickly in West Germany became a central motive, and this was tied to the idea that aid for Germany would be more acceptable, especially to the French, if it were part of an aid package granted all Western European countries. To pacify France, it was necessary to bet on it, and not on Great Britain, to help it assume a leadership role in Europe.

Even during subsequent years, the Franco-German dilemma of American policy was never wholly overcome. Its clearest formulation appeared in a report submitted by General Clay in November 1948:

... as the German economy recovers, we will be subject to increasing attack from French politicians reflecting the real and imaginary fears of the French people and of the French Government. I cannot help but feel that this conflict of policy is at a critical stage. With each compromise our efforts at German recovery will be retarded. Without compromise, we will be faced with an intensive French opposition which will result perhaps in developing a real anti-American sentiment in France. Certainly, there is no easy solution to this problem. I am convinced that German recovery is essential to European recovery and to any real stability in Europe which could make for peace. Nevertheless, if this recovery can only be obtained by the loss of French support, then stability would probably not result either.[12]

During the preparatory talks, General Marshall had explained that to avoid being accused of dividing Europe, the Russians would have to be invited to participate but that one could rely on their finally rejecting the offer since he would demand that they give complete information on their economic and financial situation. And this is precisely what happened. It was probably Stalin's most serious diplomatic error, and may have come from the fear of a "westernization" of the Central and Eastern European countries.

Initially, however, he was willing to enter negotiations. At the invitation of the French and British governments, Molotov, Bidault, and Bevin met in Paris on June 27 to July 2, 1947. After the failure of the conference, the delegates of sixteen countries that convened in Paris from July 12 to 16 accepted the U.S. aid offered them. Spain and Germany had not been invited. In the "Report of the Sixteen" signed on September 22, the total amount the United States would have to provide for the period 1948–51 was fixed at $22 billion. President Truman had some difficulty rallying the majority of American public opinion to an aid program which called for outlays amounting to 15 percent of the budget and 3 percent of the national revenue.

Meanwhile, Europe's situation was deteriorating visibly. On August 20, Great Britain suspended the convertibility of the British pound. On August 28, France—and Italy and other countries soon thereafter—saw itself obliged to stop purchasing nonvital goods in the dollar zone until the end of the year and tried to compensate for this lack by liquidating its last foreign currency reserves and enforcing any number of additional measures. Faced with this situation, President Truman asked for urgent relief for certain particularly threatened countries. On December 17, 1947, Congress granted aid in the form of a gift to three countries—France, Italy, and Austria—for the period extending to March 31, 1948. The dollar equivalent of the gift came to $520 million and was supplemented by an additional $55 million in March. The share of France came to $284 million during the first period and to $28 million during the second. An agreement signed on January 2, 1948, established how the aid was to be used and provided for the creation of a special fund which would derive from the proceeds of the sale of the goods received and finance projects for the strengthening of the French economy. This aid, which was referred to as "interim aid" and consisted entirely of free supplies of goods and services, gave France the opportunity to avoid an excessively severe rationing of food supplies and a decline of economic activity during that winter. The 780,000 tons of flour sent to France at that time represented 66 percent of the official bread ration, and 60 percent of the oil and 20 percent of the coal requirements were assured by this help.

In Italy, and more especially in France, the deterioration which set in during the fall of 1947 had still another reason, and that was the change in attitude of the Communist parties due to the establishment of the Cominform. From September 22 to 27, the delegates of nine Communist parties from the Soviet Union, Yugoslavia, Bulgaria, Rumania, Hungary, Poland, Czechoslovakia, France, and Italy met in Poland at Szalarka Poreba, the former Schreiberhau.[13] The German Communists (or rather, the two German parties, the SED and the KPD) were not invited, doubtless because Stalin did not wish to disavow his own official policy which aimed at the creation of a united and neutralized Germany. The French Communist Party was represented by Jacques Duclos and Etienne Fajon, the Italian by Luigi Longo and Eugenio Reale, the Soviet by Malenkov and Shdanov. In his report, Shdanov laid down the new political line, which diverged considerably from the policy the French and Italian Communists had followed up to this point.

In agreement with the Soviet delegates, the Yugoslavs Edvard Kardelj and Milovan Djilas violently criticized the reports submitted by Duclos and Longo. Duclos had presented an impressive balance sheet of the economic upswing in France and expressed his delight that "with every day, the French Communist Party emerges more clearly as the party of order." Concerning foreign policy, he had noted: "Our present policy turns its back on the true interests of France. The attitude of the Popular Republicans toward Germany, the Ruhr question and reparations was correct. . . . Now, the Vatican has demanded a change in this attitude." Duclos was quickly given to understand that he had got it all wrong. And when he exclaimed, "We will turn to the people and say: 'We want to retain the friendship of the English, the Americans and the Soviets,'" that slogan was rejected as malicious and opportunistic by Anna Pauker. Djilas reproached the French and Italian Communist parties for always having wanted to stay within the limits of legality, for having failed to accomplish a revolution, and even for having begun to seriously believe in parliamentarianism. And he added: "The French delegates have turned into poor representatives of Soviet policy before the entire French nation, which is not afraid of fighting, as we well know." Shdanov wanted to know why the party still insisted "on seeing itself as the government party, as

Thorez had reaffirmed at the Strasbourg congress in June." When
Etienne Fajon did not answer, Duclos retreated: "I admit that the
removal of the Communists from the government was not a question
of domestic politics (prices, etc.) but the result of American pressure.
But we have also emphasized that, though not as much as we should
have. . . . Immediately after we left the government, it is true that a
measure of irresolution developed. . . . There was opportunism, a
rigid clinging to the principle of legality, parliamentary illusions . . ."

But this self-criticism was entirely inadequate, and Shdanov concluded: "What is at stake are not minor shifts but a fundamental
change in the politics of both parties." On October 5, the conference
promulgated a resolution which announced the establishment of a
Communist Information Bureau, the so-called Cominform, and issued
a statement which concluded an analysis of the world situation with
these words:

Two camps came into existence in this fashion: the imperialist, anti-
democratic camp whose principal goal is the global rule of American imperialism and the destruction of democracy, and the anti-imperialist and democratic camp whose principal goal is the undermining of imperialism, the
strengthening of democracy, and the liquidation of the remains of fascism. . . . The treasonable policies of right-wing Socialists such as Blum in
France, Attlee and Bevin in England, Schumacher in Germany, Renner and
Scherf in Austria, Saragat in Italy, etc., have a special place among the tactical
means of the imperialists. . . . That is the reason Communist parties have to
take the lead in resisting the plans of imperialist expansion and aggression in
all spheres, the governmental, the political, the economic, and the ideological.

After October 5, 1947, the attitude of the PCF was submission to the
very letter of this text. At the meeting of its central committee on
October 29–30, the break with the tactics of the National Front and
the Popular Front was confirmed. Maurice Thorez criticized himself:
"The inestimable merit of this conference of the nine Communist
parties consists in having enlightened the workers, democrats and
friends of peace throughout the world about the essential changes that
have occurred in the international situation as a result of the Second
World War." Now the slogan was: struggle against American imperialism as embodied in the Marshall Plan and its stooges, i.e., yesterday's partners in government, especially the Socialists. There was a
return to the attitude of the Communist parties during the years
1928–34. The "Socio-Fascists" who had become "warmongers,"
"traitors," "agents provocateurs," "corruptible mercenaries," and
"American puppets" were accused of paving the way to a new fascism,
and all political, economic, and social facts were measured by this
same simplifying doctrinal yardstick. On October 31, for example, the

Communist *L'Humanité* wrote: "Is Schuman going to follow the instructions from Washington and propose devaluation today in the Council of Ministers?" Or on November 9: "The Americans want to ruin the French railroads."

In June, large strikes had occurred. They had been provoked by economic distress and fanned by the PCF, which wanted to demonstrate how much of a mistake it had been to push it out of the government. In November, the wave of strikes almost took on the dimensions of a rebellion. The government—the Prime Minister was the Popular Republican Robert Schuman from Lorraine, and Jules Moch, who had once been secretary-general of the Popular Front government, was Interior Minister—called up reservists and submitted a law for the protection of the Republic. On November 29, during the course of a parliamentary debate that lasted for four days and nights, Jacques Duclos greeted Robert Schuman's arrival with the words "There's the German pig!" Jules Moch had to submit to insults such as "oppressor of the workers" and "henchman," and while the words "Truman will be pleased with you" were hurled at him, François Mitterrand, Minister for Veterans' Affairs at the time, was told by Maurice Thorez, "Provocateur, you talk like Goering!"[14]

The government stood its ground, and the strikes finally collapsed but led to the breakup of the large union federation, the Confédération Général du Travail. Founded in 1895, the CGT had gone through a first split in 1922 when the Communists had set up the Confédération Général du Travail Unitaire (CGTU). A reunification under the aegis of the Popular Front had occurred in 1935, but in reaction to the Nazi-Soviet friendship treaty, the former CGTU leaders had been expelled in September 1939. In April 1943, unity was reestablished in the Le Perreux accords, this time under Communist dominance. One of the two secretaries-general, Benoît Fachon, a prominent member of the PCF, ran the union apparatus, while Léon Jouhaux, secretary-general of the CGT since 1909, had close ties to an organized minority called Force Ouvrière (FO). Even in October 1947, the FO leaders still hoped to avoid a split in the name of a "third force" which would be created on both the national and international level. One of them wrote: "On the one side, we see big American capital, which will not supply what we need in the form of goods or in cash unless it can make maximal profits from it. On the other side stands the Soviet Union, which tries to ruin our economy and plunge our country into a severe crisis. . . . We must therefore not categorically reject U.S. aid nor allow ourselves to be enslaved by either of the two power blocs."[15] The rank and file finally forced the moderate leaders, Léon Jouhaux among them, to leave the CGT toward the end of December and to found the new CGT-FO, which was now in the minority vis-à-vis the Communist-led CGT, just as in 1922 the CGTU had been vis-à-vis the CGT, which had been led by the very same Jouhaux.

To protect its organizational structure and its capacity to act, the CGT-FO received financial help from the Labor Minister, the Socialist Daniel Mayer, from the Swiss federation of unions, from British unions, and especially from the CIO and the AFL. The treasurer of the American Federation of Labor, David Dubinsky, came to Paris and promised sizable aid in the form of loans that would not have to be repaid.[16] It was at this time that the AFL began to play a significant and often criticized role in the activities of Western European unions and also in those of non-European countries which tried to shake off the yoke of colonialism (see Chapter 5). The criticism was at least partly due to the fact that the funds it made available apparently came from a newly created organization, the Central Intelligence Agency.[17]

The CIA was established by the National Security Act which Congress passed on July 24–25, 1947. Congress also defined its status in 1949. Thirty years later, a Senate committee wrote: "This country's intelligence agencies have played an important role in the diplomatic and military activities of the United States during the last three decades. Intelligence information has helped shape policy, and intelligence resources have been used to carry out those policies."[18]

Between 1947 and 1949, CIA activities were primarily confined to providing financial support. The methods used in South America and Asia for which it was later criticized found no application in Western Europe. Contrary to the ideas many Europeans were to entertain about the CIA in subsequent years, its activities initially differed quite markedly from those of the later McCarthyism (see Chapter 4): at that time, the struggle against a threatening Communism still largely meant support of the non-Communist Left, especially of the Socialists that were quarreling with their erstwhile partner.[19] The aid given the Force Ouvrière is in line with this perspective.

The same is true for Italy, except that there the majority of the Socialists continued to identify with the goals of the Communist Party, and this in spite of the 1947 rift. The result was that it was primarily the Christian Democrats that received financial support. Official American representatives certainly intervened much more massively in Italian domestic politics than the intelligence services, especially during the April 1948 elections, which saw the victory of the Christian Democrats (48.5 percent as compared to 31 percent for the Socialist-Communist alliance), and during the union rifts in September 1948 and June 1949, on which Clare Boothe Luce, U.S. ambassador in

Rome at the time, was to comment many years later: "We did not want the Communist Party to obtain control of the union movement . . . so we did an excellent job with the support of the AFL and created both the CISL and the UIL."[20] Yet this endeavor was doomed to fail, since in spite of all efforts the unification of non-Communist unions did not come about.

ECONOMIC AID AND ITS CONSEQUENCES

As of the fall of 1947, both American intervention and nonintervention had a more or less direct impact on domestic politics in both France and Italy. When inadequate international supplies seemed to make a reduction in the bread and dough rations unavoidable in Italy, the U.S. ambassador in Rome was instructed to discuss the matter with de Gasperi to "minimize repercussions and avoid if possible furnishing issue of high propaganda and political value for extreme left campaign against Ital. Govt."[21]

In Washington in April 1948, Jean Monnet tried to obtain an increase in the daily bread ration in France from 200 to 250 grams by referring to a letter from Léon Jouhaux according to which such an increase would enable the Force Ouvrière to deal more effectively with the rhetoric of the CGT which was calling for a 20 percent wage hike. The answer was negative: American officials "have got white hairs trying" to maintain the 200-gram ration and even that amount was not absolutely assured. At the moment, and probably until the wheat was harvested, he was told, an increase in the bread ration could not possibly be considered.[22] But at this time, European aid was getting under way. In July 1947, France and Great Britain had convened the Paris Conference, which, in addition to themselves, included Belgium, Denmark, Greece, Ireland, Iceland, Italy, Luxembourg, the Netherlands, Norway, Austria, Portugal, Sweden, Switzerland, and Turkey. On September 27, a general report specified total requirements. After various difficulties in Congress, the Economic Cooperation Act came into force on April 2, 1948, and on April 16 the agreement on economic cooperation was signed in Europe. The sixteen delegates of the year before were now joined by the three commanders-in-chief of the occupation zones, who functioned as the representatives of Germany since they still exercised supreme authority there. This agreement produced the Organization for European Economic Cooperation (OEEC), which was joined by Spain in 1959 and survived the Marshall Plan. During 1960–61, it became the Organization for Economic Cooperation and Development (OECD), to which the United States, Canada, and Japan also belonged.

In bilateral texts, the details concerning the aid to be granted each country were set down. The agreement with France was signed on June 28. The American government set up a special office to administer the resources of the European Recovery Program (ERP) and the Economic Cooperation Administration (ECA), which had already begun functioning in April 1948 and was headed by Paul G. Hoffman, who had come from the private sector. The ECA set up branches in several capitals which had only loose connections with the respective embassies.[23] The allocation of resources and drawing rights to the individual European countries was handled by the OEEC council. In September 1948, the resources for 1948–49 were allocated, in September 1949 those for 1949–50. In September 1950, the participating countries took an additional step in monetary cooperation and established the European Payments Union.[24]

The general system of Marshall Plan aid functioned with relative simplicity. The flow of dollars from the United States served two distinct purposes. It enabled receiving countries to import goods. In addition, each government would use its own currency to repay the equivalent of the dollar amounts it received into a special fund. Ninety-five percent of the funds transferred into this account were placed at the disposal of the government on the condition that they be used for the reconstruction and development of the national economy. The ECA could use the remaining 5 percent to finance administrative costs, information programs, and technical aid. The country which made most frequent use of this system of counterpart funds was France, with Germany following at a considerable distance.[25]

In spite of this, it was precisely in France that the Marshall Plan was most controversial. Everywhere else, its champions soon carried the day, especially in the United States, where the advocates of this expensive enterprise mobilized the most diverse groups and associations on its behalf, from the unions (AFL and CIO) to the U.S. Chamber of Commerce, from the National League of Women Voters to the National Council of Churches, although many interest groups, such as shipping lines and tobacco farmers, demanded special benefits for themselves.[26] The speech that attracted the most attention was given by Senator Arthur Vandenberg, an erstwhile champion of isolationism. On March 1, 1948, he said in the U.S. Senate: "This legislation, Mr. President, seeks peace and stability for free men in a free world. It seeks them by economic rather than military means. It proposes to help our friends to help themselves in the pursuit of sound and successful liberty. . . . It strives to help stop World War III before it starts. . . . It sustains western civilization. It means to take western

Europe completely off the dole at the end of the adventure. It recognizes the grim truth—whether we like it or not—that American self-interest, national economy, and national security are inseverably linked with these objectives."

In Great Britain, the anti-American mood continued rather strong. In August 1948, the American ambassador sent the Secretary of State a detailed analysis of it as he had observed it "in and out of the government."[27] There are times, he wrote, when attitudes toward the United States "border on the pathological." The reasons are different in nature: "Almost every day brings new evidence of [Britain's] weakness and dependence on the United States. This is a bitter pill for a country accustomed to full control of her national destiny. . . . [The British] regard as short-sighted and ill-considered any policy of ours which insists on treating the U.K. on the same basis as other Western European powers." The same mood is also reflected in an amusing parody of the Lord's Prayer which made the rounds in London in 1948:[28]

> Our Uncle which art in America
> Sam be thy name,
> Thy navy come, thy will be done,
> In London as 'tis in Washington.
> Give us this day our Marshall aid,
> And forgive us our un-American activities,
> As we forgive your American activities against us;
> And lead us not into Socialism
> But deliver us from Communism,
> For thine is our Kingdom,
> The Atom power and the Tory,
> For ever and ever: G-men.

Yet in general, reaction to Marshall Plan aid was positive. Most often, people saw it in the same light as the Lend-Lease Agreement, "the most unsordid act in history." They were especially receptive to the idea that present aid had the object of making later aid unnecessary and of restoring Great Britain's independence from the United States. In the Labour Party also, fewer critical voices were heard. In January 1948, Richard Crossman told the Commons that his view of the United States had changed a great deal over the preceding six months. He had not believed it possible for Washington to offer enormous aid "with as few political conditions," he said.[29] For the government, the Marshall Plan had the immense advantage that it eliminated the monetary and financial tensions which had time and again poisoned Anglo-American relations since about the middle of the war—although it could not overcome the internal difficulties which would finally lead to a drastic devaluation of the pound on September 18, 1949.

In the Scandinavian countries, the only concern of the governments was that the Socialist policies they had embarked upon not be questioned. They also wished to prevent any inflationary consequences the desired opening of the borders might entail. Anti-Americanism played as insignificant a role there as in Belgium or the Netherlands.[30]

In Italy, the Marshall Plan appeared as a last-minute rescue operation, though it was denounced by the opposition. Pietro Nenni, speaking for the Socialists in parliament in November 1948, referred to it as an "economic tool of the Truman doctrine and Wall Street politics."[31]

In France, matters were more complex. As early as the summer of 1947, the belief that *both* superpowers were striving for hegemony was much more widespread than in England, the Netherlands, or Norway.[32] But when the French were asked: "What country in your opinion helps France most to get back on its feet?" 70 percent of those questioned in February 1948 said the United States (7 percent the USSR, 2 percent Great Britain, 6 percent "no country"), and another 6 percent said: "France will get back on its feet by its own efforts." When Marshall Plan aid was fully under way in July 1949, the answers were more nuanced. Asked "Do you think the Marshall Plan is good or bad for France?" 25 percent answered "good," 20 percent "pretty good," 8 percent "pretty bad," and 15 percent "bad," while 32 percent expressed no opinion. If the answers are broken down according to party affiliation, however, there emerges a clear dividing line between Communist voters (2 percent said "good" or "pretty good," 17 percent "rather bad," and 70 percent "bad") and voters from other parties (Socialists 50 percent positive, 18 percent negative; Gaullists 64 percent positive, 6 percent negative).

The idea of an integrated Europe, on the other hand, found rapid acceptance and was to prove considerably more popular in the long run among voters than among politicians and intellectuals. Asked "Would you be in favor of a West European economic union with France, Belgium, Great Britain, Holland, Luxembourg, Italy, and West Germany?" 68 percent already answered in the affirmative in February 1948, and this increased to 74 percent in March (as compared to 16 percent negative).

In principle, the public debate was unambiguous. On one side stood the Communists with their clear rejection of "enslavement," of the "plan for the subjection of Europe," "the plan for the destruction of Europe," "the plan to save private enterprise, i.e., monopolistic capitalism." A Communist study[33] ends with these words: "The Marshall Plan ultimately means that the import programs set up by European countries in view of their needs will be replaced by export programs set up by the U.S. government in view of American production surpluses. . . . The American people will never profit from this. Exports within the framework of the Marshall Plan only serve its exploiters." In the opposite camp were those who sided with the government, notably the Socialists, who pointed to the benefits of U.S. aid, and a number of favorably inclined commentators such as Raymond Aron[34] even though they introduced certain qualifications, or the economist François Perroux, who wrote in his study of the Marshall Plan: "The pursuit of their own interest by the Americans goes hand in hand with an undeniably realistic generosity. The perfectly sincere desire to spread prosperity does not exclude the notion of doing so with increased dividends. . . . The new and possibly weighty fact is that certain American elites have developed a marked instinct for that historical and global responsibility which a situation that is unusual in every respect creates for them."[35]

The insecurity of the "innovators" of this immediate postwar period clearly expressed itself in a special edition of the journal *Esprit* entitled "The Marshall Plan and the Future of France." On the one hand, the edition contained very positive contributions by "technocrats" working with Jean Monnet (and who would continue doing so for some years to come). For J. van Helmont, J. R. Rabier, and Pierre Uri, the Marshall Plan and the incentive to reconstruct Europe pointed in the same direction as the renewal of France pursued in Monnet's modernization plan. But the edition also contained contributions by union leaders and intellectuals who not only feared American dominance but also a permanent rift between Communists and non-Communists in France and argued in favor of a barrier that would have to be erected against any form of economic and social restoration. In conclusion, there were sympathetic allusions to the attitude of the Communist Party, yet the idea of aid and its "technical possibilities" was also accepted. Marshall's policy, they stated, should not be confused with that of Wall Street or the American general staff. Instead, an attitude of "watchful independence" should be taken and instilled in the sixteen treaty countries so that "a new independent peace power" might constitute itself in Western Europe.[36]

All of this was a variation on the thesis that had already been developed in the "Manifesto for Peace and a Socialist Europe" in November 1947 which the same journal had put forward and which read in part: "Since each power bloc tries to defend itself through the subjection of Europe, it attempts to enlist partisans and fellow combatants in our country and to kindle through its acts the fears and retaliatory acts of the opposing bloc. . . . A divided Europe may become the cause of another war; united, it can serve peace. From a continent that has recovered its sovereignty the USSR and the U.S. would have much less to fear than from a motley bunch of impoverished nations whose only freedom is the choice which of the two blocs it will subject itself to."[37] The Europe envisaged here still embraced both Eastern and Western countries.

In France, this objective was always kept in mind. Yet at least at the time, it had little connection with real developments except on one point: the conditions imposed by the United States in the bilateral agreement of June 28, whose harshness had already been mitigated compared to the text originally proposed,[38] were seen by many of the deputies during the parliamentary ratification debate in July 1948—and this included even those who finally voted for them—as an expression of a "colonizing" intent. In addition to commitments assuring domestic financial stability, the text of the agreement contained the following clauses:

Article V (Access to Materials)
1. The Government of France will facilitate the transfer to the United States of America, for stockpiling or other purposes, of materials originating in France which are required by the United States of America as a result of deficiencies or potential deficiencies in its own resources . . .
2. Recognizing the principle of equity in respect to the drain upon the natural resources of the United States of America, and of the participating countries, the Government of France will, when so requested by the Government of the United States of America, negotiate where applicable
(a) a future schedule of minimum availabilities to the United States of America for future purchase and delivery of a fair share of materials originating in France which are required by the United States of America as a result of deficiencies or potential deficiencies in its own resources . . .
(b) arrangements providing suitable protection for the right of access for any citizen of the United States of America or any corporation, partnership, or other association created under the laws of the United States of America or of any state or territory thereof and substantially beneficially owned by citizens of the United States of America, in the development of such materials on terms of treatment equivalent to those afforded to the nationals of France . . .

Article IX
1. The Government of France agrees to receive a Special Mission for Economic Cooperation which will discharge the responsibilities of the Government of the United States of America in France under this Agreement . . .

This mission exercised no control whatever over French foreign policy. It even carefully avoided establishing contact with the Quai d'Orsay and worked only with the technical ministries and a new government organ that had been created on June 17, 1948, the Interministerial Committee for Questions of European Economic Cooperation. There were times when its activity was seen as interference in French monetary and economic policy; there were others when it seemed the symbol of a creative cooperation which did away with the formality of traditional diplomacy, and this was the way the High Commissioner, Jean Monnet, who was on good terms with the chief of the special commission, David Bruce, understood it. For more than one member of the American commission, the possibility of intervening directly and sometimes even dictatorially in the workings of the French government, even when this was done in the name of France's true interest, was to have long-term consequences. When these men returned to higher positions in France many years later, under the Fifth Republic, they tended to forget that the situation had changed and that a style which was both direct and patronizing was no longer appropriate.

Yet the bilateral mechanisms played a much less significant role than the multilateral ones, and this particularly in regard to the allocations of the burden each country would have to assume and which disadvantaged Great Britain and favored the small nations.

The British government certainly succeeded in limiting the power of the OEEC, while the French would have liked it to have more precisely defined tasks and greater autonomy vis-à-vis the member states. But in its effort to maintain a special relationship with the United States and to assume a leadership role in European monetary matters, England saw itself constantly isolated. The greatest pressure from the United States was being directed at Great Britain, while in Paris the suspicion of a secret understanding between England and the United States continued unabated.

The recovery of the Benelux countries—both individually and in their totality—began as early as July 1947. In the multilateralization of the international payments system in Europe, the decisive impetus came from Dutch and Belgian memorandums. During the deliberations of the sixteen, France's refusal to allow the German economy to recover was violently attacked by the Belgian, Dutch, and Luxembourg delegates, who had agreed on a common position.[39] The election of Paul-Henri Spaak as president of the Council of the OEEC already had symbolic character, although less so than the appointment of Dutch Foreign Minister D. V. Stikker as political mediator of the organization in January 1950.

Actually, the Belgian Prime Minister would have liked to play a more important role. Spaak enjoyed the support of the American government, which considered him one of the two most active promoters of the idea of European integration. The other was Jean Monnet, but he had turned down the position as secretary-general of the OEEC. On his recommendation, the position went to his young associate in the Commissariat Général au Plan, Robert Marjolin, who initially had no international prestige. In October 1948, Averell Harriman, special American envoy to the ECA, asked Spaak to give up his position as head of the Belgian government and dedicate himself entirely to the OEEC. A position as director-general would be created for him. But primarily because of British opposition to so integrationist a politician, nothing came of this. With Sir Edmund Hall-Patch at the head of the executive committee, the British were in a position to control and limit unification efforts.

In principle, the ECA had purely economic tasks: it was a matter of speeding the reconstruction of Europe by getting Europeans to unite in a common task to the greatest possible extent. But the borderline between economic and political issues was fluid. When the Senate Foreign Relations Committee initiated an inquiry on aid to Europe in 1949 and Senator James W. Fulbright asked ECA administrator Paul Hoffman about the scope of the ECA mission, he was told that the ECA was exclusively concerned with economic integration: "I am certain we do not belong in the political field." But then he reconsidered and gave this more precise formulation: "I think that there must be a greater unity among the free nations of western Europe. *The whole difference is a question of method,* and I felt certain that *as far as ECA was concerned, the Congress intended us to deal on the economic front* and intended us also *to so restrict our efforts* with the clear understanding that you cannot operate in an airtight compartment. What we do has political repercussions and vice versa."[40]

What sort of repercussions were these? The political effects of economic changes are not always immediately perceptible. This is also true of a form of aid which is less visible than material and financial gifts. "We must export our skills as well as our dollars," Paul Hoffman wrote. "The special skills and short cuts that our American workers and technicians have learned the hard way we often refer to as 'know-how.' The export of this . . . is the basis of the 'technical assistance' (TA) program at ECA. . . . I never forgot what I had seen in London, and through the years that followed, the conviction kept burning within me that the adoption of American labor and management practices would be a great boon to European labor, European management and the European consumer. My chance to do something about it came one warm summer day in Paris in 1948. Sir Stafford Cripps, Britain's ascetic Chancellor of the Exchequer, and I were talking over the economic recovery obstacles that lay ahead. 'If we are to raise the standard of living in Great Britain,' he said, 'we must have greater productivity.' My heart quickened; this was the kind of talk I wanted to hear from a European. . . . Within weeks Sir Stafford had thrown his amazing . . . energies into the creation of an Anglo-

American Council of Productivity. Top figures like Philip Reed of General Electric and Victor Reuther of the CIO were enlisted to represent American management and labor. The late Sir Frederick Bain, deputy chairman of the Board of Imperial Chemical Industries, and Lincoln Evans, general secretary of the Iron and Steel Trades Confederation, were brought in for the British. . . . The first British team to arrive in the United States represented labor and management in the steel industry. When they returned to England they sat down and wrote a report so much of an eye-opener that it sold twenty-five thousand copies in a fortnight and went into three extra printings. Its gist: productivity per man in American foundries was from 50 to 90 per cent higher than in British foundries: the latter must mechanize and raise output or national living standards could not rise as they should.

With this auspicious start in Britain, I had high hopes that the technical assistance idea would be embraced with equal enthusiasm by other countries. It did not happen that way. . . . From the standpoint of its infinite potentialities, TA has not accomplished as much as it should. On the other hand, some three thousand Europeans, either in teams or in groups of twos and threes, have been given a grounding in American techniques under ECA's Technical Assistance Program. They have not been confined to factory people. Dutch farmers came to study grain growing on Iowa farms, Norwegians our coal mines, Italians learned how to raise hybrid corn and Turks analyzed American civil aviation and public-roads building."

The balance of Paul Hoffman's report is characterized by an unshakable optimism concerning American society and the admiration it could not fail to elicit among the invited British, Belgian, and French unionists.[41] Yet there was at least one factor which did justify his idyllic perspective, and that was the spectacular success of the central element of the aid program, the economic and financial recovery of Western Europe.

All in all, dollar aid was considerable, with Great Britain and France clearly the largest beneficiaries, as is apparent from Table 1, which we have copied from a study that is exceptionally critical of American measures.[42] The effects of the dollar flow as they combined with those of the multilateral mechanisms which had in turn been created as a result of the "Marshall Plan stimulus" proved noteworthy on a number of levels. The agricultural and industrial production of Western Europe rose rapidly, and imports of foods from the United States decreased appreciably. As compared with 1947, industrial production in 1951 had risen by 35 percent in Denmark, 33 percent in Norway and in Belgium, 32 percent in France, 54 percent in Italy, and 56 percent in the Netherlands.[43] The free exchange of commodities

TABLE 1

Allocation of U.S. Credits to Countries Participating in the Marshall Plan (April 1948 to January 1952)
(in millions of dollars)

Country	Total	%	*Distribution*					
			Subsidies	%	Loans	%	Conditional Aid	%
All countries	12,992.5	100	9,290.2	100	1,139.6	100	1,517.2	100
Distributed as follows:								
England	3,165.8	24.4	1,956.9	21.0	356.9	29.6	532.1	35.1
France	2,629.8	20.2	2,212.1	23.8	182.4	16.0	61.4	4.0
Italy	1,434.6	11.0	1,174.4	12.6	73.0	6.4	87.2	5.7
West Germany	1,317.3	10.1	1,078.7	11.6	—	—	213.6	14.4
Netherlands	1,078.7	8.3	796.4	8.6	150.7	13.2	31.6	2.1
Austria	653.8	5.0	556.1	6.0	—	—	4.6	0.3
Greece	628.0	4.8	514.9	5.5	—	—	—	—
Belgium/Luxembourg	546.6	4.2	32.4	0.3	68.1	6.0	446.0	29.4
Denmark	266.4	2.1	217.3	2.3	31.0	2.7	9.1	0.6
Norway	241.9	1.9	196.0	2.1	35.0	3.1	10.9	0.7
Turkey	184.5	1.4	62.4	0.7	72.8	6.4	17.3	1.1
Ireland	146.2	1.1	18.0	0.2	128.2	11.2	—	—
Sweden	107.1	0.8	—	—	20.4	1.8	36.7	5.7
Portugal	50.5	0.4	5.5	0.1	36.7	3.2	8.3	0.5
Spain	26.8	0.2	15.9	0.2	4.3	0.4	3.5	0.2

SOURCE: Procurement Authorization and Allotments, Mutual Security Agency, Division of Statistics and Reports, 29 February 1952.

among European countries increased internal trade within the OEEC framework from $5.9 billion in 1947 to $13.1 billion in 1951, while imports from the United States decreased absolutely and even more so relatively: they had amounted to $5.6 billion out of a total of $15.2 billion in 1947 and been reduced to $4.4 billion out of a total of $20.6 billion in 1951. Exports to the United States rose during that same period from $0.73 to $1.81 billion.[44]

These results stood in sharp contrast to the analyses the Communist Party had made about the aims and foreseeable effects of the Marshall Plan. But another result also contradicted the pessimistic prognoses of many advocates of the plan: the so-called dollar gap—the European dollar deficit—was made up so rapidly that as early as 1951 the balance of goods and services of most countries had been corrected or even showed surpluses after 1950.[45]

Almost everywhere, favorable balance sheets of the results of the Marshall Plan were drawn.[46] Only in France a kind of silence fell. When Jean Monnet, president-designate of the High Authority of the European Coal and Steel Community, submitted the review of a five-year modernization effort to the French government in 1952, he underlined the decisive importance of investments but his extensive report failed to make any reference to the Marshall Plan, so it is left up to the reader to reflect on the importance of the first line of Table 2 which is inserted in the midst of considerations dealing with taxes and domestic loans.[47] Actually, the dollar amounts were used for the most important investments: coal, electricity, steel, cement, agricultural machinery, means of transport. State-owned enterprises received the lion's share. Why, then, was there a reluctance to discuss the matter? Fear of having to be grateful to the Americans was certainly part of it, but there was also the feeling that economic aid was merely a forerun-

TABLE 2
Resources of the Modernization and Construction Fund
(in billions of francs, late 1951 value)

Resources	1948	1949	1950	1951	Total
Counterpart of U.S. aid	168	328	201	53	750
Borrowings by the Treasury	94	123	235	244	696
Special assessments	54	—	5	—	59
Own Capital (repayments and interest)	—	—	21	34	55
	316	451	462	331	1,560

ner of the military aid which began replacing it after 1950–51 and thus raised two equally unpleasant problems for France: the Indochina war and German rearmament. There was the additional circumstance that, as early as 1948, there had existed something like a French certainty that American aid would ultimately benefit a recovering Germany more than it would France.

Such a certainty cannot be wholly explained by traditional resentments. It also had some connection with the well-founded opinion that economic and political recovery were closely linked for West Germany. The "Frankfurt Charter," through which the two occupying powers appointed a sort of economic government with an executive and a parliament in the Anglo-American bi-zone on February 9, 1948, was the beginning of a rapid development in both areas.

Besides, economic recovery in West Germany was much more spectacular than in the other European countries. In 1951, industrial production was 312 percent above that of 1947—a percentage which was nearly ten times higher than in Great Britain or France. The reason was that Germany had been much more seriously destroyed: the 312 percent corresponded to an index of 106 (1938 = 100), while the French 39 percent corresponded to an index of 138. As late as 1947, the 1938-based index had been 99 for France and 34 for West Germany. It also turned out that the devastation had not been as great as it had seemed: on the day after the drastic currency reform which was imposed on the recalcitrant German leadership by the American occupying power, it suddenly became apparent that the German economy had been paralyzed rather than destroyed. The moment the hoarded goods appeared on the market and the worthless Reichsmark was replaced by the generally accepted Deutschmark, the machinery started moving again. In 1948, 65 percent of West German imports were still financed by U.S. aid. By 1951, 88 percent were paid for by German resources.[48] But West Germany, which had meanwhile become the Bundesrepublik Deutschland (BRD), had its own financial problems: on December 13, 1950, the young Federal Republic was the first country to obtain a sizable special credit from the European Payments Union.

The necessity of reconstruction gradually caused American and German officials to forget about the very idea of German reparations payments to the countries that had been victimized by Hitler. It is true, of course, that the French position on the dismantling of industrial installations always reflected France's general attitude: under pressure, much more was given up later than had originally been demanded in a fair trade. The Thyssen steel works are an example: in

1949, Foreign Minister Robert Schuman rejected the secret offer to have Thyssen become French property if France in turn renounced dismantling them. A few weeks later, under American pressure, he resigned himself to having this giant enterprise struck from the dismantlement list without France's deriving any benefit whatever. Yet American aid did function as a break with the past—a function which was often criticized in France and willingly endorsed in Germany.

Aid was also much more strongly emphasized in Germany than in the other countries, for here, and especially in Berlin, the vast difference between a Soviet victor that remorselessly plundered his occupation zone and a victorious power which quickly helped "its" Germans regain prosperity had to be underlined. It hardly mattered that this benevolent victor conducted himself rather dictatorially; for example, berating the minister-presidents of the German *Länder* like schoolboys when they did not observe American directives as they worked out their constitutions.[49] What was decisive was the political import of the aid being received. When the delegates of the new German state made their appearance at the OEEC on October 31, 1949, one of the principal aims of the Marshall Plan had been realized.

The plan was thus always remembered positively in the German Federal Republic. The establishment of the German Marshall Fund in 1972, which was intended to finance transatlantic cultural exchange, testifies both to the extent of German recovery and the persistence of a genuine feeling of gratitude—which was given especially vivid expression in 1977, on the thirtieth anniversary of General Marshall's Harvard address.[50]

THE SECURITY OF THE EUROPEANS

Germany's economic rebirth and its return—or more precisely, the return of three Western occupation zones—to existence as a state were not only closely connected with the economic needs of Europe but at least equally with its striving for security. The fears aroused by Soviet policy prompted the French government in particular to gradually give up its reservations about Germany in order to obtain more American military aid. When the North Atlantic Treaty and treaties between the three Western occupying powers that would help launch the new Bundesrepublic—which was still quite restricted in its freedom of action—were signed in Washington on April 4 and 8, 1949, a twofold filiation became apparent: the Atlantic Pact and the Bonn government were the twin children of the Cold War, as it were.

In the development of the German situation and the security problem, the Berlin crisis played an important role. It arose because the

Big Four had failed to reach any agreement and the three Western powers carried out the currency reform of June 18, 1948, which would apply only in the Western zones. On June 23, the Soviet military administration also ordered a currency reform in the Eastern zone, which would apply to all of Greater Berlin. The supply of electricity and coal to the Western sector was cut off. On June 24, the commanders of the Western sectors decided to introduce the slightly modified Westmark as means of payment in their area of jurisdiction. On June 28, the American authorities announced an airlift to deal with the blockade of Berlin's Western sectors. And after July 1, 1948, the Allied military command no longer met.

The problem of access to Berlin was complicated, and involved a test of power rather than a juridical dispute. According to the Soviet government, there never was a blockade, although restrictive measures had already been taken toward the end of March. In the elections to the city parliament on October 20, 1946, the SED had obtained only 19.8 percent of the vote, as compared to 48.7 percent for the SPD, 22.1 percent for the CDU, and 9.4 percent for the FDP. Since that time, Berlin had become a kind of touchstone in the struggle for prestige and power between East and West. A second municipal council was not installed in the Eastern sector until November 30, 1948, and this meant that the administrative division of Berlin became a fact. The Soviets apparently did not believe that the airlift could be sustained during the winter and assumed that the Western powers would give up the city. But the United States made this issue a question of prestige. By its airlift, coal and food were more or less adequately supplied to the three Western sectors. A counterblockade of the Soviet zone was ordered, and in February 1949 negotiations began to resolve the crisis. On May 5, they led to an agreement lifting all traffic and transport restrictions on Berlin and the Eastern zone.

The airlift had not only saved Berlin but also determined the course of West German policy, and especially foreign policy, for a long time to come. German-American solidarity established itself during that winter of 1948–49. And while not only American planes had been used to supply the city, it was the government in Washington and General Clay who had been responsible for the airlift and mobilized what had been largely American resources.

Any German foreign policy which was not based on gaining the confidence of the Americans so that they might continue extending their protection to Berlin and West Germany seemed unacceptable henceforth. Besides, the crisis defined something like a moral turning point. Overnight, as it were, Berlin, once a symbol of Prussia and the Hitler dictatorship, had become a symbol of freedom. The East-West

conflict imposed very heavy burdens and the privations of the population were real, but at the same time, there was the satisfaction of
finding oneself in the same camp as the greatest superpower and of
being recognized as the champion of high moral values. The threat to
the freedom of two million Berliners was a concrete fear, and if it
persisted after the crisis, it was because the threat also proved to be a
permanent state. Nor was it really so very unpleasant to feel such fear,
for it permitted a long yearned-for change of role: many Germans were
all the more willing to become the accusers of a neighboring totalitarian regime since that meant that they no longer had to play the role
of the accused and be constantly reproached for their own totalitarian
past.

In addition, the Berlin crisis made possible a daily, indispensable
cooperation between American and German authorities, especially in
Berlin. The founding in West Berlin of the Free University by professors and students who had moved from Humboldt University in East
Berlin, where it had become a monolithic institution, symbolized the
close tie between the defense of intellectual freedom and German-
American cooperation. And the Germans in Cologne, Frankfurt, and
Munich were much more impressed by the unanimity of Berlin as
embodied in Ernst Reuter, the Social Democratic mayor of West Berlin, than by the fears of Kurt Schumacher, the head of that same party
who untiringly stressed the dangers of the situation and pointed out
that the American-supported political and moral recovery was really
tantamount to a total and definitive partition of Germany.

The fears of the other Western Europeans had initially been directed at Germany. The treaty which France and Great Britain signed
at Dunkirk on March 4, 1947, stated in its preamble that it was designed to prevent "that Germany should again become a danger to
peace," and in each of the three principal articles Germany was mentioned by name. But the object of the treaty was no longer the conclusion of a triangle of security pacts which would have tied the signatories to the Soviet Union. Rather, what was involved here was the
creation of a European security system, and that tendency became
more pronounced after the rifts of the following months. And it was
hoped that the United States would guarantee such a system. Toward
the end of 1947 and in early 1948, contacts and initiatives became
more frequent. Their principal European initiators were the Englishman Ernest Bevin, the Belgian Paul-Henri Spaak, and the Frenchman Georges Bidault.

Things speeded up considerably as a result of the coup d'état in
Prague on February 24, 1948. While the Politbureau of the French
Communist Party saluted the "splendid victory Czechoslovak democ-

racy had won over reactionary forces acting on the instructions of foreign imperialists" in *L'Humanité*, the other political forces in Europe interpreted the coup in Prague as suggesting a direct Soviet threat to their security. But a different analysis probably came much closer to what had really happened. It interpreted Soviet policy after 1947 as a reaction to the "containment" inaugurated by the Truman Doctrine and the Marshall Plan. "In view of the American counteroffensive which represents an answer to Soviet conquests in Eastern Europe and the pressure of the USSR on the Mediterranean (Iran, Turkey, Greece), it is the aim of the USSR to strengthen its influence in those countries where Western interests are not directly at stake. The USSR plays all its trumps and does all it can to create mischief but refrains from and will continue to refrain from any direct attack and any provocation which harbors the risk of war."[51]

But the sense of an immediate military threat carried the day in London, Paris, and Brussels, and also with General Clay in Frankfurt. The negotiations between Great Britain, France, and the Benelux countries, which had been under way for several weeks, now took on a different tone. The West European union they prepared was now to have a military as well as economic, social, and cultural aspects. In the treaty signed in Brussels on March 17, 1948, Germany was mentioned only in one of the eight declarations of intent in the preamble: the five signatory countries expressed their determination "to take any and all steps which might become necessary should there be a return to a German policy of aggression." In the ten articles of the treaty, Germany is not mentioned again, and this omission was most significant in Article IV: "If any of the High Contracting Parties should be the object of an armed attack in Europe, the other High Contracting Parties will, in accordance with the provisions of Article 51 of the Charter of the United Nations, afford the Party so attacked all the military and other aid and assistance in their power." Article IX expressly stated that the "High Contracting Parties may, by agreement, invite any other state to accede to the present Treaty."

The document had barely been signed when Georges Bidault asked General Marshall to work out a common defense system in which the five signatory states, the United States, and other European countries were to be represented. This was the birth of the Atlantic Alliance. On April 3, the five defense ministers convened to work out a plan for the common defense of Western Europe which would eventually be supported by an American security guarantee. But the U.S. government did not have the right to enter into alliances outside the American continent during peacetime. On June 11, passage of the "Vandenberg Resolution" by the U.S. Senate eliminated this obstacle.

From October 1948 until March 1949, during the time the airlift saved West Berlin from starvation, the five signatories, Canada, and the United States negotiated almost ceaselessly. Because Truman was reelected in November, delays were avoided, but three complex issues slowed down the elaboration of the final text: Was the United States to supply arms to the Europeans free of charge? Were overseas territories to be included in the treaty, as had been the case in the Marshall Plan? And finally and most important: What form was the American security guarantee to take? The Europeans wanted it to have maximal diplomatic efficiency; in other words, intervention by American forces should be automatic. But the American negotiators were convinced that a clause specifying automatic U.S. intervention would prevent Senate ratification of the treaty.

On April 4, the foreign ministers of Belgium, Denmark, France, Great Britain, Iceland, Italy, Canada, Luxembourg, the Netherlands, Norway, Portugal, and the United States signed the North Atlantic Treaty in Washington. The most important of the fourteen articles read as follows:

Article 5: The parties agree that an armed attack against one or more of them in Europe or North America shall be considered an attack against them all, and consequently agree that, if such an armed attack occurs, each of them, in exercise of the right of individual or collective self-defense recognized by Art. 51 of the U.N. Charter, will assist the party or parties so attacked by taking forthwith, individually and in concert with the other parties, such action as it deems necessary, including the use of armed force, to restore and maintain the security of the North Atlantic area . . .

Article 6: For the purpose of Art. 5 an armed attack on one or more of the parties is deemed to include an armed attack on the territory of any of them in Europe or North America, on the Algerian Departments of France, on the Occupation forces of any party in Europe . . .

Article 9: The parties hereby establish a Council, on which each of them shall be represented, to consider matters concerning the implementation of the treaty. The Council shall be so organized as to be able to meet promptly at any time. It shall set up such subsidiary bodies as may be necessary . . .

Article 10: The parties may, by unanimous consent, invite any other European State in a position to further the principles of the treaty, and to contribute to the security of the North Atlantic area, to accede to the treaty . . .

In other words, any reference to automatic intervention by the United States had been struck (Article 5), Algeria and West Germany were included in the treaty (Article 6), admission of a new member state was subject to the veto of the original signatories (Article 10), and finally, the treaty provided for the creation of permanent structures (Article 9) which were to make up the North Atlantic Treaty Organization.

The official aim of NATO was a more rational organization of the joint defense efforts, though it was equally important to create compulsory structures which would entail the automatic participation of the United States in any response to an attack in Europe. For the Europeans—primarily the French and the English—NATO was an indirect means of securing a total commitment by the Americans which would appear more credible to a potential adversary than the letter of the treaty.

The governments signed and the parliaments empowered the heads of state or government to ratify. But this certainly did not mean that membership in the treaty organization was greeted enthusiastically everywhere, as if there had been something like a conviction shared by all except for the Communists and their allies.

In Denmark, for example, the decision to accede was made in the Folketing, the Danish parliament, on March 24, 1949, on the basis of a clear vote: 119 in favor and 23 against. The Social Democrats, who constituted the government, were supported by the two most important opposition parties, the Conservatives and the Liberals. But a poll conducted at the time showed only 47 percent "yes" votes against 26 percent "no" votes, and 27 percent who weren't quite sure what to make of Denmark's membership in NATO.[52] For the signing of the treaty in Washington meant a fundamental break with Denmark's past, which was neutral or at least free of membership in blocs and alliances. During the immediate postwar era, hope had been placed in the U.N. and the World Security Council. In 1947 and 1948, futile attempts had been made to set up a Scandinavian treaty. Now the country was suddenly separated from Sweden. There was the additional circumstance that the United States considered the distant, gigantic Greenland, which was part of Danish territory, an indispensable element of its security system. Wasn't this a threat to Danish sovereignty? Theoretically, NATO offered the possibility of placing military installations on Greenland under multinational control, and the island was in fact directly integrated into the Atlantic Alliance in the spring of 1951. But the bilateral problem between Denmark and the United States persisted.

For Belgium and the Netherlands, the Atlantic obligation also meant a profound change from the prewar period. But the development had begun much earlier and much more decisively. Since the invasion by the German armies, Paul-Henri Spaak had definitively abandoned the policy of neutrality which he had earlier helped establish in spite of the threat Hitler posed. Perhaps it was partly the never-admitted guilt feeling over his former mistake which now made him one of the most committed NATO adherents and one of the most irreconcilable enemies of the Soviet Union. His speech about fear which he gave in September 1948 before the U.N. in the Palais de Chaillot in Paris was a particularly pointed denunciation of the USSR. "Never yet had anyone in the United Nations adopted such a tone toward the Russians," he later wrote with considerable satisfaction.[53]

The abandonment of neutrality by the Dutch had been announced during the war by the Foreign Minister of the government-in-exile. His speech on December 28, 1943, made clear how much the security of Holland, Belgium, France, and Great Britain (i.e., the powers that would sign the Brussels agreement) depended on their ability to make the United States understand the degree to which its own fate was tied to that of the Europeans. After the war, he had said at the time, a powerful Western bloc which would also include Canada would have to be created to balance a strong Russia in Europe. "In this manner, we would be dependent, it is true, on the Western powers, but these powers would, conversely, have a need of us. It is difficult to think of a stronger position for our country."[54] Between 1945 and 1947, these ideas had receded somewhat into the background. The Atlantic Pact realized them, yet this development did not set off the violent internal conflicts that occurred in Italy. Italy found itself in a special situation, and that in a twofold sense. For one thing, it was the only defeated country to which accession to the new defensive alliance was proposed on terms of equality. But because the United States "pursued the fundamental aim of creating and maintaining conditions in this key country" which would be advantageous to its own security,[55] should it not be possible to obtain advantages in exchange? Alcide de Gasperi and his Foreign Minister from 1947 to 1951, Count Carlo Sforza, had to let themselves be reproached for having enthusiastically agreed without first having asked for and obtained the consent of the treaty partner to the reestablishment of Italian rule in Libya and Eritrea and a more advantageous solution of the Trieste problem.

There was also the fact that even while the Atlantic Alliance came into being, it was an important element in Italian domestic politics, since in 1948–49 the dividing line in Italy was not nearly as defined as in France. The victory at the polls of the Christian Democrats was not that of a unified party. Organized socialism was not immune to rifts and regroupings. Immediately preceding the decisive parliamentary debate in March 1949 on empowering the government to sign the NATO treaty, the Christian Democrats still had to agree which position it would unanimously advocate. The resolution to accede to the Atlantic Alliance as a defensive and assistance pact in the interest of civilization, democracy, and peace was passed "after extensive discussion," but Giuseppe Dossetti, the leader of the left wing of the party, voted against it while Giovanni Gronchi, president of the Chamber of Deputies, abstained. Both politicians questioned Italy's joining a military bloc. Gronchi was thinking of an Italy that would embody the principle of a third force, and both felt little enthusiasm for an inner split which would push the Christian Democrats far to the right.[56] The Socialists had to decide between the vehement "no" of Pietro Nenni, who accused de Gasperi of unleashing greater mischief than Mussolini once had by signing the "Pact of Steel," and the decided "yes" of Giuseppe Saragat. The neutralism of small moderate groups, some of which were independent, some integrated into Nenni's party, precluded any alliance with the Social Democrats. But Nenni's attitude, which was close to the point of view of the Communist Party, essentially contributed to strengthening the Communists at the expense of the Socialists. Thus Italy's ultimate alignment with the policy proposed by the United States was both a consequence and a cause of internal political evolutions.

In France, the Communist Party was all the more isolated, as it had taken categorical positions. The theme "France will never wage war against the Soviet Union" led Maurice Thorez to such formulations that on February 24 the other parliamentary parties approved a declaration which stated: "The National Assembly takes note of the fact that the Communist Party feels that the French people should offer no resistance to the invader, should a conflict erupt between France and a foreign power, and should even collaborate with him." In the course of a meeting on March 16, the cabinet merely worried how the public might react and examined in some detail whether the content of the treaty should be published before or after the next district elections.[57] On March 18, the text was made public and Foreign Minister Robert Schuman stated on the radio: "Today, we attain what we hoped for in vain between the two wars: the United States recognizes that there can be neither peace nor security for the United States if Europe is in danger."

But even among the advocates of the Atlantic Alliance, fears were expressed. Would the economic independence of Europe which the Marshall Plan was to bring not be pointless if now the necessity for rearmament created a new dependence on the United States? And above all, what would now happen with Germany? Immediately after the signing in Washington, Hubert Beuve-Mèry, editor-in-chief of *Le Monde,* wrote in the April 6 edition (*Le Monde* always carries the date of the following day): "Whether one cares to admit it or not, the rearmament of Germany is embryonically contained in the Atlantic Alliance."[58] To which Robert Schuman replied before the National Assembly on July 25 in the course of the ratification debate: "Germany does not yet have a peace treaty. It has no arms and will have none. ... It is inconceivable to France and her allies that Germany should be permitted to join the Atlantic Alliance as a nation capable of defending herself or of contributing to the defense of other nations."

Finally, there was the problem of the non-European defense of France: Wasn't security in Europe necessarily tied to defending Indochina against Communism?

There were three Western European countries for whom a defense confined to European soil was not sufficient, and they were Great Britain, the Netherlands, and France. In Belgium, the idea that the Congo might become a problem had not yet sufficiently entered public consciousness in the years 1945–49 to give rise to genuine concern.

Seemingly paradoxically, Anglo-American relations were not disturbed by the greatest and most difficult British undertaking—the decolonization of India—while a question which was ultimately of subordinate importance for the British—the Palestine problem—produced serious tension. The decolonization initiatives of the Labour government—from Sir Stafford Cripps' mission in the spring of 1946 to Lord Mountbatten's efforts which led to the passage of the Bill of Independence by the House of Commons on July 15, 1946, and to the independence of India and its partition into the two states of India and Pakistan four weeks later—met with approval and indeed admiration rather than criticism in the United States. The bloody struggles which occurred later did not affect the conviction that Great Britain had acted intelligently and liberally, especially because at that time neither Nehru in India nor Jinnah in Pakistan had any Communist affiliations and their conflict in no way affected the American voter.

The situation in Palestine was something different. Under pressure from Jewish voters, President Truman had already applied to Attlee in August 1945 to immediately admit 100,000 Jewish refugees to the British mandate. "One of our main problems," he wrote later, "was that Palestine was not ours to dispose of. It had been legally entrusted to the British by action of the League of Nations—to which we did not belong—and the British were, in fact, in possession of Palestine."[59] In November, a joint commission of Englishmen and Americans had been set up, which submitted its report in April 1946. It recommended that 100,000 immigrants be admitted immediately and showed prudence and foresight concerning the political status. Palestine, it stated, must be neither a Jewish nor an Arab state. Jews should not rule over Arabs, nor Arabs over Jews. Since any attempt to proclaim independence would inevitably unleash a civil war, the status of a mandate would have to be maintained.

But the British government was not prepared to go this route unless the military and financial burden arising as a consequence was to be shared by the United States. The American diplomats, however, requested the President to help the British only if friendship with the Arabs were cultivated at the same time. Wasn't it the best solution to let Great Britain see to the suppression of the Zionist terrorists, whose cause seemed as just to influential elements of the American electorate as to those Europeans who felt compassion for the survivors of Hitler's frightful genocide?

In fact, neither the tragic odyssey of the overcrowded refugee ship *Exodus* in 1947 nor the crisis of 1948 which led to the voluntary surrender of the mandate and the withdrawal of British troops on May 14 gave rise to any dispute over Palestine between the French and the Americans, but on both sides of the Atlantic similar reproaches were leveled against Great Britain.[60]

A short time after its establishment, the State of Israel was recognized by the United States (and the USSR). Formal recognition by Great Britain was delayed until April 1950.

The Indonesian drama had a much closer connection with the partners of the Atlantic Alliance. As early as the end of 1945, the U.S. government had tried to mediate between the Dutch government and the Indonesian leaders. In November 1946, an agreement was concluded in which the Netherlands recognized the Indonesian Republic as the de facto power in Java and Sumatra and which provided for the formation of a Dutch-Indonesian Union.[61] But on July 21, 1947, Dutch troops carried out a "police action" in these two principal parts of the country which was sharply condemned by the United States and Great Britain. On August 3, the government in The Hague ordered a ceasefire. Before the U.N., the United States supported the Netherlands against the USSR, Australia, and India, which demanded that the Dutch troops withdraw. Finally, on January 19, 1948, a Good Offices Committee, made up of a Belgian, an Australian, and an American, succeeded in obtaining an agreement which granted the Netherlands extensive benefits. But this agreement was not kept. Renewed negotiations failed, partly because elections in Holland had resulted in a harder line on the part of the government. On December 19, 1948, the Dutch launched another military operation during which parachute troops captured the political leaders of the Indonesian Republic.

These leaders had just successfully suppressed a Communist-led rebellion and thereby increased the sympathy felt for them in the United States. The American government found itself in a difficult position. On the one hand, it had to deal tactfully with a European ally who had been one of the initiators of the Brussels Treaty and of the Atlantic Alliance, which was then being prepared. But it also had to continue supporting the non-Communist national independence movement and especially take American public opinion into consideration. On December 23, CIO secretary Philip Murray stated: "I voice the hope, on behalf of the members of the CIO, that the Government of the United States will continue to take every feasible step in the realm of diplomacy and economics to help terminate the Dutch aggression in Indonesia, and to assure a speedy settlement recognizing the rightful interests of the Indonesian people in their quest for democratic self-rule. You may rest assured that the State Department will enjoy the full support of American workers in whatever steps it may take in this direction."

The decision went against the Netherlands. In the Security Council, Philip Jessup, the U.S. delegate, severely condemned the Dutch government. To forestall a congressional resolution which would have demanded a cutoff of all U.S. aid to the Netherlands, the ECA ordered a temporary suspension of Marshall Plan Aid to The Hague[62] and thus set a unique example for political sanctions within the framework of transatlantic economic cooperation.

The Netherlands gave in. As early as August 1949, the complete and unconditional surrender of sovereignty over the entire territory of the former Netherlands East Indies (with the exception of New Guinea) to the Indonesian Republic was decided on. The bitterness in Holland was considerable. Only Belgium had given diplomatic support, while the United States and Great Britain had been hostile and France silent. What good was the Atlantic Alliance? What meaning did Article 3 have if an alliance partner was frustrated in its military efforts by an embargo when, instead, its power to counteract anything it considered aggression anywhere in the world should have been strengthened?[63] Such questions were not asked again in the Netherlands, but they did recur in Belgium in 1960, remained relevant for France until 1962, and were finally asked by the United States when that country waged its war in Vietnam.

Even where the United States was not prepared to intervene on behalf of national movements suppressed by its European allies, it was considered a potential liberator after the war, as happened in Madagascar in 1947, for example. A revolt which had broken out there was brutally suppressed by France. From an eyewitness account, it can be inferred in whom the rebels had placed their hopes: "The people of Ambila saw the airplanes flying over Manakara [they were actually French] . . . and continued to believe firmly that the Americans had landed in Manakara to support the rebels against the French." A French noncommissioned officer "with reddish facial color reminiscent of the color of Anglo-Saxons and in American uniform, which was often worn by the French after the liberation" was greeted with great joy. "With an American accent and a smiling face, he told the crowd in deliberately broken French that their suffering had come to an end and that the Americans had landed ." In this fashion, he succeeded in escaping the massacre of the local French by the rebels.[64]

American policy was actually much more nuanced where newly arising problems were involved, as can be seen, for example, in a long memorandum of the Policy Planning Staff dated March 22, 1948, and marked "top secret." After a detailed analysis of the situation in North Africa, particularly Morocco, we read: "We should point out that in our view any disorders or untoward events in the Moroccan area would not only invite the danger of communist exploitation but be a matter of concern to us because of their adverse effects on France's own world position, which it is in our own interest to maintain. . . . While we should strongly support the position of France in Morocco, making it emphatically clear that we are not attempting to disrupt French rule, we should not lose sight of our policy to favor the gradual evolution of dependent peoples toward self-government."[65] Should it be possible to convince the French to pursue a liberal policy, the United States could help them by exerting a moderating influence on the nationalist leaders. The only concern was that the French would continue acting according to the formula "too little and too late."[66]

Such a concern explained in part the support given the "Third Force—the then-government in Paris—against de Gaulle, who had shown an especially conservative attitude in the question of overseas territories in 1947, particularly with reference to Algeria, to which the Ramadier government had granted a status that was less unfair to the Muslims.

But what position was the United States to adopt when the nationalist leader was also a Communist one? There was a man who was both an old-time militant of the Third International and a hero of a national independence movement. Up to his death in 1969, Ho Chi Minh was seen by the French and American governments now in one role, now in the other, and opinions about him rarely coincided.

They did coincide, however, when Jean Sainteny, delegate of the French High Commissioner in Indochina, signed an agreement on March 6, 1946, which stated among other things: "The French government recognizes the Republic of Vietnam as an independent state with its own government, parliament, army, and currency which is part of the Indochinese Federation and the Union Française." But just a few months later, all unanimity was a thing of the past. The disputes involved independence—a word the French did not like to use—of Cochinchina with its capital Saigon, which was a French colony in the eyes of the French but part of Vietnam for Ho Chi Minh, who had come to France for negotiations. After a series of incidents, a terrible naval bombardment of Haiphong took place on November 23, 1946. The many thousand Vietnamese casualties largely account for the tension which led to the attack by General Giap's army on Hanoi on December 19, its murders and atrocities. Jean Sainteny, who had tried until the last moment to achieve a compromise, was seriously wounded. For almost all of the French public, the attack on Hanoi has since come to symbolize the start of the Indochina war.

In the inaugural address of the first government of the Fourth Republic on January 21, 1947, Ho Chi Minh was no longer considered a partner in the dialogue. Two decisive arguments militated against him: he had unleashed the war, and he was a Communist. But in the eyes of the Western and Asiatic peoples, the principal reason for the long and bloody struggle that now began was the indecisiveness of the French political leadership and the aim of the war was the independence of a colonial people. On January 22, 1947, *The New York Times* wrote that France was the only European country that tried to keep its colonies in Asia by force. And on March 23, Saravane Lambert, a deputy without party affiliation who represented the Indochinese possessions of France, declared during the debates on military aid: "You have adduced arguments for continuing the struggle and for not negotiating with Ho Chi Minh. Perhaps you are right. But from the point of view of the populations of the overseas territories—and I am saying this in all frankness—you are wrong. . . . The National Assembly votes military aid for Indochina and not a word is being said on behalf of the Vietnamese, whose policy you condemn. But you should not forget that these Vietnamese whom you condemn are nonetheless patriots who love their country. . . . The arguments you have advanced here will have no meaning whatever in the overseas territories. In the eyes of the population there, the Vietnamese are an oppressed people."

Soon, France was to negotiate with Vietnam, though only in South Vietnam, in Saigon, with the emperor Bao Dai, who had abdicated in August 1945 in favor of the "Republican Democratic Government" of Ho Chi Minh. Since Bao Dai could not be put off so easily, he had to be offered—at least on paper—what had been refused the Viet Minh, against whom war was now being waged in Tonkin. At the same time, the hesitant United States had to be urged ever more insistently to support France in this struggle on behalf of the interests of the West, a struggle which the United States still considered a colonial war.

On June 5, 1948, France solemnly recognized "the independence of South Vietnam, whose task it would now be to realize its unity in freedom. For its part, Vietnam declares that it will remain with the Union Française as a state associated with France. The independence of Vietnam is subject to no restrictions other than those its membership in the Union Française imposes on it." In actual fact, this independence remained as fictitious as the unity of Vietnam which Saigon was to achieve. But in the agreement concluded between President Auriol and Bao Dai on March 8, 1949, South Vietnam was granted the right to its own army and diplomatic status. It provided also for the unity of Vietnam as soon as the population could be consulted. On April 23, a Cochinchinese National Assembly, chosen by a few hundred, voted for the incorporation of Cochinchina in Bao Dai's Vietnam. The "consultation" had been a farce, and the National Assembly was not even asked to ratify it. Yet Bao Dai's popularity was tenuous. Would all these advantages have accrued to him if the Viet Minh forces had not constantly kept the French troops at bay at that time?

When France officially surrendered sovereignty to Vietnam on December 30, 1949, the Ho Chi Minh government declared that *it* now was a fully authorized actor on the international stage. On January 18, 1950, Radio Peking announced that the government of the People's Republic of China had decided to recognize the Democratic Republic of Vietnam. And along the Tonkin borders, Mao Tse-tung's troops, who dominated the entire Chinese mainland, gave concrete expression to that recognition.

The war in Indochina now took on a different aspect and confronted the governments in Paris and Washington with entirely new problems, although one central element had remained unchanged: while the institutions of NATO had been created, while there was increasing talk of German rearmament in the interest of European defense, the elite of the French professional army was in Indochina.

PART TWO

Harmonies and Turbulences of the 1950s

INTRODUCTION

The Atlantic Treaty and the birth of the Federal Republic in Germany, the arrival of Mao Tse-tung's victorious troops on the border of Indochina, the Schuman Plan and the outbreak of the Korean War all show clearly that the year 1950 constitutes a break. A new period begins.

But when does it end? Several answers can be given, and we prefer the most inclusive. One might be tempted to have it end in 1953. In January, President Eisenhower took up residence in the White House. On March 5, Stalin died after a quarter-century of unlimited power. But the immediate changes in course, be it in Washington or Moscow, were not very significant.

The changes that occurred in 1954 and 1955 were more incisive. During the seven months and seventeen days Pierre Mendès-France headed the government in Paris, the French version of the Indochina war came to an end but the war in Algiers broke out. The European Defense Community was buried, but the Paris accords were signed and this resulted in the Federal Republic of Germany joining NATO. This set of events had a direct effect not only on French relations with the United States but on the relations of all European countries with the United States. And even the Cold War, which had been waged with such intensity and had set both the international climate and the climate of the various individual countries, seemed to be drawing to a close in 1955. The Soviet Union's silent acquiescence in the Paris accords, the sudden thaw which made possible the conclusion of a treaty between Austria and the four occupying powers, the summit conference of the Big Four in Geneva, Adenauer's Moscow trip, are all events that clearly define a change of course— and yet it can be shown that that is all it was, and not a true break.

This is all the more true since, in the fall of 1956, two events occurred which in both their immediate reality and their symbolic import were at least as significant as the events of 1954–55. The failure of the Anglo-French Suez expedition was first of all a spectacular humiliation of Great Britain and France by their American partner. And the suppression of the Hungarian revolt by the Soviet Union showed in tragic fashion how limited the possible consequences of détente were, and how profound and seemingly immutable the partition of Europe had meanwhile become. But German hopes for a reunification of the nation had not yet been entirely dashed, while Suez was merely a stage along the path of French disillusionment over Algiers.

What, then, about 1958? A new Berlin crisis, the introduction of the Common Market subsequent to the Rome Treaty of 1957, and, even more important, the fall of the Fourth Republic and de Gaulle's return to power. Isn't this return the significant break in our theme, especially when note is taken of the later tensions between the President of the Fifth Republic and the United States? But largely because the war in Algeria continued, a confrontation did not immediately occur. The field of international relations generally and of transatlantic relations in particular had hardly changed.

But things look different when one considers the early 1960s. The independence of the Belgian Congo in 1960 and that of Algeria in 1962 together mark a significant turning point. The Europeans gradually stopped appearing as colonial powers in the eyes of the rest of the world, while the United States could no longer deflect the reproach that it was imperialist by engaging in an anti-colonialist criticism of its European allies. The liquidation of the Algerian mortgage gave de Gaulle the feeling of finally having his hands free for a global policy which would be implemented by distancing himself from the United States.

But before this, 1961 was to bring decisive changes in Germany's situation. John F. Kennedy's accession to power in January already resulted in a noticeable change in climate in the relations between Bonn and Washington. But compared to the consequences of August 13, this was secondary: the Berlin Wall permanently changed the German conception of East-West relations. There was unquestionably more continuity between the policy of Gerhard Schröder, who became Foreign Minister in November 1961, and the Moscow and Warsaw treaties signed by Willy Brandt in 1970 than between Adenauer's attitudes before and after the demonstration of Western impotence in face of that Wall around which the definitive partition of Germany took permanent shape.

But the construction of the Wall signaled the Soviet will to confine itself to the territory acquired in the immediate postwar era, while the installation of missiles in Cuba in the following year expressed the sudden desire to become active in close proximity to the territory of the other superpower. Yet this desire was short-lived, for after the Soviet-American crisis of October 1962 a new and different climate established itself permanently between Moscow and Washington. Without this new climate, the transatlantic relations of the 1960s cannot be understood.

It can now be seen why the 1950s must be taken as a sort of unit, and this in spite of the turbulence and the real discontinuities that occurred then. Such a division does of course create two methodological problems which we have mentioned before: if one wishes to bring a measure of clarity to the analysis, neither a piecemeal presentation of the actors nor chronological distortions can be avoided.

This is especially true for the national actors, i.e., the acting states. After a short sketch of the Federal Republic of Germany and its first Chancellor, we will therefore have to break up and present in different chapters of this book our account of German actions and reactions during the period the young state was not yet a principal actor in the events being analyzed. Italy, whose course had been approved by a majority in 1948 and only barely confirmed in the 1953 elections, plays only a secondary role in the conflicts of the 1950s if one omits the economic confrontation with the American oil companies which Enrico Mattei successfully weathered from 1953, when he founded the state-owned energy combine ENI, to his tragic death on October 27, 1962. Conversely, Great Britain's permanent and universal presence in all conflicts which affected the relationship between Europe and the United States makes unavoidable a fragmented presentation of British positions. This is regrettable, particularly since it would have been tempting to set forth a synthetic overview of the multiplicity and scope of Anglo-American agreements and disagreements both at the beginning and at the end of the period being investigated.[1] But for our purposes, it makes more sense to deal with British preoccupations at the appropriate place in the various sections dealing with the entirety of the relations between Europe and the United States.[2]

The antagonisms between Labourites and Conservatives (the latter returned to power for thirteen years after the elections of October 25, 1951) and the opposition between the majority and the Bevin supporters within the Labour Party notwithstanding, Great Britain seemed to be acting with much greater unanimity during this period than France, whose internal discord over Indochina, Europe, and Algeria was directly connected with American policy, and even more with the image the conflicting groups in France had of the United States.

Beginning in the 1950s, Europe was no longer just a concept that could be interpreted in a variety of ways. Gradually, a configuration called Europe developed as an independent actor on the international stage, where it took such institutional forms as the High Authority for Coal and Steel and later the EEC Commission; or in a less easily defined manner, such as conferences of the Six Foreign Ministers; or wholly informal meetings of politicians, union leaders, or industrialists of different nationality but identical spirit.

The breakup of the chronology expresses itself in the treatment of themes and facts which, though scattered over the following chapters, are actually so closely connected that they influenced each other profoundly. French military policy during this period, for example, was undoubtedly a whole, even though the disputes over a European force will be treated separately from the military problems created by the wars in Indochina and Algeria and from the implications of the decisions already made under the Fourth Republic to create a French nuclear force. The Suez expedition and the suppression of the uprising in Budapest were not just simultaneous events. The course of one was to partly determine that of the other. And how can one overlook the fact that in French domestic and foreign policy after 1951, Indochina and Europe became ever more closely enmeshed until, in the spring of 1954, American and French politicians could no longer bring up one of these problems without also discussing the other?

Thus author and reader will constantly have to try not to overlook the connections which our thematic breakdown severs. But for an understanding of the period under consideration, such a discontinuous presentation seems to make more sense than a merely chronological one. From the American intervention in the Indochina war to Robert Murphy's mission which hastened the disintegration of the Fourth Republic and on to the false hopes General Challe placed in the United States when he organized his putsch against the Fifth Republic in the name of an Algérie Francaise, there runs an unbroken line which must be traced. The recovery of Germany also took place without interruptions, yet the role of the Federal Republic in the efforts toward European unification and its place in the changing strategy of the Atlantic Alliance point to two quite different complexes. And though McCarthyism may have profoundly influenced debates concerning the organized reconstruction of Europe, it facilitates understanding if the analysis of the mood during the Cold War is separated from a portrait of the American presence in European politics. It is true, of course, that both can be dealt with in the same chapter.

4 JEAN MONNET'S EUROPE DURING THE COLD WAR

THE INSPIRER

Community Europe, which has been in existence for more than twenty-five years, is already . . . a remarkable achievement. . . . The positive balance sheet that can be drawn up at the end of this first stage . . . we owe in large measure to the boldness and breadth of vision of a handful of men. Among them, Jean Monnet has played a leading role, whether as inspirer of the Schuman Plan, first President of the High Authority, or founder of the Action Committee for the United States of Europe . . . . Jean Monnet recently retired from public life. He has devoted the best of his ability to the European cause. It is only fitting that Europe should pay him a particular tribute of gratitude and admiration. This is why the Heads of State and Government of the Community, meeting in Luxembourg as the European Council, have decided to confer on him the title of Honorary Citizen of Europe.[3]

Does this resolution of April 1, 1976, consciously point back to the press conference General de Gaulle had held twenty-three years earlier, on November 12, 1953, right in the midst of the dispute over the European Defense Community? At that time, Monnet had not been mentioned by name. He had been quite simply "the inspirer with his panacea called fusion," the inspirer whom de Gaulle according to his own testimony reluctantly listened to twice, once in 1940, when the issue was Anglo-French unification, and again in 1943: "Three years later, when the Americans had set up an organization that competed with de Gaulle's France Libre in Algiers which did not function well, the inspirer came to their aid by suggesting that the generals Giraud and de Gaulle be brought together in the same government. At that time, I agreed to that mixture because I suspected what would happen. And what did happen surprised no one—not even the inspirer."[4]

This formulation is ambiguous. Monnet is being accused of having merely wished to satisfy an American desire by his proposal. But if he foresaw that de Gaulle would emerge as the victor, hadn't he simply seen to it that this victory was achieved in harmony with the United States?

Such questions must be asked with respect to the entire European unification policy during the 1950s. The Americans wanted the unification of Europe. Jean Monnet did everything to make it possible. Does it follow that he "inspired" the Europeans only so that an American plan might be implemented? Anyone who affirms this would also have to accept two implicit assertions: first, that every American desire necessarily went counter to the "true" interests of the Europeans, and second, that Monnet's "inspiration" was effective only in one direction, in other words, that he did not also inspire the American leadership.

Neither the first nor the second assertion corresponds to what really happened. It is possible, of course, to base any analysis on the idea that the weaker is never in a position to influence the stronger. But that would be a doctrinaire conception of power relationships and not the result of an unprejudiced examination of the facts. It is true that the U.S. Congress showed all sorts of impatience over the dragging process of European unification.[5] But this does not allow the inference that every effort to hasten it was tantamount to an act of submission to American wishes.

Quite the contrary! A Dutch participant in Monnet's effort on behalf of Europe describes matters in these terms: "He influenced American statesmen and American officials and used his influence on European statesmen and politicians. His relationship with people like Eisenhower, Dulles, David Bruce, McCloy, Douglas Dillon, Tomlinson, Butterworth, Bowie, George Ball, Stanley Cleveland, Robert Schaetzel and a few others is unique in the sense of how one individual from a foreign country can influence leading statesmen and officials of a very powerful and in many respects decisive nation. There cannot be a formal proof of this great and permanent influence. The history of American policy toward the process of European unification cannot, however, be explained without recognition of Monnet's influence on the formulation of that policy."[6]

The philosophy of this "inspirer" that governed his conduct can be summarized in a single sentence: "Nothing is possible without men: nothing is lasting without institutions."[7] During the 1950s, Monnet was actively involved in helping found a number of institutions, from the European Coal and Steel Community on May 9, 1950, to the Organization for Economic Cooperation and Development (OECD), whose founding charter was signed on December 14, 1960. The work and friendship ties he had with men from the most diverse countries were so intense that even historians given to explaining everything by infrastructures and profound trends find themselves obliged to take account of them.

Monnet placed his friends and loyal associates in the French Planning Commission at strategic points, as for example, Robert Marjolin into the OEEC and Pierre Uri some years later into Paul-Henri Spaak's team when the latter proposed the negotiations which were to lead to the Common Market. When the Belgian Prime Minister later described how Uri was sent to him, he wrote: "The Spaak report was largely his work. . . . Our collaboration was a success. He had many more ideas than I did. But perhaps I made up for this by knowing how to present these ideas and advocate them."[8] And, more important, he had the political weight Uri lacked. Yet what counted in the negotiations on the Schuman Plan and the Common Market was much more the common will of the politicians and their deputies than their hierarchical relations. Thus George Ball, one of Monnet's American friends, reports: "The negotiation that followed was a model of its kind. It took place in an eighteenth-century building on the rue Martignac on the left bank which was the headquarters of the French Plan, and during a year of intense effort, Europeans worked together in common purpose, each seeking, as one said to me with awe and astonishment, to find ways to make progress, not to block it."[9]

And concerning the following years, which preceded his appointment as Under Secretary for Economic Affairs and then to the position of Under Secretary of State under President Kennedy in 1961, Ball writes: "For me these were yeasty years during which—from time to time, for long or short periods—I worked with Monnet officially and unofficially, professionally or simply as a friend, in connection with all of these enterprises. When in Paris I usually occupied a small office down the hall or under the stairs, but our most fruitful hours together were quite as likely to occur during the night or over the weekend at his country house in Bazoches as in his office during the day. I was one of Monnet's dialectical punching bags. My normal assignment was to try to express on paper his evolving conceptions, for he is a man who thinks by a process of refining successive formulations of an idea. Thus it was a rare paper of any importance that did not go through at least seventeen or eighteen drafts, for we thought together as we wrote together."

George Ball, who was Monnet's legal advisor in the Planning Commission and later in Luxembourg, was an extreme case. An English journalist, commenting on his influence on Kennedy, had this to say: "Ball was a much-travelled American lawyer who had known Monnet for many years. He had been employed as Monnet's legal representative in Washington when Monnet was running the Coal and Steel Pool. On Capitol Hill, Ball's foreign ties were not forgotten, and at a secret joint committee meeting, when he seemed to be stating a pro-

European case, an intemperate senator sharply asked him to remember he was in the pay, not of M. Monnet, but of the United States."[10]

But other friendships were no less lasting, as for example with Ambassador David Bruce or his young financial adviser William Tomlinson, who before his death at thirty-six played an important role in U.S. relations with Europe without his especially cordial relations with Monnet ever being adversely affected.[11]

But above all was the friendship with John Foster Dulles. Monnet's relations with Dean Acheson, Secretary of State from 1949 to 1953, had already been so close that in his memoirs the American statesman names Jean Monnet—along with Churchill, Alcide de Gasperi, Adenauer, the Dutchman Dirk Stikker, and the Norwegian Halvard Lange—as the only Frenchman among the "colleagues from other countries who inspired respect and affection."[12] But in the case of Acheson's successor, who would run American diplomacy from January 1953 until April 1959, the relationship was of a different order: "A man is judged by his friendships. In the case of a Secretary of State, partly by his friendships abroad. With Dulles, two foreign friends counted for most. One was an exceptionally gifted Frenchman. It was the longest, most intimate and deepest of Dulles' ties overseas. The other, of shorter duration, was with an octogenarian German of historic stature."[13]

The friendship between Dulles and Monnet went all the way back to the Versailles conference in 1919, and they had kept up personal and business relations between the two world wars. They were the same age (born in 1888), whereas George Ball, for example, was twenty years younger than Monnet. At John Foster Dulles' burial, Jean Monnet was the only foreigner among the ceremonial pallbearers, and he was also the only friend to whom Janet Dulles left her husband's confidential papers.

But international team spirit can also lead to interventions that are intensely controversial from the point of view of states whose foreign policy is affected by them. An example would be the 1950–51 negotiations concerning the agreement for the planned ECSC. In principle, they ought to have been held by the representatives of the six countries concerned. In practice, the collaboration of Monnet's American friends extended all the way to the drafting of entire treaty articles, and this was due to the technical competence of Robert Bowie, the legal advisor to the American High Commissioner in Bonn, John McCloy, who, like Bowie, belonged to the so-called "Society of Europeans."[14] And in 1963, immediately after the Franco-German friendship pact was signed by de Gaulle and Adenauer, Monnet intervened in Bonn. "Meanwhile, we had written a gloss on the Franco-German Treaty which the parliamentary strategists turned into a Preamble. The Bundestag passed it unanimously on April 25," he writes ingenuously.[15] It was this preamble which offended the French head of state, especially the sentences dealing with transatlantic relationships (see Chapter 7).

Naturally, there were those who did not belong to the "Society of Europeans." More precisely, there were two or perhaps even three kinds of outsiders. There were, first, those statesmen and politicians whose negative attitude toward both the United States and the reconstruction of Europe made almost all contact impossible. Among Germans, this was true of Kurt Schumacher. In France, Vincent Auriol, head of state until January 1954, jotted in his diary: "The Americans are stupid, naïve, and understand nothing."[16] Reading his personal thoughts on the United States or on German politics, one is tempted to make a similar judgment about him. Then there were politicians who originally pursued other aims and whose intentions became suspect when they came into power because they had not frequented the "Society of Europeans." The year 1954 remains incomprehensible if one underestimates the weight this suspicion had in the policy of Pierre Mendès-France. Finally, there were those whose incompatibilities were of a personal nature; the antipathy between Anthony Eden and John Foster Dulles, for example, existed long before the Suez crisis. Eden attempted to talk President Eisenhower out of choosing Dulles as his Secretary of State, and Dulles for his part never tired of suspecting Eden of a lack of loyalty.[17]

All these interpersonal relations were important, but Jean Monnet's influence also extended to organizations. When he resigned as president of the High Authority of the ECSC in 1955, he did so in order to advance European unity in a rather original fashion, i.e., through an organization which had neither official standing nor power but merely an influence and whose president and champion he was to remain for twenty years. When he gave up that office on May 9, 1975, the anniversary of the Schuman Declaration, the organization dissolved after first publishing a retrospective in its final "information bulletin":

The Action Committee for the United States of Europe was founded in 1955 on the initiative of Jean Monnet by the Socialist, Christian Democratic and Liberal Parties and the non-Communist unions of the six countries making up the European Coal and Steel Community. Its aim was to guarantee the united action of the member organizations in order to bring about the United States of Europe by concrete measures.

. . . The Committee was organized in such a way that the domestic political basis necessary to the continuing implementation of European action was consolidated and stabilized in every country by having majority parties, opposition parties and non-Communist unions unite to achieve concretely defined goals. In 1968, the three great British parties accepted the invitation of the Committee to join it.

The parties and unions belonging to the Committee were represented at its meetings by personalities with great responsibilities: heads or secretaries-general of parties and unions, and heads of parliamentary parties. The names of these men are given below.*

Some of them also continued to collaborate at times when they exercised important functions in the government, as Heads of government or Foreign Ministers. Most of those who regularly attended the meetings of the Committee did so for years. This constancy in the face of all difficulties was due to the commitment of these personalities to the cause of European unity and the personal relations which had been formed between them and Jean Monnet, the President of the Committee. . . .

The Committee always championed the policy of European integration and the transfer of the powers necessary to the solution of common problems from the member countries to the institutions of the Community. In 1956, the Committee played an important role in the preparation of the treaties of the Common Market (EEC), the European Atomic Energy Commission (Euratom) and, after 1957, in the ratification of these treaties by the parliaments of the six member countries. When the Committee foresaw the danger of an increasing dependence on the oil from the Mideast, it called for the development of a construction program of nuclear power stations in order to assure the economic independence of Europe (1957). After the EEC and Euratom treaties came into force, the Committee especially supported the efforts of the European Commission and of those governments who had finally abolished import tariffs and quotas since these measures had made it possible to progressively create an extensive European market and a common policy which would open for our countries possibilities of a step-by-step development comparable to that of the United States.

During the sixties, the Committee advocated that the Germans now living apart be brought together within the European Community, that Great Britain become a member, that relations on a basis of equality be established between the two great units, Europe and the United States, that economic cooperation with the Soviet Union and the countries of Eastern Europe be promoted and that official relations be established between the European Community and the People's Republic of China.[18]

---

* *Frenchmen among the Committee members:* Guy Mollet, Gaston Defferre, Pierre Pflimlin, Alain Poher, René Pleven, Valéry Giscard d'Estaing, Antoine Pinay, Maurice Faure, André Bergeron, Eugène Descamps, Edmond Maire.

Germans: Erich Ollenhauer, Fritz Erler, Willy Brandt, Herbert Wehner, Rainer Barzel, Karl Carstens, Kurt-Georg Kiesinger, Helmut Kohl, Franz Josef Strauss, Walter Scheel, Walter Freitag, Heinz Oskar Vetter, Walter Arendt, Otto Brenner, Eugen Loderer.

Englishmen: George Brown, Denis Healey, Roy Jenkins, Michael Stewart, Arthur Douglas-Home, Edward Heath, Reginald Maudling.

Italians: Pietro Nenni, Giuseppe Saragat, Emilio Colombo, Amintore Fanfani, Mariano Rumor, Mario Scelba, Giovanni Malagodi, Ugo la Malfa, Giovanni Pastore.

ADENAUER GERMANY, EUROPE,
AND THE UNITED STATES

Without the internal development of the Social Democratic Party of Germany, Monnet's Action Committee would not have come into being in 1955. And if the Federal Republic could appear as Adenauer Germany during a fourteen-year period, this was not merely due to the personality of the Chancellor. Initially, he had benefited from the negative image people in other countries had of the SPD and especially of its leader, Kurt Schumacher, for until his death on August 20, 1952, this man was seen as a bogeyman not only in anti-German circles but also among those whose attitude toward the reconstruction of the new German state was positive.

One would hardly believe that Kurt Schumacher had spent the entire Nazi period in a concentration camp and now headed a foreign sister party if one could have heard the Socialist chief of state Vincent Auriol say to a visitor in 1951: "Schumacher is a Nazi, for between him and Hitler there is no difference except that he isn't cruel. . . . Schumacher is a madman, the head of that German Social Democracy about which I wonder if it has not already become the successor of National Socialism."[19] When Dean Acheson first came to Bonn in November 1949, he was very favorably impressed by Adenauer. Subsequently, he met Schumacher and found that he "combined a harsh and violent nature with nationalistic and aggressive ideas."[20] Already at that time, the American Secretary of State found the two deputies Erich Ollenhauer and Carlo Schmid "much more attractive." Later, he said that after Schumacher's death the SPD had become more positive. Other Americans soon made a very simple distinction: German democracy is Adenauer, Adenauer's adversaries are no democrats.[21] Of course, the image Schumacher had of the United States was neither better nor more correct than the image American politicians and journalists had of him.[22] And the head of the SPD did not listen to those in his party who had come to know the United States through personal experience.

Yet this personal element should not be overestimated. The policy of the SPD, its rejection of European integration and of rearmament without political equality, was more important as an explanation of American incomprehension than of Schumacher's personality. When Fritz Erler had some friendly words to say about the United States during his first major address before the Bundestag but at the same time proposed a policy that diverged from that country's,[23] he was not listened to as much as after 1955 when his party, whose deputy chief and generally respected spokesman in foreign policy and defense he had meantime become, had accepted the Europe policy of the Chancellor, at least in its essential aspects.

It is never easy to determine the share of an extraordinary personality among the causes of a historical process, and the case of Konrad Adenauer is no exception.[24] Germany's partition was an accomplished fact before he became Chancellor, and any other chancellor would have considered it the most urgent foreign-policy priority to acquire the right to have a foreign policy of his own. For the occupation statute that was applicable to the Federal Republic when it was founded specified among the spheres over which the three occupying powers reserved total authority all "foreign affairs, including international agreements which are being concluded by or for Germany" and "control over foreign trade and foreign exchange."

And any other chancellor would also have endeavored to shake off the tutelage of the three High Commissioners in matters of domestic politics as he would also have suffered from a "Potsdam complex"— more justified on the basis of the facts than the French Yalta complex—i.e., the fear that Germany might remain or again become a mere object in the hands of the 1945 victorious powers. But neither Konrad Adenauer's fundamental decisions nor his practices or frame of reference can be separated from his person and his will. To exploit East-West tensions for the benefit of the Federal Republic though without attempting to play one of the occupying powers off against the other, to talk vaguely of reunification and strongly of security, to advocate rearmament less for its own sake than to give Germany—now shrunk to the dimensions of the Federal Republic—more room to maneuver, and, finally, to strive for the fusion of Western European sovereignties as the ultimate goal of a path leading toward German sovereignty: all these were fixed points on a course which did not necessarily and certainly not automatically suggest itself in 1949–50.

Even though the idea that it was of primary importance to gain the trust of the United States so that necessary trust might be placed in the Americans had been felt to be a fundamental premise by an overwhelming majority of Germans since the Marshall Plan and the Berlin crisis, it is nonetheless true that relations with the United States could not have been handled as skillfully by just any politician. The Americans in question were not only the governing elite but also the public, and Adenauer was probably the first foreign statesman to hire a publicity agency to win over public opinion. He also was better than others at utilizing the press to sensitize the public of both countries. He even preferred using the American press when he was about to send up a trial balloon. And it did not have to be an important paper such as *The New York Times,* to whose Bonn correspondent the Chancellor confided his concerns about the defense of the Federal Republic in August 1955. In December 1949, he authorized the small Cleveland *Plain Dealer* to publish his first confidential remarks about this subject. What was involved here was a well thought out policy. When a Social Democratic representative criticized an interview and told the Chancellor, "The press, Chancellor, is not a suitable instrument of foreign policy," Adenauer told him, "Look, Mr. Kingsbury Smith is a very well known American journalist whose articles appear in 2000 American papers. . . . I believe it would be quite unintelligent not to profit from the opportunity to enlighten wide circles of the American public on certain points."[25]

The Chancellor was not merely anxious to flatter the American public but to present himself as a true friend with the right to inform it, to explain his actions and attempt to change the ideas and the politics of those he addressed. Already during his first trip to the United States in April 1953, he found the right tone. Of course, his prestige at the time was very high and the reception he was given in Washington (which he describes with some measure of vanity in his memoirs) made his task an easy one.[26] But the important addresses he gave at the time, especially to the American Committee on United Europe or, three years later, the much more critical one before the Council on Foreign Relations,[27] were certainly more than stylistic exercises. Beyond that, he saw to it that his representatives made the widest possible contacts, as was true of the loyal and even subservient Heinrich von Brentano, his Foreign Minister from 1955 to 1961, or a special envoy like the representative Kurt Birrenbach, to whom, in October 1961, he entrusted the task of turning around the mood in the United States by any number of discreet exchanges at a time when relations with the White House were not precisely the best. The diversity of the circles addressed was astonishing.[28]

The conviction which Brentano expressed in a long personal letter to his boss in March 1957 on a visit to the Grand Canyon was certainly shared by Adenauer: "I believe . . . that it is largely within our power to determine the policy of the United States during the next few years. The growing strength of Europe ties the Americans closer to us."[29] The trust shown the Chancellor in the United States, to which Brentano referred in the same letter, was due in equal measure to his decisive policy, his friendly influence, and the international situation. The first chance to use that influence was provided by his excellent relations with Secretary of State Dean Acheson and his close ties to the U.S. High Commissioner John McCloy, though the fact that he was related to Adenauer (Mrs. McCloy was a cousin of the Chancellor's deceased wife) hardly had anything to do with this. What was much more important was the sense of political solidarity which favored the return of the Federal Republic to a minimal degree of sovereignty. From the fall of 1949 to March 1951 when the "little revision" of the occupation statute made possible the creation of a Foreign Ministry at Bonn with as yet limited authority, the Chancellor found Acheson and McCloy sufficiently sympathetic to obtain extensive freedom of action in spite of the statute. After he had become his own Foreign Minister, he persuaded his colleagues Dean Acheson and Robert Schuman to instruct their High Commissioners in Bonn not to interfere with the German chancellor, who was subordinate to them until the High Commissioners were finally replaced by normal ambassadors in May 1955.

When John Foster Dulles succeeded Acheson, a new confidential relationship developed, though this did not prevent occasional harsh disputes, as the one over the Radford Plan in 1956 or the landing of American troops in Lebanon in 1958 (see Chapters 5 and 6). But although Adenauer and Dulles could not converse without an interpreter, they completely agreed in their moralizing view of the international situation, as has been clearly testified to by Adenauer's preferred interpreter.[30] Defense against atheistic Communism was the central topic the two men discussed, and this partly explains a paradox that was hardly noticed at that time or later: John Foster Dulles' emotional preferences were for France, not for Germany, yet his *Weltanschauung* prevented him from understanding the psychological and political realities in France, while he got along perfectly well with Konrad Adenauer, who was firmly rooted in the dominant ideology of his own country.

But his personal relations with Dulles caused Adenauer to overlook two things. The first was President Eisenhower's role in foreign policy decisions. It is true, of course, that Dulles had a fairly free hand during the six years he was Secretary of State, and the President's decisions were largely based on his suggestions. But the conversations between the two men show that that influence was by no means one-sided.[31] The second factor was the human and political change that came with John F. Kennedy and his team. Nor could George Ball's presence in the State Department bridge the gap between the young President and the old Chancellor: the gap between a group of men who proposed to act rationally rather than emotionally and who turned their attention to new continents, and a champion of a moralizing politics which revolved exclusively around the confrontation with Communism.

HYSTERIA RAMPANT

Jean Monnet's activity was both facilitated and hampered by the Cold War.[32] The Western European governments unified more readily when the forces that sustained them felt a common fear, and the United States supported an organized Europe the more willingly as it feared the pressure of the USSR on the countries of an excessively weak Europe. But inside each of these countries antagonisms became more pronounced or were renewed under the twofold pressure of Soviet and American politics and of the image people in each country had of either superpower: the terrifying vision of a Soviet Union that brutally suppresses its satellites with trials and executions whose victims are heroes of the Communist revolution, and the distorted face of an America with its anti-Communist hysteria. Both of these factors strengthened the opposite camp in its self-confidence and got those into trouble who had raised the one or the other to the level of a moral model.

In 1950, the United States experienced a rapid and extensive spread of that aggressive reaction of fear which had been apparent since 1947 when Harry S Truman's loyalty program for public servants had become law. In 1948, Harry Dexter White, the American creator of the International Monetary Fund and the World Bank, was accused of espionage by two confessed traitors. He was able to defend himself for a while but succumbed to a heart attack three days after he had been called before the House Committee on Un-American Activities. In 1953, the Attorney General could calmly allege that White had been a Soviet spy and that Truman, though fully aware of that fact, had nominated him to the International Monetary Fund.[33]

Two things happened in 1950: North Korea attacked South Korea, and in the name of the U.N. the United States intervened in the war, which soon was also fought against troops of Communist China. In addition, a new wave of fear of espionage was sweeping the country. In February 1950, Klaus Fuchs, a British atomic scientist of German birth, admitted that since 1942 he had been passing on to the Soviet Union all the information to which he had access.[34] And the balance of power between the USSR and the United States had in fact changed when the Soviets exploded their first atom bomb on July 14, 1949. The feeling of insecurity increased when Stalin's successor Malenkov publicly proclaimed on August 8, 1953, that the USSR now also had the hydrogen bomb, while the first American H-bomb had just been tested on November 1 of the previous year. Still a matter of secondary importance during the 1948 elections, the defense against treason and subversion became a preferred weapon in 1952 in the hands of

Richard Nixon, who in his campaign for the vice-presidency violently attacked the Democratic presidential candidate Adlai Stevenson.

Shortly after his inauguration, Eisenhower was confronted with the case of two persons who had been sentenced to death and whose appeal for clemency he rejected. They were executed on June 1, 1953. Denounced in June 1950 by a relative, David Greenglass, who at the same time had admitted to spying for the Soviet Union, Julius and Ethel Rosenberg were indicted in January 1951. And in March they became "the first Americans to be sentenced to death in peacetime for espionage," as Eisenhower wrote later.[35]

Even on the assumption that the statements of an accuser who derived personal advantages from his denunciation were both valid and well founded, the question arises why the convicted were refused a pardon—which was demanded all over the world by both enemies and friends of the United States, including even Pope Pius XII— considering that the act of espionage in question had been committed in 1944–45 on behalf of an ally and that the accused, a couple with two small children, were surely a touching case in purely human terms. Because their execution answered the cry of all those Americans who saw their country threatened from within and without and believed that the technical achievements of the USSR could only be explained by treason. President Eisenhower gave in to their pressure, since to a considerable extent he was one of them, as can be gleaned from the letters he wrote his son and friends at the time to justify his decision.

But if Eisenhower was subject to pressure, this was only because he put up with the noisy agitation of Senator Joseph R. McCarthy.[36] After McCarthy had trained himself adequately in verbal aggressiveness and bluff tactics in April 1949 in the course of hearings by the Senate committee investigating the massacre of American prisoners of war in Malmédy by SS troops under Joachim Peiper, he began attacking the State Department in February 1950, charging that it had been infiltrated by Communists. In 1953, McCarthy's power reached its zenith. While his assistants Roy Cohn and David Shine engaged in a clean-up of American libraries abroad, particularly in Germany, he called before his committee whomever he chose, accused without proof, insulted his victims to his heart's content, negotiated on his own with Greek shipowners to strengthen the blockade of China, and humiliated an army general and the Secretary of Defense to such a degree that the London *Times* wrote: "Senator McCarthy achieved today what the generals Burgoyne and Cornwallis never achieved, the surrender of the American army."[37]

McCarthy frightened everyone, including John Foster Dulles. But he especially scared the Liberals, who occasionally preferred denouncing others to escape being accused by the senator. The purge within the Administration proceeded according to the principle that the government need not prove punishable conduct on the part of the accused but that mere doubt about the compatibility between continued service and national security interests sufficed.

McCarthy's fall was as rapid as his rise. After the Senate finally passed a resolution on December 2, 1954, which condemned the witch hunter for violating the traditions of the Senate "in word and in deed,"[38] he was soon forgotten. Some of his direct and indirect victims were gradually rehabilitated. On December 2, 1963, President Johnson conferred a decoration on Professor Robert Oppenheimer "in the name of the people of the United States of America." The "father of the atom bomb," who had been suspended and disciplined in 1953 because he had opposed building the hydrogen bomb and had championed the cause of the Spanish Republicans before the war, was thus honored. But McCarthyism was to continue for a long time to affect the image of the United States in Europe. The same is true of the idea of the so-called rollback which enabled John Foster Dulles to make sensational pronouncements which terrified friendly countries much more than any potential enemy.

In reality, of course, the strategy of simple containment was never renounced by any U.S. President, neither by Truman, who recalled General MacArthur on April 11, 1951, for wanting to extend the Korean War to Chinese territory, nor by Eisenhower, who, like his Secretary of State and his ally Konrad Adenauer, was anxious to do nothing that might look like intervention when on June 17, 1953, Soviet armor was used in East Berlin to suppress the first workers' uprising against a regime that considered itself Socialist. But the "saber rattling" language of the American leadership permitted other interpretations of its acts and intentions.

This all the more so as spokesmen for social forces outside the U.S. government vied with each other in denouncing any "softness" toward Communism and equated the drawing of any distinctions with treason against the West. Thus Francis Cardinal Spellman, archbishop of New York, emphatically supported McCarthy in a particularly vehement speech in Brussels in October 1953: "The anguished cries and protests against 'McCarthyism' are not going to dissuade Americans from their desire to see Communists exposed and removed from positions where they can carry out their nefarious plans."[39] Yet although other bishops and numerous American clergymen expressed themselves along the same lines, the fact remains that Cardinal Spellman was less representative of American Catholicism than George Meany was of the union movement.

For Meany, who became president of the American Federation of

Labor in 1952 and, after their merger, head of the AFL-CIO, did not content himself with supporting those French and Italian unions which refused to be run by Communist leadership. He made himself the watchdog of his European colleagues in the International Federation of Free Unions (IBFG), which had been established in 1949 as a counterorganization to the World Federation of Trade Unions created by Stalin.[40] Within the IBFG, the pressure from the American unions was most vigorously resisted by the British trade unions, while their conflicts with the French CGT-FO derived from the problems of decolonization (see Chapter 5).

It is hardly surprising that the German Federal Republic should have been that European country where the increasing harshness of the political climate was most noticeable. Wasn't it especially preoccupied with its security? Didn't it have to worry about Berlin and the stability of an as yet insufficiently stable political system? And wasn't it advantageous to demonstrate that it was the most reliable European partner of a disquieted America? On September 19, 1950, the West German government initiated disciplinary measures and dismissal procedures against officials, employees, and workers in the public sector who might "support" one of eleven listed organizations,[41] including three extreme right-wing ones, the German Communist Party (KPD), and the Union of Victims of the Nazi Regime (VVN), which undoubtedly was under Communist influence but also constituted a movement of survivors of widely diverging political views. After the government had requested the Bundesverfassungsgericht (Federal Constitutional Court) on November 19, 1951, to find the radical right-wing Sozialistische Reichspartei (SRP) illegal, it made the same request three days later for the KPD. But while the court did proclaim the SRP unconstitutional in October 1952, the decision concerning the KPD was delayed for almost five years. The result was that the German Communist Party was not outlawed until August 17, 1956, in an entirely different political climate.[42]

In Italy, the center coalition—the Christian Democrats and smaller partners—ran into danger through the rise of the Communists and the Nenni Socialists in the early 1950s. In spite or perhaps because of repeated interventions by the American ambassador Clare Boothe Luce, who proceeded even more massively than the AFL-CIO against the Confederazione Generale Italiana del Lavoro (CGIL), the large union federation run by the Italian Communist Party, they only barely won the elections on June 7, 1953. "In 1955, Mrs. Boothe Luce . . . promoted a new policy to undermine the CGIL further. The United States Dept. of Defense used to award 'off-shore' contracts to European manufacturers for the production of military equipment that the US govt. was furnishing its allies. Mrs. Luce succeeded in having the Defense Dept. proclaim that no further contracts would be awarded to Italian firms in which the CGIL candidates won over 50% of the votes in the elections to the internal commissions. (The internal commission represents the workers in a plant in all dealings with the management regarding the application of work rules, etc.)"[43]

The action of the Church was undoubtedly even more effective. Although in Italy it did not use Cardinal Spellman's style, it also passed through a period of internal hardening promoted by the Vatican. The consequences of this process, which must be explained both by tendencies in the circle close to the aging Pope Pius XII and the tensions of the Cold War, were especially noticeable in France. For French Catholicism, the 1950s meant not only the condemnation of more or less rebellious peripheral movements on the left wing of the Church but also the sanctions which Rome imposed on the Jesuit theologians of Fourvière, the ban on worker-priests, and finally, in 1956, subsequent to a dispute with the episcopate on the nature of its mission, the decision of the Association of Catholic Youth Organizations to disband. In this process, the episcopate itself became a kind of marginal group within the Church as a whole.[44] Between numerous Catholic movements and those Catholics who headed the MRP and made their party an ally of other Christian Democratic parties in Western Europe, a deep rift developed over social problems and the assessment of the international situation. This rift had direct effects on the image these movements had of the United States and of American policy—particularly since they could not fail to be aware of the intensive propaganda of the Communist Party. As early as 1947–48, the PCF had adopted an aggressive tone. It had called General Marshall the "new Führer" and referred to his speeches as an American version of Hitler's *Mein Kampf*. "It's almost as if one were reading a document discovered in the ruins of the Reichskanzlei (chancery) or the vaults of the Adlerhorst (Eagle's Nest) in Berchtesgaden. The great attack plan of American imperialism is not even being disguised."[45] The Korean War, which the PCF immediately attributed to an attack by South Korea, unleashed additional eruptions of hatred, especially during the retreat of the North Korean troops. The American soldiers were called "worthy successors of the murderers of Oradour." André, Wurmser, an editorialist at *L'Humanité*, threatened the American commander-in-chief: "I believe you won't get the chance to become much older before they hang you from the gallows at Nuremberg. But if just punishment should be some time in coming, I can assure you, General MacArthur, that it will be a beautiful sight for my old eyes."

The United States was accused of waging bacteriological war. The most prominent scientists of the PCF, Nobel laureate Frédéric Joliot-Curie among them, supported this campaign, which attracted considerable attention before it was forgotten again after China had refused to admit an investigative commission of the Red Cross.[46] Later, one of the most zealous of the agitators wrote: "Those who invented this extraordinary diversionary maneuver—for everything was obviously invented from A to Z—had political talent. . . . Falsification of news, incitement to hatred, the entire arsenal of those things that dishonor a journalist is represented here. That I was manipulated myself does not relieve me of responsibility for the manipulation to which I contributed."[47] General Matthew Ridgway, commander-in-chief in Korea, continued to be referred to as Ridgway the Plague in France. And what a boon it was when he was appointed commander-in-chief of NATO in Europe! His predecessor had been General Eisenhower, whom it was difficult to attack since he had liberated France in 1944 and been celebrated by the PCF in eulogies, which only had to be reprinted in 1951 to tear the L'Humanité editorial to shreds.[48] But against Ridgway, the party organized a protest demonstration in grand style which deteriorated into a riot.[49]

The date of the demonstration was May 29, 1952, and now it was necessary to mount a vigorous attack on the European Defense Community Treaty (EDC), which was being signed at that time. For this purpose, it had to be shown that the American troops in France were simply the successors of the German Wehrmacht. In an article entitled "The Invasion" (January 1951), we read: "They have established themselves all over the place. They put their feet on the tables, move into our best apartments and our ministries, our harbours, our newspaper stalls, our factories and our cinemas, in uniform or in civilian clothes, as is proper for the secret service. They control our administration. Our armed forces are under their command. They interfere everywhere: in the formation of the government, the budget, the school system and the factories, either to buy them up or to close them."[50] And André Stil, a PCF writer, received the Stalin prize for his three-volume novel Le Premier Choc, which was published in 1951–53 and which describes the struggle of dockworkers in a French port against the American "occupiers," who are portrayed as raping women, expropriating houses and land, and creating unemployment.[51]

The execution of the Rosenbergs was received with an indignation that was sincere but also manipulated in a twofold intent. When L'Humanité wrote on June 20, 1953, "We have had a close look at these infamous gentlemen, these murderers who have the insolence to pose as the guardians of freedom and democracy. What cowards, what hypocrites they are! The Nazi murderers were what they were, wild animals, murderers in short, but at least they didn't come here to preach us sermons!'' two things were involved: there was, on the one hand, the fight against European and Atlantic policy, and on the other, the effort to make people forget the show trials, the executions and repressions in the USSR which at an earlier time had sometimes been denied in the face of all evidence and approved with loud applause at others. Denial and approval had been so violent that the party found itself in a very embarrassing situation when the report filtered through in which Nikita Khrushchev revealed at the Twentieth Congress of the Communist Party in February 1956 that what had been denied had been only a small part of the horrible reality, that what had been approved had been nothing but crimes and hypocrisy. Already during the détente of 1955, the anti-American campaign of the PCF lost much of its virulence. The Twentieth Party Congress and even more the Soviet repression in Budapest disturbed many party members, although *L'Humanité* tried to present the Hungarian rebels as notorious fascists.

It was also Budapest that put an end to the loyalty of "fellow travelers" such as Jean-Paul Sartre. Writing about the execution of the Rosenbergs and McCarthyism in 1953, he had still said: "It is a legal lynching which stains an entire people with blood and once and for all uncovers in a flash the failure of the Atlantic Alliance. . . . We, your allies? How absurd! Today, our governments are your servants, tomorrow, our peoples will be your victims, that's the whole truth. . . . Do you believe we are going to die for McCarthy? Do you believe we will die to defend the culture of McCarthy? The freedom of McCarthy? The justice of McCarthy?''[52] At the time, Sartre was deliberately silent about everything he knew of the inhumanity of the Soviet regime and the acts of violence in the countries under Soviet rule. Budapest made him change his attitude, though without causing him to question the vehemence and extent of his condemnation of the United States. The same was true of other "fellow travelers."[53]

But how was the concept "fellow travelers" to be defined? It certainly differed from that of "neutralists," though there was perhaps a kind of transitional zone from the one to the other, particularly in the early 1950s when the Communist-inspired "Stockholm Appeal" of the World Peace Movement received millions of signatures in all of Western Europe.

"Neutralism" is quite a vague term which included rather different realities, especially in terms of attitudes toward the United States. In Great Britain, for example, the tone of the *New Statesman and Nation* was often already sharper than that of its chief initiator, Richard Crossman, and other members of the Labour Left.* In the *New Fabian Essays* which were published in 1952, Crossman had said about the Cold War: "We must realize that a victory for either side would be a defeat for socialism. We are members of the Atlantic alliance; but this does not mean that we are enemies of every communist revolution. We are opposed to Russian expansion, but also to an American victory. Our object is to keep the Cold War cold. . . . The success we seek is a balance of world power and in that balance the restraining influence of a communist China on Russia may be as vital as that of a socialist Britain on the USA. If neutralism is a blind alley, ideological detachment is a requisite for those on both sides of the Iron Curtain who are seeking to strengthen the social conscience in its struggle against totalitarianism."[54]

In Germany, neutralism had many shadings without ever really representing a political force, unless one wants to call neutralist the Social Democratic rejection of rearmament (i.e., of a rearmament which the SPD did not reject in principle but only on the conditions laid down by Adenauer) or takes the "without me" attitude of many young people in face of the suddenly renewed call to arms as the expression of a reasoned estimate of worldwide antagonisms. The commitment of the overwhelming majority of the citizens and of the political forces in the anti-Communist camp was much too great for small splinter groups or isolated voices like Martin Niemöller's to have much significance.

Primarily because two political trends came together there, the situation in France was altogether different: first, there was the Left, which did not wish to widen the gap that separated it from the Communist Party and which, confronted with a Soviet Union that was still socialist in spite of everything, did not care to side with capitalist America. And secondly, there was the nationalist trend, which also rejected submission to the superpower America.[55] Here, the development of anti-American themes by the leading brains of the Rassemblement du Peuple Français and its founder, General de Gaulle, played a special role in 1952—53.[56] For the Left, an entire typology would have to be drawn up, and was in fact sketched out by the editor-in-chief of *Le Monde,* the very paper whose "neutralism" was the subject of incessant controversies at the time. Hubert Beuve-Méry distinguished a number of possible positions vis-à-vis the United States,[57] giving preference to a kind of Europeanism which recognized the necessity of American protection, yet also strove to distance itself

---

* On the attitude of Aneurin Bevan, see Chapter 6.

as much as possible from the United States. But was that a reason for carrying the criticism of the United States too far, as some accused his paper of doing, and for muting the analyses of Eastern European realities? Did this not mean that *Le Monde* had entered that hazy gray area inhabited by those intellectuals whose only common trait was to apply different yardsticks to East and West, the United States and the Soviet Union, and to live in that universe of illusions Raymond Aron was criticizing so vigorously at the time in his *L'Opium des Intellectuels?*[58]

Or did it simply express the conviction of many Frenchmen from diverse social strata that the Cold War was being waged between the United States and the USSR and that it was therefore in the interest of France to stay out of it as much as possible? Such a conviction expressed itself less in the answers than in the formulations of a poll conducted in 1953 by the Institut Français d'Opinion Publique: "Is it your opinion that a West European Union would be a restraining or an aggravating element in the conflict between the United States and the USSR?"[59] The distribution of answers (41 percent said "restraining," 21 percent "aggravating") showed that Europe was seen as a possible third force.

FROM THE SCHUMAN PLAN TO THE COMMON MARKET

"The key to progress toward integration is in French hands. In my opinion France needs, in the interests of her own future, to take the initiative promptly and decisively if the character of Western Germany is to be one permitting healthy development in Western Europe. Even with the closest possible relationships of the U.S. and the U.K. to the continent, France and France alone can take the decisive leadership in integrating Western Germany into Western Europe," wrote Secretary of State Acheson in October 1949 in a note addressed to the U.S. ambassadors in Europe.[60] After the French Foreign Minister Robert Schuman had adopted Jean Monnet's project and proposed on May 9, 1950, "to place the entire Franco-German coal and steel production under a joint Highest Authority within the framework of an organization which would also be open to other European countries," he gave the impetus that the American leadership wanted without merely bowing to an American wish. He simply broke with a foreign policy style which had consisted in delaying tactics accompanied by recriminations and had never envisioned a creative initiative. And he also showed that such an initiative might be beneficial to France, if only to enhance its prestige.

France's prestige in Europe: the positive reaction of five countries on the European continent was not only due to the interest the Federal Republic and Italy had in finally being placed on an equal footing with a former victorious power, or the interest of Belgium, Luxembourg, and the Netherlands to participate in an enterprise which also included the small states in the decision-making process. There was also genuine relief that the end of traditional rivalries and conflicts had come, and this at a moment when the real problems were of new and wholly different dimensions. The personal ties between the Lorrainer Robert Schuman, the Rhinelander Konrad Adenauer, and Alcide de Gasperi, who came from Trent, are not to be explained so much by loyalty to the Catholic Church as by their common situation as men from border regions.

France's prestige in the United States: the idea of a united Europe enjoyed such popularity in Congress and in the American press that on a four-week trip through the United States in April-May 1952 Jean Monnet was everywhere received in triumph. A year later, in early June 1953, he returned to Washington as president of the High Authority of the Coal and Steel Community, accompanied by his two deputies, one of whom was the German Franz Etzel, a circumstance which gave tangible expression both to European integration and Franco-German rapprochement.

The Europeans had the full support of the Americans, whose motives were political rather than purely economic. But there was one exception: the abolition of tariff barriers between the countries of Europe seemed desirable in itself—not only because an undivided market promised to be a better outlet but also because, in contrast to the French industrialists who had vigorously opposed the establishment of the Coal and Steel Community, the Americans and Germans believed that elimination of these barriers would promote growth in all the countries concerned. And it is true that steel production in all participating countries rose remarkably, whereas the prevailing French economic ideology had been that total demand would always be the same, which also meant that total volume would be constant and that therefore a reduction in French production would necessarily result from any increase in German output.

The support took a variety of forms and ranged from speeches by leading politicians to the more or less direct financing of the activities of public and private organizations.[61] Its primary aspect was undoubtedly the continuing aid given the Europe of the Six against the British ally, who enjoyed no privileged position of any kind during the 1950s.

Basically, both Jean Monnet and Dean Acheson wanted Great Britain to participate in the Europe of the Schuman Plan, but only on the condition that it accept structures other than the elastic coordination in the style of the OEEC and forms other than the ineffectual shell of the European Council. Ernest Bevin immediately refused. And when the Conservatives returned to power in the fall of 1951, they emphasized the British desire to remain outside. Churchill especially suffered from the inequality with the United States. "They have become so big and we are now so small. Poor England!" he complained to his physician, who spoke of "that sense of inequality that devours him like a cancer." But this did not induce him to join the Europe of the Six. On the contrary: "I love France and Belgium," he admitted in confidence in January 1952, "but we must not allow ourselves to be pulled down to that level."[62]

It was therefore important to demonstrate as convincingly as possible that influence could be brought to bear on the United States, and Clement Attlee's trip to Washington in December 1950 was intended to serve this purpose. In Great Britain, it was called a decisive step to keep President Truman from using the atom bomb in the Korean War, a war which was especially unpopular in England, and not only with the Left.[63] But no pressure could be exerted to dissuade the U.S. government from giving support to the Six. In view of all American attempts to urge it to adopt a more positive attitude toward this Europe, the British government could do no more than remain firm in turn.

The British refusal had various results. In the Federal Republic, it served more as a justification than a reason for the SPD to refuse to go along. In France, it made it possible to present the Europe of the Six as either a Catholic or a German-American enterprise. In Italy, it aggravated the anti-British trend, which was marked in any event. In a poll conducted in November 1953 to determine which country was felt to be the most "sympathetic" (the choice was between England, France, Germany, and the United States), a mere 3 percent of the Italians questioned put England first, while 47 percent put it at the bottom of the list (the United States ranked first with 56 percent, while 6 percent placed it last; for France, it was 12 percent as compared to 4 percent; for Germany, 22 percent and 20 percent), with the majority holding the view that since the war England's hostility toward Italy had been greater than that of the Soviet Union.[64]

But did the Europe of the Six correspond to the Schuman Plan? Certainly, if one considers the one-and-one-half-month period between Schuman's statement of May 9, 1950, and the outbreak of the Korean War. After that, the great dispute over German rearmament and the European Defense Community overshadowed for more than four years the negotiations dealing with the treaty establishing the European Coal and Steel Community—which was signed on April 18, 1951—and the installation of the High Authority in August 1952.

Almost everywhere, especially in France and Germany, the Schuman Plan had been welcomed as a fruitful initiative. The political forces that fought it therefore used defensive arguments of the type "The idea is good, but the modalities are bad." In Bonn, the Social Democrats protested that they were not against Europe. Even after their success at the polls on June 1951, which had made them the strongest party, the Gaullists in Paris tried to distance themselves from the old nationalist Right and recalled the words de Gaulle had used during a press conference in March 1950 in answer to Adenauer's overtures to France: "If one did not force oneself to look at things soberly, one would be almost blinded by the prospect of what German valor and French valor could jointly achieve if the latter were enhanced by Africa."[65] In the question of German rearmament and the European army, there was a total switch: now the "Europeans" were on the defensive and had recourse to formulas such as "We are aware of the weaknesses and drawbacks of our proposals but . . ."

Once it was recognized that the Atlantic defense system required the presence of numerous divisions in Western Europe (see Chapter 6), the problem of German rearmament became inescapable. Could the American general staff afford to do without the human potential of a country whose population voted 95 percent anti-Communist and rely on France, whose voters gave the Communist Party 25 percent of their vote and whose professional army was in Indochina besides? But Acheson and the other American politicians also knew perfectly well that German rearmament harbored the risk of provoking violent disputes in England, France, and in Germany itself. So why risk conflicts when no direct Communist threat had been apparent since the lifting of the Berlin blockade in May 1949?

The outbreak of the Korean War on June 25, 1950, created an entirely new situation. Just one day later, Acheson stated before a Senate committee that it was urgently necessary to mobilize European forces. On August 11, the Council of Europe in Strasbourg passed a resolution by Winston Churchill which called for the immediate creation of a unified European force. As early as March 16, Churchill had proposed the creation of a German contingent within such a force in the House of Commons, but the Labour government did not adopt that project. On September 11, the Conference of Foreign Ministers of the "Big Three" of the Atlantic Alliance began in New York, and four days later the ministerial council of NATO convened. The French government had foreseen that Acheson would raise the question of German rearmament.

But Robert Schuman was in for two surprises. The American Secretary of State did not ask for vague agreements but energetically demanded a concrete decision. In contrast to the French, Ernest Bevin supported the American point of view. Initially, Schuman refused categorically, invoking public opinion and expressing the fear that the Pentagon might side with Germany. During the NATO session, everyone opposed France, the Dutch minister being particularly vehement. Jules Moch, French Minister of Defense, engaged in heated debates with his colleagues, especially British Minister L. Shinwell, who reproached the French with a lack of realism. Finally, the French delegation yielded on the fundamental points after Moch had raised the idea of limiting German units to less than regimental strength. On September 16, the communiqué of the NATO Council stated: "The Ministers agree that Germany must be placed in the position of contributing to the defense of Western Europe." Three days later, after another session, the Big Three worked out a communiqué which was a masterpiece of diplomatic formulation: "The Ministers are in complete agreement that the creation of a German national army would not be in the best interest of Germany and Europe. They also believe that this view is shared by the vast majority of the German people. But the Ministers have taken note of the views recently expressed both inside and outside Germany which plead for German participation in an integrated army for the defense of European freedom."

The result was the Jean Monnet—inspired Pleven Plan, in which the head of the French government proposed the creation of a European army. Monnet was unquestionably concerned with promoting European integration along new paths. But in actual fact, it was an attempt to make the unpopular idea of German rearmament appealing by painting it in the popular colors of "Europe." And the EDC treaty with its incredible complexity and elements that were profoundly shocking to the French public—such as the abolition of national military academies—was to be presented as a means to control a feared Germany by allowing oneself to be closely controlled by it.

The French government and Jean Monnet succeeded in convincing the initially very reserved Americans of the scope of the idea of a European army. General Eisenhower, who had been commander-in-chief of Allied Forces in Europe since April 1951, was at first particularly averse, but in a single conversation Monnet induced him on June 21 to change his mind. Now the entire weight of U.S. diplomacy, of the Congress and the American press, rallied behind the French plan, and this especially as French hostility to it increased. At this moment, the massive American support had an adverse effect on the EDC project, particularly when it degenerated into a kind of extortion that climaxed in the speech John Foster Dulles made on December 14,

1953, in which he threatened an "agonizing reappraisal" of American policy in Europe should the May 27, 1952, treaty fail.

In Germany, the policy of rearmament created a profound change in the political climate. The first plans for a German contribution to European defense had been discussed at a time when glider planes and fencing were still forbidden because they were "military exercises." This would be merely ridiculous if it had not been the very principle of rearmament that indicated a profound transformation in the idea of democracy. A young German who expressed his antipathy to uniforms was still showered with praise in 1949. He was considered the model student of the accusers. A year later, he was the accused. There was undoubtedly continuity in the thinking of those Hitler opponents who persisted in their opposition to any form of totalitarianism, but many who had been on the other side felt that they were once again becoming indispensable.

The fight for and against rearmament was long, stormy, and very confused. Neither of the two camps was homogeneous. Not only sincere "Europeans" or those democrats who were convinced of the danger of Soviet aggression but also resigned skeptics, people who had been "humiliated" and now saw a chance for revenge, and political realists who scented a great opportunity for the Federal Republic endorsed the Chancellor's policy. The naysayers included not only democrats worried about the future of German democracy or the chances for reunification, but also spineless and anarchic "without me's," conscientious objectors with high moral standards, people who had been denazified and now demanded that first they be apologized to, and finally nationalists who considered unacceptable the restrictions Germany would have to submit to.

By and large, public opinion gradually came around to the Chancellor's policy.[66] But although the SPD shifted from a total rejection of rearmament to a criticism of its modalities and finally to limited acceptance,[67] the conflict nonetheless left profound traces which affected the German-American relationship in a twofold fashion. On the one hand, they produced a strengthening of the sense of solidarity, especially thanks to the unlimited support John Foster Dulles had given the Chancellor even though the French hesitated. But they also produced the idea that American policy had more or less deliberately divided Germany further and reversed prevailing currents in the Federal Republic. For rearmament strengthened social and intellectual neoconservatism and reduced any critical spirit to near irrelevance. When the former Minister of the Interior and later President Gustav Heinemann, whom the rearmament issue had caused to resign in October 1950, wrote in an article in September 1953 that Adenauer had won the "Dulles elections,"[68] he was speaking quite pejoratively and referring to this very development.

For its most resigned adherents on both the German and the French side, the rearmament of Germany was the price that had to be paid the Americans for guaranteeing Europe's security. But the Germans could claim an additional compensation: rearmament also hastened the return to equality, for both problems were officially tied together in the treaties signed in May 1952 and October 1954. But to many in France, the American-supported German recovery appeared as the cause or sign of French decline. It is certainly true that feelings were contradictory, that one wanted a German army that would be weaker than the French, yet also stronger than the Russian. More important, however, there was the sense of being subject to a twofold pressure: the pressure exerted by the United States, and the claims to equal status of a Germany that people had assumed to be permanently weakened. The result was a conjunction of anti-German and anti-American sentiment whose importance would only emerge by and by.

From 1952 to 1954, successive French governments were paralyzed by the quarrel over the EDC, while public debate became so heated that everyone was reminded of the Dreyfus Affair. For the dividing line ran across political parties and almost threatened to split them, the only exception being the Communists and the Gaullists, the two most powerful EDC opponents. When Pierre Mendès-France became Prime Minister on June 20, 1954, in order to put an end to the Indochina war, he wanted to rid himself of a problem which pitted his ministers against each other, and tried to obtain modifications in a treaty which he did not especially care for himself but wanted to make palatable to the majority of deputies. But he came up against a united front of statesmen and politicians who were convinced that his prestige sufficed to assure the successful passage of the treaty in the National Assembly. At the Brussels Conference (August 19–22) he found himself completely alone against the five other countries, which were vigorously supported by the United States as represented by David Bruce. The isolation of the French representative, who was subjected to the joint pressure of other Europeans and the Americans, was a situation which General de Gaulle and Maurice Couve de Murville would point to during the 1960s as precedent and explanation for their diplomacy within the Europe of the Six.

The most important reason for the intransigence of the partners was the false information with which the French members of the "Society of Europeans" flooded them. Adenauer, Dulles, and Spaak believed the Socialists Guy Mollet and André Philip, the Popular Republicans Robert Schuman and Pierre-Henri Teitgen when they assured them that the EDC treaty had a good chance in France. Churchill and Eden also pressured Pierre Mendès-France when he requested them in vain to have Great Britain take at least a step toward Europe to dissipate French fears. On August 30, 1954, the National Assembly refused by 319 to 264 votes to even take up proper discussion of the treaty, which was shelved as a consequence.*

The Western capitals reacted to the vote with consternation, and Moscow without undue enthusiasm. The adversaries of German rearmament who had hoped that the Soviet Union would be prepared to accept the reunification of a demilitarized Germany, i.e., the "desovietization" of East Germany, were disappointed, as was a certain number of French diplomats and advisers of Pierre Mendès-France, for the Soviet government made no new proposals after the failure of the EDC. Had it done so, the French government would still have been helpless, for the British and Americans would certainly have refused to negotiate with Moscow from a position of weakness. John Foster Dulles felt betrayed by Mendès-France. In the Federal Republic, Adenauer had so thoroughly equated the EDC with the idea of European unity and portrayed French foes of the treaty as so many irreconcilable enemies of Germany that the disappointment was immense, even among the German opponents of the EDC, especially the young, who had found in the unification of Europe an ideal in line with their hopes. A new beginning had to be made.

Surprisingly enough, this was accomplished within a few weeks. Anthony Eden took on the role of mediator and contributed to a possible solution by letting Great Britain take a forward step. The 1948 Brussels Pact was revived by allowing Italy and the Federal Republic to accede to it. Since 5 plus 2 = 6 plus 1, Great Britain now saw itself allied with the Europe of the Six, at least in matters of defense. Mendès-France convinced both John Foster Dulles and Adenauer of his sincerity and finally got the National Assembly to approve a generally accepted solution: the Federal Republic would join the Atlantic Alliance and NATO as an alternative to EDC—a reversal of four years earlier, when the French government had launched the idea of the EDC as an alternative to the Federal Republic's joining NATO.

On October 23, 1954, the treaties and agreements were signed in Paris, and on December 30 the National Assembly authorized their ratification. They came into force on May 5, 1955. Before that date, in November 1954, Mendès-France made a triumphal visit to the United

---

* The majority against ratification was even greater since several deputies known as EDC opponents had voted along with its advocates in order not to simply cut off the debate.

States, where John Foster Dulles praised him to the skies as a "superman." At the same moment, Jean Monnet announced that he would not ask that his term of office as president of the High Authority of the European Coal and Steel Community be extended. It expired in February 1955.

Monnet made this decision because he wanted to dedicate himself to relaunching the idea of European unity, which had been dealt a severe blow by the failure of the EDC. The rallying of the German opposition contributed much toward making the discussion of this renewal less emotional. Now its principal point of departure would no longer be defense or political unification (the latter idea had suffered a quiet but decisive defeat in 1953) but the economy. From the Messina Conference in June 1955 to the signing of the Rome Treaty on March 25, 1957, by which the EEC and Euratom were created, progress was made quickly. The negotiators of the six participating countries, with outside support from Monnet's American friends, were largely members or associates of his Action Committee for the United States of Europe, in part because international negotiations had never before been teamwork to such an extent, in part because the project of a Common Market once again seemed the key to a better future, as had once been true of the Schuman Plan. True, the National Assembly that agreed to ratify the accords on July 10, 1957, was no longer the same as in 1954, if only because the Gaullist group had shrunk from 121 to 21 deputies during the elections of January 2, 1956, but the tone of the debate certainly was different. In opposition to Pierre Mendès-France, who feared that an opening of the borders might have negative consequences for the fragile French economy, the rapporteur, the Socialist Alain Savary, who had voted for the Schuman Plan and against EDC, advocated acceptance of the treaties in the name of the opportunities for economic development.

According to its spokesman, the Gaullist faction had voted against "Mr. Monnet's Europe." When the Fourth Republic ended in June 1958, one could therefore ask oneself what would now become of the Common Market, which was not yet fully functional. But to everyone's surprise, de Gaulle not only accepted the legacy but made the treaties practicable in the first place by strengthening France's external finances through a drastic currency reform, which was carried out by his Finance Minister, Antoine Pinay—the same who had been Prime Minister when the EDC treaty was signed and Foreign Minister during the new drive for European integration. Continuity was thus greater than both Gaullists and anti-Gaullist "Europeans" maintained.

A further surprise during the elaboration and ratification of the

Rome Treaty should really have been caused by the small importance given the question concerning future relations between the EEC and the United States. For during the last years of the Fourth Republic, hostility toward the United States had again grown markedly, though not because of any economic threat to France: the center of the crisis now was North Africa.

5 INDOCHINA, SUEZ, AND ALGERIA

FRENCH WAR AND AMERICAN TAKEOVER

When the Korean War began, the French professional army had been fighting in Indochina for three and a half years. When that war ended with the armistice of July 27, 1953, the Indochina war was raging more violently than ever and was being waged with ever increasing American aid. But with what aim? To reestablish French rule over northern Annam and Tonkin? To contain and push back the Communists? To give the southern part of the country true independence so that it would become a national center for those Vietnamese who still hesitated to rally to the Communist nationalism of Ho Chi Minh?

"Delay or equivocation in implementing complete independence could only serve to bolster the Communist claim that this was in reality a war to preserve colonialism. . . . It was almost impossible to make the average Vietnamese peasant realize that the French, under whose rule his people had lived for some eighty years, were really fighting in the cause of freedom, while the Vietminh, people of their own ethnic origins, were fighting on the side of slavery," President Eisenhower wrote later.[1]

Such a statement contradicted a reflection French President Auriol entrusted to his diary in October 1950: "At this moment, I notice a rather violent anti-American mood. On the one hand, Americans make themselves rather unpopular by pressing for German rearmament. On the other, they exert pressure on the Sultan of Morocco and on Indochina. What they give us for Indochina while they say that we are defending this country against Communism is limited aid so that it doesn't look as if they were abandoning us. But in reality, they do it to make us go along with their policy of total independence [for South Vietnam]. They give us money, and we pay for it with a piece of independence: that is infamous."[2]

It is a fact that at the time the French leadership insisted ever more vigorously that the independence of Emperor Bao Dai and his government was real and that what France was fighting for in Indochina therefore was certainly a defense against Communism. A defense, in other words, which was of direct interest to the United States. In the course of a conversation with John Foster Dulles, who was the Republican adviser of the State Department at the time, President Auriol said on May 6, 1952: "We are the supporting pillar of the defense of the West in Southeast Asia; if this pillar crumbles, Singapore, Malaysia and India will soon fall prey to Mao Tse-tung. You have understood that perfectly well, and I thank you for it."[3] Dulles understood it so well that President Eisenhower used almost the very same words on April 7, 1954, when he presented his "domino theory," which was to be decisive for American policy for almost twenty years: "You have . . . what you would call the 'falling domino' principle. You have a row of dominos set up, you knock over the first one, and what will happen to the last one is the certainty that it will go over very quickly." And after Indochina the President named Burma, Thailand, the Malay Peninsula, and Indonesia, and then Japan, Australia, and New Zealand.[4]

If France was fighting for the West, the other Western countries owed it support and solidarity. The French defeats at Cao Bang and Lang Son caused the National Assembly to call on the French government as early as the fall of 1950 to "emphatically call the attention of the free nations to the international character of the conflict started by the Viet Minh because it casts doubt on the future of Southeast Asia, and to also insist on the need for a common effort in facing present dangers and in the search for the possibilities of a lasting peace." During inauguration ceremonies at the dam of Donzère-Mondragon, Auriol told a number of ambassadors in an important speech on October 25, 1952:

What you see here is the rapid but authentic result of French labor, finished on time according to our first modernization and building plan. Undoubtedly, the Marshall Plan helped, and we have often acknowledged its blessings with gratitude. But unfortunately, the defense of freedom in Indochina has practically cost us twice what we received under that plan and in the form of military aid, 1600 billion [francs] as compared to 800 billion. And so that justice may be rendered us, must we also mention our irreplaceable losses in human lives? And for what did our officers, our non-commissioned officers and our soldiers sacrifice themselves? For our interests? No, but for a cause which is not ours alone: for the defense of the young, associated and friendly states [Vietnam, Cambodia and Laos] to which we brought prosperity and to which we gave independence in order to defend freedom in Asia and thereby to defend freedom and security in Europe and the world.

We shouldered this burden when we still had not rebuilt our homes, when we had to multiply our efforts to put our national defense on a firm footing. In view of this, who can still be surprised about the reactions of this country when it is treated unjustly, when one overlooks its sacrifices or seems to minimize them, when its warnings are clearly ignored?[5]

In this sense, French diplomacy achieved an obvious success when, on December 17, 1952, the NATO Council adopted a resolution expressing "its profound admiration for the courageous struggle being waged indefatigably by French forces and the armies of allied states against Communist aggression," and went on to say that "the campaign being led by the forces of the Union Française in Indochina deserves the unrestricted support of the Atlantic governments." Alluding to this resolution, Prime Minister René Mayer affirmed in his inaugural address on January 8, 1953: "This position will soon have consequences regarding the easing of the burden France has now been carrying in Indochina for nearly eight years." This relief could amount to a total assumption of that burden. On March 16, 1953, *L'Aurore*, a Paris paper that was both sympathetic to the EDC and hostile to any liberalism overseas, stated: "If America were to take on the cost of defending Indochina, France could concentrate all its efforts in Europe and Africa without needing help from anyone."

The Americans were perfectly willing to listen to the language of solidarity. Early in 1952, a long document of the National Security Council which defined the aims of Southeast Asia policy stated that the United States would have to continue "to assure the French that the U.S. regards the French effort in Indochina as one of great strategic importance in the general international interest . . . and as essential to the security of the free world," and went on to say that it might even be necessary "to oppose a French withdrawal."[6] In the following year, the National Security Council stated that the loss of Indochina "would be critical to the security of the U.S." and that "any negotiated settlement would mean the loss of Indochina and the whole of Southeast Asia."

For Ho Chi Minh, who, after 1944, had hoped for American aid against the return of the French and then against their army, this position meant an about-face. In January 1953, in a message to the Vietnamese, he denounced the "French colonialists," who were merely acting "on the orders and with the support of their masters, the American interventionists . . . whose servants they have now become."[7]

The more difficult the military situation in Indochina seemed, the more American help was given. "Between that time [i.e., June 27, 1950] and the fall of Dien Bien Phu in May 1954, our $2.6 billion worth of military and economic aid to the French in Vietnam paid for 80% of the cost of the war against the Vietminh."[8] Actually, the financial help served largely as a means to balance the general finances of France at a time when Marshall Plan aid was running out, and this was a solid though unavowable reason for not ending the war in Indochina, even though it was not really supported by any part of the French public.

Growing aid had the result that more and more Americans went to Saigon, some on official business, to work with French generals and high-ranking officials, and others with no such mission. "There can be no doubt that almost all of the official American representatives had good relations with the French administrative and military authorities and showed themselves generally understanding and cooperative. But General Navarre frequently complained about the interference of certain American businessmen who made no secret of their desire to divert part of the flow of trade necessary to the Indochinese economy to America. . . . The commander-in-chief also frequently complained about American special services, which, as he showed, also acted under the cover of more or less official missions but received their instructions directly from their headquarters in Washington, whose political line often deviated from that of the State Department. All these organs eluded the authority of the American ambassador and clearly were parts of parallel hierarchies," wrote General Ely, one of the French commanders-in-chief, in his memoirs.[9]

Though local conflicts were not precisely infrequent, the most serious ones occurred at the governmental level. On October 8, 1952, the French Prime Minister Antoine Pinay called the American ambassador M. Dunn to his office and returned to him in the presence of Foreign Minister Robert Schuman, Defense Minister René Pleven, and Felix Gaillard, Secretary of State of the Council of Ministers, a note which Dunn had handed Gaillard two days earlier. The note had criticized certain uses to which American aid had been put, and in the eyes of the French government this constituted an inadmissible interference in French internal affairs.

This protest preserved the initial principle: the Atlantic partners, the United States above all, had to show an active solidarity, but only France would wage the war and be solely responsible for the use to which any aid might be put. But already in the following year, the war appeared so hopeless, weighed so heavily on French political life, and even threatened the existence of the French officer corps, which lost an entire class in Indochina every year that subsequent governments— René Mayer's after January 1953 and especially Joseph Laniel's after June—attempted to internationalize the conflict.

But internationalization could mean two things: expansion of the war or, and this especially after the armistice in Korea, the search for an international means of ending it. And if the latter could only be considered when a favorable military situation had been secured, the effort could actually lead to an expansion of the war to obtain it although in principle France wanted the internationalization of peace.

American ambivalences were different in nature. John Foster Dulles attributed great importance to the Indochina war but did not care to see the United States directly involved. He took the defense of Europe to be much more important and therefore saw the financial and military support of France as the price to be paid if France was finally going to ratify the EDC treaty.

The connection between these two problems became evident in late 1953, at the Bermuda Conference, where President Eisenhower, Winston Churchill, and Joseph Laniel and their respective foreign ministers met in a particularly unsatisfactory atmosphere. The Berlin Conference of January 1954, where the three Western powers would be facing the Soviet Union on the German question, was being prepared. Its only result was contained in a communiqué of February 18 which announced that a conference on Korea would be convened on April 26 in Geneva. It added that the ministers agreed that the question of a return to peace in Indochina would also be discussed at this conference, to which the representatives of the United States, France, Great Britain, the Soviet Union, the People's Republic of China, and other interested states were being invited.

Had the announcement of the conference weakened the military position of France, or was it the start of an honorable withdrawal? In any event, even before the Geneva meeting the most serious of all French defeats in Indochina seemed inevitable. The forward base of Dienbienphu, an isolated position three hundred kilometers from Hanoi which the French high command had senselessly made the cornerstone of its tactics, had been continually attacked since February and seemed lost in mid-March unless the enemy batteries could be silenced by a massive air strike. The French air force was not strong enough for this, and so the question arose if the Americans should be asked to send their bombers. For an entire month, incessant and dramatic negotiations about "Operation Vulture" were carried on.[10] In spite of all French urgings, and although Admiral Radford, chairman of the Joint Chiefs of Staff, and even Vice-President Nixon advocated intervention, President Eisenhower finally refused, allegedly only because such an action would have required Congressional approval and the consent of the British government and neither would have agreed. But did such refusal not merely furnish a welcome pretext which permitted a very hesitant Eisenhower not to spell out his own?

Would Dienbienphu have been saved by an intervention of the U.S. Air Force? Would that perhaps have unleashed a Chinese reaction, which would not only have led to the failure of the Geneva Conference but also to an expansion of the war? In retrospect, and particularly when one considers the restraint of the Chinese during the American bombings of the 1960s and the ineffectiveness of these bombings, both of these questions should probably be answered negatively. Dienbienphu, in any event, was taken on May 7. And on June 10, President Eisenhower definitively decided against American intervention, although Georges Bidault, the French negotiator at Geneva, still believed that such a threat was a card he might play: the American President declared that it was not his intention to request Congressional approval for such an action. Two days later, the National Assembly overthrew the Laniel government and on June 17, by an overwhelming majority, elected Pierre Mendès-France, who for years had denounced the illusions and contradictions of French Indochina policy. He committed himself to either make peace by July 20 or to step down.

The Geneva Conference was held under the joint chairmanship of Great Britain and the Soviet Union, i.e., of Anthony Eden and Vyacheslav Molotov. The United States was represented by Undersecretary of State Walter Bedell Smith, who had arrived with very clear instructions, particularly as regards the definition of what was and was not acceptable and the limits of possible contacts with the representatives of Communist China, i.e., Foreign Minister Chou En-lai.[11] Great Britain had recognized the People's Republic of China as far back as 1950, and Anthony Eden had an excellent first contact with the new French head of government, whom Eisenhower and Dulles mistrusted. The initially rather pronounced tensions between the English and the Americans were mitigated by a visit Eden made to Washington that ended with a confidential *aide-mémoire* which spelled out to Mendès-France under what conditions Great Britain and the United States could accept an agreement on ending the war. It was a document which strikingly anticipated the formulations which would be accepted on July 20.[12]

John Foster Dulles, however, was convinced that France would yield even if its conditions were not met and therefore did not want General Bedell Smith, who had been recalled to Washington, to return to Geneva. On July 13, Mendès-France succeeded in convincing Dulles of the firmness of his intentions and of the necessity of American diplomatic support. After a long conversation with him in the presence of Anthony Eden, Dulles sent Mendès-France a message stating: "I admire and respect the honesty with which you attack the central problems facing us today. Indecisiveness is the greatest evil and you have done much to remove it. . . . Now that you must make historic decisions in Geneva, be assured that the numerous friends of France support you with their wishes and their prayers. I am happy that we have found a way by which we can express our support for you in Geneva and do so, as I hope, without doing violence to our principles or the danger of future disagreements."[13]

Days and nights of complicated negotiations followed in which Eden and Molotov but also Chou En-lai acted as mediators. During the night of July 20, the following results were finally achieved: three military agreements on Vietnam, Laos, and Cambodia, respectively, six unilateral declarations, thirteen short concluding speeches, an exchange of letters, and an unsigned final declaration which provided for free elections for the reunification of Vietnam in July 1956. The agreement between France and the Viet Minh partitioned the country, the demarcation line being the 17th parallel of latitude, which was closer to the 18th, which had originally been proposed by France, than to the 13th, which the North Vietnamese delegation had demanded. And the French army was to withdraw from the North including Hanoi and Haiphong, within ten months.

No one felt any enthusiasm about the Geneva agreement. The French parliament approved it by a vote of 462 to 13, with 134 abstentions, after almost all speakers had acknowledged that there was no other solution. *Le Figaro*, a paper with a "European" orientation and more than reserved toward the French head of government, wrote on July 21: "This is an occasion for mourning. Half of our positions in the Far East are gone, half are more than shaky. And it is also an occasion for mourning for the Free World, which must abandon yet another region to Communist expansion in Asia. But as matters stood, a failure by Mendès-France in Geneva would have made the immediate future very cloudy indeed. Let us be grateful to him for his success. Soon, French blood will no longer flow in a hopeless battle. . . . The conditions are cruel but they at least leave our honor intact and do not compromise that unity of the West whose disintegration would be the only irreparable catastrophe." At the same time, President Eisenhower told American journalists that he could not criticize the Geneva results since he had had no other solution to offer.

Now that the accords had been signed, could the French government stop taking an interest in the future of the two Vietnams, Laos, and Cambodia? While the political forces in France and especially the press immediately turned to other matters, Mendès-France decided

during the second half of August to have the United States share in the
guarantees which were to protect the South against any attack from the
North. The idea of a defense treaty as advanced by Dulles was accepted. The French delegation to the Manila Conference, where this
pact was worked out and signed, was given the following instructions
by Mendès-France: "I reject any policy in South Vietnam which will
sooner or later lead to an attempt at reconciliation with North Vietnam. Should such a perspective exist, it will soon become known and
unavoidably affect all political action. . . . I very much wished us to be
officially represented in Hanoi, but it is no less indispensable to preserve the independence of our policy in the South. It is indispensable
that the political course to be taken in South Vietnam be carefully
examined in concert with the United States, with which we have more
than enough difficulties in other areas as it is. We need no additional
reasons for antagonism in Vietnam. It will therefore be necessary to
use the Manila Conference to examine with them the decisions that
must be taken and to conclude an indispensable agreement on policy
in Saigon."[14]

On September 8, 1954, the Manila Conference created the Southeast Asia Treaty Organization (SEATO). But the decisive step in
American "sharing" in the responsibility of France was taken in
Saigon. Practically speaking, it was a regular substitution: after a few
months, joint assistance to the South Vietnamese head of government
Ngo Dinh Diem turned into unconditional support of his increasingly
authoritarian regime and the Americans were urging the French representatives to agree to this support. Diem himself did not hide his
pro-American and anti-French feelings. The Franco-American mission for the training and organization of the South Vietnamese army,
which had been created by Generals Ely and Lawton Collins in February 1955, barely functioned: the South Vietnamese army was given a
purely American form. The French expeditionary corps was repatriated much earlier than planned, in part because it had to be used in
Algeria, in part because such was the desire of the governments of
Diem and the United States.

The independence of Vietnam, so frequently promised by France,
was now implemented step by step, at least in the army and in economic organization. On January 1, 1955, the country was given
sovereignty in customs and monetary matters. But actually the Vietnam government was controlled much more directly by the United
States than it ever had been by France. And it was a government
which was becoming increasingly unpopular as all observers agreed.
To respect the independence of South Vietnam in order to unify all
nationalist elements against Communist North Vietnam was the

course the American government had incessantly recommended to the French for more than seven years, and it was precisely what it failed to do itself, the moment American officers and political advisers had replaced the French. The opinion—widespread in France in any event—that American anti-colonialism was merely a pretext for substituting an American for the European presence in the former colonial territories was thus confirmed, especially since the identical situation seemed to be recurring in North Africa, and the Guatemala affair had shown that American anti-Communism was clearly more than a defense of freedoms.

ANTI-COMMUNISM AND NATIONAL LIBERATION MOVEMENTS

"In May 1945," Anthony Eden recalls, "Sir Roger Makins, our ambassador in Washington, was told by Mr. Dulles that the United States Navy had been ordered to establish what amounted to a blockade of the Guatemalan coast. Any suspicious vessels were to be searched for arms, with the permission of the governments concerned if there was time to obtain it, and Mr. Dulles asked for our cooperation. He said that, whatever the law might be and the formal view we might take, he hoped that we would in practice agree to whatever action was necessary in order to prevent further arms reaching Guatemala. I thought this was a strange way of phrasing a request from one democratic government to another."[15]

But the British government went along, while the French and the Dutch protested against the search of freighters by the American navy. When, faced with the danger of being overthrown by an armed invasion, the government of Guatemala appealed to the U.N. in June, its complaint was not placed on the agenda because there had not been the necessary votes in the Security Council, France and Great Britain having abstained. In the memoirs which he wrote after the failure of the Suez expedition, Anthony Eden had this to say: "Her Majesty's Government agreed to cooperate with the United States Government, or at least not to oppose them, taking the view that first priority must be given to the solidity of the Anglo-American alliance. If allies are to act in concert only when their views are identical, alliances have no meaning."

President Jacobo Arbenz Guzmán of Guatemala had been elected in 1950 by a large majority. He had created new social legislation, launched an anti-illiteracy campaign, and pushed through a new, very liberal constitution. He had also begun an agrarian reform and expropriated lands belonging to the powerful United Fruit Company that were not under cultivation. Alleging that there were also Communists in the unions and among the officials, both the United Fruit Company and Dulles construed the idea of a threat to the entire Western Hemisphere by Communist imperialism. In December 1953, the U.S. government made the secret decision to have the CIA send a "liberation army" into Guatemala. The military invasion under the leadership of Colonel Carlos Castillo Armas was successful and brought him to power. He suspended the agrarian reform, returned its land to the United Fruit Company, repealed the freedom of the unions, and disenfranchised the illiterates, who made up two-thirds of the population.[16]

George Meany was also an enemy of Arbenz. In February 1954, he had sent him an open letter in the name of the AFL in which he expressed "profound apprehension" over "the extensive subversive activities of the Guatemalan section of the world Communist party in your country." After Arbenz had been removed, he said the AFL "rejoices over the downfall of the Communist-controlled regime in Guatemala" and expressed the hope that the new government would "restore as quickly as possible absolute respect for civil liberties and human rights and [would] preserve the social gains codified in the Guatemalan labor and agrarian legislation."

But at that very moment, other American union leaders were already stating openly that the expedition had had no other aim than to help the United Fruit Company abolish the social legislation, and added: "We supported the wrong people."[17]

Actually, American unions had frequently supported the cause of the exploited against the owners in Latin America, even when the owners were Americans, as for example, during the strike of the tin miners in Bolivia or that of the banana pickers against the United Fruit Company in Honduras. In Guatemala, they accorded priority to anti-Communist solidarity, and thus many perceived their efforts in support of social and national liberation movements on other continents as hypocritical and as primarily designed to substitute American interests for the rule of others. This view was especially prevalent in France, for the U.S. government and the American unions never wearied of criticizing French policy in North Africa when it was designed to prevent indigenous political and social elements from obtaining more equality with French nationals living there and greater independence for their country from France.

In the early 1950s, it was Tunisia's and Morocco's turn. Both were French protectorates. Theoretically, the bey of Tunis and the sultan of Rabat would therefore have to be free to govern their countries while they were being represented in their dealings with the outside world by French governors. But in practice, both countries were directly administered by France and many Frenchmen in Tunisia and Morocco had greater economic and administrative power than the Tunisians and Moroccans.

After a liberal period which began in 1947 and culminated in June 1950, policy hardened in Tunisia. This expressed itself in the rejection, on December 15, 1951, of demands that had been raised by the government of the bey, the Neo-Destur Party, and the Tunisian union UGTT, and soon thereafter by the arrest of the ministers and the Neo-Destur head, Habib Bourgiba. The French government imposed strict military measures, and certain Frenchmen in Tunis resorted to terrorism. On December 5, 1952, the secretary-general of the UGTT, Ferhat Hached, was murdered. In Morocco, the struggle against the nationalists, especially the Istiqlal Party, led first to the deposition of the sultan by the French governor on August 20, 1953, and then to his exile to Madagascar.

In May 1952, President Auriol had told Dulles: "We are being unjustly accused because of Tunisia and Morocco . . . Bourgiba is backed by the Communists, and so is the Istiqlal."[18] But neither the U.S. government nor the American unions accepted this view. Rather, it turned out that the French unions had established a firm foothold among the French in Morocco and more especially those of Tunisia and that their interests ran counter to those of the Tunisian unions. This was particularly true of the Force Ouvrière, which was waging a difficult fight within the International Confederation of Free Trade Unions against the anti-colonialist tendencies of the organization, which was dominated by American unions. The conference during which the ICFTU had been established in December 1949 had proclaimed "the right of all nations to unlimited national independence and governmental autonomy" and announced that it would fully support "all efforts to create the conditions necessary for the implementation of this right within the shortest possible time." In July 1953, the general council adopted a motion for support of those unions of nonautonomous countries "which are allied with a national popular movement . . . if the national movement works toward the establishment of a democratic government." The FO delegation abstained from the vote, especially because the ICFTU had just exluded the Tunisian "department union" of the FO in favor of the indigenous UGTT. The North African activities of Irving Brown disquieted the FO as much as the then French government. But the entire political line of the ICFTU was at stake. At its congress in 1956, the CGT-FO passed an unambiguous resolution: "The congress demands that the ICFTU consider the CGT-FO its natural and official branch in the territories of the Union Française. It requests that the ICFTU only become active in the territories of the Union Française after previous consultation with the FO."[19] For American unionists as for the American government, this was precisely the sort of rejection of liberal policies which could not fail to benefit Communism. In June 1954, a few weeks before Mendès-France set French policy in Tunisia on a new course, George Meany, Walter Reuther, and John L. Lewis, the three best-known union leaders, sent Vincent Auriol a rather undiplomatic telegram: "We believe that the repression of Tunisian workers gives comfort to the unyielding enemy of free trade unions, the Soviet Union. . . . We are distressed at the stubborn colonialist policies still pursued by several democratic countries to the detriment of free trade unionism." Henri Bonnet, the French ambassador in Washington, attempted repeatedly to make George Meany change his mind. After a long lecture by a French expert, he asked Meany if he had any further questions. "Just one," the American answered. "When are you fellows going to stop kicking the Tunisians around?"[20]

When Tunisia and Morocco finally gained independence in the spring of 1956, tensions between France and the United States persisted. Now they were due to the war in Algeria, which had begun on November 1, 1954. Once again, it was a question of the AFL-CIO and Irving Brown, whom the French minister and governor in Algiers, the Socialist and unionist Robert Lacoste, referred to as a helper's helper of the National Liberation Front (FLN). And again, the question concerning the position of the American government arose in the U.N.: from 1952 to 1962, from the moment the Moroccan and Tunisian issues had been put on the U.N. agenda up to the time of Algeria's independence, the French governments of the Fourth and Fifth Republic engaged in different tactics toward the international organization, but all complained at different times about weak American support, American pressure on France, or the hostile vote of the American delegate.[21] Yet Franco-American tensions over the protectorates and Algeria were quite secondary compared to the crisis which erupted when the Suez Canal was nationalized and the U.N. sent the "blue helmets" to Egypt, although for the French government, the Suez expedition had a direct connection with the war in Algeria.

THE LION, THE ROOSTER, AND THE TAMER

"The Anglo-American schism" is the title Harold Macmillan gave the long chapter on the Suez crisis in his memoirs.[22] It was a startling crisis in several respects: for once, France and Great Britain were joining forces, though in an undertaking the United States first advised them against and which it then openly fought. A usually divided France was almost unanimous in its enthusiasm for war, while Great Britain, famous for showing national unanimity on important occasions, was deeply divided, the most vehemently anti-American group advocating the U.S. point of view and the advocates of unity with the American partner seeing themselves severely punished by the United States because their confidence in its support had been excessive.[23]

The two partners had different reasons for their joint action. For while it is true that the nationalization of the Suez Canal, which Colonel Gamal Nasser had announced with much fanfare on July 26, 1956, furnished both with the immediate occasion, the canal by itself would hardly have warranted such a commitment, had it not been part of a double context. The French context was the war in Algeria, which Guy Mollet's government wanted to end but in which it was becoming ever more deeply involved, and this in spite of the election campaign promises which had led to the victory of the Republican Front on January 2. Nasser supported the Algerian freedom fighters. Wouldn't the defeat of Nasser therefore mean a quicker victory in Algeria or at least a favorable negotiating position?

The British context was the disappearance of their presence, indeed of any influence, in the Middle East. This was true in Egypt: as stipulated in the 1954 treaty, the last British units had withdrawn on June 19, 1956, five weeks before the nationalization, and thus left a country which Great Britain had once ruled. Then there was Iran, where the nationalization of the assets of the Anglo-Iranian Oil Company in March 1951 had been the prelude to a series of defeats and humiliations. While it is true that the overthrow of Prime Minister Muhammad Mussadegh in August 1953 had fundamentally changed the course of Iranian foreign policy, this had only benefited the United States, not Great Britain. And Great Britain's military association with Iran, Iraq, Turkey, and Pakistan in the Baghdad Pact (1955) had been undertaken under the impression that the United States did not wish to tie itself down and therefore left responsibility to the British ally, thus retaining greater freedom of action in the economic sphere.

The Aswan Dam is an example. The abruptness and brutality with which John Foster Dulles told the Egyptian ambassador on July 19 that the United States was withdrawing its offer of massive financial aid for the giant project served Nasser at least as a pretext for his decision to nationalize, which he announced a week later.[24] And the American decision had not been made in consultation with Great Britain. Nasser had constantly threatened to go to the Russians for help; Dulles had wanted to put an end to these extortions and been encouraged in that direction by Secretary of the Treasury George Humphrey, who was skeptical about Egypt's ability to repay. It may also be assumed that American cotton growers were hardly interested in seeing their Egyptian competitor strengthened, and thus made their influence felt.[25]

But neither Dulles nor Humphrey accepted the idea that the decision of July 19 could have had any connection with the step the Paris and London governments saw themselves driven to take, and which Macmillan, Anthony Eden's Chancellor of the Exchequer at the time, explained to his old friend Robert Murphy, who had come to see him for exploratory talks on behalf of the State Department a few days later: "We and France must accept the challenge or sink into the rank of second-class nations."[26] More than free navigation on the Suez Canal was thus involved even though the sea lanes to the Far East and access to the oil fields of the Persian Gulf seemed threatened. It was a matter of prestige. There must be no capitulation to a dictator. For in the French and British speeches and in the minds of leading politicians such as Guy Mollet and his Foreign Minister Christian Pineau or of Anthony Eden and Harold Macmillan, Nasser was associated with Hitler and Mussolini, and a refusal to take steps against him meant another Munich.

The hesitations, the indecisiveness, the infelicitous declarations of Dulles and Eisenhower, infuriated them. They were willing to participate in international conferences and negotiations but saw with exasperation that the American President and Secretary of State so clearly excluded any use of force that Nasser felt encouraged to reject all mediating proposals and compromises.[27] Eisenhower seemed an amateur who preferred playing golf to taking seriously the worries of his allies, and the Secretary of State a hypocrite who wanted to direct the wrath of the Third World countries at France and Great Britain so that no one would raise the Panama Canal issue when the internationalization of sea lanes was brought up.[28] "The United States cannot be expected to identify itself 100% . . . with . . . the colonial powers," lectured Dulles. "It is really preposterous that we should have to listen to lectures on colonialism," retorted the Conservative leader of the House of Commons, R. Butler.[29] There was in fact an underestimation of the resolve of the American leadership to avoid any act of war, for they were concerned that potential Soviet intervention might lead to a serious confrontation of the two superpowers.

The military operation had been prepared since June. Originally, it had been planned as a direct Franco-British intervention and then as a "pacification" action in a conflict between Israel and Egypt. This also was carefully prepared; there were no direct contacts between the British and the Israelis, the French serving as go-betweens in the initial phase. Then a highly secret meeting of the three took place on October 22 in Sèvres, near Paris, in which British Foreign Minister Selwyn Lloyd participated and which was kept so secret that the participants were still denying the entire affair years later.[30]

Secrecy was preserved from most of the British and French ministers, diplomats, and high officials, and also from Eisenhower. While statements had already been made in July that force might be used, the United States was informed neither about the real preparations nor the decision that was finally reached. The British government even saw to it that its ambassador was absent from Washington between October 11 and November 8, undoubtedly to spare him the fate of his French counterpart, Hervé Alphand, who, appointed on September 11, was called in to Eisenhower on October 30 just after the President had been advised of the Israeli attack. The ambassador affirmed that he knew of no plan by his government to wage war and reassured the President. He had barely returned to the embassy when the text of the Franco-British ultimatum arrived. "I will never again trust the word of a French ambassador," John Foster Dulles told him to his face.[31]

The idea was that Eisenhower, in the midst of an election campaign, would probably not intervene but would certainly raise objections should he be consulted, whereas keeping the plan secret would enable him to be perfectly sincere as he made a few critical though inconsequential comments. Yet the President had warned his friend Anthony Eden seriously and at length, pointing to the dangers of a spread of the conflict and asking him for proof of his sincerity.[32] It is true, of course, that he had not uttered any precise threats and left Eden unclear about what he would do should France and Great Britain ignore his warnings. Thus both the public and the secret action of the American government became the decisive factor in turning a military victory into a diplomatic catastrophe.

Already on October 30, a day after the invasion of Egyptian territory by Israeli troops and on the day of the spurious Franco-British ultimatum to Israel and Egypt, the United States mobilized the Security Council. Resolutions for an immediate cease-fire and the withdrawal of the Israelis which the Soviets and Americans submitted were vetoed by the French and British. On October 31, French and British planes began bombing Egypt. In an extraordinary session on November 1, the U.N. General Assembly passed an American resolution demanding an immediate cease-fire by 64 to 5 with 6 abstentions. On November 5, British and French parachutists were dropped over Port Said and Port Fuad, and the pound sterling began to fall in New York. On November 6, Great Britain, France, and Israel agreed to an armistice. On December 3, France and Great Britain announced the withdrawal of their troops, which were then replaced step by step by the "blue helmets" of the U.N. On December 22, the withdrawal ended.

What had prompted the British and French governments to yield was not so much the violent opposition of the Labour Party and still less Marshal Bulganin's ultimatum, but rather the brutal pressure of the American government on the British pound. The Federal Reserve Bank had sold large quantities of sterling "but certainly . . . far above what was necessary as a precaution to protect the value of its own holdings," Macmillan wrote later.

I would not have been unduly concerned had we been able to obtain either the money to which we were entitled from the International Monetary Fund, or, better still, some aid by way of a temporary loan from the United States. The refusal of the second was understandable; the obstruction of the first is not so easy to forgive. We had a perfect right under the statutes to ask for the repayment of the British quota. . . . I telephoned urgently to New York; the matter was referred to Washington. . . . I received the reply that the American Government would not agree to the technical procedure until we had agreed to the cease-fire. I regarded this then, and still do, as a breach of the spirit, and even of the letter of the system under which the Fund is supposed to operate. It was a form of pressure which seemed altogether unworthy. It contrasted strangely with the weak attitude of the Americans toward Egyptian funds and "accounts" after the seizure of the Canal.[33]

While the State Department persuaded President Eisenhower to cancel his invitation to Eden to come to Washington immediately after the end of hostilities, George Humphrey proved especially brutal when he told the British ambassador, "You will not get a dime from the United States government if I can stop it, until you have gotten out of Suez! You are like burglars who have broken into somebody else's house. So get out! When you do, and not until then, you'll get help."[34] And Great Britain did not get the oil it had requested until the withdrawal had been completed, which forced the British government to temporarily ration gasoline.

The last days of October and early November 1956 were especially dramatic since the short Suez war coincided with the Hungarian tragedy. The uprising in Budapest had begun on October 23. A first Soviet intervention had occurred and then Imre Nagy had announced the withdrawal of Soviet troops from the capital. But on November 2, the same day the full U.N. Assembly voted on the cease-fire in Egypt, the Red Army intervened a second time. In this bloodiest intervention, Soviet armor again entered Budapest on November 3. On the fourth, the full U.N. Assembly passed two resolutions: one on the Canadian proposal to send a U.N. force, and another which condemned the invasion of Hungary after the USSR had used its veto to prevent any decision by the Security Council.

The problem was that the coincidence of these two bloody interventions could be interpreted in different ways. For the American government, it was enough if the one was not condemned without the other. As far as many European critics were concerned, one had to go further, indeed almost as far as those students in Hamburg who demonstrated with placards which read: "Eden, murderer of Budapest." The Suez adventure had made it easier for the Soviets to suppress the uprising in Hungary and, more important, it had kept the African and Asian countries from condemning the Soviet Union with sufficient decisiveness, particularly since the latter supported the Egyptian cause. The champions of the Suez expedition, on the other hand, were shocked by the enormous disparity between the treatment of the two democratic countries (obligatory withdrawal, dispatch of U.N. troops) and the merely moral sanction which took the form of a resolution against the totalitarian regime that could scoff at condemnation by the international organization with impunity. And why were no American measures taken against the Soviet Union?

In France the advocates of force against Nasser had been in a considerable majority, and had certainly been more than a small minority in Great Britain. In Paris, only a few voices had called attention to the fact that the legal problem of internationalizing the canal was complex and Nasser's proposal that compensation be paid was perfectly reasonable. Since the Egyptian President's gesture had been full of passion, the reaction was no less so. Even a paper as critical of the use of force as *Le Monde* had let one of its writers, the law professor Maurice Duverger, state on August 1: "The example of the years 1933–39 is clear. Faced with the megalomania of a dictator, one cannot answer with ineffective judicial procedures which render the law a mockery but only with force." And on August 14: "Egypt must be beaten back militarily if all other means fail." On October 30, when Guy Mollet had announced in the National Assembly that Great Britain and France intended to occupy the canal, the deputies had approved 368 to 182 (against the Communists, the progressives and the Poujadists) and in the Council of the Republic, the vote was 289 to 19.

Yet concern was also voiced. Mendès-France had abstained after warning the President the evening before. But even the failure of the expedition did not suffice to change public opinion. On the contrary. In December 1956, as withdrawal operations were in full swing, 42 percent answered in the affirmative and 33 percent disapproved when asked: "Do you generally approve or disapprove the use of force by France and Great Britain in Egypt?" Twenty-five percent expressed no opinion. In March 1957, when it became clear that the undertaking had yielded no favorable results whatever, it was approved in retro-spect by 44 percent of the Frenchmen asked.[35] In a rather isolated position, the author of this book tried the day after the cease-fire to understand what had happened and published the following reflec-tions in *La Croix,* one of the few papers that had kept its sangfroid:

As one reads the greater part of the French press these last few days, one cannot fail being surprised by so much self-assurance: we were right, the rest of the world was wrong. Or perhaps I should say: it doesn't matter whether we were objectively right or wrong, provided we won quickly and the result was advantageous to us. . . . It is certainly true that there are arguments that can be adduced against our foreign critics: a jockeying and contradictory American diplomacy torpedoed the Anglo-French project to internationalize the canal, encouraged Nasser, and forced Israel to prepare for the day when the Arab armies, equipped with Soviet-American weapons, will jointly attack the country. For years, France has been called on to show sympathy for all na-tional movements, be it in Africa or in the Saar, to always accept the use by others of such concepts as national sentiment and national interest but to rise above such dusty, antiquated ideas.

The Charter of the United Nations was elaborated in 1945 and was based on the old conception of a directorate of major powers. After the founders recog-nized at that time that none of these five major powers could be made to submit to a constraint by the majority, why is it that France should now accept what the other major powers did not want?

For the last twenty years, the aggressor has always been victorious in spite of any moral condemnation by the "world public." Manchuria, Ethiopia, Aus-tria, Finland, Czechoslovakia, and now Hungary. What good did it do them to have the right and general sympathy on their side? And what about the prin-ciple of nonintervention during the Spanish Civil War?

But when all this has been said, further reflections must follow. If one is accustomed to act in accordance with international law, it is not so easy to proceed skillfully when one's attitude changes. Everyone knows that the well-behaved schoolboy who suddenly begins cutting up appears much more guilty than the scamp who knows all the tricks. The incredible clumsiness of the ultimatum to Nasser ("You are being attacked. We are assaulting you to reestablish peace"), and then a majority of 64 against 5 who condemn us. It certainly was an operation that was carried out without diplomatic precau-tions. The whole thing would have been less serious if during the last nine years our foreign policy had not insisted on strengthening the Atlantic Al-liance and on creating an integrated Europe. Did those who pose as champi-ons of such a Europe with a common foreign policy realize that the Anglo-French action would be disapproved by the other member countries of the ECSC? . . . The anti-American wave presently sweeping France must not make us forget that it was we who asked for the Atlantic Pact, not the United States; that the Americans have rendered us at least as many services during the last twenty years (and this is a euphemism) as we did them. We should notice here how far the anti-American phobia has swung to the right recently. Sometimes, it is precisely those who once raised the identity of views be-tween France and the United States to the level of dogma that today attack it most systematically.[36]

The same phenomenon was also apparent in Great Britain, though with significant differences. In the first place, the government only had a majority of 270 against 218 on October 30 after a debate in the House of Commons in which it had to submit to violent attacks by the Labour opposition. But the tone or, more accurately, the tones it took differed. The criticism of Nasser began immediately, in July, and continued severe: "If the sending of one's own police and soldiers into the darkness of the night to seize somebody else's property is nationalization, then Ali Baba used the wrong terminology," Bevan said.[37] Party chief Hugh Gaitskell, Bevan, and the *Tribune*, the organ of the Bevan supporters, took different positions which did not merge until November. The campaign against the government was so animated, so noisy, and so well orchestrated that even Eden finally believed he no longer had the support of the majority of voters—which was both true and untrue. Initially, his policy and especially the military action were disapproved by a majority on November 1 and 2, but after the 10th, rejection and approval were divided about equally, and after that date and in spite of the lack of success, approval increased, as in France.[38]

On the Left, rejection of the military action went hand in hand with the criticism of American policy. But the Conservatives, especially the most inveterate who felt the greatest allegiance to the Empire, turned acrimonious in their anti-Americanism. One of them demanded a confrontation with the United States, for "the United Nations has become a cover plan for American imperialism and the Americans want to take our place in the Middle East and they want to take the place of France in North Africa." Another affirmed that for the last ten years, one had constantly seen the "undermining of British interests, authority and prestige" by the United States. The influence these arch-Conservatives had on the party as a whole was greater after the failure than normally. Toward the end of November, a text stating that the attitude of the United States was "gravely endangering" the Atlantic Pact received 127 signatures from members of the Conservative Party, while another requesting the government to "help restore active cooperation with the United States" received only 26.[39]

Perhaps reactions in France and Great Britain were best summarized in a French cartoon of that time: an old, worn-out lion and a rather badly plucked rooster are sitting inside a cage. Leaning against the cage, a whip in his hand, stands an animal tamer who looks like Eisenhower. The lion asks the rooster: "Do you remember Waterloo?" and the rooster answers: "Yes, those were the days!" Days when even in defeat one remained a great country.

ALGERIA UP TO THE FRANCO-AMERICAN ACCORD

But the "Anglo-American schism" was quickly surmounted, while French resentment proved deeper and more enduring. One of the reasons was that Great Britain did not have a war in Algeria.

When Harold Macmillan succeeded Anthony Eden on January 10, 1957, he certainly felt the new temptation which many diplomats and high officials in the Exchequer shared: to draw closer to the Six, for Suez had shown how weak Great Britain was by itself. But it seemed more useful and important to him to reestablish the close and—if possible—privileged relations with the United States, since the failure had shown even more clearly that nothing could be accomplished without the American ally, and even less against it.

On January 5, Congress had passed a resolution which would henceforth be known as the "Eisenhower Doctrine": it empowered the President to intervene in the case of a "direct" Communist attack on any country in the Middle East. What had become of the principle of rejecting any and all military action? And in the following year, at the request of President Schuman after a change of power in Iraq, Eisenhower sent 10,000 soldiers to Lebanon. He telephoned Macmillan to advise him of the decision when the American fleet was already approaching Beirut. The Prime Minister noted later: "I said, 'You are doing a Suez on me,' at which President laughed."[40] He supported the American action by sending 2,500 English parachutists to Jordan.

At this time, Macmillan had already attained amazing success in his negotiations with Eisenhower on nuclear policy, first at Bermuda in March 1957, and then in October in Washington. The climate had become so friendly that the London *Times* emphasized: "In terms of the Anglo-American alliance, participants in the talks have known nothing like them since the war-time conferences of Cairo and Casablanca."[41] It had been agreed that only Great Britain would obtain access to the secret nuclear projects of the Americans, and the priority both sides once again gave the Anglo-American alliance was to have serious consequences for Anglo-French relations (see Chapters 6 and 7).

For the French, the Suez defeat had consequences of entirely different scope. It meant neither a merely temporary humiliation nor a military pullback with no direct effect on national defense. In Algeria as in Indochina before, France was once again fighting for the cause of the Western world, but this time even more clearly for the security of France. In Tonkin, that security had hardly been threatened. It no longer was threatened on the Rhine, and only very little along the Elbe. The country's line of defense was now the Paris-Algiers-

Brazzaville axis, and this was not just the conviction of military men and right-wing politicians. The Allies had to be told "because they have not yet understood it with sufficient clarity, perhaps because it has not yet been explained to them with sufficient clarity that meanwhile the Mediterranean has become the axis of our security and thus of our foreign policy. It is no longer the Rhine," François Mitterrand stated on September 30, 1957, in a debate on Algeria. Thus the defenders of the nation and those of the West united to justify the military commitment in that country.

Disapproval of the United States for not only having no sympathy for the French position but also for wishing to take the place of France by supporting the North African national movement had been voiced in the early 1950s, and already in 1952, right in the midst of the Indochina war, right in the midst of the conflict over the EDC, Dean Acheson had had to answer these reproaches when they had been raised by French ministers and high officials.[42] But after Suez, they took on an especially dramatic tone, particularly because now the war in Algeria increasingly crystallized French political life. In a "Letter to the Americans" which was published on January 9, 1957, in *Le Figaro*, the most "European" and "Atlanticist" of all Paris papers, Thierry Maulnier wrote:

With three hundred million Arabs looking on, you humiliated us before a Nasser. . . . By taking sides against us in Algeria, you abandon North Africa to the Russians. Perhaps you believe that the worst that could happen to you would be to have to take our place. The French have reason to believe that such an eventuality doesn't altogether displease you. Take care: it would not be good for you if it were to look once again as if you confirmed their suspicions. . . . It would be a mistake for you to rely too much on our need of you, for the fact is that we need each other. We cannot break the Atlantic front but neither can you. The breaking of ties between Europe and the United States would not only be the beginning of our end but of yours as well.

One does not take from an old, still proud nation the one thing that lays the foundation for the only future worthy of its past without running the risk of driving it—perhaps against its own interests—to unforeseeable outbursts of passion.

In North Africa, France defends its *last chance*. Don't force it to choose between its African vocation and its friendship with America.

At the same time, many voices in the United States began criticizing official American policy as excessively pro-French. On July 2, 1957, John Foster Dulles defended France against John F. Kennedy, who had submitted a resolution which provoked the most violent indignation in France and Algeria. For the young Democratic senator had claimed that the solutions envisaged by the French were outdated, that Algerian independence was unavoidable in the long run, and that the United States would have to actively participate in the search for a solution, given the fact that its abstention had "furnished effective ammunition to anti-Western propagandists in Asia and the Middle East." Roger Duchet, secretary-general of the Centre National des Indépendants (CNI), a key figure on the French political stage, answered Kennedy: "With a great deal of frankness and vanity, you give France lessons. Youth does not excuse everything. But since you still have a few years before you until you embark on a real career, it will do you no harm to learn a few lessons in history and geography."[43]

Didn't the allies of France even go so far as to support the enemy, albeit only indirectly, by sending military matériel (allegedly to prevent the Soviet Union from supplying it) to countries which then passed it on to Algerian partisans? An explosion of indignation occurred in France when it was learned on November 15, 1957, that Great Britain and the United States had shipped arms to Tunisia. On that same day, the French delegation to a NATO conference decided to no longer participate in the sessions since now, as its leader declared, "every effort to achieve an Atlantic solidarity as desired by all the participants in this conference has become pointless" (and this was a convinced MPR man). And a poll brought out that 82 percent of the French people knew about these arms shipments, while a mere 53 percent had ever heard of the Common Market Plan.[44]

In February 1958, the French air force bombed the Tunisian village of Sakiet after Algerian partisans had attacked French units from Tunisian soil. The government, which had not been informed, took responsibility for the operation. Sharp protests were made in France and abroad. General Ely reports: "On the tenth, at 19.30 hours, Prime Minister Gaillard had me come to the Matignon. He was pale and very tired. He had just received a telegram from Alphand, who reported a very agitated discussion with Dulles, who had shown himself quite irritated. The Mideast was unanimously and decidedly against us. The 'situation is very dramatic,' he said to me. 'The entire world condemns us.'"[45] The Tunisian ambassador Masmoudi had to return to his country, though not without first having received expressions of sympathy from de Gaulle and Mendès-France.

In March, the United States and Great Britain persuaded the two countries to agree to mediation. In measured tones, General Ely reports: "This mission was entrusted to Harold Beely for Great Britain and Murphy for the United States. During the American landings in French North Africa in 1942, Murphy had played an important role. [See Chapter 1.] He found little sympathy in French military circles. The French government had expressed the desire that the two diplomats not touch on the Algeria problem, which was to remain an internal French question. Nonetheless, the mediation mission soon became unpopular, especially in the army. The intervention of Great Britain, which had just shipped arms to Tunisia, and the presence of Murphy filled our soldiers with bitterness. It should be added that the mission found as strong a response in France as it did in Algeria."[46]

The Murphy mission did in fact appear so markedly as American interference and a humiliation of the French that it led to the over-throw of the Gaillard government when it defended the results before the National Assembly. It thus triggered the events of May 13, which, beginning with a coup in Algiers, finally put an end to the Fourth Republic and brought General de Gaulle to power.

When the constitution of the Fifth Republic was approved by 79.2 percent of the votes cast in the referendum of September 28, 1958, it was largely an act of faith: the French, frequently disunited and torn between the desire to keep Algeria and the desire for a solution that might end the war, placed their fate in the hands of de Gaulle. He was brought to power by the most intransigent element, an element that was violently critical of any attempt preceding governments had made to change the status of Algeria. But at the same time, he had often let it be understood that he was not averse to liberal solutions.

De Gaulle became President of the Republic early in 1959, and at first, the choice he would make remained unclear. But everyone attributed great importance to the speech he gave on September 16, 1959. While he indicated a preference for a sort of limited autonomy for Algeria in this address, he also recognized its right to self-determination. For President Eisenhower, this was no surprise, for during an official visit to Paris between September 2 and 4, he had had long talks with de Gaulle. Before then, he had been to Bonn and London. Adenauer had been very much preoccupied with the Algerian problem, and it had been Eisenhower's impression in Bonn that he saw it primarily under the aspect of Communist support for the FLN, a perspective which did not at all coincide with the American view. In Paris, he had then had the pleasant surprise that while de Gaulle, with whom he had difficulties in military matters, also spoke of the Communist threat and criticized the stand the United States had taken at the U.N., he also seemed ready to promise the Algerians a free vote on their destiny within a few days.[47]

Since after an intervention by Moscow, the PCF also came out for the policy of self-determination, it may be said that de Gaulle now had the support of those who had opposed his election. They were men some of whom, like Prime Minister Michel Debré, now went along with a policy which was moving far beyond anything the leaders of the Fourth Republic had dared dream, while others now fought him, some with weapons in hand.

This did not mean, however, that a relationship of genuine trust now developed with the Americans. When the new President John F. Kennedy prepared a visit to de Gaulle late in May 1961, he asked for advice from the American journalist who knew him best. Cyrus Sulzberger wrote: "He has long looked with skepticism at American diplomatic activities. Although he was not yet in power when Mr. (Robert) Murphy joined Mr. (later Sir Harold) Beeley in the 'good-offices' mission after the Sakiet incident, his suspicions are intense. He is always prepared to lend an ear to anyone who tells him that American oil companies wish to grab control of the Sahara or that the U.S. wishes to fill a power vacuum in North Africa after France leaves. Therefore we must exercise particular care both in our actions and in our statements concerning sensitive areas. De Gaulle was enraged when minor members of Cabot Lodge's UN mission attended an Algerian FLN party. He was more than enraged when Ambassador Walmsley in Tunis was instructed to confer with two FLN leaders. In fact, I am told that for a while he seriously thought of cancelling or deferring the visit of President Kennedy."[48]

The moment decolonization became the issue, however, the mistrust of the United States was also shared by the most convinced "Atlanticists." But thanks to the support de Gaulle had received from Kennedy during the generals' coup in Algiers in April, his former reservations about the American President were largely gone by May.

Paul-Henri Spaak, whom Michel Debré had accused of being "the gravedigger of France" and "in the pay of mythologists, the Americans and the Germans"[49] in European and Atlantic affairs, had nonetheless defended French Algerian policy in the U.N. in 1956. And in 1960, he appealed to Atlantic solidarity in the Congo question. When Spaak resigned from his post as secretary-general of NATO in 1961, he wrote a reproachful memorandum to President Kennedy on February 13:

The last disappointing example occurred just a short time ago in the debate on future policy in the Congo. In the form they were made public, American ideas could be approved neither by the French, the Belgians or the Portuguese nor, it seems to me, by the English, that is to say, by those who have the most direct interest in African problems. The so-called American plan was never discussed in NATO. The allies of the United States heard of it at the same time as its enemy. . . . Common sense tells one that one cannot be solidary in one part of the world and enemies in another.

I am perfectly aware that all of this will create problems and additional difficulties for a big country such as the United States which must defend its interests all over the world, but I remain convinced that an essential choice has to be made. For the moment, this choice can be summarized as follows: what is more important to the United States, the U.N. or NATO? Or, to put the matter differently: is the United States willing, in a crunch, to sacrifice the interests of its NATO partners in order to assure itself of the support or the friendship of non-aligned countries or will it ruffle their feelings?[50]

The last question was purely rhetorical: in 1960, when the U.N. had concerned itself with the affairs of the Belgian Congo, which had just become independent, the United States had sided against Belgium when it sent troops under the pretext of protecting the lives of its citizens. And in the crisis which had been characterized by the intervention of the "blue helmets," the American government had certainly not acted in Belgium's interest.[51]

But by 1961, Algeria was no longer among the countries that created difficulties in the relationship between the United States and its European allies. This was demonstrated by President Kennedy when he supported de Gaulle unreservedly against the four generals who were in power in Algiers from April 22 to 26 and were attempting to foil the policy of creating an Algerian state which had just been approved in a referendum in France by an overwhelming majority. The leader of the rebels, General Challe, had clearly hoped for American support, for had he not just publicly advocated European and Atlantic integration? Wasn't his anti-Communism beyond all doubt, and didn't he want Algeria to remain French, i.e., Western? Of course, but the political impossibility of a French Algeria constituted a much greater danger to U.S. global policies than did de Gaulle's criticism of NATO.

In contrast to what de Gaulle himself never tired of repeating, it was not the Fourth but the Fifth Republic which followed the very policy favored by the United States—at least as regards decolonization, that most difficult and most tragic problem of postwar French politics.

And the President of the new Republic shouldered his responsibility so resolutely that he largely changed the feelings of his fellow citizens toward the outside world, especially the United States. Between 1956 and 1958, a bitter and resentful nationalism had taken hold. But what was the failure of Suez and even the loss of Indochina, where draftees had never seen action, as compared to the loss of Algeria, which, in 1955, had still been under the jurisdiction of the French Interior Ministry, or as compared to the civil war of the OAS and the flight of hundreds of thousands of "pieds noirs" back to France? But thanks to his attitude and prestige, de Gaulle succeeded nonetheless in giving this disaster the quality of greatness, as he succeeded in exorcising the danger of French isolationism by appealing for cooperation with Algeria and the other former African colonies, thus replacing the nationalism of humiliation by a nationalism of pride. And while the latter was going to create new problems in European and Atlantic issues, it also made France a more solid partner.

6 WHAT SECURITY?

DIVERGENT CONCEPTIONS

"The feeling of insecurity is not always due to a defined threat, a visibly prepared aggression. The mere imbalance of forces that is maintained by the stronger and not compensated for by serious international guarantees in favor of the weaker suffices to create insecurity." This definition which Robert Schuman gave during the ratification debate in June 1949 expresses the idea people initially had of the Atlantic Pact. But would there always be agreement as to the source of the threat? Would it always be unambiguous? What would give American guarantees the greatest credibility, what kind of organization of the alliance, and what kind of weapons? And could the weak content themselves with remaining weak because they were protected by the guarantees of the strong? And finally, if the power of the strong were to be placed at the disposal of a weak country against another strong one, would this not give the former too much power over the weak, which was thus protected and powerless at one and the same time?

Initially because of Indochina and then because of Algeria, localizing the danger had for a long time been a preeminently French problem. As late as October 1960, more than a year after de Gaulle had promised to grant Algeria self-determination, Paul Reynaud had stated during a debate in the National Assembly that it "was not normal not to meet our obligations vis-à-vis NATO under the pretext that we have to send divisions to Algeria," and had been answered by Michel Debré, the Prime Minister at the time: "The state of our divisions in Germany cannot be compared with that of the Allied divisions, nor can it be maintained that we are not meeting our obligations in Germany. Instead, we must compare the state of our divisions in Algeria with that of the forces of our allies. Anyone who claims that it is not the West we defend in Algeria uses the argument of our enemies." The Allies, especially American ambassadors and envoys who so often ignored it, were regularly reminded that Article 6 of the

North Atlantic Treaty stated: ". . . any armed attack . . . on the Algerian departments of France will be considered an armed attack on one or more of the parties." And only when Algerian independence was proclaimed in July 1962 was it officially stated that Article 6 did not refer to the new Algerian state.

Yet security was not the only issue. The absence of the French troops promised for the common defense of Europe also had to be explained and excused, indeed to be eulogized for a time, for was this not an answer to the criticism that was so often raised by the Allies against the attitude of France that it wanted a dominant position, yet make only a minimal contribution? And Henry Kissinger, a young Harvard professor, wrote in a book on strategy that attracted considerable attention in the United States: "Thus France wanted to have the best of both worlds: it wished to play a principal role in allied councils, but without assuming the responsibility for effective defense. It desired to remain a great power, while following a policy of minimum risk."[1]

"Minimum risk" was particularly the idea—more widespread in France than in other European countries—that an American military presence on French soil was not required. A European poll conducted in November 1957 asked among other things: "Taking everything into consideration, should the American forces leave [name of country] now or should they stay on"[2]

	France	West Germany	Italy	Great Britain
Number of respondents	802	813	807	800
Leave now	38%	22%	34%	27%
Stay on	26%	66%	46%	56%
Don't know	36%	12%	20%	17%

"The principal role in allied councils" was to mean that France would have a privileged place, on an equal footing with Great Britain and the United States, while the other partners would of course have to content themselves with a lesser role. And this not only as regarded military planning, but even more with reference to the political orientations the alliance would adopt in Europe and the world. As early as April 1951, the French leadership demanded that the three-power consultative body of the Atlantic organization go beyond its merely regional competence and become a kind of world directorate coordinating the global policies of the "Big Three" of the alliance.[3] Seven years later, de Gaulle was to present this same idea with greater force (see Chapter 7).

The organization of the North Atlantic Treaty very gradually de-

veloped structures. Its supreme political organ became the NATO
Council, with a revolving presidency, where members of the governments of the Allied countries met at irregular intervals. Not until February 1952, during a session in Lisbon, were permanent governmental
delegates assigned to the organization. A secretary-general was named
president of the meetings of the Council. The first to occupy this
position, Lord Ismay, was rather discreet in organizing the apparatus
of the secretariat. From 1957 to 1961, Paul-Henri Spaak attracted more
attention to the office, but the precise function of the various services
and bureaus under him was not always entirely clear.[4]

A military committee made up of the chiefs-of-staff of the member
countries became the highest military organ. Because it was too large
and convened only rarely, the committee was soon given a kind of
executive organ which consisted of American, British, and French
representatives. The "Standing Group" of NATO thus came into existence. The French General Valluy, who belonged to it from 1953 to
1956, analyzed its possibilities of action unsparingly:

Since it appeared indispensable to the Standing Group to have its seat in
Washington to facilitate contacts with the Pentagon, it set up a liaison office in
Paris for communications with the NATO Council and its secretary-general
(P-H. Spaak). Besides, the countries not represented in the Standing Group
were informed about its activities by a committee of representatives from the
military which also had its seat in Washington. While supreme commands
have integrated general staffs, however, the Standing Group is not an integrated organ. Its members have their own national general staff, and if the
proverb "To live happily let us live hidden from the world" reflected a strict
truth, the Standing Group would have had to enjoy perfect bliss in its gilded
cage at the Pentagon. . . . But the reality is less simple and the anonymity only
apparent. The Standing Group escapes the difficulties and the daily dramas of
the countries that set it up no more than it escapes their troubles and demands. . . .

The principal tasks of the Standing Group are to coordinate and to integrate
the plans elaborated by the supreme commands, to provide the planners with
an estimate of the possibilities of the enemy and guidelines for the establishment of appropriate strategic concepts, to give the nations "objective" advice
concerning the obligations and demands of defense, to provide long-term
definitions of the best way to organize the forces as new weapons or more
modern equipment are progressively introduced, and finally to direct the
activity of the organs which were gradually subordinated to it. But its apparent
homogeneity notwithstanding, the Standing Group is really a "trinity." . . . In
the last analysis, the delegations can only put forward the official theses they
receive from Paris, Washington or London, what is called "national guidance"
in the jargon of the trade. Relations to the NATO Council could be improved.
The Standing Group must not only give advice which is frequently too cautious and occasionally the result of compromise rather than an objective
analysis—it must also take initiatives and forestall misunderstandings. What is
called for is a constant dialogue between Spaak, who is waiting for just that
and even demands it, his international general staff and someone . . . who

doesn't exist. For there is neither executive authority nor responsible individuals in the Standing Group but only a director (who is merely a sort of chief mail clerk) and a liaison officer (who is simply a military attaché sent from Washington to Paris) and an occasional president whose activities and power are limited by the fact that he operates within a national framework.[5]

Actually, the most important decision of the military committee was made as early as October 1950, and that was the creation of a joint military command for Europe. On December 18 of the same year, the Council decided unanimously to request the U.S. government to appoint General Dwight D. Eisenhower as Supreme Allied Commander in Europe (SACEUR). He was appointed a day later. The Supreme Headquarters of the Allied Powers in Europe (SHAPE) was set up in July 1951 at Rocquencourt, near Paris, where the secretary-general and the permanent representatives of the member countries now also established their headquarters. The Supreme Command of the Allied Powers for Central Europe was established in Fontainebleau.

The appointment of General Eisenhower satisfied the Europeans on two counts: by virtue of his illustrious past as the victorious Allied commander-in-chief he was popular, and by sending an American general, the United States showed that it was taking the defense of Europe as seriously as its own. But did this act not also symbolize the rule of the strongest alliance partner over the entire organization? This question was to be asked with increasing insistence as Eisenhower's successors arrived: General Ridgway from May 1952 to July 1953; General Alfred Gruenther, the friend and former chief-of-staff of Eisenhower; and then, after November 1956, when the first Air Force general, Lauris Norstad, was appointed to the post, which he occupied until the end of 1962.

Eisenhower already tended to look on Rocquencourt as an American headquarters.[6] Excellent relations between the staff officers of the various nationalities notwithstanding, this tendency became more pronounced under his successors. "Toward the end of the Indochina war, it was embarrassing for a French SHAPE officer recently returned from the Far East to be tapped on the stomach by those Americans whose comrades were just demonstrating at that very moment to President Diem that the French army was no good, though their cordiality was certainly not hypocritical. At the time, General Gruenther was commander-in-chief, and his sympathetic manner and diplomatic skill prevented run-ins. His successor, General Norstad, was a cool and reserved person. Under his leadership, SHAPE largely became what public opinion had always taken it to be, an American general staff headquarters. True, the officers from fifteen NATO countries retained the same number of positions and their importance continued unchanged. But the major decisions and the most vital infor-

mation were for the Americans to make and to keep. For the circula-
tion of documents a subtle bureaucrat invented the rubber stamp
AEO: 'American Eyes Only.'"[7]

And the general problem of the atomic secret meant that Marshal
Juin, commanding Allied ground forces in Europe, was not allowed to
know the nature and number of atomic weapons he might eventually
have at his disposal.[8]

The German officers who began to arrive in Rocquencourt or Fontainebleau in 1955 did not react in the same way, partly because their
mere presence in an inter-Allied general staff symbolized the rapid,
almost incredible change in status of the Federal Republic within six
years after its birth as a state under total tutelage. And also because the
threat to its security was perceived as much more tangible than in the
other countries of the alliance, since the Federal Republic had common borders with the other, neighboring Germany and Czechoslovakia, where Soviet units were stationed. And finally, because the
survival of Berlin as an outpost of the Western world—albeit not part
of the actual sphere of NATO, yet also protected by American military
power—was a constant source of concern.

Theoretically, Berlin was protected by the treaty, since Article 6
specifically mentions "the Occupation forces of any party in Europe."
And the American, British, and French units in the three Western
sectors of Berlin, though now Allied troops on the territory of the
Federal Republic, remained occupation troops even after 1955 (and
continue such to this day), their presence being justified by the 1945
statute. Whenever there was a crisis over or in Berlin, it was not up to
NATO to reject the demands of the East or to negotiate with it, it was
up to the Three Powers, and almost always according to the identical
pattern: resolute attitude of the United States which was backed by
the resolute attitude of the French while the British tended to yield.
This pattern applied especially during Khrushchev's diplomatic offensive in November 1958 (see Chapter 7).

For Adenauer, the power of the West and principally that of the
United States was for a long time not only a guarantee for the security
of West Germany and West Berlin but also an important element in
that diplomatic game which would ultimately bring German
reunification—or at least a reduction in Soviet rule over the former
Soviet zone. A less optimistic view of the problem of German unity
did not begin to prevail in Bonn and the conception of the role of the
military strength of the West was not scaled down to the protection of
existing borders until Allied impotence in face of the construction of
the Berlin Wall on August 13, 1961, became apparent to all (see
Chapter 7).

The concerns of the other power that had been defeated in 1945 were altogether different. Italy was far removed from the line that divides Europe and runs straight through Germany. Nor was it torn between security in the east and security in the south, like France. Except for Somalia, which was to become independent in 1961, the United Nations had not conferred a mandate over its former colonies on it. Eritrea became part of Ethiopia, and Libya became independent three years later, as the Italian government had proposed in 1949.

But Italy did find itself in a confrontation with Yugoslavia over Trieste, the only foreign policy problem which really aroused Italians all the way down to the village level since it concerned a border region, a border population, and not a foreign policy problem in the strict sense of the word.[9] Besides, it had become perfectly clear after 1948 that for the British and American governments, there were two kinds of Communism: one which had to be contained, and another which was trying to detach itself from the former and therefore had to be supported, though without disadvantaging Italy, the former enemy and present ally. Italy and Yugoslavia were therefore both in a position to bring pressure or even extortion to bear, though it is true that their options were limited since both needed American aid.

The decisive crisis began on October 8, 1953, when the United States and Great Britain decided to surrender administration of the territory of Trieste, to withdraw their troops at the earliest possible moment, and to place one of the two zones—zone A with a predominantly Italian population—under Italian administration, thereby giving Yugoslavia the tacit permission to annex zone B. Alcide de Gasperi tried for more. But for other reasons, he had to resign in August 1953 (for a final time; he died a year later). During the summer of 1954, Prime Minister Mario Scelba tried again to obtain more. The rejection of the EDC by the French National Assembly provided him with an opportunity: active Italian participation in an integrated defense force could only occur after the Trieste question had been settled. On September 10, Eisenhower wrote Tito a letter in which he asked for a small concession in zone B and pointed out that American aid "could only be granted with maximal effect if an agreement were concluded."[10] Robert Murphy, Deputy Secretary of State at the time, was sent to Belgrade. His mission was a success. The agreement, which Italian, British, Yugoslav, and American representatives signed in London on October 5, 1954, finally settled the conflict. But the Italian parliament approved the settlement only by 295 against 265 votes—though the compromise was not viewed as giving in to the Americans. It was apparent that Italy did not wish to engage itself too strongly on the side of the United States. The reason for this was not so much Communist anti-Americanism as evidenced on important occasions during the Cold War (the demonstrations against NATO General Ridgway ["The Plague"] on June 16, 1952, are an example), but rather the desire for a less dramatic international situation which would contribute to calming Italian political life. During his trip to the United States in March and April 1955, Mario Scelba pleaded for a summit of the major powers. The election of Giovanni Gronchi—which Mrs. Luce, American ambassador to Rome, had vainly tried to frustrate—aimed in the same direction. Thanks to the support of the Communists and Socialists, Gronchi, a Christian Democrat who had been opposed to the official candidate of his party, was elected President of the Republic on April 29, 1955.

Italy was nonetheless a model ally of the United States. In that same year, when the Austrian State Treaty was signed, it admitted the American troops that had been stationed in Austria up to this point. And, even though a poll conducted in March 1958 had shown clear reservations in this area, the installation of American missile sites on Italian soil was approved in March 1959.* The principal reason was that loyalty toward the American ally, especially when it did not involve an excessive military effort, was felt to be a sort of price for the economic aid which continued to be needed, even and perhaps especially during the economic upswing (which was so vigorous that the London *Financial Times* conferred its Oscar on the Italian lira as the most deserving currency in 1960).

When Alcide de Gasperi turned to the American Congress in September 1951, he stressed the necessity of economic aid if Italy's social situation was to be returned to health.[12] When President Gronchi addressed Congress on February 27, 1956, he stressed the necessity of strengthening the Atlantic Alliance at the economic and social level. The final communiqué of his visit to the United States emphasized that Italy no longer needed economic aid in the narrow sense but did require investments to further its industrial development, especially in the south. When President Eisenhower visited Rome in December

———

* "Are you for or against the installation of American long-range missile bases?"[11]

	For	Against	Don't Know	Doesn't Matter
Overall sample	30%	39%	29%	2%
Elementary schooling	25%	39%	34%	2%
High school education	39%	39%	19%	2%
University education	48%	33%	15%	4%

1959, Gronchi told him that his country needed more American support.

"His country needed increased American assistance, said Gronchi. He argued that Italy had a particularly heavy defense burden because, in addition to providing its quota of troops to NATO, its geography presented a long flank exposed to Communist attack across the narrow Adriatic. The defense problem had become even more difficult, he said, with Italy's present agreement to station our Jupiter missiles in its territory; their security would require, he thought, additional Italian troops, which meant more American aid," Eisenhower wrote later.[13]

Which meant that as far as the Italian leadership was concerned, the threat against which security measures had to be taken came less from the pressure of Soviet armies than from danger to internal stability. In a way that seems paradoxical at first glance, it was thus not too different in this regard from the theses Aneurin Bevan advocated in Great Britain. The significant distinction was that the left wing of the Labour Party and the Italian Christian Democrats did not precisely agree in their definition of the society to be defended!

"Liberal principles do not thrive without roots, and these roots are fed by the contentment and therefore the love of those who see in them the prospects of progressive amelioration. It is because of these considerations that I believe the guidance given to the world by the United States administration is wrong. It has mistaken the nature of the menace, and so it not only prescribes the wrong remedy, but the remedy itself feeds the danger. The scale of rearmament urged upon the democracies by the United States would increase world economic tensions to the point where the Soviet diplomatic offensive would be assisted."[14]

The ministers Aneurin Bevan alluded to in his book and who resigned on April 21, 1951, were primarily himself and Harold Wilson, the one as Minister for Labor and National Service, the other as president of the Board of Trade. Though their resignations were triggered by a minor matter relating to the National Health Service, they did have a connection with decisions affecting the entire economy. What was involved was not only social welfare in the sense of a protection and promotion of social justice and prosperity, but also a rejection of new American aid in the name of national independence. "More and more," wrote Harold Wilson in his *In Place of Dollars*, "American aid is being voted on conditions which involve British acceptance of American strategic decisions, and control not even by Congress, but by the Pentagon."[15]

The two themes could easily be combined. One need only be convinced that as long as Great Britain followed the indicated path as Bevan declared in the House of Commons on April 23, 1951, it would have the "moral leadership of the world" and that the British example would show all mankind "where to go and how to go there."[16]

The conflict between Bevan supporters and the party majority became more acute when after the October 1951 elections the Labour Party became the opposition. In March 1955, Bevan was almost expelled from the party, Harold Wilson already having left it in the previous year. On December 7, 1955, Attlee retired as leader of the party, and on the fourteenth, Hugh Gaitskell was elected his successor by 157 votes (as compared to 70 for Bevan). Thanks to the skill of the new party leader, thanks to the changed international situation, and thanks also to intraparty developments,[17] a reconciliation was effected so rapidly that in the "shadow cabinet" of 1957 Bevan functioned as Foreign Minister and Wilson as Finance Minister and the same Aneurin Bevan went against his friends in his own party, rejected the idea of unilateral disarmament, and advocated the building of a British hydrogen bomb.

Bevan died in July 1960 without having been able to show how he would have handled power. Would he have subscribed to the theses of his adversaries? Certainly Hugh Gaitskell did much to change the image of the United States in the Labour Party. After his death in January 1963, an American liberal eulogized him because "his belief in the potential strength of American democracy [had] reinforced his conviction that the Atlantic Alliance was indispensable and the Atlantic Community indestructible," and this in spite of the fact that "the 1950s [had] consolidated the picture of the United States as a bigoted and repressive nation, irrevocably conservative, given to the persecution of dissenters, the burning of books and the protection of investments,"[18] a view allegedly current among Bevan supporters.

But was this change merely one-sided? British nuclear armament was not only to safeguard independence vis-à-vis the United States, but also to promote national and collective security. And had not the idea that defense costs must be cut to avoid jeopardizing the economic development of the European countries already been recognized by the governments of the NATO countries in 1952?

STRATEGIES AND NUCLEAR WEAPONS

The requirements of defense and the demands of the economy had already proved contradictory in the bilateral agreements which were concluded between the United States and the various Allied countries on January 27, 1950. They provided American aid to enable the European Allies to contribute more effectively to common defense. The agreement between France and the United States concerning aid for mutual defense, which was patterned like the rest, reads as follows:

The governments of the United States of America and the Republic of France; being parties to the North Atlantic Treaty signed at Washington on April 4, 1949; conscious of their reciprocal pledges under Article 3 separately and jointly with the other parties, by means of continuous and effective self-help and mutual aid, to maintain and increase their individual and collective ability to resist armed attack; desiring to foster international peace and security, within the framework of the Charter of the United Nations through measures which will further the ability of nations dedicated to the purposes and principles of the Charter to participate effectively in arrangements for individual and collective self-defense in support of those purposes and principles ... Taking into consideration the support that the Government of the United States of America has brought to these principles by enacting the Mutual Defense Assistance Act of 1949 which provides for the furnishing of military assistance to nations which have joined with it in collective security arrangements ... have agreed as follows:

Article I (1) Each Government, consistently with the principle that economic recovery is essential to international peace and security and must be given clear priority, will make or continue to make available to the other governments ... such equipment, materials, services, or other military assistance as the government furnishing such assistance may authorize. ... The furnishing of such assistance as may be authorized by either party hereto shall be consistent with the Charter of the United Nations and with the obligations under Article IX of the North Atlantic Treaty approved by each Government. Such assistance as may be made available by the United States of America pursuant to this Agreement will be furnished under the provisions, and subject to all of the terms, conditions and termination provisions, of the Mutual Defense Assistance Act of 1949, and such other applicable laws as may hereafter come into effect. ...

Article I (3) Neither Government without the prior consent of the other will devote assistance furnished to it by the other Government to purposes other than those for which it was furnished. ... *

Article VI (2) Each Government agrees to receive personnel of the other Government who will discharge in its territory the responsibilities of the other Government under this Agreement and who will be accorded facilities to observe the progress of assistance furnished pursuant to this Agreement. Such personnel who are nationals of that other country will, in their relations with the Government of the country to which they are assigned, operate as a part of the Embassy under the direction and control of the Chief of the Diplomatic Mission of the Government of such country.[19]

The text of the agreement shows a certain continuity between the conception behind this military aid and the economic aid organized in

---

* This paragraph was to have weighty consequences for the wars in Indochina and later in Algeria.

1948. The Mutual Security Agency (MSA), which was set up by the American government, certainly resembled the Economic Cooperation Agency (ECA), which it succeeded toward the close of 1951. And the fight of the American President to obtain Congressional authorization of the required budgetary allocations was at least as difficult. A case in point would be the $7.8 billion which Truman requested in March 1952 and which had been cut to $6 billion by the time the appropriation act was signed in July.

But there were also significant differences. The bilateralism of the 1948 agreement referred to a European multilateralism. The military multilateralism was no longer European but Atlantic. At the same time, it was felt that the Atlantic defense organization was much more closely integrated than the European organization for economic cooperation ever had been or intended to be, and this in spite of the fact that the aim of economic development was clearly and unanimously recognized while rather divergent opinions prevailed concerning the goal of security, as we have seen.

But everyone originally agreed that it was essential to defend Western Europe by both the counterthreat of the American atomic weapon and the presence of numerous divisions on the European continent. This included American divisions, but principally divisions the Europeans were to furnish themselves. In August 1950, as the Korean War seemed to bring the threat closer, the French government promised to increase the troops it would provide for the defense of Europe by fifteen new divisions of combat strength within three years.[20] But soon fears were voiced everywhere that rearmament might inhibit economic growth. It is true that the NATO Council decided in November 1951 to create an army of forty-three divisions by 1954 and three months later, in the course of a meeting in Lisbon, it even increased it to ninety-six divisions, thirty-five or forty of which would always be in combat readiness (twenty-five to thirty of them for the central front). But in spite of assurances to the contrary by the various governments, these ambitious figures were taken seriously by no one. On the first day of the Lisbon conference, Winston Churchill declared in the House of Commons that the British rearmament program would have to be spread over a longer period. In France, Prime Minister Edgar Faure was thrown out of office shortly after his return from Lisbon because he had contemplated a tax increase. And his successor officially informed NATO in November that the Lisbon program could not be complied with in 1953.

In spite of the German contribution, which was announced in 1950 and gradually became a reality as of 1955, conventional land forces thus remained limited. What role were they meant to play? And, more important, were they to be a coherent or even an integrated whole? The Americans had first thought of an integration which would be so far-reaching that the individual member countries would even specialize in the manufacture of certain types of armaments and weapons. But soon, mere coordination prevailed, at least until the Paris accord of October 1954 was signed. Theoretically, the Federal Republic was to join the organization on an equal footing. To control it more closely, all Allied forces on the continent (including the four divisions Great Britain had committed itself to maintain there) were put under an Allied commander-in-chief. The only exception were those troops which NATO had decided would continue under a purely national command. In conformity with the strategy laid down by the organization, SACEUR was given the authority to decide where they would be stationed and how they would be supplied and committed. Such, at least, was the theory. In practice, control and direction applied more to the Federal Republic than to France (which sent more and more of its troops to Algeria) or to Great Britain (which withdrew two divisions in 1957, claiming financial difficulties). In addition, the Federal Republic had agreed to a significant distinction laid down in the statutes: it had committed itself not to produce nuclear, bacteriological, or chemical weapons on its territory and could build guided missiles, magnetic mines, and bombers only if the commander-in-chief of NATO demanded it and if a two-thirds majority of the Council of the West European Union agreed.

It rapidly became clear that the American divisions did not play the same strategic role as the other troops of the alliance: while intended to contribute to a defense against a potential aggressor, their primary function was that of a hostage which guaranteed that the President of the United States considered the defense of Europe essential and would not content himself with a "peripheral" strategy which ultimately envisaged victory only through the liberation of a Europe previously occupied by an aggressor. On May 10, 1952, *Le Monde* published a report, erroneously attributed to the American Admiral Fechteler, which advocated such a strategy. The excitement which resulted in France made clear what was feared at that time, a time, that is, when new elements such as the obvious, continuing weakness of the conventional NATO forces, the terrible destructiveness of the hydrogen bomb, and the ability of the USSR to first use its nuclear weapons in Europe and later—perhaps by the mid-1950s but certainly by the early 1960s—against the United States as well, had not yet come into play.

In 1952, at Lisbon, the simple-minded conception that conventional troops would resist until American B-52s could carry their bombs to the USSR had still prevailed. But 1953 brought a "new look." On the one hand, American technicians had succeeded in "miniaturizing" the A-bomb; they had built "tactical" nuclear weapons which could destroy enemy units without laying waste entire regions. Besides, the enormous inferiority of the West in conventional forces proved to be a permanent condition. It consequently became necessary to integrate units with tactical nuclear weapons in the overall system. There was the additional fact that it was precisely the weakness of the NATO armies which allowed no other choice but an immediate nuclear counterstrike. The "conventional" battle would be too unequal. In October 1954, General Gruenther stated: "We have determined that our strategy in the center requires the use of atomic weapons, whether the enemy uses them or not, and we must use atomic bombs to redress the imbalance between their forces and ours to achieve victory."[21]

Such a strategy offered the Europeans a certain advantage: if the inferiority in conventional forces was no longer such a serious matter, there was good reason for not making excessive armaments efforts. But drawbacks also became apparent. The first and, for years, the greatest related to the nature of the hydrogen bomb. It was one thing to know that the United States had set off a thermonuclear explosion in November 1952 and that the USSR had exploded a hydrogen bomb in August 1953. But to fully understand in 1954 how much destruction a single bomb could cause over thousands of square miles, not to mention a much larger contamination zone, was something else. To the apprehension of the Europeans that America might shrink from using the atom bomb in the defense of their countries, there was added the growing anxiety that the United States might use this weapon and thus destroy friend and foe at one and the same time.

There was a further fear: it was apparent that the Soviet Union had launched a program of medium-range missiles. If it wished to destroy the destructive potential of its enemies with a single blow, would that not mean that the very countries which had allowed American bomber bases on their soil, and would soon also permit the installation of American missile launching pads, were the most seriously threatened? And when the first Sputnik was put into orbit in October 1957, it was not difficult to guess when the USSR would have intercontinental missiles and therefore be in a position to destroy American cities, a prospect which would involve a fundamental rethinking of the entire problem of defense.

As long as the Europeans were certain that the Russians did not doubt the assured use of American nuclear bombs should they attack Europe, they felt secure. But could the Russians still be convinced of an automatic American counterstrike if it involved a considerable risk of self-destruction? To increase security by enhancing Soviet certainty regarding an American counterstrike, at least two paths could be taken: the massive presence of U.S. troops as hostages, and an end to the American monopoly on the final decision, i.e., the development of atomic weapons by European members of the alliance. The Federal Republic insisted on the first alternative, while Great Britain soon chose the second and France gradually moved from the one to the other.

After German rearmament had been decided in principle with the coming into force of the Paris accord in May 1955, the Federal Republic still had to decide its scope. The strategic conception that Adenauer had developed and in which he believed still relied on the idea that the strengthening of conventional NATO forces would make it possible to repel any potential attack without resort to nuclear weapons. What consequences the use of atom bombs would have was revealed in the most terrifying manner in a "war game" which SHAPE carried out in the Federal Republic, the Netherlands, and North Africa in May 1955 under the code name Carte Blanche. It was discovered that a simulated attack on military targets by 335 bombs resulted in a total of 1,700,000 "dead" and 3,500,000 "wounded," and this did not include the effects of radioactive contamination.[22] Especially because the basic hypothesis of the war game had been an initially successful invasion that was then repulsed, and not the successful defense along the eastern border of the Federal Republic, excitement in Germany was considerable.

As the opposition speaker in the parliamentary debate on the German draft law, Fritz Erler expressed the view that the entire discussion was based on outdated premises: What was the point of a German army of 500,000 if the 1950 conception was no longer valid? On June 13, *The New York Times* reported that Admiral Radford, chairman of the American Joint Chiefs of Staff, had demanded a drastic reduction in conventional U.S. forces—a reduction of 800,000—and a concentration of all efforts on nuclear armaments since even a small army could have a considerable deterrent effect.

For Adenauer, this report had a "frightening significance,"[23] particularly because in the midst of a parliamentary and political battle, he experienced it as a stab in the back. Yet on the basis of numerous earlier statements, he should have been aware of the development of the American strategic concept. Besides, it was not up to Admiral Radford to make decisions, and his ideas were far from being official policy. Yet the Chancellor reproached John Foster Dulles severely for not having kept him *au courant*. On August 11, he received a long letter from Dulles, written "as a friend to a friend whom I deeply respect and admire." In it, the friend lays down everything the United States has done for common defense so far, and adds: "If the sum of all these endeavors is 'unreliability,' I should like to know what the measure of 'reliability' is and where it can be found."[24]

Adenauer was neither reassured nor convinced, particularly because the letter did not really address itself to his fears. Toward the end of September, in Brussels, he used words which were unusual for him: that the security of the European peoples lies in the hands of the United States "can and must not remain a permanent condition . . . what are vital necessities for European states are not always necessarily such for the United States and vice versa. From this fact, there may result differences in political ideas which could lead to independent political action."

The example of such independent political action was furnished him when the United States landed troops in Lebanon in July 1958 and units from American bases in West Germany were used without the Chancellor's having been advised beforehand. Adenauer's indignation explains in part his excellent relations with de Gaulle (see Chapter 7) and prefigured the reaction of another German government which conducted itself quite similarly in a comparable situation in 1973 (see Chapter 10).

But in the meantime, an extended international debate about the idea that there should at least be a nuclear disengagement of the two superpowers in the center of Europe had been carried on, and in this debate the governments in Bonn and Washington were of one mind. On March 25, 1958, the Bundestag endorsed the policy of the Chancellor, i.e., that American units with tactical nuclear weapons would remain on German soil. They were to be supplemented by German units equipped with the same weapons, but under American control. The German-American agreement went hand in hand with the abandonment of all the more or less confused notions concerning a demilitarized zone in the center of Europe which the plan of the Polish Foreign Minister Rapacki had symbolized.

This did not mean, of course, that the principal psychological problem of the *Bundeswehr* had been solved: once it had been admitted that conventional troops would not suffice to keep the enemy at bay, how could one content oneself with the role of a "fire alarm glass" which had to be broken in order to alert nuclear forces whose use did not depend on the German government? The problem became even more acute when Great Britain and later France acquired atomic weapons of their own.

British nuclear weapons were created in response to the American attitude that had expressed itself in the McMahon Act of August 1946, according to which the United States would always act independently and keep its atomic secret even from its wartime allies, including its most trusted partner. Churchill was not allowed to publish the content of the Quebec accord until 1954. But as early as 1946, it was felt in Great Britain that American policy constituted a violation of the treaty. Clement Attlee reacted with the decision to have Great Britain proceed on its own since the United States might return to a policy of isolationism someday, and that would make it essential for Great Britain to defend itself unaided. A second reason was that it had to be shown what one could accomplish.[25]

The decision to build the atom bomb was made by the Cabinet subcommittee for defense in a secret session in January 1947. At that time, it was hoped that England might succeed before the Soviet Union, which, it was believed, would not be ready before 1952, and thus to show that Great Britain had clearly remained one of the three major powers, as it had been during the war. The Soviet atomic explosion in 1949 dashed these hopes, but the national atomic program went forward nonetheless. In a vague answer to the cautious question by a member of the House of Commons, the existence of such a program had been revealed so casually by the British Minister of Defense in February 1948 that even Winston Churchill was surprised at the progress that had been made when he returned to power at the end of 1951. And it was also Churchill who announced in January 1952 that a first British nuclear explosion would be attempted on the Australian island of Montebello, and this was carried out successfully in October.

It would certainly have been possible to proceed more democratically. A poll which was conducted after the atomic program was announced gave a clear indication: 60 percent of the British approved the development of the atom bomb and only 22 percent disapproved.[26] But the secrecy also had the purpose of keeping the United States away. Significantly, not a single American observer was invited to Montebello. And this policy paid off, for faced with the British success, the U.S. government gradually agreed to go very much further in the transmission of secrets and in collaborative efforts than had been provided for in the McMahon Act and in an agreement on very limited exchanges of information signed in 1948. Acting on a proposal of President Eisenhower, Congress passed the Atomic Energy Act in April 1954, which facilitated what was still a very restricted flow of information.

It is also true, of course, that the usefulness of secrecy was not what it once had been, for meanwhile the Soviet hydrogen bomb had been exploded. During the next few years, a strictly bilateral Anglo-

American cooperation developed. In 1955, agreements providing for an exchange of information on civil and military aspects of nuclear energy were signed, the only exception being the technique of manufacture of the atomb bomb. In June 1956, the White House and the State Department persuaded the Pentagon to overcome its reluctance and give the British access to information about the first American nuclear submarine, the *Nautilus*, which had been put into service in December 1954.

But the most important British decision was made in 1954. Deliberately unilateral and based on research undertaken in 1952, it meant that Great Britain would build the H-bomb, and this for three reasons. First, large outlays could be avoided and Britain would again be able to dispense with the draft if conventional weapons were replaced by nuclear ones. Second, there would be a greater assurance of being defended, since unfortunately it could not be precluded that the United States would put its bomb to the same use to which Great Britain had put its air force in May 1940, i.e., the protection of its own territory. Third and most important, it was essential to acquire possession of the same perfected weapon which the other two major powers had if Britain wished to retain rank, prestige, and influence—and that influence, it might be added, would primarily be brought to bear on the United States.

In the parliamentary debate dealing with the Defense White Paper in 1955, Harold Macmillan, Defense Minister at the time, rejected the idea that the American deterrence potential made superfluous the building of a British hydrogen bomb: "I think this is a very dangerous doctrine. . . . Politically it surrenders our power to influence American policy and then, strategically and tactically it equally deprives us of any influence over the selection of targets and the use of our vital striking forces. The one, therefore, weakens our prestige and our influence in the world, and the other might imperil our safety."[27]

He was certainly not the only one to think this. "If we want to remain a first-class power, we cannot possibly leave to an ally, however staunch and loyal, the monopoly of this instrument of such decisive importance in these massive issues of war and peace," a retired Chief of Air Staff said. "Britain without the bomb," suggested the archbishop of York, "might become a satellite of a nation which possessed it."

Of course, the pressure the Americans exerted on the British during the Suez crisis did not seem to indicate that they considered it a nuclear power. But that hardly mattered, for already in the following year, in May 1957, the first British H-bomb was set off on the Christmas Islands, which prompted Randolph Churchill to explain to the

American Chamber of Commerce in London a short while later: "Britain can knock down twelve cities in the region of Stalingrad and Moscow from bases in Britain and another dozen in the Crimea from bases in Cyprus. We are a great power once again."[28]

The major decisions which were to be made in strategic and military policy were announced in a White Paper of 1957, at a time when confidence and collaboration between London and Washington had been reestablished. The end of the general draft was announced, and the concept of nuclear deterrence became the center of defense thinking. The reduction of conventional forces was meant to signal that Great Britain no longer had its earlier possibilities of intervening on other continents.

The British press applauded all these plans, and criticism by the opposition was restrained. A few negative aspects were mentioned only hesitantly: the announcement of a strategy of massive retaliation at the very moment the United States was thinking about graduated response and the Soviets were developing intercontinental missiles, which put the problem on an entirely new basis; American dissatisfaction in view of Britain's decision to go it alone and its renunciation of responsibilities in Asia; and finally, the shock the announcement of a reduction of the British Rhine Army and the tactical air force in Germany produced among the European partners of the alliance. Since Britain had apparently been promised American help in the development of its long-range missile at the very moment it violated its obligations to participate in the integrated defense, the idea that others would have to follow suit was quite naturally given a boost among those who had already engaged in similar reasoning in France and taken an identical position.

"Hurrah for France! Since early today, she is stronger and prouder. From the depth of my heart, I thank you and all those who have achieved this magnificent success for France. De Gaulle." This was the text of the telegram the President of the French Republic sent on February 13, 1960, to Pierre Guillaumat, the minister responsible for Operation "Gerboise Bleue" (blue jerboa), i.e., the explosion of the first French atom bomb, near Reggane in the Sahara. Of the two men who should have been singled out for congratulations, one was the principal organizer of the operation, General Ailleret. Officer in charge of special weapons and responsible for nuclear matters at the level of the chief of staff since 1957, he had had mysterious duties as commander of special units of the land forces from 1952 to 1956. The other, Félix Gaillard, was no longer a leading politician in 1960. But from August 1951 to June 1953, under four successive governments, he had been in charge of atomic energy matters and set up a five-year plan of considerable scope. And on April 11, 1958, as Prime Minister, he had given the order to manufacture the bomb, already deciding at that time that the first explosion would take place in early 1960.[29]

During his work with Jean Monnet and before he became one of the bright young ministerial candidates of the liberal "Radical Party," Félix Gaillard had developed a taste for long-range projects. When he became Secretary of State for atomic energy, the atomic energy commission which had been created in 1945 had just passed through the long crisis into which it had plunged in April 1950 when High Commissioner Frédéric Joliot-Curie was recalled because he had been active as a "fighter for peace" on the side of the Communist Party. With the new High Commissioner, Francis Perrin, who was also a renowned scientist, Gaillard worked out the five-year plan which provided for the development of "peaceful" atomic energy, but also permitted research and even preparatory work for the building of the atom bomb. At the same time, Colonel Ailleret, acting almost by himself, began to organize a pressure group to disseminate information about the innovative aspects of nuclear strategy and to persuade the government to create a national nuclear force.

Preliminary decisions were made by Pierre Mendès-France in 1954, by Edgar Faure in 1955, and by Guy Mollet in 1956, though these went no further than keeping open the option to build the bomb, should this be decided upon. But these heads of government overlooked almost entirely to what extent the preliminary work which would make the final decision both possible and inevitable had advanced in the meantime. It is also true, however, that they were better informed than the ministers, the parliament, the parties, and the press. Even more than in the United States during the war and in Great Britain after it, the activity of a small group of military men and high officials was carried on almost wholly outside the constitutional decision-making process and with an almost total absence of any democratic control. Yet an attentive reader of the budget and relevant publications such as the *Revue de défense nationale* would have had no difficulty noting that the French conception of defense was undergoing a transformation.

The chief obstacle did not come from the American government, with which relations in this matter were rather distant. Some French fact-finding missions were sent to the United States, but what they brought back was almost useless. What the "conspirators" did see as the greatest threat was the project of a European atomic community which had been launched by Jean Monnet's Action Committee in January 1956, particularly when President Eisenhower offered to assist the Europeans in the peaceful use of atomic energy by providing uranium. But the initiative taken by General Ailleret and others responsible for the "special weapons" project caused Guy Mollet to change his mind. It is true that the Rome Treaty of April 1957 had created the European Atomic Energy Commission (Euratom), but France was left totally free to put atomic energy to military use and that freedom never became the subject of a genuine debate in the parliament or the press.

The motives of the initiators of the project closely resembled those of the British. One was economic in nature. In 1953, Ailleret reports, "When I gave the concluding lecture on 'nuclear realities' at the jujitsu maneuver [of the French army], I put the headings of the various sections on the blackboard as I talked. When I wrote down 'atomic weapons are cheap weapons,' the audience burst out laughing."[30] Yet he ultimately succeeded in convincing many generals and politicians of his view.

The second motive was strategic in nature and became stronger as Soviet power grew. It found its justification in formulations such as the hardly felicitous statement Secretary of State Christian Herter made before the Senate Foreign Relations Committee in April 1959: "I cannot conceive of any President engaging in all-out nuclear war unless we were in danger of all-out devastation ourselves."[31] The third motive, connected with the second, was the rank of France, especially vis-à-vis the United States.

Yet at least two differences could be noted during the last months of the Fourth Republic. On the one hand, there was a great temptation to combine German economic strength and French technology. On March 31, 1958, the two Defense Ministers, Jacques Chaban-Delmas and Franz Josef Strauss, signed an agreement according to which the Franco-German research institute at Saint-Louis (Alsace) would be run jointly and carry out "basic scientific and technical weapons research" with the purpose of strengthening the common defense of their countries. Officially, atomic energy was not mentioned, but Strauss took a trip to the Sahara which attracted some attention. Yet Chaban-Delmas, though a loyal Gaullist, apparently did not have the blessings of the General, for de Gaulle had no sooner returned to power than he put an end to all gestures toward Franco-German collaboration in atomic energy matters.

On the other hand, France did not succeed in obtaining U.S. support, although theoretically, the Congress had provided in 1954 that the flow of information could be increased as the recipient developed greater knowledge and more know-how through his own initiative. While confidence between Washington and London had been damaged only temporarily by the Suez crisis, French anti-Americanism produced a constant mistrust concerning the diplomatic use to which France might put nuclear weapons. Great Britain was an integral part of the American defense system, after all. It had acted differently from France and, as of 1948, had raised no objections whatever to the construction of bases for American strategic bombers on its soil.

ECONOMIC HARMONY?

In matters of defense, there were privileged relations with Great Britain; in economic matters, there was support of the Schuman Plan and later of the "European renewal" which led to the Common Market without Great Britain: Doesn't this mean that American policy during the 1950s was contradictory? And wasn't there a second contradiction that must be pointed out: Wasn't the strengthening of the European economy, especially support of the unification efforts of the Six, tantamount to creating a powerful competitor for the United States?

Actually, both of these were only apparent contradictions the moment one saw the primary goal as political. The defense and power of the United States were being maintained by a global strategy which gave the militarily dependent British ally room to maneuver. They also lay in a European prosperity which stabilized the liberal political systems and promoted the global development of international trade. Economic support of Europe was the expression of an essentially political decision which was made significantly easier by the fact that the enormous progress of the Europen economies up to about 1958 led to the creation of a new flow of goods rather than to a redirection of existing goods for the benefit of the countries of Europe.[32]

Marshall aid, the effects of the Korean War, and rearmament as well as the progressive liberalization of trade favored a European economic development which very quickly rendered obsolete the idea of a mere recovery, a return to prewar levels.

Difficulties certainly did exist, and they were predominantly of a financial and monetary nature. The rise in the price of raw materials during the "Korean boom" first created a precarious situation for the mark and then for the franc. Growth demanded additional imports. For a country such as France, which did not yet export much at the time, additional purchases in the United States were not compensated by sales, and this meant that dollars had to be found. To an extent, military aid helped overcome this problem. But like all the countries of the OEEC, France profited primarily from the regulatory mechanisms of the European Payments Union, whose rather revolutionary principle of a solidarity of European currencies had a very favorable impact on trade and the economy as a whole.

It also had a favorable effect on the state of mind: toward the mid-1950s, France experienced both a truly enormous economic recovery and a step-by-step transition from the old protectionist ideology to the conviction that the opening of borders and the development of the neighboring country might favor its own. As late as 1953–54, French employers had discreetly but effectively participated in the fight against the EDC, not because they feared German rearmament or wished to defend the French army but in order to obviate the danger of Europe's becoming an economic unit. The confidential letter the president of the National Council of French Employers, Georges Villiers, sent on June 23, 1954, to Pierre Mendès-France, who had just been appointed Prime Minister, is characteristic in this respect.[33]

But already three years later, when the Rome Treaty had been signed and ratified, the coolness and resistance had significantly decreased. And they were even less marked when, on December 27, 1958, de Gaulle's government approved the ensemble of measures which even today is associated with the name of his Foreign- and Finance Minister Antoine Pinay and his principal economic adviser Jacques Rueff. A massive devaluation and the creation of a "heavy" franc were to guarantee the success of a liberal policy which specifically included respect for international obligations vis-à-vis the Common Market and the liberalization of trade: external convertibility of the franc, a reduction of tariffs, and the increase of quotas were measures that attracted considerable attention.

In a certain respect—though certainly not in all! (see Chapter 8)—it was precisely de Gaulle who enabled France to move closer to American conceptions in international economic issues and in the matter of decolonization.

Even before French policy in Algeria changed, political relations between the Western European countries and the United States were hardly affected by events on other continents when economic interests were involved. Sometimes, this was due to surprising arrangements, as in the case of the uranium from the Congo which the president of the Union Minière of Upper Katanga had begun shipping to the United States as early as 1940 when he was informed that the Germans were working on an atomic bomb. "For years we had been able to import substantial amounts of uranium ore from Katanga at prices below what was paid elsewhere, but now the Union Minière justifiably felt it was entitled to a price increase. This amounted to a number of million dollars annually, and I was summoned home to participate in the negotiation. The appropriate agencies in Washington thought we should approve the sum the Belgians were asking, and so did I. But as a matter of negotiation I felt that if we agreed at once to the entire increase, our friends might regret they had not asked for more. So I suggested that we offer half the amount requested. To my surprise, the Belgians promptly accepted the offer and both sides were quite happy," Robert Murphy reports.[34]

The replacement of the Anglo-Iranian Oil Company by American firms produced a different kind of malaise (see Chapter 5). But that conflict was not as acute as the one which erupted later, in part because of Iran, between the oil companies of global rank—the "international majors"—and the Italian ENI under Enrico Mattei.

The Ente Nazionale Idrocarburi had been created on February 10, 1953, by a law which gave it the exclusive right to drill for oil in the Po valley. The battle for this monopply (which included neither exploration in the southern Italian oilfields nor the sale of oil products) had been strenuous and marked especially by the interventions of Mrs. Luce on behalf of private enterprise—i.e., the petroleum companies—and who had allied herself with private Italian companies against the state monopoly Enrico Mattei wanted.[35] Subsequently, the ENI developed increasingly in areas other than oil production, which finally proved a failure in northern Italy. Thanks in part to the discovery of natural gas, ENI could totally transform Italy's energy situation. To an extent, this success was due also to initiatives its president took in the Middle East.

Mattei was also president or chairman of the board of six other companies of the concern,[36] which he never stopped enlarging until he died in the crash of his private plane on October 27, 1962. Excluded from the Iranian arrangement because ENI was too small, he revenged himself in 1957: his contract with Iran benefited Italy and simultaneously affronted the "majors" since the arrangement was much more favorable to the producing country than was normally the case. Profits were shared on a 75:25 instead of a 50:50 basis, and half of the members of the board of directors were to be Iranians while the chairmanship went to an Iranian by statute.

Enrico Mattei used his power exclusively to Italy's advantage and certainly had no intention of creating a European front against the American oil companies, in part because the latter were associated with the former (with a Dutch and an English company), in part because he opposed European integration. His rejection of the Common Market and his presence in North Africa, especially his contacts with the NLF during the war in Algeria, precluded any "Europeanization" of his positions vis-à-vis the United States in any event.

Nor was there any need for confrontation. The perspective that was current during the 1950s was really the one Robert Marjolin, secretary-general of the OEEC, had presented to the Americans in 1951: "An essential part of the answer to both of our first two questions—how to secure a continuously expanding economy and how to obtain the raw materials the expansion would call for—can, I think, jointly be found in the effort now being made, although as yet on an insufficient scale, by the United States and Europe to develop the underdeveloped areas of the world. This is where we shall find, at the same time, the outlet for our greatly increased industrial production and the raw materials we need to keep our system going."[37]

The absence of feelings of rivalry explains why the Americans supported the creation of the European Economic Community, although they initially gave Euratom more direct aid.[38] Their support was especially evident when, in the spring of 1958, the EEC was accused before GATT* of having by its very structure violated the rules of international trade which the members of the organization had committed themselves to respect.[39] The external tariff provided for by the Six did not seem too dangerous to the Americans since it merely set mean values between the previous national tariffs. Besides, the planned consolidation of the European economic area was to make American investments simpler and more rational.

Support in GATT was strengthened by the support given by the Six in the face of Great Britain's efforts to prevent the creation of the EEC. In November 1958, when de Gaulle for the first time broke off negotiations on the possible creation of a free trade zone between the Six and eleven other countries of the OEEC with Great Britain among them, the Americans did not react strongly.[40] And the creation of the "small free trade zone" one year later did not give rise to the idea that special help would be granted this grouping that had come about through British initiative, and this for two reasons. There were three neutral members—Switzerland, Sweden, and Austria—among the six member countries, and of the three member countries of NATO— Norway, Denmark, and Portugal—one had an especially strained relationship with the United States. Denmark had resisted various demands and pressures and had refused in 1956, 1957, and 1958 to approve the stockpiling of atom bombs and nuclear warheads on its territory.[41]

But toward the end of the 1960s when it became obvious that rapid economic development in Europe could not but lead to the creation of a power that would be an economic competitor albeit a political ally, a clear change in the American attitude became observable. There was, first of all, the order of magnitude: steel production of the Six rose from 36.6 million tons in 1952 to 62.9 million in 1959, while the United States stagnated (84.8 as compared to 84.5 tons), as did Great

---

* General Agreement on Tariffs and Trade; see Chapter 1.

Britain (16.6 in both years). And secondly, as regarded the pace of development: on the basis of 1948 = 100, the United States and Canada were at 130 in 1953 and at 131 in 1958, while figures for the Six were 172 and 246 respectively.[42] But most important were the terms of trade: while the dollar gap had still been evident in 1957, the American trade deficit suddenly rose in 1958. This was due primarily to a spectacular decline of the trade surplus from $6.1 to $3.3 billion, while the moderate surplus in the European balance of trade, which had hovered around $1.5 billion ever since 1953, rose to $4.1 billion.[43] Europe was well on its way toward exporting as much as the United States. In a parallel development, gold reserves in the United States began to decline, while those in Europe, primarily in the Federal Republic, began to increase.

A change of such magnitude could not but jeopardize the priority of politics in the American attitude toward European unity. But it had been so little foreseen during the preceding years and was recognized so imperfectly when it occurred that leading circles in the European countries continued for a long time to cling to the ideas and perspectives of the 1950s[44]—the only exception being de Gaulle, whose vision differed from that of his predecessors in France and his colleagues in Europe.

PART THREE

The 1960s: Confrontations at a Time of Prosperity

INTRODUCTION

We are faced once again with the problem of the temporal and spatial articulation of our subject. For the 1950s, it was relatively easy to isolate the transatlantic difficulties which resulted from decolonization, i.e., difficulties which concerned other continents. But during the 1960s, the common and disputed themes are much more enmeshed, especially during the mid-decade.

It is possible, in fact, to distinguish a middle period which runs from 1963 to 1968 and which was both preceded and followed by a longer period. So far, we have been discussing the former. The second extends to 1971–73.

De Gaulle's return to power in June 1958 was unquestionably a turning point in French politics, but however important relations with the United States might have been to him, he waited for the end of the war in Algeria before really going on the offensive and making the attempt to change their nature. It was only in connection with American-Soviet relations, to which the Cuban crisis of October 1962 gave a new direction, that his policy became apparent.

The defeat of the Republicans by the Democrats and the accession of John F. Kennedy undoubtedly brought about a certain modification in the relationship between Adenauer's Germany and the United States. But the tensions which had existed between Bonn and Washington since Khrushchev's Berlin ultimatum in November 1958 underwent a change in meaning on August 13, 1961, when construction of the Berlin Wall symbolized and cemented the partition of Germany, and this probably resulted in the most marked break in

West Germany's foreign policy since the establishment of the Federal Republic.

In 1961 and 1962, two seemingly kindred visions of Europe came into conflict: John F. Kennedy's "grand design" and Europe according to the Fouchet Plan as de Gaulle conceived it. The core of the problem was the place and role of Great Britain in Europe, and especially in the relationship of Europe to America. At a press conference in January 1963, de Gaulle put an end to the grand design by rejecting British membership in the EEC. In April of that same year, the German Bundestag unanimously passed a preamble to the law authorizing ratification of the Franco-German treaty and thus ended de Gaulle's efforts to create a Europe that would be detached from the United States.

The articulation of the years 1961–63 is thus quite clear, and their fundamental elements are precise. This also applies to the structure of the closing years of the decade, and this not only because the May-June 1968 crisis in France decisively weakened de Gaulle's position and finally led to his defeat and resignation in April 1969. Nor is it simply that the invasion of Czechoslovakia in August 1968 signaled the brutal end of the transformation in Eastern Europe and its possible effects on East-West and transatlantic relations, and concurrently a certain shift in the positions of the major Communist parties in Western Europe. More important in this connection is the fact that it was in 1968 that the Western monetary system passed through a crisis which, on August 15, 1971, produced the notable decision concerning the inconvertibility of the dollar. This was no less significant a stage in the growing crisis of the economy of the West than the quadrupling of oil prices in November 1973. And the beginning of the economic crisis coincided with a kind of termination of the provisional status of the Federal Republic by the treaties and agreements that were signed in Moscow, Warsaw, and Berlin between 1970 and 1972.

Here also, the period where changes in course occurred is relatively easy to determine, although many fundamental features obviously persisted throughout the decade and others changed during its middle period. To judge the true importance of the latter is especially difficult, for here more than at other times, the spectacular event was not necessarily the most important. Based on a policy of entente with the Soviet Union, de Gaulle waged an offensive that included antagonism over currency questions, withdrawal from NATO, condemnation of U.S. policy in Vietnam, and opposition to the United States in Latin America, the Mideast, and Canada. What impact did all of this have on transatlantic relationships as a whole?

Had the general prosperity not come from a factual interdependence which became more pronounced the longer it continued? But didn't the asymmetry of this interdependence justify the growing interest with which the "Americanization" of the European countries, the role of American firms in Europe, the benefits that accrued to the United States from the monetary system, were now being discussed?

France's withdrawal from the Atlantic organization and de Gaulle's fight for the introduction of the gold standard were perhaps only episodes in a development during which one discovered the paradoxical phenomenon that the Federal Republic was becoming increasingly dependent militarily and at the same time ever stronger economically, and especially monetarily, until it threatened to assume the position France and Great Britain were after.

How can de Gaulle's political will and the economic power of the Germans, which grew ever stronger even relative to the United States, be reconciled with phenomena of an entirely different nature? What about the Vietnam War, with its consequences for the image the United States had of itself and the world, and the image of America in Europe, or the social and intellectual transformations which manifested themselves in the student movements of the late 1960s and were simultaneously hastened by them? Those movements, whether in Berlin or Berkeley, certainly had a connection with the war in Vietnam but also resulted from a change that occurred in the Catholic Church: the criticism of Western societies led to a transition from the vision of an East-West opposition which produced self-satisfaction to a vision of a North-South difference which produced self-criticism. The pronouncements of the Second Vatican Council would thus shape the attitudes of many Europeans toward the United States more significantly than the gestures of General de Gaulle or even the denunciations of the multinational corporations.

7 A GREAT AMBITION VERSUS A GRAND DESIGN

THE POLICY OF GENERAL DE GAULLE

When de Gaulle once again found himself at the head of the French government, the substance of French foreign policy changed less than its nature and the world view underlying it. In Algeria, it went counter to the hopes of those to whom he owed his return to power. He accepted and consolidated the European Economic Community, which had been bitterly rejected by the Gaullists. And it had been the profoundly despised preceding government that had decided to build the atom bomb. But foreign policy was something for de Gaulle which it had not been for the parties of the Fourth Republic. It was the only true politics, compared to which economic, social, and cultural policies were nothing more than means. There was more behind this conception than a mere "primacy of foreign policy" as in Adenauer's case, more than a personal preference and a certain estimate of the relative importance of constraints. What did lie in back of it was an ideology, a *Weltanschauung* at whose center the nation functions as the highest political value.

Domestic policy and the economy are means which must be placed at the service of action that is taken in the outside world in the name of the nation. This view becomes manifest in a variety of texts, as for example in the 1963 New Year's Eve address: "Our prosperity reaches an unprecedented level, our social progress is unexampled. To the extent that the conjunction of recovery and reason leads us to power, France recovers her rank, her attraction, her possibilities."[1]

The outside world is the totality of nations. Ideologies and regimes certainly exist. During the war, many of the General's texts speak not just of Germany but of Hitler Germany, and as of 1947 and after 1958 many evoke the totalitarian nature of the Soviet regime. But regimes must only be fought or denounced as provisional entities. They are transitory forms in which the immutable nations manifest themselves.

During the press conference of January 31, 1964, in which he announced recognition of Mao Tse-tung's People's Republic, de Gaulle said, "The regime which presently rules China . . ." and when he mentioned the Atlantic Alliance in a message he sent to parliament on December 11, 1962, and referred to it as "presently necessary for the defense of the free world," the adverb was to be understood in the same way. The alliance arises from a transitory constellation, a conjunction, which may last for some time but is nonetheless merely a conjunction, a specific constellation in the life of the French nation. The Atlantic organization can be justified by expediency. But expediency will never justify trans- or supranational structures which would change the substance of the nation as a whole, and permanently, simply because a particular conjunction exists.

France is one nation among others and simultaneously one that differs from others. As a nation among others, it must know what de Gaulle had already written before the war in his book *The Edge of the Sword:* ". . . prerequisite of movement and the midwife of progress . . . force has ruled empires, and dug the grave of decadence: force gives laws to the peoples and controls their destinies." What he expressed in his important address to the officers of the higher military academies on November 3, 1959, follows from such a view: "In everything that constitutes a nation, and principally in what constitutes ours, nothing is more important than defense." But this defense must be more than just that: military policy must furnish the arms that will discourage or repel a potential aggressor, and it must furnish diplomacy the means it needs in a world where strength means so much—be it the diplomacy that deals with a potential enemy or the diplomacy vis-à-vis the partners within an alliance. But France occupies a special place among nations in part because it is loved, in part because it must play a special role. When de Gaulle tells of his 1945 visit to the United States in his *Mémoires de guerre,* he writes: "The explosion of enthusiasm which had marked this occasion revealed the extent of the city's [i.e. New York] extraordinary love of France."[2] And on December 31, 1967, he stated in his New Year's Eve address: "Our action is directed toward goals which are connected and which, because they are French, reflect the desire of all men." Such formulations did not shock his audience and were not even called attention to by commentators. We will see in the following chapter to what extent the idea of a special mission of France was and still is accepted by the most diverse and even antagonistic political currents in the country.

Every nation worthy of its name must have ambitions. As de Gaulle describes his visit to devastated Germany in 1945, he says compassionately: "For many years, the ambitions of the German nation and the aims of its policy would necessarily be reduced to the level of survival and reconstruction."[3] But France's fundamental ambition must be the rank, the place it has to occupy as a great Western nation in the global game, and this as much in 1958 as in 1945.

As a Western nation: this adjective seems indispensable to us if we wish to understand de Gaulle's policy. He certainly often placed the two giants, the United States and the Soviet Union, on one and the same level. But the fact that France belongs to the West involves a distinction which can sometimes be played off against the one, sometimes against the other. Whenever a more or less physical threat comes from the Soviet Union, France, because it is Western, feels complete solidarity with the West. The general's firmness in the Berlin crises of 1958 and 1961 did not only reflect his will not to cross Adenauer or his fundamental attitude which consisted in pleading for inflexibility in every situation of weakness; that firmness undoubtedly also derived from the sense of belonging to a community which had to present a united front. In October 1962, during the Cuban crisis, his attitude was the same. "In Western Europe support was general though there were waverings in Britain and Italy," President Kennedy's adviser and memoirist wrote later. "In Paris General de Gaulle received Dean Acheson, the President's special emissary, and, without waiting to see the aerial photographs Acheson had brought along, said, 'If there is a war, I will be with you. But there will be no war.' De Gaulle went on to wonder whether the quarantine would be enough, and so did Adenauer, but both strongly backed the American position."[4] President Eisenhower had already been impressed by this solidarity. In his memoirs, he writes that after a difficult exchange about the U-2 incident at the Paris summit in May 1960, de Gaulle touched him on the elbow and said: "Whatever happens, we are with you."[5]

But when there is no threat (or no sense of one), France—precisely because it is a Western country—must strive for independence and influence in its relations to the United States. Being a Western country, it hardly has any connections with the USSR. As a Western country, it finds itself economically, technologically, militarily, and culturally in a situation of unequal interdependence with the United States. America must certainly be powerful to keep Soviet power in check. But the moment the USSR is kept at bay, American preponderance has to be confronted in order to raise France's rank vis-à-vis its ally.

The political vision is complemented by emotions. The most negative, inextricably intertwined were resentment and mistrust, and both of them were crystallized in the concept "Anglo-Saxons." On March 13, 1960, de Gaulle visited Prime Minister Harold Macmillan, who mentions in his notes that he asked his guest in the course of a very friendly conversation why he had continually harped on the theme of the "Anglo-Saxons" in his memoirs. Macmillan found the answer not only in De Gaulle's jealousy of Anglo-American relations at that time, especially in the close friendship between Macmillan and Kennedy, but primarily in unforgettable memories of the Roosevelt-Churchill hegemony, of Syria, of D-Day, of Yalta, etc. And Macmillan's answer obviously did nothing to shake the General's certitudes.[6] When the first volume of de Gaulle's *Memoirs of Hope* appeared in 1970, it became apparent that his grievance had roots that went back even further: "But was it not primarily the 'Anglo-Saxons' cry of 'Halt!' that brought the sudden cessation of hostilities on November 11, 1918, at the very moment when we were about to pluck the fruits of victory?"[7]

In his rather superficial report on the period 1958–61, however, Couve de Murville, French Foreign Minister from 1958 to 1968, sets forth a rather different situation which yet accurately reflects an unavoidably contradictory reality. "De Gaulle and Eisenhower had known and esteemed each other since the war in North Africa and the liberation of French territory. Dialogue between the two came about easily and frankly, without obstacles and preliminaries. Thanks to circumstances, i.e. the Soviet Berlin initiative, the two Presidents met frequently, four times in two and one-half years. Every time, things went smoothly and in an atmosphere of trust and cordiality. The American President's visit to France in September 1958 was a meeting of long-lost friends. The population of Paris played its role by showing touchingly and cordially how it remembered General Eisenhower from the war. The reception the American authorities and the American people gave the French chief of state eighteen months later, in April 1960, was a fitting response. . . . Franco-American relations were never closer than during that time."[8] Though it is true that at that time, as Couve de Murville immediately adds, "there could be no question of entering into a debate concerning fundamentals with America, i.e. the future" until the Algerian question had been resolved.

This memorandum which de Gaulle sent to President Eisenhower and Prime Minister Macmillan on September 17, 1958, shows one of the possible goals of French ambition: complete equality with Great Britain and even with the United States, with the Big Three of the Atlantic Alliance forming a special entity. Since this text remained secret for a very long time, it is useful to reprint it here in its entirety:

Recent events in the Middle East and in the Taiwan Strait have contributed to the recognition that the present organization of the Western Alliance no longer does justice to those conditions which are necessary for the security of the entire free world. The indispensable cooperation in the taking of decisions and the bearing of responsibilities does not correspond to the solidarity in the risks that have been assumed. The French Government finds itself in a position to draw certain consequences and to make certain suggestions.

1. The conception and implementation of the Atlantic Alliance occurred in view of a potential sphere of action which no longer corresponds to political and strategic realities. In view of the present global situation, an organization which, like NATO, limits itself exclusively to the security of the North Atlantic can no longer be considered efficacious as if what happened in the Middle East or Africa, for example, were not of direct and indirect interest to Europe, and as if the indivisible responsibilities of France did not also extend to Africa, the Indian Ocean and the Pacific, as do those of Great Britain and the United States. On the other hand, it must be said that the range of today's ships, planes and missiles makes so limited a defensive system appear militarily outdated. It is true that we had initially agreed that the unquestionably decisive nuclear weapon would remain a monopoly of the United States for a long time, and this may have appeared as justification for practically conferring on the government in Washington all decisions concerning questions of global defense. But here also it must be recognized that such a state of affairs, though accepted in the past, no longer corresponds to the actual situation.

2. It is therefore not the view of France that NATO in its present form can do justice either to the security requirements of the free world, or to its own. *It therefore seems to France that an organization comprising the United States, Great Britain and France should be created and function on a world-wide political and strategic level* [italics added]. This organization would make joint decisions in all political questions affecting global security and would also draw up and, if necessary, implement strategic action plans, especially as regards the use of nuclear weapons. In this way, it would be possible to foresee and organize eventual theaters of operation which would be subordinate to the general organization (such as the Arctic, the Atlantic, the Pacific, the Indian Ocean, for example) and which could be subdivided into subregions, if necessary.

3. The French Government considers such an organization of security indispensable. As of now, it will make all further development of its present participation in NATO contingent on it and intends, should that become necessary, to invoke the revision procedures of the North Atlantic Treaty as set down in Article 12 for this purpose.

4. The French Government suggests that the questions raised in this memorandum be made the object of consultations between the United States, Great Britain and France at the earliest possible moment. It proposes that this consultation take place in Washington and, initially, through the embassies and the Standing Group.[9]

The answer of the American President was sent on October 20, 1958. As much as a year later—and even after its publication in the fall of 1966 in an American journal[10]—the French repeated time and again that Eisenhower had not answered at all, or only in platitudes. Although the idyllic picture he painted of the consultative mechanism within NATO admittedly did not correspond to any political reality, it is nonetheless true that he emphatically stressed a decisive point in his letter: "We cannot afford to adopt any system which would give to our other Allies, or other Free World countries, the impression that basic decisions affecting their own vital interests are being made without their participation." In addition, the President referred to the numerous difficulties an expansion of the Atlantic Pact area would cause and declared his willingness to have the matter examined by the appropriate authorities.

A precise French proposal was never made. Not because the aim had been given up but because the sentence of the American President quoted above made an answer almost impossible for anyone who spoke of a Europe founded on the equality of its members. For how could one concede that de Gaulle's conception of the equality of nations should entail the demand that France be equal to those who were more equal than the rest, that there be five to decide in the U.N., four to decide on Germany, and three in the Western world? The central demand of the memorandum of September 17 soon became known and shocked the Common Market partners. Not without reason, they felt that the General's attitude toward the weaker in Europe resembled the one for which he justifiably reproached the United States on the transatlantic level. But there were two major differences: he did not have the same preponderance vis-à-vis the weaker, and could not give them protection.

If one was to speak of European unity, one should therefore not invoke the idea of a tripartite organization too often. But to want a united Europe can also mean a search for the same goal by a different route. If France could speak to the outside world in the name of a strong Europe, it would have a special weight among the three Western powers since the strength of Europe would represent a more significant means of influence than the "special relationship" which it was believed Great Britain had with the United States. But this would only be true if Great Britain was not part of this Europe and if the European partners did not really share the wish of France to play a world political role, especially if this meant distancing themselves from the United States. Or, more precisely, they did not share it *as nations* but accepted it for a Europe within which the French nation would be the only one to have this desire.

Belgium, the Netherlands, and Luxembourg in any event were too small to feel called to a world political role, once Indonesia and the

Congo had been lost. Italy was preoccupied with its internal problems, satisfied to once again find itself in a "normal" situation and finally rid of its status as a defeated nation. This left the Federal Republic, which could throw the weight of a constantly growing economic power onto the scales of world political influence. But this was counterbalanced by its Nazi past and the partition, which forced it to pay more if not exclusive attention to the East rather than to other continents. It was therefore with Germany that de Gaulle proposed to lay the foundations for the kind of Europe he envisaged, although he knew that the anxious glance that country cast toward the East conferred special importance on American protection and that the Europe which Konrad Adenauer and Jean Monnet had built did not merely aim at a simple federation of states.

During the following years, the implicit dialogue between the German Chancellor and the French President therefore necessarily took the following form:

"I do not understand you. You want a Europe with a loud voice but without a body."

"I do not understand you. You want a Europe with a body but you permit its soul to be American."

But from 1958 to 1963, the differences of opinion and contradictions were less noticeable than the consequences of the twofold surprise of September 14, 1958. It was surprise at the two attitudes and was felt in both countries and elsewhere. Here was de Gaulle, far from repudiating the Franco-German rapprochement of the preceding regime and actually anxious to continue and deepen it. And Konrad Adenauer, far from distancing himself from a man who had indefatigably and with great passion fought the rebirth of the German state and the entire European policy of integration, actually proclaimed the unity of views with a warmth which not even Robert Schuman had shown. And there was the surprise of the two men themselves: everything indicates that they had not expected such love at first sight when they met for the first time in Colombey-les-Deux Eglises.[11]

"From then until mid-1962," de Gaulle recalls, "Konrad Adenauer and I were to write to each other on some forty occasions. We saw each other fifteen times, either in Paris, Marly or Rambouillet, or in Baden-Baden and Bonn. We spent more than a hundred hours in conversation, either in private, or with our ministers in attendance or in the company of our families." After describing the reception given Adenauer in Paris in July 1962, the military ceremony at the camp of Mourmelon (where they stood "side by side in a command car," inspecting "a French and a German armored division"), and a religious ceremony in the cathedral at Rheims, the French President concludes: "Subsequently, and until the death of my illustrious friend, our relations were to progress at the same tempo and with the same cordiality. By and large, everything that was spoken, written and evinced between us was to do no more than develop and adapt to events the friendly agreement concluded in 1958. It is true that circumstances would produce some divergences of view. But these were always surmounted."[12]

In his memoirs, Konrad Adenauer put more emphasis on the disagreements, the most important of which concerned the organization of Europe rather than relations with the United States, at least during the early years when the General presented himself as the most resolute defender of the Federal Republic against the pressure of the Soviet Union, though without appearing hostile to the USSR. Vis-à-vis Nikita Khrushchev, who visited France from March 23 until April 3, 1960, de Gaulle defended the Federal Republic and its desire for peace. But sometimes he also shocked the Germans, as when he stated during his press conference on March 25, 1959, that reunification in freedom was certainly "the normal destiny of the German people" but only on the condition that it "not question its present borders in the North, the South, the East and the West"; in other words, the Oder-Neisse line.

Respectfully received by the British parliament on April 5 and by the American Congress on April 25, 1960, de Gaulle had what may have been the most stunning success of his presidency on May 14 of the same year. This was the first day of the Four Power Conference, which he hosted in Paris and at which he appeared as the loyal ally of the United States, as a good friend of Great Britain, as a privileged partner in his dialogue with the Soviet Union, and simultaneously as the spokesman of the Federal Republic. This was the kind of situation which best corresponded to his global vision and yet did not necessitate the slightest conflict. But that vision dimmed with the immediate failure of the conference, for under the pretext that Soviet air space had been invaded by an American spy plane, Khrushchev broke it off. The framework of the Four had burst, and de Gaulle was once more confronted with the problem of France's standing in the West—and that at a moment when the USSR again seemed a threat.

ADENAUER, KENNEDY, AND BERLIN

Khrushchev's visit in France could not offend that country's American ally since the Soviet leader had already visited the United States in September 1959 and conferred for two days with General Eisenhower at Camp David. The topic of their discussions had been

German problems, notably the Berlin issue. The communiqué of September 27 had hinted that new negotiations on the fate of the city were to take place, and during the following two days, first Eisenhower and then Khrushchev stated that these negotiations would not be limited to a specific period of time.

At the time, two interpretations of these exchanges presented themselves. Since the matter did not seem urgent, the ultimatum of November 1958 in which Khrushchev had threatened to terminate the Four Power agreement on Germany and to sign a separate peace treaty with the DDR unless the Western powers immediately consented to a new status for West Berlin could be considered a thing of the past. It was to become an "independent political entity," and this was presented as a concession when compared to the "most correct solution," i.e., the incorporation of West Berlin into the DDR. But in Adenauer's and de Gaulle's interpretation, Eisenhower's willingness to enter negotiations in the first place already represented a retreat of the West, since any change in the status of Berlin would only come from unilateral Western concessions.

Was the spirit of détente to be allowed to increasingly undermine German positions? Already at the Geneva Big Four Conference of May-June and July-August 1959, the Federal Republic had had to accept a serious setback. Although it felt that there was only one German state, since the other political entity was merely the "Soviet-occupied zone" or Mitteldeutschland (to distinguish it from the former German lands in the east that had been annexed by Poland), its delegation of observers had been placed at a small table next to the conference table on the same side as the American delegation, while the observers from East Germany had sat at a table of the same size as the conference table on the side of the Soviet delegation. Were the Western powers about to forget their solemn obligations of October 3, 1954? At that time, the governments of the United States, France, and the United Kingdom had stated that they "considered the government of the Federal Republic as the only freely and legitimately constituted German government and therefore entitled to speak for Germany as the representative of the German people in international matters."

The declaration went on to say: "The security and well-being of Berlin and the maintenance of the positions of the three powers in that city are considered by them as essential elements of peace in the free world in the present international situation." And this was their version of the meaning of Article 2 of the treaty signed on October 23 concerning the relations between the Federal Republic and the Big Three: "In view of the international situation which has so far prevented the reunification of Germany and the conclusion of a peace treaty, the Three Powers retain the rights and obligations they have exercised to this point as regards Berlin and Germany as a whole."

Since November 1958, Khrushchev had been threatening the Western powers with nothing less than the unilateral termination of the Four Power agreement of 1944–45, the removal of West Berlin from Western responsibility, and the turning over of access routes to the city to the Ulbricht regime. Eisenhower and his advisers, torn between a desire for détente and the determination not to surrender anything of what they had, now felt the temptation to obtain guarantees for what they had, namely West Berlin, and to exchange them for juridical concessions in what they no longer had, i.e., the other German state and the border with Poland. Such a conception was unacceptable to both Adenauer and de Gaulle. Their consent to the summit of May 1960 was therefore contingent on the condition that the Western powers make no concessions, and this demand doomed the conference to failure from the start. Adenauer's stand appeared all the more rigid at that time, as a year earlier, in March 1959, the SPD had already presented a "Deutschlandplan" that had attracted considerable attention for advocating the rather utopian proposal that reunification in freedom should be brought about by negotiations on equal terms between the Federal Republic and the DDR and through the creation of a sort of Common Market for all of Germany.

The SPD plan was already dropped in 1960, but in view of the elections announced for September 1961, the Chancellor felt he had to prove that his inflexibility was being supported by the United States and that it would not affect chances for reunification, while the opposition reproached him for irrevocably sealing Germany's partition by his very rigidity. The Berlin drama of 1961 was played out against the background of this internal political dispute. And the protagonist in the Western camp was no longer Eisenhower but Kennedy, with whom Adenauer never established good relations.[13]

De Gaulle and Adenauer, the former discreetly, the other openly and thus shocking the American press, would rather have seen Richard Nixon elected. The German Chancellor wanted a maximum of continuity. In actuality, he found himself pushed aside as an old and wise councilor for the same reasons which were to make the young President popular both in America and Europe: the team of intellectuals around him was more sensitive to the changes than to the constants in the world and paid more attention to the continents undergoing rapid transformation than to the petrified situations in Europe. Kennedy had wanted to surround himself with "the best and the brightest",[14] and they really were full of ideas. But they were also

short on modesty and experience in affairs of state and their dilettan-
tism became apparent in the Berlin crisis. In a study published in
1969, the SPD leader Helmut Schmidt put the "intellectual arrogance" of certain cabinet members and associates of Kennedy on the
same plane as the "incorrigible and obstinate vanity of power" of de
Gaulle when he tried to explain the problems of the Western alliance
in the early 1960s.[15]

The Kennedy era began with a defeat. Because he approved a decision made by his predecessor in March 1960 and had confidence in
the CIA, the new President ordered an expedition against Fidel Castro's Cuba. In principle, the force was to consist entirely of Cubans.
The total and humiliating rout of this expedition in the Bay of Pigs
in April 1961, Schlesinger writes, had devastating consequences:

In western Europe I found widespread disenchantment. In the brief time
from the Inaugural to the Bay of Pigs, Kennedy had come to seem the last
hope of the West—a brilliant and exciting hope. He had conveyed an impression of United States foreign policy as mature, controlled, responsible and,
above all, intelligent. Western Europe in return had made a heavy political
and emotional investment in him. Now he suddenly seemed revealed as a
mere continuator of the Eisenhower-Dulles past. The New Frontier looked
like a collection not only of imperialists but of ineffectual imperialists. 'Kennedy is to be regarded as politically and morally defeated,' said the
Frankfurter Neue Presse. 'For the time being, Moscow has not only maintained but strengthened its outpost on the threshold of America.' 'In one day,'
said the *Corriere della Sera* of Milan, 'American prestige collapses lower than
in eight years of Eisenhower timidity and lack of determination.' . . . The
same sense of shock prevailed in Paris and London. 'It was a terrible blow,'
Lord Boothby said, 'and it will take a long, long time for us to recover from it.'
'It was a great blow,' Hugh Gaitskell said. 'The right wing of the Labour Party
has been basing a good deal of its argument on the claim that things had
changed in America. Cuba has made great trouble for us. We shall now have to
move toward the left for a bit to maintain our position within the party.' Yet, at
the same time, it was clear that the fund of goodwill toward Kennedy, though
somewhat dissipated, was far from destroyed, even on the democratic left.
Men like Ugo La Malfa of the Republican party and Fabio Cavazza, editor of *Il
Mulino* in Italy, Pierre Mendès-France and Jean-Jacques Servan-Schreiber in
Paris, as well as Gaitskell and R. H. S. Crossman in London, were sure that
Washington could achieve a quick comeback."[16]

In certain respects, the defeat was too ludicrous to destroy the
positive image of a Kennedy who had less narrow views about the
Cuban regime than his predecessors. But for many of the political and
intellectual left-wing forces in Europe, Fidel Castro was a sort of hero
of the good-natured, popular, and anti-imperialist socialism to which
the hopes disappointed by Tito during the 1950s had shifted. American policy toward him was seen much more negatively than it had

actually been at first when Castro had triumphantly entered Havana late in 1958. The Bay of Pigs expedition thus acted as a strong shock, but Kennedy's positive image quickly recovered.[17]

Among European governments, and particularly in London, the reputation of the American President soon rose to the highest levels, and in spite of differences in age and education, a surprising friendship developed between Kennedy and Macmillan. With de Gaulle too there was an auspicious beginning when John and Jackie Kennedy visited Paris from May 31 to June 2, 1961. But the conversations with Adenauer which took place on April 12 and 13 in Washington were not precisely marked by sympathy and mutual understanding. Was that because the one was forty-four, the other eighty-five years old? It was probably rather due to the fact that Kennedy saw his interlocutor as a survivor from another era, a man who was incapable of perceiving the changes in the world, and that Adenauer could not really bring himself to trust the President. But he himself did want to inspire trust, and when the German ambassador in Washington, Wilhelm Grewe, sent a telegram to Bonn at the end of May in which he cautiously criticized Kennedy in the name of the Chancellor's policy, Adenauer wrote a furious letter to his Foreign Minister, asking him to consider transferring the ambassador. Grewe was mistaken in his criticism, the Chancellor wrote, adding, "President Kennedy is an intelligent and farsighted man. He has good advisors . . . I am frightened and indignant about his [Grewe's] telegram and his judgment, however veiled it may be."[18]

The triangular situation between Kennedy, de Gaulle, and Adenauer in the spring of 1961 was rather odd. The German Chancellor felt close to the French President, although de Gaulle's ideas about the Western system were quite different. At the same time, he failed to impress Kennedy when he expressed a thought which really ought to have pleased the President, a thought which had already been stated in a preparatory letter by Heinrich von Brentano and was that central idea de Gaulle had rejected for France: from the global responsibilities of the United States there derive obligations for that country which are not to be submitted to consultations within the Atlantic Alliance—as in Indochina, for example. At most, one could participate in the struggle against Communism in Africa, Asia, and Latin America by providing development aid.[19] On the other hand, American leadership within NATO had been too restrained. The United States had to inject new life into that organization. Misunderstanding de Gaulle's policy, Adenauer told Kennedy that the paralysis of NATO was the reason the French President was turning away from it.[20]

The most important problem was in Europe, in any case. The pressure on Berlin continued, and the difficult meeting between Kennedy and Khrushchev on June 3 and 4 in Vienna certainly did nothing to alleviate it. In Washington, the President's advisers were divided. Dean Acheson pleaded for inflexibility, and Kennedy remained convinced that one had to negotiate. The Italian Prime Minister Fanfani and Foreign Minister Segni did not contradict him when he received them on June 13 before they traveled to Moscow early in August and let them know that he did not feel that the "opening toward the Left" in Italy, i.e., toward the Socialists, was a bad thing. In a press conference and a television address on July 19 and 25, Kennedy defined the three essentials on which the United States could make no concessions. They were the American presence in West Berlin, free access of the United States to that city, and the security of the population and their right to freely choose how they wished to live.

Was this a resolute attitude? Yes, insofar as it showed his determination to defend West Berlin. No, insofar as he did not discuss the rights of the Four Powers over all of the city. In other words, Kennedy seemed to leave the other side considerable freedom of movement in East Berlin.

The Soviet Union meanwhile had to come up with an answer to Walter Ulbricht's questions. What could be done to stop the stream of refugees, which was weakening the country he ran? Already in 1960, almost 200,000 Germans had gone to the West, 152,000 of them via Berlin, that being the most normal route. One could reach East Berlin without difficulty from any place in the DDR, since for the East German government, it was one and the same country. Then one went on to West Berlin, for in spite of its two administrations and two political systems, it was one and the same city as East Berlin. From there, one was taken to the Federal Republic by plane, for in many respects West Berlin was part of the Federal Republic and Air France, Pan Am, and British European Airways had free access. In 1961, the stream of refugees continued to mount. There were more than 30,000 in January and February, 21,000 of which escaped via Berlin. And there were 42,000 in March and April. Nor were these just old people or idlers whom the economy of the DDR—whose population was stagnant in any event—could do without. In 1960, 49 percent of the refugees were under twenty-five, and 23 percent between twenty-five and forty-five years of age. A large number of them were craftsmen or highly qualified technicians.

When the foreign ministers of the United States, Great Britain, France, and the Federal Republic convened in Paris from August 5 to 7 to prepare the measures to be taken in face of the Berlin crisis, the wave of refugees took on exceptional proportions: on August 6 alone, 2,305 persons arrived in West Berlin. What was surprising was the surprise of all the governments, in Bonn as in Washington, when on August 13 the demarcation line between the two parts of Berlin was suddenly transformed into an impenetrable barrier, with all the terrible consequences such a measure involved, especially within the city. Workers lost their jobs since they could no longer travel back and forth, families were torn apart, etc.[21]

No countermeasures of any sort were taken. While Adenauer was silent, indignation among Berliners raged from the *Bild Zeitung*'s outburst "The West does nothing," to the mayor's, the Social Democrat Willy Brandt, letter to Kennedy: "Inaction or merely defensive action could provoke a crisis of confidence in the Western powers." The vehemence of the letter made Kennedy bitter. Initially, he saw it as part of the German election campaign, but then decided on August 16 to send Vice-President Johnson and General Lucius Clay to Berlin. The latter had meanwhile become the chairman of a private concern but immediately declared his willingness to take temporary leave to help the people of Berlin once more. The following day, Kennedy answered Brandt's letter. He restated the guarantees for West Berlin and announced the dispatch of additional American troops, but also appealed to the mayor to see to it that peace and order were maintained along the new border, which could only be done away with by a war no one wanted.

On that same day, August 17, all three Western governments sent almost identical protest notes to the Soviet government. The analysis of the situation was firm:

All this is a flagrant and particularly serious violation of the quadripartite status of Berlin. . . . The boundary between the Soviet sector and the Western sectors of Berlin is not a State frontier. The U.S. Government considers that the measures which the East German authorities have taken are illegal. . . . Moreover, the U.S. Government cannot admit the right of the East German authorities to send their armed forces into the Soviet sector of Berlin. . . . It is to be noted that this declaration [i.e., of the Warsaw Pact powers of August 13] states that the measures taken by the East German authorities are "in the interests of the German people themselves." It is difficult to see any basis for this statement. . . . It is evident that no Germans, particularly those whose freedom of movement is being forcibly restrained, think this is so. This would be abundantly clear if all Germans were allowed a free choice and the principle of self-determination were applied in the Soviet sector of Berlin and in East Germany.

But no countermeasures were taken. During the course of his Berlin stay from August 19 to 21, Vice-President Johnson had nothing concrete to declare. The people of Berlin cheered him enthusiastically nonetheless.

During the course of the following weeks, it became increasingly clear that nothing would be attempted to prevent a complete partition of Berlin, although the French urged a hard line, as did General Clay, who was less and less listened to in Washington and finally returned there in May 1962, a bitter and disappointed man. December 9 saw the first tragic manifestation of the determination of the Western powers to do nothing outside the strictly defined borders of their sectors. Shot down by East German border guards during an escape attempt across the wall, a student went through a three-hour death struggle a few meters away from the British sector without anyone going to his aid. The case of the eighteen-year-old construction worker Peter Fechter was even more dramatic. He died on August 17, 1962, under identical circumstances, but this time outside the American sector.

In its detachment, the language of inaction was perfectly clear: as on June 17, 1953, in Berlin, as in 1956 in Budapest (and as later, in August 1968, in Prague), the Western superpower did not go beyond the containment as defined in 1947. Within its sphere of influence, the USSR had perfect freedom of action, and the Four Power responsibility for all of Berlin was of little consequence vis-à-vis the Soviet presence in East Berlin.

For Adenauer, this was a severe defeat. He had always maintained that his European and Atlantic policy was reconcilable with the efforts toward German reunification. August 13, 1961, proved that his method had failed in terms of the national problem. At the same time, untold illusions on both sides of the Wall crumbled. In the East, the regime was consolidated, if only because a large number of its citizens now resigned themselves to a government they would have preferred to see abolished. In the West, August 13 constituted the clearest break in the development of German foreign policy since 1949. From now on, a new policy had to be found if the abyss between the two Germanys was not to become deeper still and if one was not going to be excluded from the détente which was creating more and more openings between the two camps at the very moment the door between Germans and Germans slammed shut.

When Adenauer formed his fourth government after his relative lack of success at the polls on September 17, there was a significant change in the Foreign Ministry. Heinrich von Brentano, who had been convinced of the permanence of the Cold War and a loyal executor of the Chancellor's policy, was succeeded by Gerhard Schröder, who would soon show that he had other ideas and was willing to carry them out.

Relations between the German Chancellor and the American President continued to be troubled. But John F. Kennedy's image in Germany and especially in Berlin was a different matter. Never had the enthusiasm of the Berlin population been greater than during the visit he made there in June 1963, perhaps because de Gaulle had deliberately avoided Berlin during his triumphant tour through the Federal Republic in September 1962; but principally because Kennedy appealed to the masses with a warm-hearted speech which he concluded with the German words "Ich bin ein Berliner." He restated the unconditional American guarantee to the Federal Republic and West Berlin and also pleaded for contacts with the East and collaboration between the superpowers, though this was less well understood. But above all, his "I am a Berliner" created a misapprehension. The population of Berlin could assume that if the American President said something like that, it meant that he saw their city as the hub of world politics, whereas he actually perceived the Berlin problem as an irritant in his overall policy.

Kennedy's popularity remained enormous even after his tragic death on November 22, 1963, and indeed precisely because of it. Adenauer's prestige was first to suffer repeatedly before it consolidated itself in memory as that of the greatest German statesman of all time.[22] But in 1968, a year after his death, when the population of Berlin debated hotly if the Kaiserdamm should be renamed after him, his grandchild wrote in a letter to the *Frankfurter Allgemeine:* ". . . there is one point in which I will agree with you, and that concerns the frenzy to rename places after Kennedy. I consider it wholly unjustified and unworthy. If one asks about merit, and surely the merits involved here are those on behalf of Germany and Berlin, not America, there isn't much to be found in Kennedy except words. I assume here that Kennedy's real thoughts and intentions are known. I do not think it necessary to subject my grandfather to a comparison with Kennedy on that score."[23]

Kennedy's popularity in Europe proved lasting. In November 1977, on the occasion of a visit by President Carter, *L'Express* conducted a poll on the popularity of American postwar Presidents among the French public: Kennedy was an easy first with 68 percent. He was followed by Eisenhower with 8 percent, while the rest got 3 percent and 1 percent of the answers.[24] It is certainly true that the Dallas assassination transfigured John F. Kennedy, but there is something more profound in this popularity—perhaps above all the desire for a positive image of America. Positive, because it was young and looked toward the future, and was open and firm at the same time. And people saw the proof of this firmness in the Cuban crisis.

When, on October 28, 1962, Khrushchev announced the dismantling of Soviet missile launching pads which had been installed on the island at the very doorstep of the United States, everyone breathed a sigh of relief because the danger of a nuclear war seemed to have been averted and people admired the American President who had stood his ground in a poker game. But the governments deduced divergent consequences from the crisis. The Soviet Union stopped its threatening behavior, which it could do all the more easily since Kennedy had done everything to keep it from losing face and to continue his policy of creating openings. This led to that extended phase of détente which was initiated by the signing of the Soviet-Anglo-American Test Ban Treaty in Moscow on July 25, 1963. It also resulted in the "friendship treaty" between the USSR and the DDR which was signed on June 12, 1964, and which differed very clearly from a peace treaty: Its Article 9 expressly refers to the Potsdam agreement, i.e., the Four Power status of Germany. In a word, it said the opposite of what Khrushchev had announced in November 1958.

But did this mean that the United States would now enjoy a recognized superiority over the Soviet Union? American and German government circles did not take that view. Their reflections went something like this: Kennedy did not threaten Khrushchev with a nuclear retaliatory strike if he did not remove the missile bases but threatened an intervention with conventional forces, and Khrushchev could not counter this threat. He had no navy and no air force in the Caribbean, and the threat of a nuclear counterstrike would not have been credible since it would have implied the self-destruction of the USSR for the sake of a distant goal like Cuba. But as regards Berlin, the situation was and continues to be the reverse. At a place so far distant from the United States where one faces the clear-cut superiority of the USSR, the West is in a position of weakness and must continue to do everything to convince the Soviets of the seriousness of the American commitment and of the danger of an escalation in response to the most minor intervention in the West.

To de Gaulle, however, the resolution of the Cuban crisis proved American superiority, a superiority which was so unreservedly acknowledged by the Soviets that any genuine threat from their side came to an end. And this had to permit French policy to open up toward the East and to show more toughness toward the West. After the ending of the Algerian war in June, the Cuban crisis thus became the second factor that permitted de Gaulle in 1962 to take up more clearly defined positions toward the United States.

GREAT BRITAIN, THE "GRAND DESIGN," AND ALL-AROUND FAILURE

At the very time the Berlin Wall cemented German reality and ushered in the process which led to the recognition of that reality by

200 THE WESTERN ALLIANCE

the Federal Republic—i.e., the accepted permanence of the Eastern border of the European Common Market area—a new movement, a profound transformation of the West, seemed to set in. Between the end of June and early August 1961, first Great Britain and then Denmark, Ireland, and Norway announced their candidacy for accession to the European Common Market. On October 10, negotiations with the Six began. They promised to be long and difficult.

Harold Macmillan's decision had been taken against the opposition of the Labour Party and sizable segments of his own. Among the many, mutually contradictory arguments, those which concerned the nature of relations between Great Britain, Europe, and the United States occupied a special place. Was one going to dispense with a triangular situation in world trade and politics which appeared all the more justified since the United States, the European Common Market, and the sterling zone had divided up the larger part of world trade into roughly equal shares? But hadn't the sterling zone long since become a fiction, wasn't Great Britain weakened and therefore in no position to stay away from the EEC? Hadn't the United States neglected its British ally since the beginnings of the Common Market and favored the European unity that was being formed? But wasn't it also true that the idea of European integration had an "anti-American flavor"?[25] And if this was particularly so since de Gaulle's accession, wouldn't Great Britain's membership change all that?

It was in part this last argument that prompted President Kennedy to launch the idea of a reorganization of transatlantic relationships, which then took on the spectacular form of a "grand design." But only in part: the book by that title is based on different considerations. For the author, it was a matter of urging his countrymen to see the abolition of customs tariffs through negotiations between the United States and a genuine European partner as an important national concern and not merely the concern of one part of the nation (as in France, for example, where "the Common Market Treaty was put through by the combined efforts of an arch-capitalist, Jean Monnet; an arch-Catholic, Robert Schuman; and an anti-clerical arch-socialist, Guy Mollet"[26]). For such an abolition of customs barriers seemed necessary if the American economy, the Western economy, and indeed the world economy were going to develop.

Kennedy's address in Independence Hall in Philadephia on July 4, 1962, did in fact mark a halfway point between a bill which had been introduced in January and would give the President authority to lower tariffs and the announcement of the Trade Expansion Act on October 11. But the central phrase of the speech to which it owed its exceptional resonance had a wholly different scope: "But I will say here and now, on this Day of Independence, that the United States will be ready for a declaration of interdependence, that we will be prepared to discuss with a United Europe the ways and means of forming a concrete Atlantic partnership, a mutually beneficial partnership between the new union now emerging in Europe and the old American union founded here 173 years ago."

The idea of a "partnership" between the United States and a powerful Europe as a presupposition for the best possible future of the Atlantic community had already been publicly expressed in December by McGeorge Bundy, one of the President's closest advisers. And in a speech entitled "Toward an Atlantic Partnership," another adviser, George Ball, had pointed out in February 1962 how closely this idea corresponded to the aim of the builders of Europe, among whom he had good reason to count himself (see Chapter 4). He stated: "As long as Europe remained fragmented, as long as it consisted merely of nations small by modern standards, the potentials for true partnership were always limited. It was in recognition of this fact that since the war we have consistently encouraged the powerful drive toward European integration. We have wanted a Europe united and strong that could serve as an equal partner in the achievement of our common endeavors—as an equal partner committed to the same basic values and objectives as all Americans."[27] The Action Committee for the United States of Europe had expressed the same idea in a statement which had been published on June 26, eight days before Kennedy's Philadelphia speech: "The Action Committee which comprises the vast majority of the political parties of our six countries as well as the free and Christian trade unions representing ten million workers is of the opinion that only through the economic and political unification of Europe, including the United Kingdom, and the establishment of a partnership of equals between Europe and the United States can the West be strengthened and the conditions created for peace between East and West."[28]

A strong, associated Europe on an equal footing with the United States: at first glance, it might seem as if there existed no essential difference between the visions of Monnet and de Gaulle, for hadn't the latter declared when he toasted President Lübke in Bonn on September 4: "Union! Why union [between France and Germany]? First of all, because we are both directly threatened . . . and then, because the alliance of the free world, in other words, the mutual obligation of Europe and America, can only maintain its self-confidence and solidarity over the long term if there exists on the old continent a bulwark of power and prosperity that is similar to that of the United States on the new continent."

Actually, there was ambivalence here, in part because the General did not really want an equal and united Europe. The Italian ambassador in Paris was probably not altogether wrong when he confidentially told an American journalist: "De Gaulle sees clearly that Britain's membership in the Common Market will completely change the kind of Europe he wants. It would be dominated by Britain and Germany instead of by France with German support."[29] Besides, unification with its unavoidable limitation on national autonomy would—if it were acceptable at all—make sense only between countries sharing the same vision, and that meant de Gaulle's vision of the independence Europe would have to manifest vis-à-vis the United States.[30]

But the ambivalence lies principally in the concept of "partnership." In everyday speech and in the language of sports, the term refers to individuals temporarily joining forces in a deal or a game. In American legal and commercial terminology, the term designates an association of partners who run a joint enterprise. And a clearly defined hierarchy can certainly exist between these partners. For de Gaulle, the community of interests and ideas between Europe and the United States was only partial, only defensive. Above all, Europe must not be a "junior partner," least of all in so central a problem as defense. Instead, it had to unite without reference to the desires of the great ally and certainly could not have a permanent partnership with it. Such a position weakened Kennedy's in the United States, since even more than during the late 1950s, people there now began to wonder whether such a "a united and powerful Europe [would] continue to be a friendly partner of the United States and thus add to Western strength? Or would transatlantic relations become antagonistic and hostile, thus producing a fatal weakness in the Western position?"[31]

The complicated negotiations over the Fouchet Plan and its failure were inseparably tied to these ambivalences. The way an eventual political union was to be organized was just a partial aspect of the discussions which started after de Gaulle's press conference of September 5, 1960, in the course of which he had proposed a collaboration between the states. The question as to the form relations between Europe and the United States were to take in the future and the further question of Great Britain's accession to the EEC took up an equally important place in the conferences and negotiations which dragged on until April 1962.[32]

Already at the meeting of the six heads of state or government on February 10, 1961, in Paris, a conflict developed, though not between de Gaulle and the other five but between Dutch Foreign Minister Joseph Luns and all the other delegations. Although the Dutch statesman certainly did not represent the unanimous view of his nation in matters of foreign policy, his was the decisive voice in successive cabinets from 1956 to 1971, when he became secretary-general of NATO.[33] In 1961, his position within Europe was not unlike de Gaulle's within NATO: he called for equality with the great powers which were supported by other small ones. His demands were and remained contradictory: Europe had to be "supranational," and Great Britain would have to be part of it although that country resisted supranationality. Supranationality and the membership of Great Britain, however, were only a means to make impossible a Europe as de Gaulle conceived it, i.e., a Europe based on the joint predominance of France and the Federal Republic. That the Dutch fight in favor of NATO was led with such vigor was due in part to the fact that the distant superpower, the United States, was perceived as less oppressive than the neighboring medium-sized powers and their striving for dominance in Europe.

The decision was made to set up a study commission which would submit proposals to the six EEC countries. The former French minister and then ambassador to Denmark, Christian Fouchet, was elected its president. On July 18, 1961, the Six agreed to the joint "Bad Godesberg Declaration," which was to give rise to many quickly disappointed hopes. In it, the heads of state or government expressed their conviction "that only a united Europe that would be allied with the United States and other free nations would be in the position to counter the dangers which threatened the existence of Europe and of the entire free world," a formula which obliged no one to undertake anything of consequence. On October 19, the French plan was submitted to the Fouchet commission. This "Fouchet Plan" was a "draft treaty for the establishment of a union of states" in which the contracting parties declared their willingness "to admit other European countries which are ready to accept the same responsibilities and the same duties." In principle, there was nothing supranational about the planned union of states, since it was to be based on unanimity in all matters. But its goal was to be the adoption of a common foreign and defense policy. In the course of the tough negotiations this proposal gave rise to, Paul-Henri Spaak switched sides and joined Joseph Luns in a threefold battle for supranationality, Great Britain's immediate participation in the preparation of the plan, and the emphasis on Atlantic relations, the last two points finally taking on greater importance than the first. Belgian and Dutch inflexibility in turn prompted de Gaulle to go back on his earlier concessions. "Fouchet Plan II" (actually, it was the third), which was presented on January 18, 1962, went less far than the first draft and served its enemies as a reason or pretext for extending their opposition to the entire enterprise. Three months later, the six foreign ministers announced failure and went home.

If April 17, 1962, is "a decisive date in the history of European politics,"[34] it is so principally because it revealed a conflict concerning the kind of Europe to be created. At the very moment Paul-Henri Spaak published an article in a French periodical in which he wrote, "An integrated Europe must not and cannot have the will to become a third world power,"[35] de Gaulle ridiculed the idea of supranationality in a press conference on May 15. For it is nations that are the political reality. But there was also a second reason. In such an integrated Europe, there would perhaps be no policy at all, " . . . but then, perhaps, it would follow the lead of some outsider who did have a policy. There would perhaps be a federator, but the federator would not be European."

The failure of the Fouchet negotiations was to harden the General's attitude, and all the more so as the development of the military problems seemed not only to demonstrate the bad will of the United States in the question of partnership but also revealed the inability of Great Britain to really decide in favor of a European solidarity that would clearly differ from a transatlantic one.

What could equal "partnership" mean for de Gaulle after the American Secretary of Defense Robert McNamara had presented his strategic conception for NATO at the meeting of the NATO Council in Athens in early May, and that without any prior consultation? And he had also emphasized once more that the United States did not want the development of a nuclear force which would not be at the disposal or under the control of the United States. In the fall of that same year, and after Kennedy's address, McGeorge Bundy and George Ball said the same things publicly in Europe.[36] On July 20, General Norstad submitted his resignation as commander-in-chief because he had been refused permission to set up a nuclear force that would be distinct from the American.* In June, McNamara annoyed all the European partners by trying to force them to buy missiles which would remain under American control, and Prime Minister Macmillan punned maliciously in his notebook: "This is not a European rocket. It's a racket of the American industry."[37] Both commercial and political concerns came together here. Sulzberger had already written in April that General Gavin, the American ambassador in Paris, "is haunted by a fear that Macmillan is going to offer de Gaulle nuclear aid in ex-

---

* On the development of American strategy, see Chapter 8.

change for his OK on England joining the Market. This will leave the U.S.A. on a hook and getting no benefit from the orders for nuclear equipment."[38]

The British attitude was actually rather contradictory, and this not only because of conflicts between the government and the opposition but also—and this was more unusual—because of conflicts within the conservative government itself. The Minister of Defense, Peter Thorneycroft, was a "European" who was not opposed to a "Europeanization" of defense, including nuclear weapons.[39] Would it really be possible to achieve all of these things: obtain admission to the EEC, maintain privileged relations with the United States in atomic matters, and retain an independent nuclear force within this framework?

Toward the end of the 1950s, the British nuclear force had been added onto an outdated arsenal. When the project of an English nuclear missile proved too costly, Macmillan had, in March 1960, obtained Eisenhower's consent to Great Britain's purchase of the American Skybolt as soon as it went into production. Since Skybolt would be fired from planes and thus differed from the Polaris, which had to be installed on submarines, the bombers of the Royal Air Force could continue to be used. But did it make sense to bank on a vulnerable air force when the projected nuclear submarines were going to be practically invulnerable? Eisenhower's Secretary of Defense did not feel that it did, and cancelled the Skybolt program.

His successor Robert McNamara initially started it up again but then decided to stop it, without realizing that in the meantime Skybolt had become a symbol of independence in Great Britain, especially since in exchange for the promise to provide it, the Scottish naval base Holy Loch had already been placed at the disposal of the American submarine fleet. The decision to cancel the program was delayed for reasons relating to the internal decision-making process of the Americans. Poorly worded hints were not understood in London. And when McNamara visited the city on December 11 and presented Peter Thorneycroft with the *fait accompli* (though stating his readiness to negotiate an alternative solution), this happened at a moment when British newspapers and parties were indignant over a speech his predecessor, Dean Acheson, had given at West Point on December 6. Here, the former Secretary of Defense had stated: "Great Britain has lost an empire and has not yet found a role." Since neither the "special relationship" with the United States nor a structureless and powerless Commonwealth any longer made sense, he had emphatically called on it to join Europe. In answer to a protest by diverse British personalities, the Prime Minister wrote at the time: "Mr. Acheson has fallen into an error which has been made by quite a lot of people in the course of the last four hundred years, including Philip of Spain, Louis XIV, Napoleon, the Kaiser and Hitler."[40]

American assurances that Acheson's views did not reflect those of the government did nothing to improve the atmosphere of disarray in London when Macmillan left to meet de Gaulle in Rambouillet. On December 15 and 16, he asked that Great Britain be admitted to the EEC, while the legal and economic aspects of this accession continued to be laboriously negotiated in Brussels. In the flush of the victory he had just won in the referendum establishing the election of the President of the Republic by universal suffrage, de Gaulle showed himself both benevolent and much more negative than prior to the failure of the Fouchet Plan.[41] No common perspectives resulted, and this all the less so since the fate of the British nuclear force had been made contingent on the decisions which the American President and the British Prime Minister would make during their planned meeting in Bermuda on December 18.

The Nassau Conference was unquestionably the most difficult of all Anglo-American meetings of the postwar era—in part because it had been poorly prepared and got off to a bad start, in part because the American partner, still suffused with the glow of his most recent success in the Cuban crisis, saw himself facing an ever more controversial British head of government, and finally because the problems to be discussed were exceptionally thorny. For Kennedy, it was a matter of pushing Macmillan toward Europe, which meant that Great Britain could not be granted too many privileges, though he was ready to help him calm the anti-American furor in London. He also had to permit England a nuclear force of its own, yet place it under American control. Macmillan, on the other hand, was anxious to boost his prestige without offending de Gaulle.

A long communiqué, accompanied by an even longer statement on nuclear defense systems, was issued on December 21, 1962.[42] The signatories affirmed the necessity to develop a multilateral NATO nuclear force. The United States would place Polaris missiles without warheads at Great Britain's disposal which that country would install on submarines of its own construction and provide with warheads it would manufacture itself. These submarines would be integrated in the NATO forces. The Prime Minister clarified that British forces developed under the plans discussed "will be used for the purposes of international defense of the Western alliance in all circumstances except where her Majesty's Government may decide that supreme national interests are at stake."

The same system was also offered de Gaulle. While Kennedy believed he would accept it after tough negotiations, Macmillan rightly feared that however de Gaulle might feel about its contents, he would reject it because it had been worked out bilaterally. There was the additional circumstance that France did not as yet have submarines under construction which could accommodate the Polaris missile. Finally, and above all, it was felt in Paris that the passage dealing with exceptional cases was an empty formula. "The Anglo-American Bahamas agreement," the French Foreign Minister later wrote, "illustrated the fact that the ideas people had about the future Europe on this and the other side of the Channel were unfortunately at odds the moment the time for practical action arrived. The difference between a nuclear force as part of NATO and a national nuclear force is the difference between an Atlantic Europe and a European Europe."[43]

On January 14, 1963, in a press conference that was to have weighty consequences, de Gaulle spoke at length about the Nassau pact and set forth his negative interpretation. But most important, he said no to Great Britain. Among the many reasons he gave for his rejection, there was the idea that Great Britain's accession to the EEC would be followed by that of many other countries, which would mean that Europe would lose its cohesion and "turn into a gigantic Atlantic Community that would be dependent on and be run by America and absorb the European Community."

On January 23, the Chancellor and the General solemnly signed a treaty in Paris which would bring about closer Franco-German collaboration. Adenauer had not been too severely affected by the rejection of Great Britain and welcomed de Gaulle's desire to create his own nuclear force, although he asked him to understand that the Federal Republic could not refuse to participate in a multilateral organization.[44] But this attitude was shared neither by his Foreign Minister Gerhard Schröder nor by the other leaders of the governing party or the Social Democratic opposition, all of whom had wanted admission of Great Britain and were now upset with the General. And the manner in which Maurice Couve de Murville terminated the Brussels negotiations with Great Britain in late January increased their irritation.[45]

This irritation expressed itself during the parliamentary debate on the ratification of the treaty in the unanimous adoption of a preamble in which the Bundestag stated its willingness

to promote by the application of this treaty the great aims which the Federal Republic together with the states allied with it has striven for for years, and which govern its policy, namely the preservation and strengthening of the union of free nations, especially of a close partnership between Europe and the United States of America — the implementation of the right of self-determination of the German people and the reestablishment of German unity — the common defense in the framework of the North Atlantic Alliance and the integration of the armed forces of the states in this alliance — the unification of Europe along the path taken with the creation of the European Community including the admission of Great Britain and of other states willing to accede, and the further strengthening of this Community — the abolition of trade barriers through negotiations between the European Economic Community, Great Britain and the United States as well as other states within the framework of GATT.

In short, an inventory which apparently went counter de Gaulle's policy. And the French President certainly understood the import of this text which changed the meaning *he* wanted to give the treaty and his entire Franco-German policy. During a press conference on October 28, 1966, he stated: "It is not our fault if the preferred and permanent ties Bonn has contracted with Washington have deprived this Franco-German treaty of its spirit and substance. . . . Our neighbors beyond the Rhine . . . did not apply our bilateral treaty but the unilateral preamble which completely changes its meaning and which they added on their own initiative."

After all this, it can be said that Kennedy's "grand design" died on January 14, 1963, in Paris, and that de Gaulle's "grand ambition"—the creation of a Europe on the basis of German support for French policy—failed in Bonn on May 8. Adenauer and Macmillan had to surrender power in October, and Kennedy was murdered a month later: 1963 had turned out to be a ghastly year. What survived it was economic in nature: the Common Market with six partners whose development progressed, and the "Kennedy Round," that important negotiation within the framework of GATT which had resulted from the American Trade Expansion Act to which the *Bundestag* had alluded in its preamble quoted above and which would finally and after many difficulties attain success.

8 THE TRANSATLANTIC ECONOMY AND VIETNAM

DE GAULLE'S OFFENSIVE

Beginning in 1963, de Gaulle's attitude toward the United States hardened. It attained its greatest rigidity in 1967, when one might justifiably have called it a fixed idea.[1] His irritation at Lyndon Johnson's America was certainly a factor. Because neither of them wanted to take the first step, the two Presidents met only twice, the first time at John F. Kennedy's burial, the second at Konrad Adenauer's in April 1967. As early as August 1963, however, the French ambassador in Washington had jotted in his notebook: "The situation has probably never been this confused, and never before have the misunderstandings between France and the U.S. been as profound. De Gaulle is filled with the deepest mistrust because he fears both the hegemony of the U.S. and its disengagement."[2] In fact, it was not just mistrust but a mixture of resentments and clear-sighted analyses, of the will toward self-affirmation and mythical vision. It was a thirst for action, the feeling of being confined by the United States, and the certainty that he risked nothing if he opposed that country.

The resentment surfaced in the General's dramatic absence from the great ceremonies on the twentieth anniversary of the Allied landings in Normandy,[3] though at that time his public criticism of the United States was still moderate. During the course of his trip to Latin America in September and October 1964, he did not mention America in his speeches to the enthusiastic crowds. But the important themes he did speak of, such as the solidarity of Latin-speaking peoples, the possibility of economic aid without political interference, and the rejection of all hegemony, would have emerged much more clearly if—as his advisers had suggested—he had spoken more in the name of an economically strong Europe than in that of a France whose means were limited.

But those limited means did not keep him from sounding his sensational "Long live Free Quebec" to the tumultuous crowds in Montreal on July 24, 1967. For he was addressing a Quebec which was filled with a "widespread anxiety caused by the ever-increasing hold of the Anglo-Saxons" in a Canada which was apprehensive lest it become "an appendage of the giant neighbor across the great lake," as the General had noted during his first visit in 1960.[4]

Already in 1963, the criticism of American Vietnam policy had been barely veiled, but the first dramatic diplomatic comment on a U.S. action was made during the American intervention in Santo Domingo in April–May 1965. The triumvirate of generals that had been wielding power there had been overthrown by officers loyal to the former President, Juan Bosch. Part of the army having taken sides against them, President Johnson decided to send his marines to prevent Bosch's return. For although Bosch and his revolutionary party were certainly no Communists, they allegedly stood under Castro's influence. In the U.N. Security Council, this American view was only feebly supported by the delegate of the British Labour government, while the French ambassador, Roger Seydoux, clearly distanced himself from it. On May 6, after a cabinet session, de Gaulle made known that "France disapproved of the American intervention and desired the withdrawal of American troops." Two weeks later, the Security Council unanimously passed a short French resolution which demanded that the temporary armistice in Santo Domingo be made permanent. Earlier, the Security Council had rejected a Soviet text, the United States, Great Britain, Nationalist China, the Netherlands, Bolivia, and Uruguay voting against, and France, the Ivory Coast, Malaysia, and Jordan abstaining.

In this affair, France paraded as the spokesman of the Third World and the moderate opponent of the United States because it intervened against governments it did not like on the American continent. At the same time, American advocates of this intervention recalled that France had acted in Gabon under very similar circumstances the year before, and even Americans critical of their President viewed the French position less as a positive expression than as a kind of retaliation for the stand the United States had adopted in the U.N. during the affairs in which France had been involved in the course of decolonization.

Compared with the Vietnam War, whose prolongation and indeed existence de Gaulle increasingly blamed on the United States, the Santo Domingo expedition was a minor episode. But the subject of Vietnam became increasingly central as it was tied to criticisms or actions in other areas, especially that of economic and monetary relations, for the shaky dollar and the considerable difficulties this created for everyone were inseparably connected with the expenditures caused by the war (see below). It was more surprising that in his comment on the Arab-Israeli conflict in June 1967, de Gaulle should have reminded his listeners of it: "One conflict always produces the next. The war in Vietnam which has been unleashed by American intervention . . . will necessarily cause unrest elsewhere." This statement, which was put out after the cabinet session of June 2, a few days after the Israeli victory, provoked strong reactions.

De Gaulle's critical attitude toward Israel was certainly not entirely attributable to his global criticism of the United States, but it was connected with it. In the first place, because the Six Day War had demonstrated the weakness of France as compared to the real powers. What could it possibly mean to the Foreign Minister of Israel that de Gaulle should promise that France would never permit the destruction of his country? The French proposal for a Four Power conference to resolve the conflict was not taken up because the United States and the USSR alone attempted to limit the consequences of the war.[5] The second reason was that French Arab policy as resumed after the war in Algeria wore a special aspect for de Gaulle, which he explained once to a journalist during a discussion on Arab civilization: "If we wish to create around this Mediterranean—the cradle of great cultures—an industrial civilization which does not follow the American model and in which man is not merely means but purpose and aim, then our cultures have to open up toward each other."[6] For him, Israel was more or less a reflection of the United States. The bitter tone he took in 1967 can perhaps be partly explained by his disappointment that the twofold reorientation of the preceding year had brought so few successes. The development of the Mideast crisis proved that neither the dramatic rapprochement with the Soviet Union nor the dramatic withdrawal from the Atlantic organization had really changed France's international standing. For the failure of the policy toward Germany in 1963 had led to a kind of reversal of the yardstick by which the order of rank vis-à-vis the United States was determined. French recognition of the People's Republic of China in January 1964 implied the idea of a certain symmetry: the relations that were established between Paris and Peking could be viewed as the expression of similar aspirations for independence within both camps. The rapprochement of the two superpowers as symbolized by the 1963 Test Ban Treaty was welcome only if it did not strengthen a joint domination over the rest. Thus France's opening toward the Soviet Union was a further means to prevent the feared tête-à-tête of the two superpowers, and at the same time a gentle pressure was exerted on the Federal Republic because it was clearly too submissive toward the United States.

After increasingly frequent contacts between Paris and Moscow in

1964 and 1965, de Gaulle's trip to the USSR from June 20 to July 1, 1966, represented the climax of what was largely just a dream: if Russia were not the Soviet Union, if Communism were to disappear in Eastern Europe ... The phrase with which de Gaulle opened his address on Soviet television was typical: "My visit to your country is a visit of eternal France to eternal Russia." Only such a myth permitted as generous a vision as was put forth during the press conference on February 4, 1965, in particular: "Europe, the mother of modern civilization, must attempt to develop its immense resources from the Atlantic to the Urals in harmony and cooperation. In this way, and together with America, its child, it will then play its appropriate role in the progress of two billion people who are so much in need of it." ·

Meanwhile, the strategic organization of the Atlantic Alliance was an object of conflict not only between Paris and Washington. Before as after January 14, 1963, the history of the Multilateral Force which began in 1960 was also filled with tension and opposition between the American and European governments. Were the nuclear submarines of the various nations to be made a European weapon which could be employed without U.S. consent? Would Germany's participation be tantamount to a recognition of the Federal Republic as a nuclear power? The confusion was all the greater because, with the possible exception of Norway and Denmark, which had voted against it from the very beginning,[7] all participants in the discussion were quarreling with each other.[8] In Great Britain, the Labour Party, which had returned to power in October 1964, had as many reservations about the Multilateral Force as the Conservative Party. Harold Wilson, who had become head of the party in February 1963 after Gaitskell's death, did accept the Polaris legacy but decided at the same time that the nuclear submarines would have to be wholly placed under NATO and that there would be no British "nuclear pretence."[9]

In the Federal Republic, the Multilateral Force was viewed as a kind of consolation for the subordinate role vis-à-vis France and Great Britain, although it had to be foreseen that one would share a greater part of the cost without receiving any more say-so than the smaller countries. Within the CDU/CSU, Adenauer and Franz Josef Strauss fought the position of Chancellor Ludwig Erhard and Foreign and Defense Ministers Gerhard Schröder and Kai Uwe von Hassel, who felt that the Multilateral Force would have to be accepted since that was what the Americans wanted, while Washington believed that it was necessary to give the Germans this dreary satisfaction. After finally taking up the problem, President Johnson discovered in December 1964 that the Senate was against it (no sharing of atomic secrets!), that the new Wilson government had other ideas, and that opinion among the Germans was divided. He put an end to the undertaking, and this naturally embittered its advocates in Bonn, who were thus being disavowed and even made ridiculous.[10] In compensation, a "Nuclear Planning Group" was set up within NATO in which the Federal Republic would be a permanent member.

But the Multilateral Force was only one aspect of German-American problems in strategic questions. General de Gaulle's procedure almost made one forget that "the real conflict of national interest built into the Atlantic Alliance pits the German Federal Republic against the United States. Both want to prevent any war, big or little; but Germany, on the front lines, is reluctant to accept a strategy which, by reducing the chances of escalation, increases those of minor aggression, while the United States, removed by several thousand miles from the potential theater of ground operations, is determined to prevent escalation even at the cost of what, from that distance, appear to be mere minor skirmishes."[11] Such a situation provoked widely differing reactions in the governing party in Germany. Some of the Christian Democrats once again joined Strauss against Schröder, who was rather close to the Social Democratic opposition.[12]

While these debates had a lasting effect on Franco-German relations, they barely influenced the decision de Gaulle made in 1966. Its motivations, its presentation, its implementation and consequences, were so largely political that one might even say that the French withdrawal from NATO had little to do with military policy.[13] The letter de Gaulle sent President Johnson on March 7, 1966, and which was published immediately, emphasized the distinction between the alliance and the organization and announced the withdrawal of France from the latter:

Our Atlantic Alliance will in three years' time complete its first term. I wish to tell you that France is aware to what extent the defensive solidarity thus established between 15 free Western nations contributes to ensure their security, and especially of the essential role played in this respect by the United States of America. France therefore plans, as of now, to remain, when the time comes, a party to the Treaty signed on April 4, 1949, in Washington. This means that, unless in the three coming years events change the basic facts directing East-West relations, she would, in 1969 and beyond, be determined, as today, to fight on the side of her Allies in the event that one of them should be the object of an unprovoked aggression. Nevertheless, France considers that the changes which have taken place since 1949, or are now taking place, in Europe, Asia and elsewhere, as well as the development of her own situation and forces, do not justify, as far as she is concerned, the arrangements of a military nature made after the conclusion of the Alliance either in common in the form of multilateral conventions or by special agreements between the French and the American Governments.

This is why France is determined to regain on her whole territory the full exercise of her sovereignty, at present diminished by the permanent presence of Allied military elements or by the use which is made of her air space; to cease her participation in the integrated Commands: and no longer to place her forces at the disposal of NATO.

Regarding the application of these decisions, it goes without saying that she is ready to determine with the Allied Governments, and above all that of the United States, the practical measures concerning them. Furthermore, she is ready to reach agreement with them as to the military facilities to be accorded mutual use in the event of a conflict in which she would take part on their side, and as to conditions of co-operation between her forces and theirs in the event of common action, especially in Germany.

On all these points my Government will therefore establish contacts with yours. But, in order to comply with the spirit of friendly frankness which must inspire relations between our two countries, and . . . between yourself and myself, I wanted, first of all, personally to tell you what were the reasons . . . for which purposes, and within which limitations, France had considered herself compelled to modify the form of our Alliance, without altering its substance.

In his answer, President Johnson expressed his regret over the unilateral character of the decision, affirmed after consultation with the other fourteen members of NATO that they did not have the same view of their interests as the present French government, and added, "I am puzzled by your view that the presence of Allied military forces on French soil impairs the sovereignty of France. These forces have been there at French invitation pursuant to a common plan to help ensure the security of France and her Allies."

But it was precisely this presence that seemed the fundamental problem to de Gaulle, for the other one, the integration of national military forces in NATO, was largely a secondary issue since such integration was always only provisional and revocable in peacetime (except in the case of the German forces). Neither France in Indochina and later Algeria, nor Great Britain in its dispatch of troops to Malaysia, nor Greece and Turkey in their threat to annihilate each other on account of Cyprus, had found any difficulty providing the necessary forces and arms. But the presence of NATO meant inter-Allied general staffs, military bases, depots, and pipelines.[14] To put an end to all this, de Gaulle took rather drastic measures. A "calendar" which was sent to the Allied governments at the end of March set the date, July 1, 1966, by which the withdrawal of France was to be completed, and April 1 of the following year as the day by which the general staffs, installations, and depots of the Allied forces would have to be moved out of France—and that, it might be added, without any compensation for fixed installations from which France would benefit. All existing agreements, both those that had been made public and those kept secret up to this time but now published by the American government and whether signed under the Fourth or the Fifth Republic, were partly terminated, partly ignored.

The Americans did not fight back. President Johnson wrote later:

Many people expected me to denounce the French leader's move and to resist his disruptive tactics, but I had long since decided that the only way to deal with De Gaulle's fervent nationalism was by restraint and patience. He would not remain in power forever, and I felt sure that the fundamental common interests and friendship of our two nations would survive. To have attacked De Gaulle would only have further enflamed French nationalism and offended French pride. It would also have created strains among the nations of the European Common Market and complicated their domestic politics. As I told Bob McNamara, when a man asks you to leave his house, you don't argue; you get your hat and go. McNamara and our military leaders moved U.S. bases out of France with magnificent efficiency. While NATO headquarters was being shifted to Brussels, our other allies carried on their responsibilities to the alliance with quiet determination.[15]

As a consequence of the March 7 decision, the most serious foreign policy parliamentary debates of the Fifth Republic took place between April 13 and 20. Prime Minister Pompidou and Foreign Minister Couve de Murville developed the theses of the President of the Republic with precision: The Foreign Minister stated, "At bottom, this is a change in the relationships between the U.S. and Europe." Both speakers mentioned the danger that members of NATO might become involved in a nuclear war in Asia. To which René Pleven replied, "Assuming the outbreak of a conflict between China and America in Asia, why should NATO become involved since the area covered by the treaty is limited to Europe and the North Atlantic? Did NATO become involved in the Korean War? And when we engaged ourselves in Indochina, NATO was certainly not dragged into the conflict. You yourself keep insisting that nuclear weapons are only good for deterrence and that since Russia has acquired atomic weapons which are capable of a direct strike against the U.S., the Americans would no longer use this weapon to protect any of their allies. How then can you maintain at the same time that the U.S. would not use them to protect Europe but would to defend South Vietnam or to attack China?"

A central criticism was expressed by Guy Mollet: "The best guarantee for American engagement and thereby against any attack on Europe lies in the physical presence of Americans on our continent." To which Maurice Faure added: "The French government demands the withdrawal of American troops from France. If all our European NATO allies did the same, where on the continent would American forces remain? . . . If the Atlantic Pact had already existed in 1940, the situation would certainly have been better, but if NATO had already existed at that time, there would have been no war."

Actually, de Gaulle never expressed the desire that American troops leave Europe altogether. What was valid for France was not valid for Germany, and since the Federal Republic luckily lay between France and the USSR, the mechanism of American protection through the presence of troops on European soil did not change. And this very presence also kept the German neighbor in a state of inferiority.

Outside of political circles the effects were barely felt, although de Gaulle had weathered a difficult reelection just a few months earlier. To the question "Do you agree with de Gaulle's policy toward the United States or not?" the answers varied significantly but not dramatically:[16]

	May 1962	Jan. 1963	Sept. 1965	April 1966
Yes	32%	47%	46%	41%
No	15%	17%	21%	29%
No opinion	53%	36%	33%	30%

In the other countries, there was considerable agitation, and disapproval was almost universal. In Germany, the French decision was felt to be all the more shocking and irritating, as neither the government nor the opposition wanted to be confronted with the necessity of deciding between Washington and Paris, and should they have to do so, it was clear that their choice would be Washington.[17] The disquiet increased when de Gaulle's trip to the Soviet Union was announced. But finally the General succeeded in convincing Chancellor Erhard of the firmness of his ties to the West—though not without severely testing the German government in December by affronting them in the question of the status of French units that would remain in Germany after his withdrawal from NATO.

In Great Britain, the problem of defense quickly lost importance as the plan for renewed candidacy for admission to the Common Market came up. In January 1967, Harold Wilson visited the French President and had to submit to questions about Great Britain's attitude toward the United States. "The whole situation would be very different if France were genuinely convinced that Britain really was disengaging from the U.S. in all major matters such as defence policy and in areas such as Asia, the Middle East, Africa and Europe," the British Prime Minister wrote later.[18]

In early May, the British candidacy became official. A few days later, General de Gaulle ended a press conference with the statement that Great Britain was not yet ready for the Common Market and that its admission "would lead to the creation of an Atlantic zone which would deprive our continent of any real character." There was a second rejection in December. Among the reasons not explicitly given was also the one Harold Wilson had already quite clearly recognized in April when he was subjected to a kind of test by Georges Pompidou, Maurice Couve de Murville, and the economic expert Jacques Rueff, during which only Finance Minister Valéry Giscard d'Estaing, who was at odds with the others, had supported him: "It was clear that I had failed to pass the examiners. I had not, at least not yet, shown the degree of economic perception qualifying me for entry to the anti-American, anti-liquidity gold club."[19]

AMERICAN CHALLENGES

The Franco-American confrontation over the monetary system was only one aspect of transatlantic economic problems. Their dramatization came primarily though not wholly from France. While increasing prosperity was creating a calm climate in which it might be hoped that obstacles perceived as secondary could be jointly resolved in a common development,[20] it was also true that Europe's economic upswing and its growth, which was considerably more rapid than that of the United States, also made inequality much more difficult to bear. The smaller the difference, the greater the desire to eliminate it altogether. When reciprocal dependence brings benefits to both sides, everything that makes them asymmetric seems a provocation, a stimulus to reestablish or create more balanced relations.

For this reason, the simultaneity of "Americanization" and anti-Americanism was not at all paradoxical. The spread of fashions and eating habits, of entertainment styles (dance music, songs, movies, television), and of certain methods of management went hand in hand with a feeling of domination which had to be denounced all the more vigorously as it had all the characteristics of foreign rule. The responses given in a poll in France in April 1968 are typical. Answers to the question "Which of the following people [the German, the American, the British, the Italian] resembles the French most closely in its lifestyle, and which the least?" showed that the most similarity was felt with the Germans (33 percent) and the Italians (28 percent) as compared to 5 percent with the English and 4 percent with the Americans, while Americans were felt to be the most dissimilar (43 percent as compared with 22 percent for the British, 8 percent for the Italians, 7 percent for the Germans).[21] At the same time, the concept "Americanization" permitted the ascription of everything that was perceived as negative in the social consequences of economic development to a harmful outside influence.

While European engineers and managers studied in the United States, and MIT and the Harvard School of Business made Cambridge, Massachusetts, a place where ambitious young Europeans felt they could obtain the finest education, a twofold complaint was being voiced. It was expressed with particular emphasis by Robert Marjolin, vice-president of the EEC Commission, when he addressed the European Parliament: "If the Six countries remain, as they probably have done for a generation, the main world importers of discoveries and exporters of brains, they will be condemning themselves to a cumulative underdevelopment which will soon render their decline irremediable."[22]

Concern in face of the technological gap was expressed at the same time by the Italian Foreign Minister Amintore Fanfani and the British Prime Minister Harold Wilson.[23] Gaston Defferre had already made it the centerpiece of the accusations he had raised in the name of the Socialist opposition during a discussion of the fifth modernization plan in November 1964. He charged that "the failure of the French Government to assist industrial research and production was leading to the 'colonization of France by the United States.' The Gaullists . . . are taking France not to the independence of which they speak so much but to economic enslavement and finally to political enslavement."[24]

The primary goal of de Gaulle's industrial policy may not have been the achievement of equality, but it certainly was an attempt to redress the technological imbalance and was frequently interpreted as a prestige operation. The way progressive French techniques were fought or ignored in the United States was resented not only by the French head of state. The Caravelle jet, which had been built under the Fourth Republic, was not accepted in the American market. The French color television system was hardly tested on the other side of the Atlantic, yet the Soviet Union adopted it. In a sense, Aleksei Kosygin's visit to France in December 1966 stood under the slogan: "Technological proletarians of both parts of Europe, unite!" What was at stake was to be better or at least as good as the United States in a wide variety of fields, and it was this spirit that was behind the development of the supersonic commercial aircraft.[25] The agreement on the joint Anglo-French production of the Concorde that was signed in November 1962 in London was rather more a demonstration of prestige and avant-garde thinking than of a sober, commercially competitive position, for the reasonable project of a solid but less spectacular Super-Caravelle had been turned down. Hardly recognizable at first, the "computer war" began when the United States refused in 1963 to sell France an electronic calculator which was considered indispens-

able for development work on the Force de Frappe, the French nuclear force. The "Plan Calcul" of 1966 was to help France build its
own computer system (see Chapter 11), while the launching of the
Redoutable, the first French nuclear submarine, on March 29, 1967,
appeared to prove that one could get along without American assistance.

The "brain drain" primarily affected Great Britain, whose experts
had no language difficulties when they moved to the United States.
The American call for European scientists and engineers had become
especially loud in 1957, after the first Soviet satellite, Sputnik, had
been sent into orbit. In 1966, "Lord Bowden, principal of Manches-
ter's Institute of Science and Technology, burst out angrily:
'. . . America is stripping other countries of their technologists,'"[26] and
that at the expense of the taxpayers who had financed their training. In
1967, the government presented a rather pessimistic report on the
"brain drain" to the House of Commons, though without taking very
much account of the fact that the harsh tax policy of the Labour Party
was about to once more accelerate an emigration that had just slowed
down somewhat.

But what weight did this inconvenience due to membership in the
"community of English-speaking peoples" have when one compared
it to the language problem many Frenchmen experienced? In Germany also, there were complaints about the infiltration of numerous
American terms, indeed of an entire vocabulary, into everyday language. But German at least was not considered a universal language,
whereas the global ambition of France was predominantly cultural,
the language being considered the indispensable support of civilization. The concept "francophonie" is purely political. Whether it was a
question of the predominance of English in the international organization, in Quebec, in West and Equatorial Africa, in South America or
Rumania, the preservation or diffusion of French was always connected with prestige and influence.

It was here that the conflict with the United States took on a special
dimension, though it was certainly nothing new since the themes of
the 1930s recurred (see Chapter 1). To denounce more effectively the
harmful influence on the language, to rebel more vigorously against
the economic and political predominance, American culture and society were painted in the most ghastly colors. The book that attracted
the widest attention among those combating the "Yankee cancer" was
written by René Etiemble, a cosmopolitan university professor who
usually violently criticized Communist regimes, a fact which further
contributed to the effect of his polemical treatise "Parlez-vous
Franglais?"[27] In a wild satire on "Atlantic jargon," he turned on the

"French bourgeoisie which had not managed to become a German colony and now spent all its time dreaming of a Yankee protectorate." "If we keep up this Atlantic gibberish for only a little while longer, veiled anti-Semitism, virulent racism, sexual hypocrisy, the worship of the dollar, scientific superstition and science à la Christian Science will soon become our daily bread." Why bother, then, with the cultural and scientific reality of the United States, the massive American representation in the natural and even more the humane sciences? What did it matter that the most positive aspects of France's past and present had often been researched through the efforts of American sociologists and historians?

Nor were hardly any comparisons made that might have reflected unfavorably on the state of culture in France. "During a stay in the United States," writes an eminent expert on the Middle Ages, "I had to write an article on Bertrand de Born. I happened to be in Detroit at the time. In the municipal library there, I discovered that the system of classification which our libraries have meanwhile begun to adopt was of such quality that I had no trouble whatever locating the book I was looking for on the shelves. What is there for any reader at all on the other side of the Atlantic is not even available to the privileged user of the Bibliothèque Nationale (he is admitted only after showing his university diploma). Nothing proves more clearly the narrowness of the cultural notions among us who are so proud of our prestige as a nation of culture."[28] Such remarks were ignored. The struggle to maintain the purity of French combined with a kind of cultural contempt of others which itself had a political dimension.

The emigration of experts and linguistic imperialism, however, were only secondary themes in comparison with the debate on American enterprises in Europe. It was a debate which was carried on with particular vehemence during the mid-1960s and which will probably never end (see Chapter 11). Already at that time, it combined to a considerable extent with economic and ideological discussion about the "multinationals," which tended to confuse rather than clarify, in part because the large enterprises with truly multinational capital are only rarely American. Royal Dutch Shell and Unilever, both of them Dutch-British companies, are much more multinational than General Motors, for example. Besides, large firms with subsidiaries in various countries (either under direct central management or relatively autonomous) are not a specifically American phenomenon: Péchiney, Philips, Bayer are not fundamentally different from their American counterparts, just as a Fiat or a Volkswagen is not fundamentally different from a Ford. Finally and most important, the massive establishment of American companies in Western Europe gave rise to special problems which are connected with the nature of power relationships and the reciprocal influence between Europe and the United States. What is at issue is the American, i.e., precisely the *national* character, of these firms.[29]

Of course, in the mythology of this subject as it has been expatiated on in newspapers, novels, and films since the 1960s, this distinction is never made. In political discussions, "multinational" and "American" are readily put on the same plane. One simplifies what one wishes to denounce and imputes to it a rationality, a quasi demonic intentionality, and acts as if American enterprises and the American government had a common intent. People also like to pretend that the word "power" is an uncomplicated concept, as if the answer to the question. "The power of whom to make whom do what and when?" were self-evident.[30]

Yet the controversies of the 1960s were not artificial but reflected the massive installation of American firms in Europe. In 1950, for example, there were 1,000 U.S. subsidiaries in the Europe of the Six. In 1957, that number had only increased to 1,200, but by 1966 there were already more than 4,000. In Great Britain, the number rose from 700 in 1950 to 800 in 1957 and to 2,300 in 1966. The extent of direct U.S. investments emerges clearly from Table 3.[31]

There was also European investments in the United States, but during the first phase these were almost entirely shares in enterprises which continued under American control. The establishment of American subsidiaries by large European enterprises did not increase until the end of the 1960s, and remained limited (see Chapter 11). Transatlantic movement from west to east attained its apogee around 1962: while Great Britain's share decreased, that of all of the six countries of the EEC rose. The abolition of all kinds of tariff barriers and restrictions made the industrial space of the Common Market especially attractive.

But this attractiveness was much more clearly recognized by American than by French, Italian, or even German enterprises. In other words, the new possibilities the developing Europe offered were much better utilized by American than by European firms. In *The American Challenge*, which attracted considerable attention, Jean-Jacques Servan-Schreiber pointed to the harmful consequences of this development. "Fifteen years from now it is quite possible that the world's third greatest industrial power, just after the United States and Russia, will not be Europe, but *American industry in Europe.* Already, in the ninth year of the Common Market, this European market is basically American in organization."[32] As he points to the backwardness of France in particular in such matters as training, research,

TABLE 3 Book value¹ of direct U.S. investments abroad (Value at year end in millions of dollars)

	1950	1957	1958	1963	1964	1965	1966	1967	1968	1969	1970	1971	1972
Federal Republic	204	581	666	1,780	2,082	2,431	3,077	3,486	3,785	4,276	4,597	5,209	6,262
France	217	464	546	1,240	1,446	1,609	1,758	1,904	1,904	2,122	2,590	3,020	3,432
Italy	63	252	280	668	850	482	1,148	1,246	1,275	1,423	1,550	1,871	1,978
Netherlands	84	191	207	446	593	686	859	942	1,069	1,221	1,508	1,679	1,943
Belgium/Luxembourg	69	192	208	356	455	596	748	867	981	1,214	1,529	1,826	2,130
EEC total	637	1,680	1,908	4,490	5,426	6,304	7,584	8,444	9,012	10,255	11,774	13,605	15,745
Great Britain	847	1,974	2,147	4,172	4,547	5,123	5,657	6,113	6,694	7,190	7,996	9,007	9,509
Switzerland	25	69	82	672	948	1,120	1,211	1,322	1,437	1,604	1,777	1,888	1,911
Denmark	32	42	49	133	166	200	226	273	204	309	362	356	377
Norway	24	51	53	123	129	152	167	183	201	223	268	292	326
Sweden	58	109	107	221	260	315	370	438	516	607	620	689	726
Spain	31	44	48	155	196	275	408	480	582	577	737	778	903
other European	79	179	181	374	438	495	585	673	761	884	981	1,122	1,208
Europe total	1,733	4,151	4,573	10,340	12,109	13,985	16,209	17,920	19,407	21,650	24,516	27,740	30,714
Canada	3,579	8,769	9,470	13,044	13,796	15,223	16,999	18,097	19,535	21,127	22,790	24,105	25,784
Latin America	4,445	7,434	7,751	8,662	8,894	9,391	9,826	10,265	11,033	11,694	12,252	12,982	13,528
Africa	287	664	746	1,426	1,685	1,918	2,074	2,273	2,674	2,982	3,482	3,836	4,111
Asia²	1,001	2,019	2,178	2,793	3,112	3,569	3,896	4,289	4,724	5,221	5,557	6,545	7,677
(Japan)	•	•	•	•	•	•	•	•	•	(1,491)	(1,483)	(1,821)	(2,222)
rest of world	943	2,357	2,669	4,442	4,790	5,242	5,707	6,636	7,611	8,342	9,582	10,990	12,217
World	11,788	25,394	27,827	40,686	44,386	49,328	54,711	59,426	64,983	71,016	78,090	86,198	94,031

¹ Book value: U.S. net capital outflow for investments abroad plus undistributed foreign profits reinvested there (excluding investment from local sources).

² Preliminary.

SOURCE: Survey of Current Business, Aug. 1960-64, Sept. 1965-67, Oct. 1968-69, U.S. Dept. of Commerce.

and managment, Servan-Schreiber warns of the danger that the future might not see the creation of large European enterprises but of giant Franco-American, German-American, Italian-American ones which would all be under American control, which would mean that as long as the European countries did not really make joint industrial efforts, they would be faced with the following dilemma: "If we allow American investments to enter freely under present conditions, we consign European industry—or at least the part that is most scientifically and technologically advanced and on which our future rests—to a subsidiary role, and Europe herself to the position of a satellite. If, on the other hand, we adopt effective restrictive measures, we would be double losers—denying ourselves both the manufactured products we need and the capital funds that would then be invested in other countries. By trying to be self-sufficient, we would only condemn ourselves to underdevelopment."

The arguments concerning American investments differed considerably in value and weight. There were complaints about the presence of "200,000 upper level employees at American subsidiaries in Great Britain and on the continent," whose image was justifiably "not just bad but terrible," for "their abilities are either moderate or zero."[33] And they also proved brutal and incapable of social integration. People asked what role American firms might play in an eventual Americanization of Europe.[34] But to what extent did this hostility derive from a rejection of all the social change which industrialization brings with it? Is concentration American in origin, and are its effects purely negative? Does the standarization and uniformity of the products offered the European consumer destroy more culture than it creates new goods which increase the number of possible purchasers? Are the higher wages the multinationals pay due to better management, to a greater effort toward justice and efficiency, or to the simple fact that the sectors in which they have established themselves pay higher wages in any event?

Foreign firms create employment. But since the ultimate decisions are made on the other side of the Atlantic, it is only natural that the labor market of the country in which one is a guest should not be taken into account. One simply discharges part or all of the indigenous personnel. One is all for export, but overall strategy may suddenly put an export firm out of business. The technology transfer to Europe permits rapid increases in productivity, the GNP, and the prosperity of European countries, but large sums must be paid for patents.[35] There is the additional consideration that the resulting technological dependence may make supplies uncertain and jeopardize the government's freedom of decision in its industrialization policy. And this is dangerous because American enterprises establish themselves in such vital sectors as the oil, auto, aircraft, and chemical industries, electronics and banking.

Evaluations of benefits and drawbacks differed, depending on the country,[36] and in some, principally France, hinged on the role one happened to be playing at a given moment: as a minister or leader of the opposition party, one could point to the dangers, yet advocate the installation of American enterprises if one were the mayor of a locality or the deputy of a region. Generally speaking, however, everyone more or less adopted the formula Robert Marjolin had used in an address before the European Parliament in Strasbourg in March 1955: "It is not a question of protecting Europe from such investments, which often bring much benefit to our countries. It is simply a matter of avoiding excesses."[37]

Belgium and the Federal Republic were the two countries which probably welcomed American firms most. Belgium increased subsidies and tax advantages to attract the Americans even more, and this often meant luring them away from other European countries. In the Federal Republic, all parties subscribed to the economic doctrine that no restrictions be placed on investments. Rejection of a joint control of American investments was as marked in 1963 under the CDU/FDP coalition as after 1966 when the Social Democrat Karl Schiller was Minister of Economics. But after 1966, fears arose in both countries, in part because there was a shortage of workers which caused foreign enterprises to offer higher wages, in part because the investments were made in key sectors. Reacting to a rumor that Petrofina, the largest Belgian oil company, was about to be bought up, the Belgian government decreed in 1967 that the controlling interest in Belgian firms would henceforth be acquired only after previous authorization (though this decree was made less restrictive in 1971).

It was also in 1967 that Harold Wilson suddenly declared that Great Britain was on its way to becoming the industrial helot of the United States. If American industry were allowed to set the tempo, "we will turn into wood cutters and water carriers in the industrial society while they . . . will enjoy an increasing monopoly in the technologically advanced sectors of production."[38] In spite of the imposition of countermeasures, however, not a single investment application was rejected, and the share of American enterprises in British industry rose from 5.7 percent in 1957 to 10.5 percent in 1966 and 14 percent in 1970.

In France, though the phenomenon was more limited there than elsewhere, divergent political positions—the Left with its encompassing accusations of the United States for imperialism (see Chapter

9), the traditional protectionists, and the Gaullists with their striving for independence—made common cause in the denunciation of the invasion of capital. There was also general enthusiasm for the idea of "planification" and the fear that foreign enterprises might prevent the implementation of the economic plan by their mere existence. All these accusations went hand in hand with a national resentment, and this combination gave rise to a rather inconsistent attitude. People complained whatever the case: if an American firm invested in France, it was a sign of imperialism; if it invested elsewhere, it was felt to be an intolerable discrimination against France.

Partly exaggerated, partly justified, these French criticisms nonetheless had a certain continuity, which is more than can be said of government policy or at least of its practice, for its doctrine never varied: American investments are useful if they are made in sectors which are significant for the overall development of the economy and of industry in particular. Until 1962, restrictions hardly existed. In the Finance Ministry, an office was set up to promote and channel investments into regions to be developed. An agreement which assured American firms favorable treatment was signed with the United States. But within a few months in 1962–63 and at the same moment de Gaulle's attitude toward the United States hardened, a series of events brought a change in the situation. Two American firms, the refrigerator factory of General Motors in Gennevilliers, a Paris suburb, and the typewriter factory of Remington Rand in Calluire, near Lyon, discharged large numbers of employees. Libby announced that it would build a fruit-canning plant in Languedoc and sign long-term agreements with local fruit growers. Chrysler increased its interest in Simca from 25 percent to 63 percent and thus acquired control. And after 1963, complicated negotiations began in the computer industry, which first revolved around a share of General Electric in Bull. Prime Minister Georges Pompidou explained: "France is not hostile to foreign investments, however, a limitation appears desirable in practice. France does not wish that the industry of a particular region or a particular branch of industry be dominated by foreign capital, for example, American." And Hervé Alphand, ambassador to the United States, phrased it as follows: "We must, as must other countries in the world, supervise the total of investments coming from abroad. . . . It is not possible for us to leave certain sectors of our economy, certain of our large enterprises, in the hands of companies whose head offices are in Chicago or Detroit. But it is not true that we do not accept with pleasure in the great majority of cases—in fact, we have never rejected them—all American investment which may certainly constitute a large complement and a large stimulant for our policy of expansion in

France. The legend of a France which forbids the investments of American capital in the French economy is entirely false."[39] This selective policy became more stringent in 1965 and then was relaxed because it had negative results. As of 1966, the new Economics Minister, Michel Debré, behaved more hospitably. The important decree of January 27, 1967, provides in Article 4:

In the following cases, application for permission has to be made to the Minister of Economics and Finance:
1. Direct investments in France by either natural or juristic persons, public or private, having their permanent residence or headquarters abroad, or by corporations in France under direct or indirect foreign control or by branches in France of foreign corporations.
These regulations apply especially when the investment is made by the transfer of part of the assets of a corporation in France, either between natural or juristic, public or private persons with permanent residence abroad.
For a two month period after receipt of the application, the Minister of Economics and Finance can demand that the planned transaction be delayed. But he may waive the right to demand a delay before the expiration of this period.
2. The total or partial liquidation of investments in France . . .[40]

Actually, the fundamental contradiction in French policy was not just the alternation of laxness and rigor in authorization procedures, but went much deeper. A man such as Michel Debré wanted the state to influence industrial development. Faced with the United States, it became clear to him that French industry by itself did not carry enough weight and that a powerful European industry would be needed. Logically, a para- or quasi-governmental authority on a European level would therefore have to have the power to coordinate, stimulate, and control. But this logic was blocked by the dogma of absolute sovereignty. As a result, large private enterprises, particularly the American ones, could maneuver freely in Europe without colliding with a unified governmental will.

Meanwhile, France's most important partner, the Federal Republic, was caught in the opposite contradiction. It said yes to a politically integrated Europe, i.e., a Europe which would be based on the principle of majority decision and leave the Brussels Commission wide scope, but said no to any interventionist economic policy because it was committed to the *Marktwirtschaft* principle. It therefore became unavoidable that the internal development of the EEC should take a rather chaotic course.[41]

Generally speaking, it was the lack of coherence in the French position from which the other member countries suffered most, especially during the mid-1960s when the French government tried to block all progress in political integration on the one hand, yet wanted to impose a rigidly integrated system in agricultural policy on the other. It was also perfectly willing, however, to accept the Brussels Commission, on which it brought much pressure to bear as a joint spokesman for the six EEC countries in the "Kennedy Round," the most important of all world-wide economic negotiations. The crisis of June 1965 was quite characteristic.[42] The boycott of the EEC by France pursued the twofold aim of pushing through the French proposal for financing a joint agricultural policy and of imposing a "set of commandments" to modify the role and conduct of the commission, which had been run by Walter Hallstein since its creation. After tough negotiations, a number of compromises were agreed to in Luxembourg on January 30, 1966: a compromise concerning a "set of rules of conduct" for the commission; a second (which was really a sequence of contradictory statements) concerning the application of Article 2 of the Rome Treaty, which provides for a majority vote of the Ministerial Council, the executive organ of the EEC; and a third on the resumption of the agricultural negotiations.

The shock diplomacy which Couve de Murville practiced on instructions from de Gaulle did not just serve the protection of national interests. The five partners also had to be forced to accept a position which "France deemed desirable for the Community": this revelatory formulation by the head of government passed almost unnoticed, for it seemed unproblematical even to the opposition. As guest of honor at the American Club of Paris, Georges Pompidou had dedicated his address to relations between France and United States: "The old division into two monolithic blocs is a thing of the past. What emerges now is the role of France, whose geographical position and history condemn her to *play the role of Europe* [italics added]. A Europe that has long been asleep under the protection of the powerful USA . . ."[43] When, two years later, a group of high-ranking, rather anti-Gaullist officials published a work entitled *For a European Foreign Policy*, they criticized much in the substance and style of governmental policy but maintained: "For Europe, France is the laboratory of correctly posed questions,"[44] and hardly asked themselves whether the policy they proposed was acceptable to the other countries.

France knows what is good for everyone else, even though there may be differences on some important points, especially in attitudes toward the United States. In 1963, for example, a poll asked: "How great is your confidence in the ability of the United States to lead the West intelligently through today's global problems?" In Germany, 75 percent of the answers were positive and only 9 percent negative, in Italy it was 61 percent versus 10 percent, in Great Britain 51 percent versus 33 percent. In France, the relationship was reversed: 33 percent positive answers as compared to 49 percent negative ones.[45] But during the following years when Ludwig Erhard was Chancellor in Bonn, the French government faced a German partner who was particularly anxious not to displease Washington but who also wanted to maintain the best possible relations with Paris. Italy could not be relied on: the April 1963 elections, which had not gone well for the Christian Democrats, had led to an "opening toward the Left," and as a consequence, the originally very "neutralist" Socialist Pietro Nenni became Deputy Prime Minister from December 1963 until June 1968 and Foreign Minister toward the end of 1968. In spite of this, the stability of the Italian position was never in question, for de Gaulle's attitude was approved by none of the parties of the changing coalition.[46]

Yet Stanley Hoffmann is not mistaken when he keeps stressing in his books on France and the United States that de Gaulle often merely said out loud what his partners did not dare express. This was especially true of the Italian government. But in negotiations where the EEC countries had a common interest vis-à-vis the United States and also accepted it as such, the French government was much more conciliatory. And constant turmoil and internal division, notwithstanding, it is nonetheless true that the European Community acted as an entity and presented a common front in the most important economic negotiations of the postwar era.

In this message to Congress on January 25, 1962, which was to result in the Trade Expansion Act, President Kennedy pleaded for a lowering of tariffs by pointing to the significance of a common European market "which is being protected by a uniform external tariff similar to ours." For economic reasons (the uniform external tariff threatened to deprive American industry and agriculture of necessary markets) and for political reasons ("economic isolation and political leadership are completely irreconcilable"), it would therefore be necessary to start broad-based negotiations to reduce tariff barriers, particularly those between the United States and the EEC.

Five and a half years later, on June 30, 1967, Eric Windham White, director-general of GATT, was in a position to present as a notable success the agreement which had been signed in Geneva and to which he himself had contributed significantly as mediator: "The industrialized countries participating in the Kennedy Round made duty reductions on 70% of their dutiable imports, excluding cereals, meat and dairy products. Moreover, two thirds of these cuts were of 50% or more. Another fifth were between 25% and 50%. . . . All this can be stated in another way. Of the imports by the participating industrialized countries (other than cereals, meat and dairy products) 66% are either duty-free or are to be subject to cuts of 50% or more; on another 15% there are to be cuts of less than 50%, and 19% remain unaffected. As for cereal, meat and dairy products, the aim, as you know, was the negotiation of general arrangements. In the case of cereal, agreement relating to prices and food aid has been reached. Some bilateral agreements have been concluded on meat. Very little has been obtained in the negotiations on dairy products. On scores of other agricultural products, significant duty reductions were made."[47]

The negotiations were long and complicated, often tiresome, and sometimes dramatic. The preparatory period had lasted until May 1964. On May 5, 1967, failure seemed imminent because the group that was to negotiate on the chemical sector could not agree. From May 8 to 14, the American and the EEC negotiators faced each other in tough bargaining. On May 9, it was decided to end negotiations on the fifteenth. By stopping the clocks at midnight, the goal was reached: on May 15, Windham White's compromise suggestions were accepted.

The talks were dominated by a concept which all the world referred to by its English name, and by three others whose French designations have entered international jargon. The ASP, the American Selling Price, was no customs tariff but the often fictitious standard of valuation on the American domestic market by reference to which the imported product was to be taxed. It was imposed primarily on chemical products but also on shoes and canned fish. The solution which was found was *découpage:* part of the tariff reduction for chemical products would come into force in all cases, while an additional reduction would only become effective after the ASP had been done away with. But what was meant by a "significant disparity" which was to be reduced or eliminated? The EEC obtained acceptance of the principle of *double écart:* the disparity is considered significant when the tariff on a given product is at least twice that on another and when the difference between the two comes to at least ten points. And finally, in order to avoid that the linear reduction (equal tariff on all products) favor the United States, which imposed especially high tariffs on certain products, the Europeans insisted on the method of *écrêtement:* to start by cutting the highest tariffs before imposing the same percentage of diminution on all tariffs at stake.

The Kennedy Round was essentially dominated by the confrontation of the two most important collective actors, the United States and the EEC, while the GATT negotiations included numerous other countries. This was the first time the EEC had spoken with one voice, for the six countries were represented by a joint delegation which had come out of the Brussels Commission. And the participating forces and the aim of the negotiations were such that, for the first time also, a kind of equilibrium between Europeans and Americans was attained, for every agreement constituted a compromise which had been reached without one party's prevailing over the rest.

It wasn't that the two delegations had much freedom to maneuver. The Americans were constantly being watched by Congress, which was anxious to protect the U.S. market. And the European delegation had to keep negotiating with the six member countries. Nor did unanimity always prevail among the three decisive members within the commission: the Frenchman Robert Marjolin, vice-president in charge of economic questions (while the president, Walter Hallstein, was a jurist and politician); the Belgian Jean Rey, who was responsible for the overall conduct of the negotiations; and the Dutchman Sicco Mansholt, who was charged with agricultural matters. But the authority and even authoritarianism of Mansholt, and especially Jean Rey's mixture of firmness and diplomatic sense, gave the negotiators sufficient latitude. Even the French government felt increasing confidence in Rey and his ability to represent both the interests of the individual member countries and those of the EEC as a whole. When, four days prior to the signing in Geneva on June 26, 1967, the six governments nominated the Belgian statesman as president of the European Commission, which was born of the fusion of the existing communities, it was in dramatic recognition of the success of the Kennedy Round. It was largely perceived as such because the common external tariff, a decisive element in the unity of the Community, had been retained, most notably in agricultural products. ("We have no flag, we have no army, all we have is a tariff," Hallstein had said.[48])

Perhaps this was the principle reason de Gaulle agreed to the later compromises, though before that the French government had announced very tough and often quite fruitful positions, and in Brussels and Geneva there had always been fear of a negative outburst, particularly after the summer of 1965. The Kennedy Round had made it possible to put forward a joint agricultural policy which was everything that France, worried about a market for its agricultural products, could possibly ask for. And while 1965 was the year the French provoked a crisis at Brussels, it was also the year that the farm vote forced de Gaulle into a second-round run-off during the presidential elections in December. The Luxembourg compromise within the EEC and the acceptance of the progress made during the Kennedy Round were certainly connected with this domestic political event.

Even before the Kennedy Round, agriculture had been at the center of the first conflict between the United States and Europe. For years, the "chicken war" aroused considerable passion. It had begun as a regular bombardment of Europe and especially the Federal Republic with frozen American chickens, whose production had quintupled between 1948 and 1952 and whose price had constantly decreased due to growing mechanization. Chicken exports to the Federal Republic increased from 3.5 million pounds a year in 1956 to 122 million pounds in 1962. During that same period, production and consumption in Europe rose considerably, but on July 30, 1962, the EEC imposed higher tariffs. According to GATT regulations, 15 percent was permissible. But the first increase was 30 percent, and this was gradually raised to almost 70 percent. By 1965, American chickens on the German market had been almost entirely replaced by Belgian, French, and Dutch chickens. In May 1963, the United States demanded compensation according to GATT regulations, announcing that it would increase its own tariffs in order to derive an additional $46 million from European exports. The EEC considered $19 million adequate. In November 1963, GATT arbitrage set an amount of $26 million. On December 4, President Johnson announced an equivalent increase in tariffs on various products, potato flour and starch among them.

At this moment, the Kennedy Round began. From the point of view of a liberalization of trade, the results regarding agricultural products were disappointing. But protection of agriculture was mandatory for the governments on both sides of the Atlantic. A rational trading system could have been established both within the EEC and between the EEC and the United States if currency fluctuations had not led to ever greater chaos in agricultural policies.

Always present in the background of trade relations, currency problems had become increasingly important in the various areas of transatlantic relationships since U.S. gold reserves had fallen below the level of the dollar amounts held by foreign central banks in 1958, and this continued up to that symbolic date of August 15, 1971, when the American government suspended the convertibility of the dollar into gold. The new problems were recognized only slowly, and they had barely been understood when the tendency developed to project the new situation onto the past, as for example, in relation to American investments in Europe.

During the second half of the 1960s, European enterprises or shares in them were acquired ever less frequently by direct investment from the United States or reinvested profits, and ever more frequently by loans made in Europe. For a long time, Americans refused to acknowledge this phenomenon, while the Europeans tended to act as if American investments had been made with Eurodollars from the very beginning.

While it is true that the balance of trade (i.e., the difference in value between imports and exports) between the United States and the EEC remained favorable to the United States during the entire period, this did not suffice to create a balance-of-payments surplus, i.e., a surplus in the balance of all current operations, which were made up not only of trade but also of capital and currency transactions. In the United States, people now began to dream of the trade surpluses one would have if there were neither an EEC nor a European Free Trade Association. It was said that accumulated losses of American trade for the period 1958–70 amounted to $2.29 billion, based on 1958 prices.[49]

One of the reasons for the balance-of-payments deficit was directly connected with political relations with one of the most important European countries: Was it really the United States that should pay for the upkeep of American units stationed in the Federal Republic? But since these units were there for the defense of all European countries, why should the Germans be the only ones to shoulder the burden? The answer was simple: because it was easier for the United States to exert direct pressure on the Bonn government[50] (from which Great Britain also demanded payment for its Rhine army). In 1961 and 1964, the German government expressed its willingness to buy large quantities of American weapons and equipment, and these purchases were to compensate for the dollar deficit caused by the upkeep of American soldiers. Among the orders were those Starfighters whose record number of crashes were to give them a depressing notoriety. In 1966, there occurred a clash between the American desire to sell the greatest possible number of weapons during times when there was a balance-of-payments deficit ($2.3 billion in 1966 as compared to $1.3 in the preceding year) and the German wish to no longer keep all its promises since an economic stagnation limited the means of the Federal Republic.

When the first dispute between Robert McNamara and Kai Uwe von Hassel in Washington led to the American threat to reduce troop strength in Germany, the German government promised not to cut its orders. During a visit to President Johnson in September 1966, Chancellor Erhard yielded again and assumed even greater obligations. After his return, he had to request a budget increase from the cabinet, which contributed to his defeat in November.

Bilateral meetings between heads of governments and ministers became increasingly less important as monetary problems developed and these problems became an ever more central concern to the governments. Other actors such as the directors of the central banks now played a greater role, however widely their powers might vary from one country to the next. The Bank of France, for example, had much less power than the Bundesbank, and in the United States the Federal Reserve Bank of New York and, more important, the Federal Reserve Board, whose twelve governors have a fourteen-year tenure, can frustrate the government for the board sets the discount rate and this affects economic and currency mechanisms on both sides of the Atlantic. And however great American influence on the International Monetary Fund might be, that of its director-general (first the Swede Per Jacobsson and, after June 1963, the Frenchman Pierre-Paul Schweitzer) is certainly not inconsequential. There was the additional fact that parallel to existing institutions, a new structure, the "Club of Ten," was establishing itself. Including the Federal Republic, Belgium, Canada, the United States, France, Great Britain, Italy, Japan, the Netherlands, and Switzerland, it very soon found itself at the center of all debates on reform of the world monetary system.

But the newest and probably also the most decisive actor was the currency market itself. Difficult to define, it consisted of banks and enterprises, private speculators and public organs. Its significance, and its uncontrollability, grew rapidly as currency trading was liberalized and increasingly efficient means of communication made it possible to quickly recognize the situation on all the world financial markets and transmit orders directly from the New York Exchange to Frankfurt, Zürich, or Tokyo.

The currency market would have been more adequately controlled by the governments if each had coordinated its economic and currency policy with the rest. Not only was this barely the case, but American indifference to the international repercussions of U.S. domestic politics—which was aggravated further by a lack of understanding of the internal effects resulting from their laxness on the international scene—led to consequences that were catastrophic for the entire world. After 1958, Regulation Q kept the interest rate which banks paid on term accounts in the United States very low. It was therefore advantageous to invest dollars in Europe, where interest rates were more favorable, particularly because such interest could be "repatriated" and because funds that were transferred to the United States from Europe (including those of the European branches of American banks) were not subject to Regulation Q. When, in 1966, the chairman of the Federal Reserve Board, William McChesney Martin, wanted to fight the inflation caused by the Vietnam War by reducing the liquidity of American banks (and since funds could be borrowed in Europe and then transferred to the United States), there occurred an assault by American banks on London, Paris, and Frankfurt and a rise in the interest rate of the Eurodollar which was to have catastrophic consequences[51] (see Chapter 9).

The new facts were not always correctly understood by the politicians. An example would be that decisive moment in the development of currency problems, the marked devaluation of the British pound on November 18, 1967, when Harold Wilson blamed the economic consequences of the Middle East crisis, particularly the closing of the Suez Canal, and saw "the dock strikes in London and Liverpool and, following their ending, financial manoeuvring within the Six" as "proximate causes."[52] An alternate interpretation of the same event: the devaluation was really caused "by the rise of the Eurodollar above the interest rate of the communal obligations, i.e., the investment especially Englishmen living abroad preferred for their pound sterling accounts. During the first week of November 1967, large quantities of communal obligations were exchanged for dollar certificates of deposit with a life of three or six months since their interest rates had clearly become more attractive. One should not speak of chance here: when all the money changers saw how the curves of the interest rates approached toward and even touched each other, they knew what would happen. If Mr. Wilson had called Mr. Johnson and requested him to put a brake on the eagerness of people who wanted to borrow dollars from American banks, the danger would probably have been averted."[53]

The attack on the pound in any event was partly connected with a general loss of confidence in a world monetary system in which "the vulnerability of the key currencies to the functioning of the gold exchange standard is paralleled by a reverse vulnerability of the gold exchange standard itself to the fate of the key currencies upon which it rests."[54] And what about this gold standard? In his press conference on February 4, 1965, de Gaulle, a remarkable pedagogue, provided an analysis which permitted him to make his conclusions part of his overall strategy toward the United States:

Question: Mr. President, in converting part of its dollar holdings into gold, France has provoked certain reactions which have brought out the inadequacies of the present world monetary system. Are you in favor of a reform of this system and if so, how?

Question: My question, Mr. President, ties in which the earlier one: Could you give specific details of your policy concerning foreign and especially American investments in France?

Answer: I shall try to explain my ideas on these points. To the degree the states of Western Europe, decimated and ruined by the war, recover their substance, their relative situation which their weakness created seems inappropriate, not to say abusive and dangerous. I should say that there is nothing in this observation that implies unfriendliness on their part or that of France toward other countries, especially the United States. For that with every passing day, these countries wish to act more independently in all spheres of international relations is simply due to the natural course of things. This also applies to monetary relations as they have been practiced in the world since the trials it underwent caused Europe to lose it equilibrium. I am referring to the system which came into existence after the First World War and established itself after the Second.

It is well known that since the Genoa Conference of 1922 this system has conferred the privilege of functioning as a gold equivalent in international payments transactions on just two currencies, the pound and the dollar. Later, when the pound was devalued in 1931 and the American dollar in 1933, this privilege seemed in danger. But America overcame its big crisis. Then the Second World War ruined the currencies of Europe and brought inflation. Since almost all gold reserves were in the possession of the United States at that time and that country could maintain the value of its own currency because it was the world supplier, it could appear natural that the other countries accepted dollars or gold in their foreign currency accounts without distinguishing between the two and that the balances of payments were regulated by the transfer of credits, American means of payment or precious metals, and this all the more so as America never found it difficult to pay its debts in gold on demand. This international monetary system, this "Gold Exchange Standard," has therefore been the practice ever since. . . .

The conditions which earlier led to the "Gold Exchange Standard" have in fact changed. The currencies of the West European states are so firm today that the gold reserves of the six EEC countries equal those of the Americans. They would even exceed them if the Six exchanged all their dollar accounts for gold. It follows that the agreement which made the dollar preeminent has lost its basis, which lay in the fact that America owned the larger share of gold reserves. Beyond that, the fact that many countries accept dollars on the same basis as gold to eliminate deficits, which appear as credits in the American balance of payments, gives the Americans the possibility to contract interest-free debts abroad, for what they owe they pay—at least in part—with dollars which they can create at will and not with gold, which has a real value, whose possession one has to work for, and which cannot be transferred to others without risk or sacrifice. But this one-sided opportunity which America has also contributes to undermining the idea that the dollar is an impartial and international means of payment, though it is actually merely a means of credit of one state.

This situation also has other consequences, of course. There is thus in America a growing tendency to invest abroad, and this results in a kind of expropriation of this or that enterprise in certain countries.

It must be admitted that to a considerable extent, this practice has favored and still favors the frequent and considerable aid America gives to many countries and from which we also benefited significantly at one time. But today, conditions are such that one must even ask oneself what dimensions this problem would take on if countries with dollar reserves wanted to exchange them sooner or later for gold. . . . For all these reasons, France recommends that the system be changed. . . . We consider it necessary that international trade be placed on an incontestable monetary base as was the case before the two World Wars, a base which does not carry the stamp of any one country in particular.

Such a system could be conceived in a variety of ways. In 1944, Lord Keynes had wanted to introduce an ambitious project at Bretton Woods but had had to submit to the American desire for privileged treatment of the dollar. For de Gaulle, there was another answer which, at least in appearance, was very much simpler: "What is this base going to be? Actually, it is impossible to conceive of any criterion, any standard other than gold. Yes, gold, whose nature does not change, which one can turn into bullion or coins, which has no nationality and whose unaltering value as the monetary base per excellence is acknowledged everywhere and forever."

It is true that the President then spoke of the "reintroduction of the gold standard," and it is also true that his then adviser Jacques Rueff made himself the apostle of that standard which would make it possible to keep the United States from "using the secret of the painless deficit" which "permitted giving without taking, lending without contracting loans, acquiring without paying."[55] But in April 1968, Economics and Finance Minister Michel Debré stated authoritatively: "No official voice has ever called for a return to the gold standard. To allege that such is the French position is tantamount to caricature and falsification."[56]

For no one outside of France and only a few economic experts inside it accepted such a utopia, while French criticism of the international monetary system found much more response in Europe than the American leadership cared to admit.[57] But that leadership also overestimated the intensity of de Gaulle's offensive, not least because France actually did begin to exchange its dollars for gold, which decreased American gold reserves. France was part of the gold pool, a system it had set up jointly with the Federal Republic, Great Britain, Italy, Belgium, Holland, and Switzerland in October 1961 in order to contribute to the stabilization of the gold market. When it withdrew in June 1967 (a few weeks after the Bundesbank had committed itself not to exchange dollars for gold), this decision was kept secret. It was revealed in an article by Paul Fabra in *Le Monde* on November 21.

For President Johnson, matters presented themselves in this light: "The first week after devaluation, sales from the gold pool were $580. The French attitude did not improve matters. Britain's announcement was made on a Saturday. The de Gaulle government chose the following Monday to announce that it had withdrawn from the gold pool. Actually, France had withdrawn several months earlier, but the unfortunate timing of the French announcement complicated an already difficult situation. France had been building its gold reserves and was doing everything possible to force an increase in the official price. This was one of several times when I was tempted to abandon my policy of polite restraint toward de Gaulle, but I forced myself to be patient once again."

Raising the price of gold meant devaluing the dollar, which the

American government wished to avoid at all costs, even though it was told everywhere that it was too high. It preferred to pressure the Germans into revaluing the mark, and this was done on March 5, 1961, as a simple adaptation. The 1969 revaluation occurred under much more dramatic circumstances.

VIETNAM AND THE WESTERN ALLIES

Since 1966, the Vietnam War had been behind the monetary problems. But more important, it had been at the core of American worries since 1965 when the number of American soldiers in South Vietnam rose from 23,000 to 184,000 in the course of a single year. Toward the end of 1966, there were 385,000; toward the end of 1967, 485,000; and the maximum was reached in April 1969 with 543,000 men.[58] The first two American advisers had been killed in June 1959. In December of that year, the National Liberation Front of South Vietnam (NLF) had been formed to fight the Diem regime. In November 1961, President Kennedy had decided to step up American assistance, though without sending troops. The machinery of the war and the machinery of American involvement in South Vietnam politics were thus put into motion. The coup against Diem and the death of this man who had been installed as President by the United States occurred three weeks after Kennedy's murder.

President Johnson thought that North Vietnam would have to be defeated if the war was to be ended. On August 7, 1964, the Senate voted 88 against 2 to pass the Tonkin Gulf Resolution, which gave the President a free hand (and was not repealed until June 1970). The text was based on incidents in the Tonkin Gulf for which, it later turned out, the Hanoi government bore no responsibility. On February 7, 1964, the bombing of North Vietnam began, and after March 2 it became increasingly brutal. The greatest escalation, which was meant as a response to increasing infiltration by North Vietnamese into the South, took place toward the end of June 1966.[59]

The reactions of the European allies of the United States to its growing involvement varied considerably. The firmest and most unconditional support came from Germany, both from the government and the opposition. The communiqué dealing with the conversations between Johnson and Erhard that was put out on December 21, 1965, in Washington left no doubt whatever. The President "expressed his gratitude for the support of the Federal German Republic in the struggle to deter Communist aggression in South Vietnam. The chancellor declared the resolve of his government to continue supporting the cause of freedom."

In March, the *Bild Zeitung*, normally known for its anti-Communism, had published an editorial entitled "No, Sir": "We should tell Washington quite clearly that the Germans don't want to go to Vietnam. ... As everywhere in the world, in Vietnam also the right to self-determination applies, even if free elections there should not turn out favorable to the Americans. ... We cannot trample underfoot in other parts of the world the right that we demand for the Germans in the East and must therefore stand aside from this 'dirty war.' Very far aside." Two days later, Fritz Erler, deputy chief of the SPD, wrote Axel Springer, the publisher of the widely read paper: "I think it is terrible that ... the last bit of confidence in our nation by its ally is being destroyed [in this article]." In his answer, Springer, beat a retreat. In April, Erler and Willy Brandt flew to Washington and publicly proclaimed their support for American policy, and this eight months earlier than the head of government they were opposing.[60]

An eminent German professor concluded a balance sheet of the foreign policy of the Federal Republic as follows: "The fact that America protects us costs us the price of obedience, which will rise as the Americans see themselves increasingly burdened in the world."[61]

Actually, it was less a question of obedience than a kind of exaggerated interpretation of the domino theory: should the U.S. guarantee for South Vietnam prove illusory, not only the defense of Cambodia or Thailand but that of Berlin and of all of Germany would lose credibility. As Erler's formulation shows, the West Germans struck to their original thesis: in order to be able to have perfect confidence in the United States, one had to do everything one could to maintain American confidence in the Germans (see Chapter 2).

The Italian ally had no intention whatever of sharing responsibility outside the European continent. In 1966, the influence of the Socialists led to an unambiguous rejection of any and all engagements in Asia.[62] Yet one of the best-known leaders of the Christian Democrats, Foreign Minister Amintore Fanfani, had mediated between his friend Giorgio La Pira and President Johnson in January 1966 when the far-from-conformist mayor of Florence believed he could serve as a go-between after a talk he had had with Ho Chi Minh in Hanoi. But while this episode may have contributed to making the American government mistrustful of Fanfani for a period of years, it did not keep a new Moro government in which Fanfani was still Foreign Minister from presenting itself to the parliament in February where it expressed its "understanding for the position and the responsibilities" of the United States in Vietnam.[63]

Open support by the British government was less firm and Harold Wilson made more serious attempts to intervene. In February 1965, he met with a rebuff when he telephoned Johnson to suggest a meeting. He had to submit to a "Texan outburst": "If you want to help us some in Vietnam, send us some men and send us some folks to deal with these guerilas. And announce in the press that you are going to help us."[64] On June 21, 1966, Wilson declared in the House of Commons that he was opposed to the bombings in the area of Hanoi and Haiphong, and that was precisely where the escalation of the bombing began on June 29. In February 1967, the two countries that had presided at the Geneva Conference and were now represented by Harold Wilson and Soviet Prime Minister Kosygin, who was visiting London, vainly tried to have the resumption of American bombing that was scheduled for the Vietnamese Tet celebration postponed in order to sound out Hanoi.[65] In February 1968, Wilson was again rebuffed by Johnson.

In France, American policy was criticized publicly and ever more succinctly. At first, this was merely indirect, as in de Gaulle's statement on the situation in South Vietnam on August 29, 1963: the decision as to the future of South Vietnam was for the Vietnamese people to make "and no one else," he said. On April 15, 1964, a session of the Council of the Southeast Asia Treaty Organization (SEATO) that included the United States, Great Britain, France, Australia, New Zealand, Pakistan, Thailand and the Philippines ended with a rather odd communiqué: the French council member expressed the sympathy and friendship of France for the Vietnamese people who had for so long endured severe trials and striven for real independence. "The member pointed out that in view of the seriousness of the present situation, it might be advisable to refrain from making any declaration." This French member was Maurice Couve de Murville, who wrote later: "I refused the consent of the French delegation to the communiqué which my colleagues had proposed and which expressed unreserved support for the American undertaking in Vietnam. This was an unparalleled initiative which was naturally widely commented on. It was clear that France totally rejected American policy, which was fully supported by its other partners, and therefore no longer had a place in this organization. From that moment on, the French delegation stopped attending the sessions. The council meeting had been nothing more than a long quarrel between me on one side and all of my colleagues on the other, except for the representative from Pakistan. I declared that we could not support Washington's policy and that for the simple reason that we did not approve of it."[66]

The American participants in the dialogue, of whom the most intransigent and the most profoundly convinced that the United States was fighting the good fight was Secretary of State Dean Rusk, could point out that between 1947 and 1962 France had never stopped demanding the support of its allies who did not approve of its policy in Asia or North Africa. But in view of the deep-seated differences of opinion in fundamental questions, this was a secondary consideration. For the American government, it was a matter of keeping South Vietnam from becoming Communist. For the French government, "the war in progress there was not a war of aggression by North Vietnam but a civil war which had developed out of the revolt of part of the population of South Vietnam against the Saigon government."[67]

Another difference of opinion was apparently less clearly understood by either side. From Washington's perspective, Ho Chi Minh was a Communist leader, an instrument of world Communism. Paris knew him as a man with French education who was open toward France and who had been betrayed by that country in 1946. The "eternal" Minister of the Armed Forces, Pierre Messmer, had been in Tonkin in 1945 and been secretary-general of the interministerial committee for Indochina in 1946. One of the best-known journalists in Vietnamese problems, Jean Lacouture, had been press attaché on the staff of General Leclerc in Indochina in 1945. Between December 1962 and January 1966, the Ministry for French War Veterans was run by Jean Sainteny, the same man who had signed the agreement with Ho Chi Minh in March 1946 and been sent to Hanoi on an official mission by Pierre Mendès-France in 1954 (see Chapter 5). The exchange of letters between de Gaulle and Ho Chi Minh in 1966 cannot be divorced from this historic context.

On February 8, the President of the French Republic answered a letter from the President of the Republic of North Vietnam, dated January 24, in which he wrote among other things:

You know that France has been publicly stating for some time how in its view peace could be restored, which is by a return to the Geneva Agreement which had guaranteed the independence of Vietnam through the nonintervention of any foreign power in any form whatever, and on the part of Vietnamese authorities by a policy of strict neutrality. We continue to believe that the problem can be resolved and that there is no other road to peace. In other words, we exclude any military solution, nor do we approve of a continuation and thus an inevitable spread of the fighting under the pretense of ending it. . . . You will have noticed the increasing attention and sympathy, Mr. President, with which France has been following the Vietnamese drama from the beginning, for it feels tied to Vietnam by history, by human affinities and all other still existing links and remains convinced that a better understanding between the Vietnamese and the French immediately after the World War would have prevented the cruel events that tear your country apart.[68]

In June–July of that same year, in the course of a trip to Asia, Jean Sainteny visited Ho Chi Minh in Hanoi and handed him a second letter from de Gaulle: "You have known Mr. Sainteny for a long time. I wish to stress that he enjoys my esteem and entire confidence." The answer read in part: "Mr. Sainteny is now and always will be welcome as an old friend."[69] When Ho Chi Minh died on September 3, 1969, President Pompidou sent Sainteny to the funeral as the official French representative. Before his return to Paris, Sainteny stated: "There is no paradox in the assertion that the deceased, though the unswerving enemy of French tutelage and the gravedigger of our colonial empire, remained a friend of France."[70]

It was therefore no surprise that Jean Sainteny should be a mediator in eventual negotiations. The matter came up in January 1967, but de Gaulle did not want him to serve in that function if there was going to be no more than a simple contact between American and North Vietnamese representatives. Since the time for genuine negotiations had not yet come, it was preferable to stand aside.[71] Nonetheless, an attempt was made shortly after de Gaulle had gone to Cambodia, where, in a dramatic address in the Pnom Penh stadium, he did not exactly pose as an intercessor, and placed all the blame on the United States: "While your country [Cambodia] succeeded in saving its body and its soul because it remained the master in its own house, one could see how the political and military might of the U.S. established itself in South Vietnam and how simultaneously war again broke out there." The war can have no end: "While it is unlikely that American military forces will be destroyed, there is, on the other hand, no chance that the peoples of Asia will submit to the law of the stranger who came from the other side of the Pacific."

To obtain neutralization and independence, it would be necessary to negotiate. "But," the General added, "the chances for—not to mention the opening of—such extensive and difficult negotiations are naturally contingent on a prior decision and commitment by the Americans to repatriate their forces within an appropriate and fixed period of time. Today, the moment for such a resolution has not yet come, assuming that it ever will." In conclusion, he entreated the United States to take such steps, for it "would in no way hurt its pride, contradict its ideals or harm its interests." On the contrary: "How the world would applaud the U.S. from one end to the other." But if such a decision were not to be made by the United States, "no mediation would have any chance of success and for that reason France has never considered, nor does it now consider, proposing anything of the sort."

The harshest formulations to which de Gaulle put his inimitable style are perhaps those he used in a letter he wrote to Jean-Paul Sartre on April 19, 1967. In his role as president of the "Russell Tribunal," the philosopher had respectfully requested the President to permit the tribunal, which was going to judge American war crimes in Vietnam, to freely convene in France after French authorities had refused to let one of its members into the country. General de Gaulle wrote:

The initiators of the 'Russell Tribunal' propose to criticize the Vietnam policy of the United States. There is nothing here that might cause this government to restrict the normal rights of freedom of speech and assembly. Besides, you know what the government thinks about the war in Vietnam and what I myself have stated publicly and unequivocally. Quite apart from the fact that the written and spoken word are free in our country, there would be no reason to turn down private individuals, particularly those whose theses on this subject are so close to the official position of the French Republic. But what is at stake here is neither the right to free assembly nor to free speech but the duty—all the more imperative for France as she has taken a position on the basic issue which is known to all—to see to it that no state with which she has relations and which in spite of all differences remains her traditional friend become, on her territory, the object of a procedure which runs counter to general law and international custom. . . .

I will add that to the extent that certain of the persons around Lord Russell may have moral credit rather than be holders of public office, it does not seem to me that they will give greater weight to their admonitions if they clothe themselves in a robe which has been borrowed for the occasion.[72]

The situation did not change until January 1968. The Tet offensive of the NLF and the North Vietnamese was repulsed, but barely. General William Westmoreland demanded reinforcements, which Washington could not possibly send. "The limit had been reached," wrote French Foreign Minister Couve de Murville. If the war could not be escalated further, why then should the consequences not be drawn? Lyndon Johnson did so clear-sightedly when he announced the unilateral and immediate cessation of the bombing of North Vietnam on March 3, excepting only the areas along the demilitarized zone between the 17th and 19th parallels. At the same time, he declared his willingness to send his representatives to any conference which would discuss ways and means to end the war. And since public opinion in his country had already expressed itself on that score, he also refused to be a candidate for a second term in the impending elections.

The French government immediately welcomed this initiative. After the cabinet session of April 9, General de Gaulle declared: "Although it is neither general nor unconditional, the suspension of the bombing of North Vietnam is apparently a first step and therefore an act of reason and political courage on the part of the President of the United States."[73]

The adversaries decided to meet in Paris. Their first meeting—the last took place on January 27, 1971—began on May 13, 1968, in the conference rooms of the former Hotel Majestic on the Right Bank at the very moment students were putting up barricades on the Left, in the Latin Quarter (see Chapter 9).

In Pnom Penh, de Gaulle had pointed to the example of France, which "not too long ago had quite consciously put a stop to pointless struggles." But the Americans rejected any comparison with the Algerian situation and with France's negative experiences in Indochina between 1947 and 1954. They were wrong to do so. For the similarity between the statements of American cabinet members and generals and those of French ministers and generals who twenty years before had announced that victory was close if not already won leaps to the eye. And had not France already proved in Indochina and then in Algeria that it was futile to reject negotiations with those one fights against? The comparison with Algeria is not even very favorable to France: "I shall never do that," de Gaulle had exclaimed a few months before he began negotiating with the NLF after all. And he had had to discover how impossible it was to have genuine and truly free elections.

It is no exaggerated comparison to say that in 1966 the United States was more or less following Guy Mollet's plan whose three steps were: armistice, elections, negotiations (with those that have been elected). After any number of attempts, de Gaulle had finally arrived at the solution which others had proposed for some time: negotiations first; when these are finished, armistice; and then elections, which could hardly be anything other than the ratification of previously made agreements. How did the majority of South Vietnamese really think and feel? No one can say with certainty. What is certain is that if one fails to get the better of it, one finally negotiates with the fighting minority. And on the very day negotiations begin, the majority will follow. That may be a bitter observation, but the American leadership was wrong to reject the Algerian precedent without further examination.[74]

At that time, it was probably almost impossible to foresee that ultimately no elections would take place. It was possible to recognize, however, that between the American thesis (North Vietnam is the sole aggressor) and the French (merely a rebellion in South Vietnam which is being supported by the North), there was room for a third truth: support from the North was so total that, in the end, the South was purely and simply annexed by it.

9 STUDENT UNREST AND MONETARY TURMOIL

FROM VATICAN COUNCIL II TO PRAGUE: THE MODELS BECOME BRITTLE

The Vietnam War profoundly affected both the image of the United States in Europe and the idea people in that country had about their society, and this was soon to have repercussions in Europe as well. But these repercussions would have been more limited if changes, the most significant of which was presumably the inner transformation of the Catholic Church, had not already occurred during the 1960s. Pope John XXIII, who had been elected the successor of Pius XII in 1958, both revealed and hastened this process by calling a council whose fundamental note he sounded with his encyclical *Mater et Magistra* in July 1961. The document contained a statement with multiple implications, especially as regarded the definition of the impending struggles, i.e., the powers and influences to be denounced: "Perhaps the most pressing question of our day concerns the relationship between economically advanced commonwealths and those that are in process of development."[1]

Bishops had often advocated decolonization and discouraged racial discrimination before, and the definition of "neighbor" had already noticeably changed (see Chapter 5). But Pius XII had sanctioned the daring steps of French Catholicism. As before and already during the war, his chief concern was atheistic Communism, and he had therefore stressed the East-West conflict. But now a regard for greater justice gave more weight to the North-South opposition. Since Great Britain and France had finally granted their former colonies political independence, the economic domination of the rich over the poor became increasingly the central theme. And the rich country par excellence was the United States, which dominated a subcontinent where social inequality was especially pronounced and where Catholics were very numerous, i.e., Latin America.

In the new language of justice, more was said of the struggle for social liberation than of the protection of political freedoms, more emphasis placed on the injustices Western countries practiced or condoned on other continents than on the abolition of human rights under a different political system in Eastern Europe. At the same time, inequalities and injustices in Western societies were brought out with increasing sharpness.

The Council began on December 11, 1962. On April 12, 1963, the encyclical *Pacem in terris* was promulgated. It contained a denunciation of the developed nations for taking "unjust advantage of their superiority over others."[2] Yet though it became very popular thanks to its magnanimity and to the personal charisma of John XXIII, it has perhaps less significance than the Pastoral Constitution on the Church in the Modern World, which was promulgated under the title *Gaudium et spes* on December 7, 1965, after Paul VI had become the successor of John XXIII in June 1963. Part II, Chapter 3, on "Economic and Social Life," describes the process whereby "the development of economic life . . . even results in a decline of the social status of the underprivileged and in contempt for the poor." The right to property is affirmed, but St. Thomas is also quoted: "If one is in extreme necessity, he has the right to procure for himself what he needs out of the riches of others." And a long, forceful paragraph is wholly devoted to the latifundia: "In many underdeveloped regions, there are large or even extensive rural estates which are only slightly cultivated or lie completely idle for the sake of profit, while the majority of the people either are without land or have only very small fields . . . it is evidently urgent to increase the productivity of the fields."[3] In March 1967, the encyclical *Populorum progressio* largely resumed the same themes and added a very clear denunciation of liberal capitalism: "The introduction of industry is a necessity for economic growth and human progress; it is also a sign of development and contributes to it. . . . But it is unfortunate that on these new conditions of society a system has been constructed which considers profit as the key motive for economic progress, competition as the supreme law of economics, and private ownership of the means of production as an absolute right that has no limits and carries no corresponding social obligation. This unchecked liberalism leads to dictatorship rightly denounced by Pius XI as producing 'the international imperialism of money.'"[4]

This was a far cry from the certitudes of Cardinal Spellman, but also from what the German episcopate had considered as fundamental a few years before and after the Council. For while German and French prelates had acted in concert and while a spirit of protest (more characteristic of French than of German movements) had become apparent

during the German *Katholikentag* in 1968, the German episcopate
nonetheless quickly reverted to most of the views it had held before
the Council, especially because defense against the Communism in
the other Germany had remained its central concern. The French
episcopate, on the other hand, increasingly emphasized as "ethical
demands" of the Bible and as concrete, particularly urgent problems
"respect for the poor, defense of the weak . . . mistrust of wealth and
the condemnation of power through money, the exploitation of foreign
workers, the pillage of the Third World and the legitimation of the
economy through profit or the will to power of oligarchies and nations . . . "[5]

The United States became all the more readily the central target of
anti-imperialist sentiment as its economic power and penetration of
all continents now made it possible to count the old colonial countries
of Western Europe among the victims. In such a perspective, France,
though among the exploiters in other respects, could also be seen as at
least relatively underdeveloped, for it suffered from the destructive
effects of this penetration.[6]

Although it could not be analyzed in terms of purely economic
interests (unless one considered the benefits accruing to the American
armaments industry), the Vietnam War was now no longer being
judged a mere error of U.S. policy—and naturally even less a just
struggle—but was seen as the unmasking of the true face, the true
nature of America. The Western European countries were not like
that, though a few similarities might exist. Yet there was one country
which, thanks to American aid, thanks to its position in the midst of an
impoverished Arab world, thanks to its victories and its conquests,
occupied a special place among the imperialists, and that was Israel.
Whoever really spoke as a champion of the Third World also had to
take a stand against Israeli policy and ultimately against the Jewish
state. De Gaulle's attitude in 1967 could not be entirely divorced from
such ideas. Many also felt a goodly measure of *Schadenfreude:* "For
fifteen years, Europe has been attacking what it felt to be demagogic
in America's Africa and Southeast Asia policy: arbitrary simplifications, disregard for concrete facts, collusive winking while its friends
were wading through blood and filth. But how well it has now learned
to play this role."[7]

Blood and filth: it was largely moral filth which stained America's
prestige even among large sectors of the German population: "Has
your esteem of the United States increased or decreased during the
last year or two?" the pollsters from Allensbach asked. The answers in
November 1968 were as follows: increased, 5 percent; decreased, 36
percent; unchanged, 48 percent. Of the 36 percent, 22 percent gave

Vietnam as the principal reason.[8] Moral filth was the unfair war of an army that used massive and perfected means of destruction against a poor people. The aversion was reminiscent of what had once been felt toward Italy as it crushed Ethiopia. Moral filth was the barbarity of napalm bombs, of deforestation, of fighting terror by terror. The My Lai massacre was rightly associated with the massacre of Oradour,[9] but in France people forgot the Oradours of Indochina and Algeria, and they almost all tended to overlook the massacres by the other side.

"Vietnam is the Spain of our generation" was a formula many of the young endorsed.[10] For others, it did not come anywhere close to the psychological reality: the barbarous war in Asia led to a radical condemnation of a society which had made such barbarism possible, be that society German or American. In long articles on Vietnam which the journal Konkret published between 1965 and 1967, one could observe how a young woman such as Ulrike Meinhof moved from criticism to rebellion, from opposition to negation.[11] But the anti-Americanism produced or revived by the Vietnam War arose—and this was no paradox—in contact with and under the influence of Americans one felt close to and who often served as models and inspirers. On October 21, 1967, the international Vietnam Day, protest demonstrations streamed through London, Paris, Berlin, Rome, Oslo, Amsterdam, and Tokyo while tens of thousands of young Americans laid siege to the Pentagon. Two years before, on October 15, 1965, Vietnam Day had still been a purely American affair, with unrest at about thirty universities.[12]

As American as the movement for the rights of blacks, tragically marked by the assassination of Martin Luther King on April 4, 1968—a murder that shocked Europe almost as deeply as Kennedy's—was the revolt of the blacks which was promoted by the Black Panthers, who had emerged from the ghetto unrest of 1966. And the most violent denunciations of the foreign policy of the United States, which "by any objective standard . . . has become the most aggressive power in the world, the greatest threat to world peace, to national self-determination and to international cooperation,"[13] were American as well. And American finally and above all was the sociology which culminated in a radical critique of American society and thus a critique of all societies that resembled it or tended in that direction.

The Americanization of the anti-American protest in Europe was carried out through the language of student action (sit-in, teach-in), through clothes, through music. In a certain sense, anti-Americanism became a kind of fashion which derived its mode of appearance, its forms of conduct, and even its intellectual base from America.

But though American influence may be an indispensable explanatory element,[14] it is inadequate to an understanding of that transnational and even transatlantic movement which, though everywhere a failure as a political movement, threw an entire complex of values and certainties into confusion. In Holland, societal and political life changed more markedly than elsewhere. But to gauge the force of the shock waves, one need only consider the significant turn which the years 1966–68 brought to the style and content of television programs in Sweden, Germany, and Great Britain and which was hardly less pronounced than in Holland.[15] Or the similarity of the forms of speech and thought at the universities (including the Swiss) to Marxist jargon, a simplified world view, and a practice of intolerance in the name of absolute freedom. High-mindedness and systematism combined in a general and radical denunciation of national societies which became society as such, its basic pattern or archetype being American society.

The lasting traces of the 1966–68 movements are difficult to recognize, particularly because the willingness to be stamped by them was largely governed by the indigenous stereotypes in each country. The denunciation of the United States hardly came as a surprise to the French, while it shocked in Berlin. The spread of the movement to unions, the threat to the political regime, the diffusion of the patterns of thought of May 1968, were not so much evidence of power as of a certain affinity, a malleability of the surrounding society. The great counterdemonstration that took place in Berlin on February 21, 1968, when tens of thousands obeyed the call of the unions and the Senate to protest against the revolutionary students, defined an abyss, a rift which owed its existence not merely to a different cultural tradition but even more to the immediate proximity of a world in which the freedoms the students dismissed as "formal" were an unattainable dream.

The hope that these freedoms would establish themselves under the Eastern European regimes had been brutally disappointed by the suppression of the Budapest uprising in August 1956. It reawakened in 1968 when the Communist Party of Czechoslovakia underwent a spectacular transformation which was clearly supported by the population and especially the "intelligentsia." As new utopias arose—the non-authoritarian society, based on the spontaneous creativity of all, the return to nature as an antidote to the enslavements of industrialization—the old dream of a pluralistic unity, a non-compulsory planned society, a discipline that did not renounce truth, appeared to become a reality under the leadership of Alexander Dubček.

At the same time, a certain malaise set in among all those who, though denouncing the misdeeds of the United States and the evils of American society (misdeeds which had largely been uncovered by official American investigations, it should be added), yet considered it unnecessary to discover or express the truth about the regimes and societies of Eastern Europe—a truth which the Czechs now began to expose. The danger that this attitude might be contagious was so considerable that on August 20, 1968, Soviet, Polish, Hungarian, Bulgarian, and East German troops invaded and occupied Czechoslovakia. The "Prague Spring" quickly turned into a severe winter.

Except for the German Communist Party, which was coming back to life, the West almost universally condemned this intervention. For the first time, the French Communists immediately and publicly censured the Soviet action. For things had reached a point where the Communist parties of France, Italy, and the Federal Republic saw themselves being attacked from the Left, from libertarian students (part of whom surprisingly saw their utopia realized in China). It was therefore high time to end the solidarity with an undertaking tailored after the imperialist model and which was intended to suppress a growing freedom. But this could only succeed if one also stopped raising the Soviet Union to a more or less perfect model.

For many, however, this also involved a shift not in the nature but certainly in the standard of reference of their criticism of American policy and society: from now on, the United States was measured against an ideal nowhere attained. In this sense, the invasion of Czechoslovakia marked the end of the so-called fellow travelers of the Soviet Union. Yet a significant pattern of thought which raised the Vietnam War to the status of a logical and necessary consequence of capitalism persisted, whereas the destruction of the "Prague Spring" was never seen as anything like an unmasking of the true nature of the Soviet type of socialism.

The condemnation by Western governments stopped short of action. The initiative which led to the calling of the Security Council on August 21 did not obscure the actual position: nothing could be done, and there was no intention of doing anything to keep the Soviet Union from proceeding as it saw fit in the part of Europe it ruled. In this respect, the reactions of President Johnson and General de Gaulle did not differ. Nor did either care to have the Czechoslovakian tragedy adversely affect improved relations with the Soviety Union.

But this concern did not have the same meaning for the two men. The American President did not wish to jeopardize the policy of détente with the USSR which a mere month earlier had led to the signing of the nuclear nonproliferation Treaty. For the French chief of state, Prague meant at the very least a blockage of that policy of "détente, understanding, and cooperation" which was designed to create a Europe that would no longer require the American presence.

The year 1967 had already brought a number of disappointments in

Franco-Soviet relations. This time, the disappointment was especially severe, but an explanation was soon found. On the day after the invasion, the Office of the Presidency issued a communiqué in which de Gaulle's obsession with the "myth of original sin"[16] surfaced once again: "The armed intervention of the USSR in Czechoslovakia demonstrates that the Moscow government has not abandoned the policy of blocs which was imposed on Europe by the Yalta agreements, which is irreconcilable with the right of self-determination of nations and which can only lead to international tension. France, who did not participate in that agreement and does not conduct such a policy, notes and deplores the fact that the events in Prague constitute not only a blow to the rights and the destiny of a friendly nation but are also such as to work against European détente, which this nation practices, which it has attempted to persuade others to practice, and which alone can assure peace."

So Roosevelt was responsible for the end of the kind of socialism Alexander Dubček had been striving for, and the two parts of Europe were put on the same level in terms of the freedom of nations, an interpretation of history which was anything but incontestable. It was just as questionable as the even more quickly proffered explanation which consisted in placing a large part of the blame on the Bonn government: "Lately, there have been instances of imprudence and excessive zeal on the part of the Federal Republic vis-à-vis Czechoslovakia," the then French Prime Minister, Couve de Murville, wrote. Above all, there had been the persistent refusal of all German governments to create a "true Europe." Toward the end of September 1968, during the next regular Franco-German meeting in Bonn, Chancellor Kurt Georg Kiesinger and Foreign Minister Willy Brandt sat on the bench of the accused.[17]

OSTPOLITIK AND THE CURRENCY CRISIS

It is a fact that that great coalition of Christian Democrats and Social Democrats, the two powerful adversaries in the entire earlier political game, had been in power in Bonn since December 1966 and had significantly advanced the policy of an opening toward the East which the earlier government had initiated. In January 1967, the Federal Republic had established diplomatic relations with Rumania, and Chancellor Kiesinger and DDR Prime Minister Willi Stoph had exchanged letters, though the West German government had not made clear over which government of which state the East German presided.

The Federal Republic was thus no longer a kind of permanent obstacle to a policy of détente, and this should have pleased both Washington and Paris. But the satisfaction was not unalloyed. Didn't Kiesinger's government submit too much to General de Gaulle? Didn't German initiatives toward the East always harbor the seeds of a "new Rapallo"? In part, this mistrust could be explained by the composition of the Bonn government: it was made up of those elements that were called the "German Gaullists" who, like Franz Josef Strauss, were calling for greater firmness toward the United States while vigorously rejecting compromises with the East, but it also contained the anti-Gaullists such as Gerhard Schröder and the Social Democrats whose position was more "Atlanticist" and who secretly hoped to be able to conduct a policy of greater openness similar to the General's but against him. But when, in September 1969, Willy Brandt was elected Chancellor with the support of a third faction, the Free Democrats, the liberal party whose head Walter Scheel became Foreign Minister, Richard Nixon was the American President and Georges Pompidou the French. Both strongly supported Bonn's *Ostpolitik* in their official statements, though their real attitudes were more nuanced, to say the least.[18] Everyone applauded Willy Brandt for wishing to destroy the last illusions of his countrymen concerning the two key questions which had not been resolved heretofore: the permanence of the Oder-Neisse line and the existence of the DDR as a state on the international stage. That the quid pro quo for such a painful concession would have to be a new guarantee for West Berlin was all the more readily agreed to in Washington and especially in Paris since the status of Berlin was still the business of the Big Four, which meant that the German government continued to need the erstwhile victorious powers, a circumstance which gave them a certain control over its initiatives.

The treaties Willy Brandt signed in Moscow on August 12, 1970, and on December 7 in Warsaw contained the recognition of the western border of Poland. On September 3, 1971, the Four Power accord on Berlin was signed by the four ambassadors who had negotiated it, and on December 7 there followed a transit agreement with the DDR (as a preliminary step to the basic agreement on relations between the two German states in December 1972). Meanwhile, Willy Brandt had been awarded the Nobel Peace Prize on October 12, 1971, and, though no one contested this award, it was marked by political ambiguities.

The 1970–72 agreements contained important German renunciations: the renunciation of the lost eastern territories, the renunciation of its status as the only representative of Germany on the international stage, the renunciation of the transformation of West Berlin into a *Land* like any other, and the renunciation of complete sovereignty for what remained of the quadripartite sovereignty now constituted the last sign of the unity of the German nation.[19] All these renunciations were made in the interest of détente, of peace, and of personal relations with the population of the other German state, and this immediately gave rise to a certain mistrust in the West.

Renunciation in this context also meant freeing oneself of a certain obsession. Like de Gaulle after the declaration of Algerian independence, Willy Brandt now had his hands free: the problem that had been dominant up to now and had blocked the solution of all others had become less significant. But in spite of the similarity, there was a twofold difference: de Gaulle had had great ambitions in a world which had afforded him only small means, whereas Willy Brandt had no particular plans for the Federal Republic, while its allies saw it as an increasingly impressive power.

There were also personal elements. De Gaulle was no longer there, and Pompidou reacted rather sensitively to the shift of prestige from Paris to Bonn. "The hymns of praise to Willy Brandt that filled the foreign and French press irritated him," wrote Michel Jobert, his closest associate and later Foreign Minister.[20] And without quoting the President, he implied that Brandt's prestige was based "on Germany's economic success and some inconsequentialities."[21] And all resentments aside, it was in fact a question of economic power: the country which had just signed the Eastern treaties had so strong a currency that it could take on the former victors during the currency crisis in the fall of 1968 by itself, whereas America found itself in difficulties and de Gaulle was deprived of the last means of carrying out his policy. The German economy was apparently so vigorous that the ground rules of the European game changed as a result: the French government preferred Great Britain's EEC membership to a Franco-German confrontation and aligned itself with the dollar rather than the mark.

Yet the nonproliferation treaty was the first major international document the Brandt government signed: on November 28, 1969, the Federal Republic, though strongly criticized by the Christian Democratic opposition, affirmed to the world that it was not a major power and would not become one (see Chapter 10). But this renunciation of nuclear weapons did not affect its economic strength. In its relations to Kissinger's America and Pompidou's France, this ambiguity was to play an important role.

The wave of free-flowing capital which, in November 1967, brought down the British pound was merely the first of its kind. Many others followed: the entire international monetary system entered a crisis that lasted for years, and in which the period from 1968 to 1971 represented a transition from putative stability to accepted instability. And this instability also produced an illusion that was discouraging and calming at one and the same time: monetary phenomena determine political phenomena, and this permitted governments to show only their political will when they dealt with short-term monetary crises. Since it is always useful to have someone to blame if real or admitted impotence is to be justified, everyone now tended to diabolize someone else.

For the United States, de Gaulle was the guilty one. Yet while "from 1965 to 1968 the whole French posture towards the Unites States was negative, critical, non-co-operative, and obstructive," it was "never actually destructive," a perfectly impartial observer wrote. "The aim was to limit US power and influence, not to disrupt the Western world. The distinction is important. In political terms, France was playing an opposition role in the Atlantic community, not a subversive or revolutionary one."[22] And this opposition could have had a healthy effect if de Gaulle had not had a tendency toward solitary aggressiveness and clung to the utopia of the gold standard, which was wholly unacceptable to his European partners and even to the most violent critics of American irresponsibility and callousness.

Nor was France the only country to accuse the United States. "An unpredictable inconsistency in the monetary policy of the United States authorities" is denounced by an Anglo-Saxon expert in 1970 as "the result of sheer incompetence." "Without an elimination of the American deficit," he goes on to write, "there could be no hope for a consolidation of the international monetary situation. What was perhaps even worse, the sharp world-wide rise in interest rates meant a danger of a world-wide slump. There must surely be a limit beyond which producers and merchants all over the world would cease to be prepared to finance their activities with the aid of money borrowed at 10 per cent and more."[23]

The rise in interest rates had largely been due to the policy of the chairman of the Federal Reserve Board, and its negative effects combined with those of President Johnson's policy, which he was fighting. In order not to have to ask Congress for the increased taxes that the growing military expenditures of the Vietnam War made necessary, the President accepted the inflation which McChesney Martin fought by raising interest rates on short-term loans. Due to the borrowing of the European branches of American banks, this also lead to higher interest rates in Europe. "A large number of companies have debts between 11% and 13%. Since no investment returns a net profit of more than 5% . . . constant price increases will become necessary over

a period of years, and they will be due entirely to the cost of interest."
"We already had a wage-price spiral and now there is a price—cost of
interest—reduced profits—increased price spiral on top of that,"a
French expert wrote in a retrospective on the twofold process of inflation and recession.[24]

But the shock that was felt in March 1968 was not directly due to
interest rates or inflation itself. In principle, the devaluation of the
British pound was marked enough to correct Great Britain's balance-
of-payments deficit. But it seemed to foreshadow a general realignment of currencies with the price of gold. Speculation in gold attained
its climax on March 14, especially on the London market. Acting at the
request of Lyndon Johnson, who had called him the evening before,
Harold Wilson closed that market on the fifteenth. On the seven-
teenth, a conference of the central-bank governors of those seven
countries which continued playing an active role in the gold pool
(Belgium, Germany, England, Italy, Holland, Switzerland, and the
United States) under the chairmanship of American Secretary of the
Treasury Henry Fowler announced the introduction of the "two-tier
system," which, among other things, meant the end of the pool. From
now on, "monetary gold" would be the gold being stored in the central banks. It was to circulate from country to country at a fixed price of
$35.20 per ounce, but the participating countries actually agreed to no
longer demand American gold. The U.S. government and the central
banks of the six other countries announced that they would suspend
gold sales to individuals and buy none from producers. "Industrial"
gold, on the other hand, was to find its level on the free market but
would no longer enter into international currency regulations, which
would have to be established in part in a new system which the IMF
would work out.[25]

The result was the "Special Drawing Rights" whose principles had
been formulated in a long text at the meeting of the IMF in Rio de
Janeiro in October 1967 and which came into force on August 31,
1968, after acceptance by the IMF administrative council. Since this
new system tends to replace gold and since decisions about the creation of drawing rights must be made by a majority of 85 percent,
which gives the United States a veto (but also the Europeans if they
vote together), de Gaulle vigorously opposed it and the French government rejected the arrangement. But just a little more than a year
later, in December 1969, Georges Pompidou ratified the agreement.
This did not mean a turning away from Gaullism but was a result of
France's changed position.

The student rebellion and the great strikes of May 1968 had had
far-reaching consequences. During the first phase, they had consid-

erably speeded up inflation in France because wages and salaries had been raised as a consequence of the Grenelle agreement between the government, employers, and unions. At the same time, the gold reserves accumulated during the years of prosperity were shrinking rapidly, partly because production had been practically suspended for three weeks, partly because the well-to-do became frightened and turned away from the franc.

Thanks to these same reserves, thanks also to the support from the central banks of the Club of Ten countries, to foreign exchange controls, and last but not least, to de Gaulle's overwhelming victory in the June 30 elections, the situation appeared to improve somewhat. But then a new currency crisis erupted in the fall of 1968. Speculators rushed in to buy marks—hurting the franc, which everyone avoided. Two ways out of this seemed possible: a devaluation of the franc, which de Gaulle wanted no part of, and a revaluation of the mark, which the United States wanted but which did not seem acceptable to the German government a year before an election, for it would have jeopardized export and agriculture.

For the first time, the Federal Republic resisted pressure from Washington. But this stance did not precisely bring a "European Europe" any closer, since de Gaulle was not interested in listening to the proposals for the support of the franc which Karl Schiller put forward in a manner hardly designed to make them palatable. Finally, Bonn took technical measures which temporarily postponed a revaluation, while de Gaulle decided on November 23, 1968, in a particularly dramatic manner not to carry out a devaluation of the franc— which all the world had already considered certain—and to impose restrictive monetary and economic measures instead.

But actually this decision was merely a final spasm. For all intents and purposes, de Gaulle's entire policy had failed by the end of 1968. On the one hand, there was the fact that the material bases of his offensive policy toward the United States had at least been shaken: in 1960, the Bank of France had owned only $1.6 billion worth of gold while the reserves at Fort Knox had come to $17.8 billion. Seven years later, the relationship had improved to $5.2 versus $12.1 billion, but in 1969 it had deteriorated again to $3.5 versus $11.9 billion.[26]

On the other hand, it was obvious now that the "European Europe" would in the future have to take Germany's economic power into serious account. If the Federal Republic no longer gave in to the United States, was it really necessary to go along with the Germans, i.e., with the mark, and against the dollar? Was it not preferable to dispense with the "European Europe" and to bank on the accession of an "Anglo-Saxon" Great Britain to make up for German preponderance? Pompidou became President in June 1969 and shortly thereafter opened the gate to British admission to the EEC. This step is partly attributable to de Gaulle, who had already alluded to such a maneuver in a discussion with the British ambassador Christopher Soames on February 4, 1969, which had occasioned a veritable cascade of diplomatic incidents.

De Gaulle finally saw himself obliged to revise his central idea of foreign policy as the only true policy. The movement of ideas that resulted from the events of May 1968 had diffused global social criticism so widely that he felt compelled to solicit the confidence of his countrymen in a language altogether unusual for him. His statement concerning the reasons for the proposed law on "regionalization," which was to be voted on in a referendum on April 27, 1969, was sent to the entire electorate. In it, de Gaulle defined "our epoch as essentially economic and social in its nature" and spoke of the life of the French, not of France's rank in the world. This new language may have been one of the reasons he was defeated on April 27 and resigned as President. But a partial change of course in French foreign policy certainly preceded de Gaulle's departure.

A sign of this change can be seen in the cordiality of his talks with President Nixon, who came to Paris on February 28, 1969, at the end of a European trip which had first taken him to Brussels, where the most important person he had spoken to was Jean Rey, the former president of the EEC Commission. Nixon had then gone to London, Bonn, and Rome. It is true that de Gaulle had long felt kindly toward Richard Nixon, and the opinion he had already expressed about him in 1960 later came to be shared by other Europeans, the Soviets, and the Chinese: "He struck me as one of those frank and steady personalities on whom one feels one could rely in the great affairs of state if ever they were to reach the highest office."[27] But now, even the style of the conversation showed a significant modification of tone in Franco-American relations.

After de Gaulle's departure, a devaluation of the franc was expected. Franz Josef Strauss, German Finance Minister at the time, proposed a general realignment, in part because he wished to counter the growing inclination of his Social Democratic colleague in the Finance Ministry to carry out a unilateral revaluation of the mark. The notion of a compromise was rejected in Paris and Washington. Suddenly, everyone felt the mark would be revalued. On May 5, the Christian Democratic majority in the German cabinet rejected Karl Schiller's revaluation proposal.

On May 9, all records were broken: the equivalent of nearly 17 billion marks had streamed into Germany, while in November 1968 it had been no more than 9.5 billion. After another meeting of the cabinet, Kurt Georg Kiesinger announced on the evening of that same day that there would "never" be a revaluation of the mark, which the rest of the world interpreted to mean that there would at least be none before the September 24 elections. Earlier, on August 8, while the whole country was vacationing, Georges Pompidou had decided on a strong devaluation of the franc without consulting either his EEC partners or the IMF. Immediately after the result of the Bonn elections became known and the new SPD—FDP coalition was a certainty, the still governing Kiesinger let the mark float. And directly after it took over power, the Brandt government decided on an especially strong revaluation of 9.29 percent to end speculation (October 24). Large amounts of money now left Germany again, though with so handsome a speculative profit that a repetition of the entire operation could occur at any time.

Which is precisely what happened in the spring of 1971, at the very moment a new triangular conflict emerged: a callous American policy was rejected by Bonn because Paris refused to make common cause with the mark. For John Connally, Secretary of the Treasury, things were perfectly straightforward: the United States no longer felt like playing the role of an Atlas who must support the entire Western world on his shoulders. The time had come for the Europeans to relieve it of part of its burden. If they did nothing to help the United States in its currency problems, the American government would act unilaterally and compel them to.[28] In reaction, all justified German concerns, especially over inflationary pressures due to an increase in wages, raw-material prices, and rates of interest, receded into insignificance as compared to the fear that a new, powerful influx of dollars would be exchanged for marks, a process for which liberal economic doctrine provided no remedy. At most, foreign currency markets could be closed, and this was done on May 5, after more than $1.5 billion had entered the country within twenty-four hours. On May 9, the mark again began to float, which meant that its value was set by the market and the Bundesbank did not intervene to maintain a fixed rate. Before that, the German government had proposed to the French to let all European currencies float together. Because the French refused, the Germans decided to act alone. The Dutch guilder floated along with the mark, and Belgium opted for a two-tiered foreign exchange market. The pound, the Italian lira, and the French franc were in relatively little danger and remained at their former exchange rate relative to the dollar. Among other things, this meant the destruction of the plan for a common European currency (see Chapter 10).

For the American government, there was not just Europe and not just currency problems. The most serious trade and financial problem was Japan, and there was an ever-widening desire in the country for disengagement. To end the war in Vietnam, to establish equally good relations with China and the Soviet Union in spite, or perhaps precisely because, of their antagonism, to rid oneself of all constraints vis-à-vis Europe: all this provided the background for those offensive measures President Nixon and John Connally ordered without Henry Kissinger's or the State Department's direct involvement. The convertibility of the dollar into gold or any other reserve instrument was officially suspended, which this time also included the central banks, and a 10 percent surcharge on all dutiable imports was imposed as a provisional measure to compensate for "unfair rates of exchange." The whole thing was a kind of ultimatum to the other industrial countries: they'd better revaluate or else, since a devaluation of the dollar was simply out of the question.

Initial reactions were highly nuanced. The Federal Republic suggested that all European currencies float against the dollar while retaining fixed rates against each other. The French government refused and decided to maintain the same rate as before August 15. But because for the first time Great Britain joined the countries of the EEC, of which it intended to become a member, a kind of European front did come into being. In Rome on November 30 and December 1, John Connally was faced with a general desire for a devaluation of the dollar. Even the Italian government had resolved not to yield. His counterattack was to accept devaluation as a political concession but to propose a devaluation level of 10 percent—which did not at all suit his opposite numbers for trade policy reasons.[29] Even before it came to final negotiations, a conflict between the Finance Ministers of France and Germany, Valéry Giscard d'Estaing and Karl Schiller, caused European unity to disintegrate. The dispute was only settled at a summit conference between Brandt and Pompidou on December 5. And thus it was as the spokesman for Europe that the French President finally met the American President in the Azores and obtained officially what had already been obtained in fact: the devaluation of the dollar with respect to gold and the abandonment of the 10 percent surcharge.

The Club of Ten met at the Smithsonian Institution in Washington on December 17 and 18. The ensemble of decisions finally taken seemed to resolve the immediate crisis. The dollar was devalued, the price of an ounce of gold was raised from $35.20 to $38.80. Relative to gold, the French franc and the British pound remained what they had been, the Dutch guilder and the Belgian franc were revalued by 2.8 percent, the mark and the Swiss franc by 4.6 percent, and the Japanese yen by 7.7 percent. With reference to the dollar, all currencies had been revalued, especially the French franc, the British pound (by 8.57 percent) and the German mark (by 13.58 percent), which devalued the franc against the mark and thus benefited French exports to Germany.

The 10 percent surcharge was dropped, the United States did not reestablish the convertibility of the dollar, and no steps were taken to control the great speculative movements. In actuality, and in spite of a seemingly lasting realignment which involved a return to fixed exchange rates, nothing had been solved. The old Bretton Woods system no longer existed and had not been replaced by a new one, which was undoubtedly due to a lack of common political will, especially among the Europeans, who had been able to agree on no more than a few short-term technical measures. It seemed that the weakened dollar was no less dominant than the strong one had once been.

PART FOUR

In Crisis

10 THE YEAR 1973

GREAT BRITAIN CLOSE, AMERICA FAR AWAY?

The currency agreement of December 18, 1971, at least provided a breathing spell. Since the Europeans had shown relatively little unity, it did not seem impossible that further progress might be made in the direction taken at the Hague Summit in December 1969, where the six heads of state or government had decided to perfect and expand the Common Market.

In March 1970, two committees had been set up. The report of the Davignon committee, which had dealt with political collaboration under the chairmanship of a high Belgian official, had been accepted in October without much of a stir or the raising of great hopes, for its proposals were modest though not negligible: it was a matter of introducing a discreet, useful, and limited consultative mechanism. The other committee, which had convened under the chairmanship of the Prime Minister and Finance Minister of Luxembourg, Pierre Werner, had a much more ambitious task, which was to work out a phased plan for the implementation of an economic and monetary union. Although there had been differences of opinion concerning the definition of the motor (currency mechanisms had been the preference of the Belgian and the French minister—Valéry Giscard d'Estaing at that time— economic policy the preference of the Dutch and the German, Kurt Schiller), the Ministerial Council of the European Community had adopted a three-stage plan on March 22, 1971.[1] The economic and monetary union was to be achieved within ten years, and to include Great Britain, Ireland, Norway, and Denmark, since these four countries intended joining the EEC and this time there was agreement on their admission. The relevant negotiations had begun on June 30, 1970, and the three principal actors, Georges Pompidou, Willy Brandt, and Edward Heath, wanted them to succeed—although otherwise they certainly did not represent a harmonious trinity, particularly as regarded their situation and attitude toward the United States.

For Georges Pompidou, "the Hague Summit [December 1969] and

the Paris Conference [October 1972] constituted two pedal points between which it looked as if the economic and monetary union of the member states of the Common Market was the most direct route toward the independence of our continent."[2]

At the opening of the Paris Conference, which for the first time brought the heads of state or government of the nine countries of the enlarged EEC together, the French President made a long declaration in which he developed the formula by which his most important associate in European affairs would summarize his position. "Europe," he said, "has to speak with a single voice," especially in its relations with the United States, which he discussed in some detail:

Our relations to that great country, the economically most powerful in the world, with which eight of us are allied in the Atlantic Pact, are so close that it would be an absurd idea to create Europe *against* it. But it is precisely this closeness of relations which means that the European personality must maintain itself vis-à-vis the United States. Western Europe, which owes its freedom to the decisive intervention of American soldiers, which was rebuilt with American help and looks for its security in the American alliance, has so far accepted the American currency as the principal element of its foreign currency reserves, and must not dissociate itself from the United States. Yet it must also maintain itself as an independent reality. Whether it be a discussion about trade, which we are all the more willing to enter since our accounts are in good shape, or whether it be a reform of the currency system, which would have to involve a return to the convertibility of the dollar, a new definition of reserve instruments, the development of trade and a control of speculative capital, there are solutions . . .

These calm, unexcited phrases differed significantly from the tone the President had his Foreign Minister use a year later. But hadn't Michel Jobert, so aggressive as Foreign Minister since April 3, not been affable and open before when he was secretary-general of the Office of the Presidency, and had he not often and without the knowledge of the minister, the warm-hearted and eloquent Maurice Schumann, conducted important negotiations for the President, particularly with the British government? An explanation for this change in style can be found in both the men and the events, in Pompidou's terrible illness, which hardened him, and in Jobert's rise to the highest echelons, which did not exactly arouse an inferiority complex in him. One can also look for it in the failures and confrontations of 1973, which naturally also had consequences for the conduct of the participants.

But another interpretation is also possible: from the very beginning, Georges Pompidou had had both a political vision and great open-mindedness but had also felt a profound mistrust which was based on strong skepticism and considerable ignorance of foreign realities. His trip to the United States in February and March 1970 was typical. On the one hand, he spoke clearly and frankly in speeches and at press conferences, particularly about the Atlantic Pact and American investments in France:

If you ask me about NATO, I should like to say: collaboration with our allies is as natural and important for us as the fact that we do not wish to be in an integrated organization, that we wish to preserve what General de Gaulle called our independence, which means our freedom of decision. It is by our free choice that we are allies, not by compulsion.

Question: To what extent would you accept American investments in France?

Answer: If you have capital at your disposal, I should point out that we opened an office called FRIDA a short time ago in New York whose job it is to bring American investments to France. I am in favor of the movement of capital, nothing satisfies me more than to see great French companies invest abroad, in the U.S. and, in view of the means available, I am pleased that American firms can invest in France. I merely wish to say this: I would like to see that these investments not only profit the companies that make them but also benefit France, and that is the reason we may resist certain investments at the present time. If a foreign investment is a real investment which gives us something, which enlarges our productive capacity, our capacity for research, our capacity to export, we not only accept but welcome it. If it involves merely the frequently cheap acquisition of a French enterprise, we do not favor it a priori.[3]

But an incident in Chicago sufficed to make him take a rather different tone. Demonstrators who wished to protest French policy toward Israel invaded his hotel where an official dinner was being given at the moment, accosted the President, and insulted Mme. Pompidou. The very next day, they returned to France. As he left Chicago, Pompidou declared: "These demonstrators have stained America's face and harmed their own cause. But they cannot harm Franco-American friendship since it stands high above such demonstrations of impoliteness." This last sentence did not express his real thoughts. There is no question that the local authorities proved incompetent and showed too much indulgence during this demonstration. But the French President, who was used to the highly organized protection of his person and of official guests of France, hardly had any idea what the freedom to demonstrate and lack of respect for the President meant in the United States. Yet Michel Jobert may be exaggerating when he writes in his *Mémoires d'Avenir,* which are full of longstanding anger:

This trip only left a bitter taste. Mme. Pompidou was resolved never again to visit a country in which her husband had been complacently insulted. The President, who did not excuse the negligence of the American government, continued to feel bitter about the disrespectful treatment of his person and from that time on reacted to the indifference he believed he had sensed with a dryness in his analyses of the relations between the two countries which did not reflect his original inclination. Beyond reasons of protocol, the care he took to meet Nixon only outside American territory, in the Azores or in Iceland, derived from a disappointed and injured confidence. More than the personal insult, however, it was the affront to his country which kept him from feeling any friendly indulgence in the future.[4]

The meeting with Soviet leaders in the fall of that same year was more of a success and personal relations between Pompidou and Brezhnev seemed to have been initiated, although the French President remained reserved and refused to sign a friendship pact, in part because Soviet policies made him mistrustful. If one can believe a witness among whose virtues the precise reporting of confidential communications does not figure prominently, this mistrust extended to everyone, including Great Britain and Edward Heath (about whom Pompidou allegedly said that he was "the only European in Great Britain . . . True, he is anti-French but what Englishman isn't"[5]), but principally to Germany and Willy Brandt, whose *Ostpolitik* he felt gave the Federal Republic too much weight, especially in its relations with the Soviet Union (see Chapter 9).

The chronology does not in fact seem to show a Franco-German rivalry: on August 12, 1970, the German-Soviet agreement was signed in Moscow, and on October 6 Pompidou visited the USSR. In September 1971, Willy Brandt met with Brezhnev in the Crimea, and in October the latter visited France.[6] But actually the intentions were quite different. Brandt wanted Soviet support so that the other German state might be willing to make concessions on Berlin. And this support could not be obtained without American help. In exchange for its participation in arms limitation talks, the United States therefore negotiated a Soviet concession on the status of Berlin in February 1971. Pompidou needed no help of any kind, since he was not conducting genuine negotiations and pursued no specific aim.

It is also true that good relations with the United States were much less of a constant preoccupation for Willy Brandt than they had been for his predecessor. This was one of the charges his Christian Democratic opposition raised against him and which almost brought him down in May 1972 when it tried to prevent ratification of the Eastern treaties.[7] The Chancellor had to obtain the dissolution of the Bundestag in September and to triumph at the polls in November before he could recover his prestige. Meanwhile, on May 17, the opposition had approved a very important text: in its fifth article, the "joint resolution" declared it essential that the rights and responsibilities of the Big Four for all of Germany and Berlin continue in force. This meant that the three German parties not only accepted the fact that West Berlin would never be a *Land* properly so called but also that the Federal Republic was not a state like any other and never would be. Paradoxically, the Big Four represent the last vestige of national unity (see Chapter 9). In order not to destroy this vestige, the decision was made not to wholly abandon the subordinate status that dated back to 1945. The consequence was a kind of dependence on the United States and a certain inferiority vis-à-vis the European partners, France and Great Britain.

At the same time, Great Britain seemed to accept a further weakening of its position. The special relationship with the United States no longer offered any advantages. And wasn't the Commonwealth a burden rather than a means of influence? This does not mean that the British had changed into enthusiastic Europeans. The polls that were conducted simultaneously in the six EEC countries and in England showed this clearly: "Are you for or against British participation in the Common Market?"[8] On the continent, the negative answers ranged between 6 percent and 11 percent (in France), while the positive went as high as 79 percent in Holland, 69 percent in Germany, and 66 percent in France. By contrast, 63 percent were negative in Great Britain and only 19 percent positive. "If Great Britain were part of the EEC, would you then be for or against a further development of the Common Market to include the creation of a political entity, the United States of Europe?" In Great Britain, only 30 percent declared themselves in favor, as compared to 69 percent in Germany, 67 percent in France, and 60 percent in Italy. The no votes came to 48 percent, 9 percent, 11 percent and 7 percent respectively.

The British application for admission to the EEC had been submitted by the Wilson government. But it was the Conservative government, which had returned to power after the elections of June 18, 1970, that took it upon itself to oppose public opinion and try to change it. The first important vote of approval in the House of Commons came on October 28, 1971. On January 22, 1972, the solemn signing of the membership treaties of the four new EEC members took place in the Palais d'Egmont in Brussels, though at the end of September only three of them remained, for a referendum in Norway had rejected EEC membership by 53.9 percent of the vote. In October, the summit conference of the Nine approved a final declaration in which it envisaged the implementation of a European union by 1980 at the latest.

Yet enthusiasm was limited when the Europe of the Six became that of the Nine on January 1, 1973. In part, this was due to the fact that Georges Pompidou felt he saw a criticism of his conception of Europe in the near-failure of the referendum he had asked for in April (39.5 percent abstentions), though actually this merely expressed the lack of interest of his countrymen in so undramatic an issue as approval of the admission of the new EEC members. A more important reason was that the "Werner Plan" for a European economic and monetary union had already failed.

When at their monthly meeting in Basel on April 10, 1972, the governors of the central banks had established rules of procedure which set a relatively narrow range for the "snake" of the participating currencies, hopes had been high. Any fluctuations in excess of 2.5 percent in either direction would have obliged the participating banks to an unlimited intervention. As early as May, Great Britain demanded that its currency be included in the snake. But this was before it had joined the EEC and, more important, in spite of the fact that it had taken no steps to solve the problem which had been so great a concern first of de Gaulle's and then, in 1971–72, of the vice-president of the EEC in charge of currency questions, the Frenchman Raymond Barre. What was involved here was the role of the pound sterling as a reserve currency for the countries of the Commonwealth, the Middle East, and Far East. Eight weeks after it had joined the currency snake, Great Britain left it again on June 23, 1972, and the pound sterling began to float once more, while the Six expressed their intention to respect the Washington and Basel agreements. In Bonn, disagreement on monetary policy led to the resignation of Finance Minister Karl Schiller, who was succeeded by his principal foe in the cabinet, Helmut Schmidt. But the further devaluation of the dollar on February 12, 1973, merely confirmed once again the disarray of the international monetary system and the desire of the American government to play its game without excessive regard for its European partners.

The important August 1971 decision had been due in part to a change in perspective. With the "decline and disappearance of the American foreign policy establishment," a new team had moved in: "A solidary group of academicians, bankers, journalists and jurists who had played a dominant role in the shaping and implementation of American foreign policy during the postwar period. . . . The cohesion and influence of the establishment disintegrated in the confusions of the Vietnam war. The return of the bitter hawks and mutilated doves to their nests brought new faces into key positions."[9] In a certain sense, Henry Kissinger, Presidential Adviser and Secretary of State after August 9, 1973, was also one of these new men, though he had had long experience in Atlantic relationships. The man in power was no longer the same he had been at the university, and so it was perfectly proper to write: "It is sad that as Secretary of State, he does not understand what he could explain so well as a Harvard professor."[10]

Neither in currency questions nor in trade was it any longer a question of feeling co-responsible for the fate of Europe. Instead, there was the need to act exclusively for the benefit of immediate American interests and to do this so emphatically that it seemed as if there were an intent to force the Europeans to make "a most unwelcome choice—either unity in Europe or cooperation with the U.S."[11] And this especially since Europe was certainly not President Nixon's primary concern, nor that of the great traveler into whom Henry Kissinger soon developed. In 1972 Richard Nixon set out on his amazing global diplomacy. In February, he flew to Peking, in May to Moscow, thus becoming the first American President to recognize the People's Republic, and the first to visit the Soviet capital. But while Europe applauded his desire for renewal and détente, the impression of being on the sidelines dampened this positive reaction.

At the same time, the Vietnam War would not end. Yet as early as July 1969, Kissinger had tried to get the Paris peace negotiations going again by establishing direct contact between Ho Chi Minh and Nixon, and had naturally turned to Jean Sainteny.[12] But he soon got caught in a terrible mechanism: every time the enemy gained ground or the negotiations faltered, the war was escalated a little more. The American invasion of Cambodia in April 1970 was meant to destroy the Vietnamese troops there. The bombing of North Vietnam between December 26 and December 30, 1971, the worst since November 1968, had no object other than diplomatic pressure. The same was true of the bombing of Hanoi and Haiphong in April 1972 and then in December when an agreement in Paris seemed near. It was finally signed on January 27, 1973.* The last 23,700 American soldiers now began leaving Vietnam, and prisoners of war were to be exchanged within two months. The plan to set up a "reconciliation commission" in Saigon came to nothing (see Chapter 11).

A Gallup poll conducted at the time showed that the President had the support of 68 percent of all Americans. He had been reelected by a landslide on November 7, 1972. A bare year later, on November 3, 1973, the Gallup Institute announced that the President was sup-

---

* Without remembering his comments on the anti-Pompidou demonstration in Chicago, Michel Jobert writes in his memoirs: "On the occasion of the solemn signing, demonstrations occurred before the International Conference Center. They were quite unpleasant for William Rogers and the American delegation, who immediately saw a hostile French government behind them. The recent devaluation of the dollar was more serious."

ported by only 27 percent of his countrymen. The reason was that the police had surprised the so-called plumbers in the office of the Democratic Party in Washington's Watergate Hotel on June 17, 1973. And on October 10, the Washington *Post* had started a campaign which shook the entire political system of the United States and did not end until Richard Nixon resigned on August 9, 1974.

"YEAR OF EUROPE" OR YEAR OF OIL?

After the withdrawal from Vietnam had been completed and new relations established with China and the Soviet Union, one could attend to Western Europe once more. 1973 was to be the "Year of Europe." Two texts explicated this idea: a speech by Henry Kissinger on April 23 in New York, and a long passage in a report on U.S. foreign policy during the 1970s which President Nixon submitted to Congress on May 3.[13] What was involved here was the definition of transatlantic relationships in a world that had been changed by the economic development of the EEC, by détente, by the rise of Japan, which would have to be made part of the "Atlantic solutions" in many instances, and by the foreseeable depletion of energy sources for the industrialized nations.

Both texts stated that the United States had always supported European unification efforts and that it would continue to do so. Not because it was an end in itself but rather in order to strengthen the West as a whole. EEC foreign trade policy, especially as it related to tariffs and protectionist policies which limited the import of American agricultural products, demanded a new definition of the bases for collaboration between the United States and the EEC in this decade. "We will maintain our forces and not withdraw from Europe unilaterally. In turn, we expect from each ally a fair share of the common effort for the common defense." An important aspect of these new conditions was the desired combination of détente and defense efforts. The Europeans should not worry about bilateral American-Soviet relations. Wasn't it a fact that most of them also had bilateral relations with the USSR? In any event, the United States would do nothing to endanger the security of the Europeans. For all that "a concerted strategy is necessary" for which reason regular consultations and coordination would have to define a new Atlantic charter.

Europe reacted to all this with mixed feelings, though not because the fundamental problem was not clearly recognized. The U.S. economic offensive which had been under way for two years had largely derived from a sense of relative decline, which meant that it was based on the upswing of the European economies. During the period from 1950 to 1970, the U.S. share of global exports had dropped from 16.7 percent to 13.7 percent while the EEC share had risen from 15.4 percent to 28.8 percent (though half of this was trade within the EEC). And in 1970, only 15.7 percent of international reserves remained to the United States, while in 1950 they had amounted to 49.8 percent. During that same period, the share of the EEC had risen from 6.1 percent to 32.5 percent.[14] American privileges, expecially in currency matters, were all the more clearly recognized by the Europeans as they overcame their initial weakness, while the Americans noticed, with growing irritation, the one-sided advantages the Europeans were deriving from U.S. military protection and from their political support of the idea of European unity.

The proposals of Henry Kissinger and President Nixon were received positively because they were seen as a kind of recognition of Europe as a unit. They might even have the advantage of forcing the Europeans to better define themselves. But weren't there already too many disagreements among them, a large part of them on questions which had a direct connection with transatlantic relationships? Besides, the idea of a new Atlantic charter had been advanced in a situation that was generally unfavorable and was becoming ever gloomier even before a new war in the Middle East broke out.

Inflation rose significantly in 1973. In part, this was due to currency fluctuations and the earlier credit policy (see Chapters 8 and 9). And in part, it also resulted from the marked rise in raw-material prices, which had some connection with the recovery itself. "The prices for copper, zinc, tin and coffee reached unprecedented levels in the spring of 1973. . . . Speculation amplified and aggravated these market tendencies. The impact of world demand for food also showed up in dramatic fashion in foodstuffs. The prices for wheat increased two and one-half times, those for soy tripled. While the USSR purchased a total of 20 million tons on the American market during the summer of 1972, and this at very low, subsidized prices, food was suddenly becoming scarce. The large world markets which had been suffering from a surplus heretofore are presently experiencing shortfalls."[15]

This was particularly true of soybeans, for there had been a poor harvest in the United States. The American government therefore decided to limit their export. But European cattle breeding is largely dependent on soy imports from the United States. This is especially true of French cattle breeding, which a technical revolution has made increasingly dependent on a mixed feed in which soybeans provide the necessary protein. As far back as 1966, the French agricultural research institute had warned the government of a dependency on imports, particularly in view of the "foreseeable rise in world demand," and had added that national production could be substantially increased.[16] Although liberalized in early August 1973 and suspended in October, unilateral American export restrictions in the summer looked like a declaration of war or at least a cynical demonstration of an economic dominance which permitted all manner of extortion.

The soybean affair did nothing to reduce the antagonisms within the GATT commission which was charged with preparing trade talks between the United States, the EEC, and Japan. On the eve of the "Nixon Round" which took place in Tokyo in September (for which reason it was later called the "Tokyo Round"), the Nine agreed on a joint text which diametrically opposed the American. The Europeans stated: "The liberalization policy of world trade cannot be successfully continued unless a parallel effort to establish a currency system which protects world trade from the kinds of convulsion which have lately occurred is also made."

To which the Americans answered: "A functioning monetary system presupposes that governments take trade measures which facilitate the process of adjustment [of balances of payments] and make concomitant efforts to liberalize trade and improve commercial relations. These points will be kept in mind throughout these negotiations whose purpose it is to improve the international economic order in light of those structural modifications that have occurred during the last few years."[17]

Since the European text was already much weaker than the French had demanded, French participation in the Tokyo Conference seemed in doubt. In a letter to Prime Minister Pierre Messmer, François Mitterrand, first secretary of the Socialist Party, insisted that France stay away. Toward the end of July, Messmer answered him that France had decided to participate. Apparently, the government felt a desire for reconciliation at that time, and that desire became a decision in late September when Finance Minister Valéry Giscard d'Estaing recognized at the general meeting of the IMF in Nairobi that "special drawing rights are becoming the most important reserve instrument" and thus subscribed to the thesis he had rejected earlier. Already in late May, a similar tendency had emerged when during his talk with Nixon in Iceland, Georges Pompidou had referred to the presence of American troops as indispensable to the defense of Europe.

The concern that lay behind this observation was shared by the European governments at a time when U.S. relationships with the USSR kept improving. In his message to Congress, Nixon had not been wrong in saying, "Our allies wish to influence our relations with the Soviet Union to strengthen their own security. At times our allies have urged the United States to be more flexible in approaches to the Soviet Union; in other periods, they have criticized us for moving too fast or too far in relations with Moscow."

The Nixon-Brezhnev agreement on the prevention of nuclear war which was signed in Washington on June 22, 1973, reflected a phase of the latter kind, though Article 6 stipulated that it must in no way affect or jeopardize the obligations of the two signatories toward their allies. For the French, more than merely a problem of security was involved, especially since in his first address to the National Assembly on June 19, Michel Jobert had spoken of "our Soviet friends." In France, the Soviet-American agreement appeared as a "return to Yalta," as a symbol of a joint domination of Europe by the two superpowers.

The United States as a dominant power, just like the Soviet Union: this idea, widespread in France, less so in the Federal Republic and in Great Britain, received additional support on September 11 when a military coup overthrew the government in Chile, killed President Salvador Allende, and imposed an exceptionally cruel dictatorship. The Chilean tragedy was felt all the more deeply in Italy and France, as Allende had represented an entirely novel attempt to institute a Marxist government with Communist support though without therefore surrendering the liberal principles of bourgeois democracy. No direct proof of American help to the putschists was needed to immediately denounce the United States. Wasn't there sufficient proof of the activities of the CIA and the giant American ITT that had been directed toward preventing Allende's victory and later to bring about his overthrow? In his speech before the U.N. General Assembly on December 4, 1972, Allende had analyzed ITT activities in detail and exclaimed: "It has driven its tentacles deep into my country and proposed to manage our political life . . . I accuse the ITT of attempting to bring about civil war."[18]

The fact that Vice-President Spiro Agnew had to resign a month later because he had been convicted of tax evasion hardly contributed to an improvement of the U.S. image in Europe. But his departure and replacement by Gerald Ford were minor events compared to the crisis which the Egyptian and Syrian attack on Israel gave rise to.

The Yom Kippur War was the fourth Egyptian-Israeli conflict. More indecisive than those that preceded, its first phase was defined by massive U.S. arms shipments to the Israeli army and a regular air lift from the Soviet Union to Egypt. When the Israelis took the offensive, the United States tried to push through a cease-fire to prevent an Israeli invasion of Egypt. During the weeks between the Egyptian and Syrian attack on October 6 and the Egyptian-Israeli agreement of November 11 which was signed at "kilometer 101," relations between the two superpowers had been full of contradictions. There were simultaneous confrontations—most spectacularly when American troops were put on alert on October 25—and cooperation. Israel had to be saved from the Soviet-supported Arab countries, and any intervention by Soviet troops to save Egypt had to be prevented. And while the Soviet Union had to be kept at bay, its help was also needed if the belligerents were to end a war that was jeopardizing world peace. The American game was anything but simple.

It was made more difficult by marked transatlantic friction. American procedures had offended the Europeans, while Henry Kissinger felt betrayed by America's European partners. The United States demanded that the Europeans support American aid to Israel without giving them any voice in American decisions; indeed, without prior consultation on decisions that directly affected them.[19] American military bases in Germany were used to speed supplies to Israel, for example, yet the Bonn government was not informed. Chancellor Brandt protested and finally demanded that the American government at least stop using German ports for its shipments. In the government and the German press, "Gaullist" notes were suddenly sounded: Can it be called normal that the Atlantic allies should have no right to remonstrate with the principal power in the alliance the moment a crisis, albeit beyond the NATO sphere, affected the European countries?

Though the bitterness in Bonn was great, Henry Kissinger expressed disgust in Washington. Spain had refused the United States permission to use its air bases. And so had Turkey, Greece, and Italy. The Italian government had trouble enough as it was for having permitted the island of Maddalena, north of Sardinia, to be used as a port of call during the preceding year for the supply ships of American nuclear submarines. The Heath government had imposed an arms embargo to keep British-built Israeli armor from obtaining spare parts and ammunition. Before that, the British Prime Minister had requested the American Secretary of State in strictest confidence to keep secret the use of British bases by American planes. And in the United Nations, Great Britain had avoided introducing the compromise resolution the United States wanted.

In Paris, the government quickly demonstrated that its generally pro-Arab position had not changed. Already on October 8, Michel Jobert had answered the question concerning France's stand on the responsibility for the conflict with a question of his own: "Is the attempt to put one's foot back into one's own house necessarily a surprising act of aggression?" An exchange with Jean Lecanuet in the National Assembly on October 12 revealed a fundamental aspect of Jobert's attitude: he did not share de Gaulle's illusions concerning the possibility of a game *à quatre:*

> *Lecanuet:* I am now coming to your recent conduct which in my eyes again shows your partiality. I am referring to the persistence with which you seek solutions only by way of an understanding among the Big Four and not through direct negotiations. Has your view in this matter changed?
> *Jobert:* Excuse me for having to interrupt you once more, M. Lecanuet, but I did not advocate an understanding among the Big Four in the name of the French government.
> *Lecanuet:* Yet it was the policy of the government for a long time.
> *Jobert:* I did in fact mention that it was the policy of the French Government for a long time. But I will tell you something: at the time I was in the Elysée, I was entirely against that policy because I knew it wouldn't lead anywhere. And now you have the proof.

Lecanuet's centrist opposition wanted to see the arms embargo become general, but the government stuck to the concept of "countries in the theater of war." Libya thus continued receiving the promised Mirage jet fighters, even though the firm of Dassault had announced in January 1970 that the question of their possible transfer to Egypt had constantly been discussed, particularly after Colonel Qaddafi's statement in February 1971: "We can do anything we please with the weapons we bought with our gold."[20] On November 12, 1973, one day after the cease-fire was signed at kilometer 101, Jobert vehemently criticized in the National Assembly "the system of entente that has developed from an agreement between Brezhnev and Nixon" and whose effects could be most clearly seen in the "international community." "That true condominium has resulted in the community's impotence."

During the following weeks, a subject that had already been discussed with reference to a passage in Nixon's May message came up again and now brought Michel Jobert and Henry Kissinger into conflict. The American President had distinguished between the "regional interests" of the Europeans and the "global interests" of the United States. His Secretary of State turned this remark into a reproach which annoyed an ally that had expressed its readiness to assume world-wide responsibilities even more. The controversy suffered from insincerity on both sides. When Kissinger accused the Europeans of being solely concerned with regional affairs, he failed to mention that he was perfectly satisfied to be able to act without interference and pleased not to have an organized Europe rising alongside the United States. When the French complained about American ac-

tivities, they failed to mention that they had no desire whatever to
enter risks anywhere. It was not inconvenient to have America protect
Israel and keep the Soviets at bay, while one's own hands were free
because not burdened by any genuine responsibilites.

The condominium idea was certainly not confined to the government. In a resolution entitled "For a Europe on the Path to
Socialism," an extraordinary congress of the Socialist Party of France
also put the two superpowers at least on the same level:

> The two superpowers, the United States of America and Russia, who grew in
> the same measure as the Occident disintegrated, today run the affairs of the
> world. . . . This directorate resembles a coalition government of two parties
> that now agree, now disagree. When they agree, the other states are impotent;
> when they don't, the noise and the quarrels of these giants make the world
> tremble. In either case, the nations suffer from the consequences of events
> they cannot influence. Although often different from that of the U.S., the
> expansionary capacity of the USSR must be watched very closely by the EEC
> countries. We need Europe just as urgently in order to avoid domination by
> the superpowers as we need it to fight American imperialism.[21]

"Treated like a nonperson, humiliated in its nonexistence, Europe
in its energy dependence is nonetheless the object of the second
struggle in this Mideast war," Michel Jobert said on November 12.
And energy dependence was in fact at the center of the problem of
European attitudes. The share of oil in energy consumption of the
European OECD members had risen from 32.5 percent in 1960 to 59.6
percent in 1970. The percentage figures for 1973 are shown in the
table below:[22]

	Oil	Natural Gas	Coal	Other
Italy	78.6	10.0	8.1	3.2
France	72.5	8.1	16.1	3.2
Belgium/Luxembourg	62.1	13.8	23.7	0.4
Netherlands	54.2	42.3	3.4	0.1
Federal Republic	58.6	10.1	30.1	1.3
Great Britain	52.1	13.2	33.6	1.2

For a time, it had looked as if France could largely rely on the oil in
the Sahara. But apart from the fact that those resources were limited,
tensions with Algeria over oil had developed in 1971. The European
Community never succeeded in putting together a joint energy policy
vis-à-vis the Organization of Petroleum Exporting Countries (OPEC).
And this in spite of the fact that the situation in which the Europeans
found themselves was quite different from that of the United States.
While the nine EEC countries had to import 63 percent of their
energy requirements (and 98 percent of their oil), the United States
only had to import 17 percent (and 38 percent of its oil).

The very considerable restraint of the European governments when the Middle East war broke out derived from the consciousness of this dependence. Only the Netherlands denounced the unilateral Syrian-Egyptian rupture of the coexistence that had been in force since 1970. They were punished for this by OPEC, which announced an initial embargo on October 17, and then stated its tactics on November 5: from now on, oil exports would be cut by monthly installments until the Arabs had attained their aims in the war against Israel. The importing countries were divided into three groups: the United States and the Netherlands would be totally boycotted; "friendly" countries, Great Britain and France among them, would continue receiving at the same level as before; and supplies to the rest would be cut by 5 percent a month.

One might have thought that the Europeans would show a common front in face of these threats, that OPEC would in a sense hasten the unification of Europe, just as Stalin had in 1948. The French, the English, and the Germans could probably have been persuaded to accept the consequences of decreased oil imports in the name of European pride. But what actually happened was a kind of *sauve-qui-peut*, a scurrying for advantage through bilateral negotiations with this or that oil-producing country, at best a general compromise with OPEC which demanded as its first priority that pressure be brought to bear on the Netherlands to get it to join the more conciliatory "larger" European countries. But the Federal Republic, more sensitive to the fate of Israel, kept a certain distance from Great Britain and France. Late in October, the French government immediately resisted the Dutch desire for an agreement between the Nine concerning the distribution of available oil.

On November 9, President Pompidou is said to have told a friend: "You can believe me when I say that I have meanwhile come to know the Dutch. On the Quai d'Orsay, people don't seem to have understood that yet, but the Dutch can't stand the French: that is the only constant in their history. They give us lectures on Europe but all they want is to chain it to America. . . . That's the reason they sabotaged the Fouchet Plan, which was the only genuine chance for the creation of a political Europe. The U.S. didn't want it at any price."[23]

Finally, a minimal understanding was reached, in part because the Netherlands threatened to limit its exports of natural gas (which made up 40 percent of the French consumption of it), in part because it changed its attitude and became less supportive of Israel. The embargo against the United States continued until March 14, the boycott against the Netherlands until July. In point of fact, however, supplies were not really distributed unevenly, for the large oil companies decided among themselves and without consulting the governments, and sometimes against their wishes, to equalize distribution (which caused friction between the British Prime Minister and British Petroleum and between the French government and the state-owned Compagnie Française des Petroles). The companies did well for themselves but had actually usurped the place of the quarreling states.[24]

The problem of oil quantities soon took second place to that of price, for in February 1974 the oil-producing countries raised the price of a barrel of crude oil from $2.50 to about $10. This quadrupling produced large additional revenues so that total income from oil rose from $14.6 billion in 1972 to $85.2 billion in 1974,[25] while the European countries had to spend a significantly larger share of their national product for the indispensable oil. In earlier discussions between oil companies and oil-producing countries that had taken place in 1971 in Teheran and Tripoli, President Nixon had already subscribed to the view of a commission which had recommended a long-term price rise for imported oil so that domestic prices might be stabilized at a higher level and investments in national energy sources promoted.[26] In Europe and especially in France, many politicians and journalists were convinced that OPEC had acted on American wishes and that that country therefore bore a share of the responsibility for the difficulties of the Europeans.

The governments wavered between two tactics: collective negotiations with the oil-producing countries or joint action with the United States. At the ministerial conference of the Atlantic Council on December 10 and 11 in Brussels, both oil problems and the project of a new charter were discussed. Henry Kissinger and Michel Jobert expressed very different views. The following day, in London, the American Secretary of State suggested to the Western European countries and Japan that they and the United States set up a joint energy commission which the oil-producing countries should also join. The French government favored a conference of European and Arab countries. This proposal was to be examined by the heads of state or government of the EEC on December 14-15 in Copenhagen. Though a communiqué was issued there in which the conferees affirmed their common will to have "Europe speak with a single voice on the large questions of the world" and which included a "statement on European identity," the conference was wholly dominated by the arrival of four Arab foreign ministers, whose presence again reinforced differences of opinion among the Europeans.

On December 21, the conference of the United Nations began in Geneva. To prepare it, Henry Kissinger had spent days flying all over the Middle East. Convened at the insistence of the Security Council by Secretary-General Kurt Waldheim, it was presided over by Kissinger and Gromyko and ended with provisional and uncertain results on January 9. Only after some more shuttling by Henry Kissinger, an agreement between Egypt and Israel was finally reached on January 18, by which the confrontation between enemy troops along the Suez Canal was ended.

Between January 7 and 9, the representatives of the OPEC countries met in Geneva and took tougher positions, which produced strong U.S. reactions. One of them was an invitation President Nixon sent to the eight most important oil-importing countries—the Federal Republic, Great Britain, France, Italy, the Netherlands, Norway, Canada, and Japan—to a conference which was to take place in Washington on February 11 and deal particularly with the question of a meeting with oil-producing countries.

From the very beginning, this invitation became the source of new conflicts among the Europeans. At the currency conference in Rome on January 17-18, the German Finance Minister Helmut Schmidt criticized his French and British colleagues, Valéry Giscard d'Estaing and Antony Barber, for their policy of bilateral agreements with the Arab states. The German government was strongly in favor of the Washington conference, believing it would present a possibility to establish Western solidarity vis-à-vis the oil-producing countries. For the French, the bilateral action was merely the prelude to joint action by the Europeans. But a day later, this position lost much of its credibility.

On January 19, France removed its currency from the "snake," in which now only those of the Federal Republic, Belgium, the Netherlands, Denmark, Norway, and Sweden remained, and let it float. To avoid this situation, Helmut Schmidt had offered the French a $3 billion credit, but it was turned down. In the name of the Socialist Party, André Boulloche now criticized the government: "Our German partners had made proposals. But you have not officially recognized the stability of the mark vis-à-vis the sick franc and did not want to risk the creation of a zone in which the mark would be dominant. In so doing, you have destroyed a European structure. But is it in the interest of France to be alone? It looks as if the Europeans, incited by the U.S. and often with its help, intended to destroy the creation of Europe, and this without being able to count on the help of the USSR, whose attitude in this respect has never been very encouraging. What results is an extension of the de facto U.S. protectorate to all countries of the West which is being mediated by their economies."

From January 23 to 29, Michel Jobert traveled through the Middle East. Particularly on Syrian radio and television but everywhere else as well, he put matters very clearly: "'The positions of France and of the United States are diametrically opposed." In a final press conference in Damascus, he made statements which were not printed in the Syrian press: "Malicious tongues might claim that the sale of arms was one of the aims of my trip. I shall not keep it secret from you that this matter did come up." And about the Geneva conference: "There is no question that the true problem would have come up at Geneva, had France been present."[27]

On January 31, the European Commission in Brussels took an extremely unusual initiative and issued a "solemn appeal to the heads of state or government of the EEC member countries." The long text[28] mentioned the "crisis of confidence, will and clear-sightedness in which Europe found itself in face of a new situation which remorselessly exposes its weaknesses and dependence but also irrefutably proves the need for its unity." What unity? The Nine had discussed it in the middle of January. Their foreign ministers met again in Brussels on February 4 to agree on a common attitude at the Washington conference. The British Parliament now agreed to discuss energy, since it had obtained certain advantages in the matter of European development aid for underdeveloped regions. Even before that, the nine countries had persuaded the American government to invite all EEC countries. At the same time, it was agreed that the Community would be represented by two men: Walter Scheel, the German Foreign Minister whose turn it was to preside over the Council, and the president of the Commission, François-Xavier Ortoli. Michel Jobert had made the participation of France contingent on the acceptance of a text which narrowed down the possible scope of the Washington conference.

Because Pompidou had kept Finance Minister Giscard d'Estaing from attending on the same basis as his colleagues from the other EEC countries, France was represented at this conference by Michel Jobert and soon found itself alone. It seems that the other eight EEC countries went beyond the concessions they had made to France in Brussels and agreed to the creation of a permanent coordinating committee (which would develop into the International Energy Agency in November).

The final communiqué was signed by all ministers present except Michel Jobert, who rejected the most important paragraphs. On February 21, before the foreign policy committee of the National Assembly, he vigorously criticized American policy and the attitude of his European colleagues, whom, as he put it, he would greet with "Good morning, traitors" at the next meeting. Some days later, when asked why he had gone to Washington to begin with, he answered: "At first,

I did not see the necessity of going to Washington. But since we all depend on each other in this European adventure, my colleagues said to me: 'We are alone, we are weak, don't let us go there by ourselves.'"[29]

The disarray of Europe which was to have spoken with a single voice now was evident, and the course of the Washington conference seemed to mean that thanks to the oil crisis, the United States had regained its position as the leading power among the partners who were unified only when under its direction. But things were different in America, where bitterness over French policy was all the greater as it was believed there that the other Europeans had allowed themselves to be led astray by Michel Jobert's position.[30] Late in March, the French ambassador handed the State Department a note and sent a letter to the Washington *Post* in which he protested against the manner France and French policy were being portrayed in the American press.[31]

A year after its proclamation, the expression "Year of Europe" seemed mendacious or absurd. At the same time, the three most important countries of Europe changed leadership, and this entailed consequences for both the problem of its unity and its transatlantic relations. On February 28, 1974, and in contrast to 1951, the British electoral system worked in favor of the Labour Party, giving it 301 seats as against 297 for the Conservatives, while the Liberals with one-fifth of the votes got only one-fiftieth of the seats. Foreign policy has played only a minor role in the election campaign. It would not become more important until October when Harold Wilson consolidated his position by a decisive election victory (39.2 percent against 35.8 percent for the Conservatives, or 319 seats as compared to 277). In their constituencies, 80 percent of the Labour candidates had spoken in favor of once again submitting the question of England's EEC membership to a referendum.[32]

In France, the change in leadership was due to the death of Georges Pompidou on April 2. Valéry Giscard d'Estaing was elected President on May 19, with 50.8 percent of the vote, while François Mitterrand, the candidate of the Left, with 26,368,000 votes, missed victory by a mere 425,000. Michel Jobert left his office on the Quai d'Orsay and was replaced by the ambassador to Bonn, Jean Sauvagnargues.

In Bonn, Willy Brandt had to resign on May 6 because it had been discovered that one of his closest associates, Günther Guillaume, was a long-time spy for the DDR. Helmut Schmidt became Chancellor.

The men now in power in all three countries were considered more "Atlanticist" than their predecessors. The man they would deal with continued to be Henry Kissinger, who carried on as Secretary of State under Gerald Ford, who succeeded Richard Nixon on August 8 with diminished powers. The Watergate affair had led to a weakening of the presidency and a strengthening of the ambitions and possibilities of Congress.

11 UNCERTAINTIES

THE ALLIANCE AND ITS WEAPONS

On June 26, 1974, the heads of state or government of the member countries of the Alliance signed a declaration on Atlantic relations in Bonn which the NATO Council had adopted in Ottawa on June 19. This fourteen-point declaration reads in part:

The members of the North Atlantic Alliance declare that the Treaty signed 25 years ago to protect their freedom and independence has confirmed their common destiny. Under the shield of the Treaty the Allies have maintained their security, permitting them to preserve the values which are the heritage of their civilization and enabling Western Europe to rebuild from its ruins and lay the foundations of its unity.

The members of the Alliance reaffirm their conviction that the North Atlantic Treaty provides the indispensable basis for their security, thus making possible the pursuit of détente. They welcome the progress that has been achieved on the road towards détente and harmony among nations, and the fact that a Conference of 35 countries of Europe and North America [i.e., the CSCE] is now seeking to lay down guidelines designed to increase security and co-operation in Europe. They believe that until circumstances permit the introduction of general, complete and controlled disarmament, which alone could provide genuine security for all, the ties uniting them must be maintained. The Allies share a common desire to reduce the burden of arms expenditure on their peoples. But States that wish to preserve peace have never achieved this aim by neglecting their own security.

The members of the Alliance reaffirm that their common defence is one and indivisible. An attack on one or more of them in the area of application of the Treaty shall be considered an attack against them all. The common aim is to prevent any attempt by a foreign power to threaten the independence or integrity of a member of the Alliance. Such an attempt would not only put in jeopardy the security of all members of the Alliance but also threaten the foundations of world peace.

At the same time they realize that the circumstances affecting their common defence have profoundly changed in the last 10 years. The strategic relationship between the United States and the Soviet Union has reached a point of near equilibrium. Consequently, although all the countries of the Alliance remain vulnerable to attack, the nature of the danger to which they are exposed has changed. The Alliance's problems in the defence of Europe have thus assumed a different and more distinct character.

However, the essential elements in the situation which gave rise to the Treaty have not changed. While the commitment of all the Allies to the common defence reduces the risk of external aggression, the contribution to the security of the entire Alliance provided by the nuclear forces of the United States based in the United States as well as in Europe, and by the presence of North American forces in Europe remains indispensable. . . . The European members, who provide three-quarters of the conventional strength of the Alliance in Europe, and two of whom possess nuclear forces capable of playing a deterrent role of their own, contributing to the overall strengthening of the deterrence of the Alliance, undertake to make the necessary contribution to maintain the common defence at a level capable of deterring and if necessary repelling all actions directed against the independence and territorial integrity of the members of the Alliance.

The United States, for its part, reaffirms its determination . . . and states its resolve, together with its Allies, to maintain forces in Europe at the level required to sustain the credibility of the strategy of deterrence and to maintain the capacity to defend the North Atlantic area should deterrence fail. . . . All members of the Alliance agree that the continued presence of Canadian and substantial U.S. forces in Europe plays an irreplaceable role in the defence of North America as well as Europe. . . . They wish also to ensure that their essential security relationship is supported by harmonious political and economic relations. In particular, they will work to remove sources of conflict between their economic policies and to encourage economic co-operation with one another.[1]

This was certainly not a charter with precise obligations such as the American Secretary of State had proposed the year before. Actually, the text deviates only little from the draft Michel Jobert had worked out and to which his successor Jean Sauvagnargues and Henry Kissinger paid homage when they announced that they had come to a quick agreement on disputed points, though these were really not central.

Yet the declaration was important both in what it said and in what it didn't say. The reference to elementary problems of security shocked those who did not like discussing them, particularly in France. On the other hand, this was the first time that the French nuclear force—and the British, which had never created any serious problems for the Alliance—was recognized by the other members as a gain for collective security in a certain sense. And as he read Article XI, every European and American could see how ridiculous the brief allusion to economic difficulties was, at least at a moment when the security of the member countries was clearly threatened much more directly by recession and inflation than by Soviet arms. And even over the longer term, the gap between energy needs and available resources seemed much more disquieting than the constantly growing military might of the USSR.

The meetings in Ottawa and Brussels had to deal with two modifications which might have affected the security system of the Alliance. One of them was relatively minor: in March, in the midst of its dispute with Great Britain over fishing rights, Iceland had demanded the closing of the NATO base at Keflavík. The other was both more significant and more ambiguous: on April 25, the regime in Portugal had changed; Prime Minister Marcello Caetano, who had become Salazar's successor in 1968, was driven from power by a movement in the armed forces. What attitude would the new leaders take toward the Alliance? Wouldn't the weight of the extreme Left be felt, particularly since the United States had supported Salazar's dictatorship? Or was it possible on the other hand that Portugal would soon have a democratic system and thus bring it about that the proclaimed will of the signatories to the Atlantic Pact to defend political freedoms no longer appeared suspect?

Almost immediately after the declaration on Atlantic relations, the entire southeastern flank of the Alliance threatened to disintegrate. Two of its members, Greece and Turkey, were practically at war with each other,[2] the object once again being Cyprus, which had been an independent republic since 1960. The Greek military junta, in power in Athens since 1967, needed a foreign policy success. The Cypriot national guard under its Greek officers staged a coup on July 15, 1974. President Archbishop Makarios eluded assassination at the last moment. The superpowers did nothing: the American government made no bones about its support of Athens, and the USSR did not mind that Turkey should feel neglected by its NATO partners. On July 20, Turkish troops landed on Cyprus and occupied part of the island. A cease-fire was declared on the twenty-second. But in August, after futile negotiations in Geneva, the Turkish government again took the offensive to "establish bases for a new Cypriot state."

Meanwhile, Kissinger had had a change of heart. He had stopped supporting the regime of colonels which the United States had helped bring to power in 1967 and had kept there, though under strict control. Under the joint pressure of the American government and part of the Greek army, the President, General Gizikis, turned for help to the exiled politician Constantine Karamanlis in Paris, who would become Prime Minister only if democracy were restored. The wave of anti-Americanism which now swept Greece was so strong that the August 14 decision of the new government to withdraw from the military organization of NATO (though not from the Alliance) hardly sufficed to restore calm. The larger number of American bases in Greece were to be evacuated. Its troops had barely landed in Cyprus when the Turkish government came under strong pressure from the American government. In reaction to the arms embargo which was imposed, it closed the American bases in Turkey which were not under NATO control. The entire air defense system of the Alliance in the eastern Mediterranean was thus jeopardized by the anti-American attitude of the two quarreling member states. The situation did not improve until the spring of 1976 when an agreement between Washington and Ankara returned the military bases to their function. They would now be under Turkish control, for which the Americans gave the Turks considerable military aid. At the same time, an agreement between Washington and Athens brought the Greeks military assistance, though this did not restore balance between the two countries.

NATO, in any event, continued functioning on both the military and the political level. Since 1974, Greece had maneuvered itself into the same position as France in 1966: both remained in the Alliance but left its integrated command structure. But that was all; France continues in the Atlantic Council, has a voice in the appointment of the NATO secretary-general, and pays its share of the civilian budget. It even participates on a military level, in the early warning system of the United States, but because of the domestic political situation in France, this membership in the organization is never trumpeted abroad.[3]

Conversely, France is not a member of that working team outside NATO which the European members of the Alliance, except Portugal and Iceland, set up in 1968 under the name Eurogroup. In this group, the appropriate ministers meet twice a year to discuss the best ways for jointly using national finances, harmonizing conceptions relating to weapons and training, and making the presence of American troops politically, psychologically, and materially less burdensome.[4]

But organization and coordination do not suffice to overcome the internal difficulties of the various partners. The old quarrel over the possibility of a European defense system is an example. Even setting aside the old disputes over the degree of its independence vis-à-vis NATO and the United States, the fact remains that such a system can be established neither *with* Germany's sharing in nuclear weapons, since this would presumably mean the end of détente in Europe, nor *without* it, for the Federal Republic cannot indefinitely accept the status of a second-rank power relative to France and Great Britain.

The utilization of strategic nuclear weapons is also a matter of dispute: "The Europeans fear that raising the nuclear threshold too markedly might lead to a concept of conventional war which would demand costly and pointless efforts, since it is an axiom for the USSR to always retain superiority in this area. And they fear that this doctrine will lead to the return of conventional wars and their devastation, with which they have a cruel and abundant familiarity. This results in the paradoxical situation that the Europeans seem to demand the use of the weapon which might destroy them while the Americans, whose territory might remain intact, insist that the allies have means at their disposal which reduce to a minimum the compulsion to use them."[5]

As regards tactical nuclear weapons, the apparent paradox is primarily German-American: in order to avoid as long as possible an escalation which would threaten it, the United States would prefer not to resort to them until the last possible moment, while the Federal Republic would rather have the clear threat of the immediate employment of these weapons in the hope that, should deterrence fail, their use would not be too massive, for that would be the end of all German cities.[6]

But the principal problem lies elsewhere and concerns the proper handling of détente. How and about what is one to negotiate with the potential adversary? And who is to do the negotiating? The various American governments have been right to complain that their allies sometimes reproach them for *not* wanting to come to an agreement with the USSR, and at others for doing precisely that. To which the Europeans could always answer: two fighting elephants will trample the grass, but it is equally true that two loving elephants will do the same.[7]

This difficulty remained relatively limited during the long preparation for the conference on security and cooperation in Europe whose final document was signed in Helsinki by the heads of state or government of thirty-three European countries, Canada, and the United States on August 1, 1975. The European states represented included not only the members of the two alliances, NATO and the Warsaw Pact (the two German states among them), but also Liechtenstein, Switzerland, the Vatican, Sweden, Monaco, and Yugoslavia. The long history of the conference comprised three years of contacts to lay down the presuppositions, six months of preparatory talks in 1972–73, and then, after the Foreign Ministers' Conference in Helsinki in July 1973, the actual negotiations in Geneva up to the draft of the final document.

Alongside the negotiations proper, two collateral negotiations were carried on: one between the United States and the nine countries of the EEC, and a second among the nine countries themselves. The coordination of European policy never functioned as smoothly as during the preparation and implementation of the Helsinki conference. Most positions were taken jointly, and there were times when a kind of switch of roles occurred: the American delegation complained of not being adequately consulted by the Nine whenever those countries had agreed on a common position. It is true, however, that the antagonism between the French, who wanted to stress this division within the Western camp, and the Germans and especially the English, who wanted to overcome it, cast a shadow on the harmony among the Nine in 1973–74. The British Foreign Minister, James Callaghan, even went so far as to make public the annoyance of his government with the tensions between the nine EEC countries and the United States and clearly indicated that Atlantic détente was more important to him than détente within Europe.[8] But during the final phase of the conference, the Europeans repeatedly managed to reach genuine unity and to speak with a single voice.

Perhaps this was possible only because the issue at stake was not very important. When the final declaration was signed in Helsinki, everyone knew pretty well that the wonderful principles on security, nonintervention in internal affairs, and cooperation in economic, scientific, and environmental matters would largely remain theory. At least people believed they knew this: none of the Western delegations anticipated the resonance the passage on human rights would find in the Soviet Union and the other Eastern European countries. These results gave rise to contradictory feelings and attitudes: Was one going to support those who invoked the Helsinki accord, even if that annoyed the Soviet Union? Or was it better to ignore them for the sake of détente?

The Helsinki declaration was especially vague on questions of military security and disarmament, for East-West negotiations on these matters occurred within a different context. When the balance of terror had seemed threatened, the United States and the Soviet Union had initiated the Strategic Arms Limitation Talks (SALT) to deal with nuclear intercontinental weapons. At that time, both superpowers had only had a so-called second-strike capability. The missiles in underground silos and on nuclear submarines would not destroy the enemy's corresponding weapons. But when anti-ballistic missiles for possible use in a defensive system and MRVs to break through such a system were developed, the Soviets overcame their reluctance and agreed to negotiations. In May 1972, in Moscow, Richard Nixon and Leonid Brezhnev signed a permanent treaty limiting anti-ballistic missiles and a provisional five-year agreement limiting intercontinental missiles. Further negotiations—SALT II— began in November 1972 and went through alternately optimistic and pessimistic phases but have not so far brought any agreement on fundamental issues, not even on a desirable definition of parity (the same number of weapons or equivalence of the entire destructive arsenal?).

Concerning the other weapons systems, the foreign ministers of NATO decided during their meeting in Reykjavik in June 1968 to propose negotiations to the Warsaw Pact nations. The conference on the so-called Mutual and Balanced Force Reduction (MBFR) began in Vienna in January 1973. Participants were the seven Warsaw Pact nations and the twelve NATO countries, some of them as full conference members (the USSR, the DDR, Poland, Czechoslovakia, the United States, the Federal Republic of Germany, Belgium, Canada, Great Britain, Luxembourg, and the Netherlands), and others merely as observers (Bulgaria, Hungary, Rumania, Denmark, Greece, Italy, Norway, and Turkey). France had refused to participate in any form since it was opposed in principle to any negotiations between blocs or alliances, for it felt that this made things too easy for the superpowers. The communiqué of June 28, 1973, stated: "The objective of this conference is to arrive at an equilibrium of military forces in central Europe, with a reduction of force levels but without a reduction in security. It has been agreed that the security zone considered in this study would comprise the territories of Belgium, Czechoslovakia, the German Democratic Republic, the Federal Republic of Germany, the Netherlands and Poland."[9] A second reason for the nonparticipation of France was the desire not to become involved in future arms limitations or disarmament measures in a certain part of central Europe.

The Vienna MBFR negotiations proved to be as protracted and frustrating as SALT II. But their lengthiness and the constant change in negotiation topics did not keep them from causing serious disagreements and tensions between the United States and its European allies. The Bonn government, for example, had initially been positive toward the MBFR talks because their results might make it possible to strengthen contacts with the other Germany and simultaneously cut down military expenditures, but it became increasingly reserved the more clearly a decision emerged which would imply a certain reduction in the American commitment. This also explains its increasingly insistent demand for detailed consultations between the allies. And these consultations were all the more desirable because the United States was making decisions in the SALT II talks which might have a direct bearing on the security of the Europeans without their having first been consulted. This applied especially to possible limitations on the production and placement of cruise missiles, those unmanned aircraft which can fly so low that they escape detection by radar and can drop both nuclear and conventional bombs with extreme precision on their targets. Or to the neutron bomb, which destroys human life but not buildings or objects, and is presumably capable of stopping massive armored attacks on European soil.

But consultations presuppose two things: that the Americans are ready to discuss their decisions in advance, and that other countries know what they want, that they have defined clearly what weapons they need for their security.[10] In December 1977, the Nuclear Planning Group of NATO decided to place neutron bombs in Europe. France did not belong to this group and therefore refrained from influencing the decision of its partners, especially because there was no negotiating or decision-making structure in the EEC where detailed consultations on security measures might have taken place.

The Federal Republic tried hard to take a hand in the planning and the structures of NATO because it wished to assure itself of a certain influence on American decisions. Up to the time of his resignation in February 1978, Georg Leber, in office since 1973 when Helmut Schmidt had taken charge of the Finance Ministry, had been Defense Minister. He was a respected personality in the Atlantic Council and had had friendly relations with his American colleagues Melvin Laird and James Schlesinger. The appointment of General Gerd Schmückle as deputy commander-in-chief of Allied forces in Europe in early 1978 symbolized the strength of the German army within the alliance. Yet it was a rather limited strength: the Federal Republic had no nuclear weapons and had to rely on strategies which were defined on the basis of the American nuclear commitment. In 1977, the old debate over forward defense thus began anew. Would the United States, because it feared escalation, not be willing to first let the enemy invade part of German territory?

While German doubts and fears revolved around protection by the Americans, successive French governments had attempted to exploit these fears to convince the Bonn government that a common European defense would be advantageous. But from the very beginning, this argument had lacked all credibility, since it was loudly proclaimed at the same time that France was interested only in its own defense. While it is true that there had been uninterrupted contact between the French and the "Atlantic" general staffs since 1966 to coordinate action in case of a possible conflict, the French position had always remained the same, especially with respect to the short-range Pluto missile stationed in France: "We will defend you by destroying the enemy the moment he is inside your cities." The statement Prime Minister Jacques Chirac made on February 10, 1975, when he turned the first Pluto missiles over to the troops at Camp Mailly, seemed to indicate a change, however: "In the knowledge that her fate is tied to Europe, France proposes to play a role that is in keeping with her capacities in the defense of the continent to which she belongs. To accomplish this, we cannot content ourselves with making our own territory "sacrosanct" but must also look beyond our borders. In this sense and because they are French and genuinely

European on this continent, these weapons by their mere existence constitute a contribution to the defense of Europe. And it is a contribution whose scope our allies and we ourselves have not yet fully assessed."[11]

But under the twofold pressure of the opposition and the Gaullists, who were in the majority and led by that same Chirac, the French President dared go no further in the examination of new ideas, although he did support General Méry, the army chief of staff, in the controversy which his publication of an article in the *Revue de défense nationale* in June 1976 gave rise to. In a carefully circumscribed manner, General Méry had envisioned French participation in forward defense, i.e., a possible nuclear commitment in a concerted plan. In June 1977, when the new head of government, Raymond Barre, addressed the troops, only a trace of all this remained: "The concept of deterrence is used in the defense of our vital interests, which means that it applies essentially to our national territory, the heart of our existence as a nation, but also in bordering areas, i.e., those of our neighbors and allies."[12]

In the same address, the old doctrine was emphatically reaffirmed: "National independence is the law of every French government . . . but it must be equally clear that France belongs to the Atlantic Alliance and must fulfill the obligations deriving therefrom, should the occasion arise, in complete independence." And France would at the same time strive to "take her security into her own hands," which was perfectly possible since its strategic nuclear force is "effective and adequate." On May 25, 1975, President Giscard d'Estaing had already stated in a radio broadcast: "I have given much thought to this problem and have come to the conclusion General de Gaulle would also have reached, which is that France must have an independent defense."

A twofold criticism of this position was voiced. In view of a statement the President made at the same time, on May 21, 1975, it seemed that as far as the Soviet Union was concerned, independence had not been sufficiently stressed. When Giscard d'Estaing spoke of the "understandable concerns" which "the plans for an organization of European defense arouse in the USSR since it could see in them the danger of a long-term threat or a certain military pressure by the Europeans," had he not conceded a kind of veto power to the nation at whose cities French missiles were aimed? And if it was true that two contradictory aims ("to free France from all subservience to the military alliance with the U.S. and from all constraints within NATO; to continue availing oneself of the American shield over Germany without participating in common defense") could be pursued simultaneously, what had been gained? Wouldn't one finally reach the point where one strengthened Germany's position, yet did not become truly independent, simply because one's means were inadequate?[13]

But this kind of criticism has been losing ground on the political stage of France, since the Socialist Party and especially the Communist Party have fundamentally changed their attitude toward the Force de Frappe. The "Joint Program" of these two parties of June 27, 1972, had stated: "Renunciation of the strategic nuclear Force de Frappe in any form whatever; immediate stop to the further development of the French Force de Frappe; step-by-step conversion from military to peaceful atomic industry according to a precise schedule . . . immediate stop to nuclear tests and adherence to treaties banning atomic explosions and the proliferation of nuclear weapons."

As the March 1978 elections approached, the Socialist Party took a position which was somewhat unclear but in which endorsement of the French nuclear force at least in its present form, i.e., "retention," prevailed. The Communist Party even spoke like those Gaullists who had been determined to not only affirm the value of nuclear weapons but to move away from the Alliance. Even the "defense in all directions" concept which de Gaulle had never made his own reemerged.[14]

Can one expect a similar reorientation on two further counts? The Joint Program had stated: "Suspension of all arms and war material sales to colonialist, racist, or fascist movements [and] strictest regulation of future arms sales abroad."

The question of arms sales was given added importance in transatlantic relations by two consequences of the economic crisis. One was the tendency to cut military budgets,[15] which made arms purchases by one's own forces more difficult and the sale of weapons to others even more essential to the profitability of the armaments industry. The second was that the armaments industry became a privileged sector which could not only provide jobs during periods of unemployment but also help correct balances of payments.

Within the Alliance, competition had always been so strong that rationalization and standardization of weapons systems were never attained. Citing cost effectiveness and better organization, the United States had usually argued vigorously for the acceptance of its products. Attempts to standardize at the European level had consistently failed. The French wish that other European countries decide in favor of French weapons in the name of European unity was all the more difficult to fulfill as France had not become a member of the Eurogroup, and this is also the reason for the rapprochement with this group which began under the presidency of Giscard d'Estaing and is being vehemently criticized by both the Communist Party and some of the Gaullists.

In fact, competition in arms sales is becoming more severe in all parts of the world, in Latin America as in Africa or the Middle East, where military expenditures (in 1970 dollars) have risen from $1 billion in 1960 to $13 billion in 1975.[16] And not just rifles are involved. The missile market, where American, Soviet, French, British, German, Franco-German, and Anglo-French products compete,[17] is developing nicely since the number of purchasing countries in the Third World, those interested in long-range ground-to-air missiles, for example, soared from one to twenty-seven between 1958 and 1975.[18]

Political and commercial motivations are closely interwoven, but the latter tend to dominate. The argument "It is better for the peace of the world (or for the West) that I should be the seller and not someone else" often simply hides the desire to sell the greatest possible quantities to the largest number of countries. The British presence and the recent appearance of the Federal Republic on the arms market notwithstanding,[19] it is primarily the French and the Americans who, between them, compete against the Soviet Union. In 1977, France had a market share of 16 percent, which made it the third biggest arms exporter in the world after the United States (46 percent) and the Soviet Union (30 percent). Arms sales amounted to as much as 16 percent of all French exports of industrial goods, and the French armaments industry employed 270,000 (as compared to 750,000 in the United States).[20]

The promoters of these arms sales are both governments and private (or state-owned) companies.[21] In the course of a NATO conference in Brussels in 1975, for example, President Ford urged Belgian Prime Minister Leo Tindemans to purchase General Dynamics rather than Dassault planes. In the Middle East, French ministers go peddling their wares. There is a more or less constant competition between the Commission for International Logistics Negotiations, a kind of Pentagon sales promotion office, and the Direction des Affaires Internationales of the French Defense Ministry, which was run by the engineer Hughes de l'Estoile from 1970 to 1977, when he joined Breguet-Dassault as deputy director-general for international affairs after a short spell in the Ministry of Industry. The problem of corruption emerged with special clarity when Lockheed conquered almost all European markets. Owing to an especially high number of crashes, its Starfighter, which had been ordered by the then German Defense Minister Franz Josef Strauss, attained a depressing notoriety in Germany, and Prince Bernhard of the Netherlands found himself at the very center of a scandal as a highly paid Lockheed representative.[22]

Commercial rivalries, technical considerations, strategic options, and financial aspects made up a confused tangle in the "deal of the century" when American planes finally won out over their French counterparts on the European market. In September 1974, a communication the French air force general and then vice-president of the National Assembly, Paul Stehlin, sent to the French President caused a scandal. In this document, which he also sent elsewhere, he attempted to prove that the General Dynamics and Northrop jet fighters were "indisputably superior to the Mirage F-1" of Marcel Dassault, whose influence on French politics he denounced.[23] On June 6, 1975, it was learned that four NATO countries (Belgium, the Netherlands, Denmark, and Norway) had decided after months of hesitation to order the F-16 from General Dynamics. On that same day, a Senate committee under Frank Church which had been investigating the conduct of Northrop and Lockheed published a letter in which General Stehlin called on Northrop (a firm from which he received a yearly retainer) to launch a press campaign to promote the Cobra. A few hours later, Stehlin was run over by a bus in front of his office. He died a few days later. The court limited compensation to the family because of the victim's "abberant behavior" in traffic. A year later, the affair of Marcel Dassault's chief accountant, Hervé de Vathaire, revived discussion of the business practices of that concern.

Is the issue of arms sales related to the French-American and German-American conflict over exports of nuclear installations? Certainly, for it was felt by Henry Kissinger and later by President Carter that a proliferation of nuclear weapons might result from the misuse of these plants, which in principle are intended for peaceful uses.[24] But the pressure the American government brought to bear on the parties that had signed contracts for shipment (the Federal Republic with Brazil and Iran; France with Pakistan and South Africa) can also be seen as an expression of commercial rivalry, independent of any security considerations.

In spite of its having signed the nonproliferation treaty, it was hardly ever disputed that the Federal Republic had the right to export nuclear installations, especially since, on November 28, 1969, the very day it became a signatory, the German government had sent all countries with which it had diplomatic relations a note specifically reserving the right to do so.[25] The Schmidt government resisted the American pressure over its contract with Brazil in June 1976 more vigorously than the French did over their agreement with Pakistan at the same time. The discussion revolved essentially around the scope of guarantees that would keep these installations from being used for military purposes. In France, the conflict contributed to the creation of the Council for External Nuclear Policy on September 2, 1976, which would be chaired by the President of the Republic and would balance export needs with efforts on behalf of the nonproliferation of nuclear weapons. At a global level, the nuclear exporting countries which had already adopted common directives in January 1967 agreed to new guidelines on January 11, 1976.[26] The 1976 signatories (the United States, the USSR, Great Britain, France, Canada, the Federal Republic, and Japan) were joined by Italy, Belgium, the Netherlands, Poland, Czechoslovakia, the DDR, Sweden, and Switzerland. Today, the problem of nuclear energy is no longer confined to a small number of countries, and the global energy crisis now overshadows concern over the spread of weapons.

ECONOMIC COMPETITION

During the prosperity of the 1960s, people had not really been conscious of it. It took the provocative conclusions of the Club of Rome to set off a genuine discussion on the limits of available resources for an uninterrupted general growth and the extremely uneven distribution of such resources in the world.[27] Even though the economic crisis was less widespread than had been feared toward the end of 1973 when the large oil price increases occurred and the various economies underwent a marked slowdown rather than a genuine recession, the threat of a collapse of industrial production and of the monetary system has remained a heavy short-term burden for the United States and its European allies, while over the medium term the finiteness of energy sources increasingly takes on the character of an impending catastrophe.

The result is an exacerbation of existing competition and the absence of a usable form of cooperation which would make it possible to deal with this problem through a truly joint effort, especially because competition is no longer limited to the Atlantic world. Steel production is a particularly striking example.[28] In the ECSC countries, a dizzying expansion had taken place: steel production rose from 36.8 million tons in 1953 to 132.4 million in 1974,* while in Great Britain it increased only from 17.9 to 22.4 million tons during that same period. The six members of the ECSC thus reached the level of the United States, whose steel production had risen only from 101.2 to 132 million tons. The considerable development of the Soviet Union (from 38.1 to 136.3 million tons), however, did less to sharpen competition

---

* Germany from 15.4 to 53.2 million tons; France from 10 to 27; Italy from 3.5 to 23.8; the Netherlands from 0.8 to 5.8; Belgium from 4.5 to 16.2; Luxembourg from 2.6 to 6.4.

than the staggering Japanese growth rate: from 7.6 million tons in 1953 to 117.1 in 1974. For Japan can export at lower prices, because its labor cost is much smaller than that of the United States or Europe and because the indebtedness of the Japanese steel industry is minimal as compared to that of its European competition, especially that of France. In 1976, Japanese exports to the European market equaled the exports of all six countries of the former ECSC. Of the approximately 13 million tons the United States imported in 1973 and 1976, the share of the Six fell from 43 percent to 22 percent while Japan increased its share from 37 percent to 56 percent.

To save untold thousands of jobs and prevent the bankruptcy of large enterprises, thought has been given to closing the borders. And bitter competitive struggles in various forms have been waged where currency manipulation combined with investments which gave hope of increased productivity: thus the weakness of the dollar made it possible for European investment in America to succeed American investment in Europe. The same weakness also permitted an increase in exports.

But does the unleashing of competition solve anything? For a possible increase in American production can do nothing toward solving the most serious problem, the problem of energy sources in a country where energy consumption rises by 4 percent a year, and this due to waste as much as to necessity. While average per capita income in the United States, Sweden, and the Federal Republic is roughly the same, the average American uses almost twice as much energy as the average Swede or German.[29] To meet the constantly growing demand, President Nixon had wanted to stimulate the development of domestic energy sources. In an important speech on November 7, 1973, he announced energy independence for the country in the near future. The program was an almost total failure, and President Carter therefore gave priority to the energy problem. On April 20, 1977, three months after coming into office, he submitted an energy conservation program through which he hoped to reduce the yearly increase from 4 percent to 2 percent. But wasn't this an affront to the habits of his countrymen and the requirements of economic recovery? Frankly stated and less openly avowed interests combined to frustrate the realization of his projects.

Provided that they had not resulted in a recession, the European countries would have benefited from their success, for the excessive energy consumption of the United States comes from global reserves, particularly from those oil fields whose geographical location entails numerous political consequences. The United States imports ever-increasing quantities, and less and less of this oil comes from the Western hemisphere (in 1970, 90 percent of American imports came from Canada, the Caribbean, and Venezuela; in 1976, it was only 36 percent), and more and more from the Arab countries (22 percent in 1973, 38 percent in 1976, and probably between 60 percent and 70 percent by 1985[30]). Among those countries, the preferred partner is Saudi Arabia, whose oil reserves make up one-quarter of global reserves. Even though it is also France's most important supplier (which was the reason for President Giscard d'Estaing's visit in January 1977), Saudi Arabia, whose resources were developed by the American companies making up Aramco and which follows a policy of graduated and contractually safeguarded participation, continues to be America's most important trading partner. American dependence has some influence on the American stand toward Israel, but due to good relations with Washington the representatives of Saudi Arabia exert a moderating influence within OPEC. These privileged relations are also of indirect benefit to the Europeans.

But compared to the twofold advantage the United States derived from the oil crisis, that benefit is minor. On the one hand, the large oil companies have grown more than the small ones and even more than the not so small ones. When Pierre Guillaumat turned over the chairmanship of the Entreprise de Recherches et d'Activités Pétrolières (ERAP, a company which combines all French oil prospecting, production, refining, and distribution) to Alain Chalandon in August 1977, after having exercised enormous power over French oil and nuclear policy for more than thirty years, he left him an important instrument with far-reaching ramifications but also a disturbing situation which had been created by the rise of the "majors," most of which transfer their profits to the United States. It isn't that the power of the large companies had grown.* In 1975, their share of crude oil production in the non-Communist world (except for North America) amounted to only 30 percent, as compared to 73 percent in 1972, while the state-owned share in the oil-producing countries had risen from 12 percent to 62 percent. But profits from refining and distribution, where they retain 47 percent and 45 percent respectively (though less than the 56 percent and the 54 percent respectively in 1973, or the 65 percent and 62 percent in 1963), suffice to assure their prosperity.[31] The other American advantage is U.S. predominance in the International Energy Agency, which was established in November 1974 and comprises nineteen countries, including eight of the nine EEC members, President Giscard d'Estaing having remained loyal to the decision of his predecessor.

But as regards the consequences of the oil price increase and the

---

* There are five American companies: Exxon, Mobil, Gulf, Standard of California, and Texaco; and two non-American ones: British Petroleum (BP) and Shell.

danger of a drying-up of oil sources, either through a possible boycott or the foreseeable depletion of reserves, the United States finds itself in the same position as the Europeans. The quadrupling of the price in 1973–74 means a constant drain on the GNP of the Western countries. That this drain is somewhat smaller than first believed is due to the fact that a slowdown in industrial production also reduces energy demand, that the marked decline of the dollar, which is only inadequately compensated for by new price increases, has reduced real cost to both the United States and those countries whose currency followed the dollar (the franc, not the mark), and that, finally, the recycling of petrodollars, i.e., the reinvestment of the enormous sums taken in by the Middle East oil producers, occurs without excessive difficulties and benefits American banks and the European financial market. It is true, however, that where this recycling comes to more than the purchase of real estate in London or Paris, the problem of an increasing control of European industry by the oil-producing countries also arises. There was a good deal of discussion in Germany when Iran acquired much of Krupp in 1974.

Because of its newly discovered oil and natural gas deposits, Great Britain finds itself in a special situation. Thanks to the North Sea oil (and in spite of a downward revision of estimates), since 1977 it has been producing about half of the oil it consumes. For political reasons, this new wealth, which really should enable Great Britain to make up for its slower economic growth as compared to the continent,[32] must not noticeably modify its relations with the United States.[33] But it makes the demand for nuclear energy less critical than for the other countries.

"The President of the Republic has called attention to the importance of carrying out a nuclear energy program for the security and independence of French energy supplies." The concluding communiqué of the session of the French Council for External Nuclear Policy dated August 4, 1977, makes it clear to what extent commercial policy, energy policy, and technology are tied to each other in France. The same holds true for the Federal Republic. In both countries, public debate over increased construction of nuclear power stations is very lively and led to acts of violence in 1977. But the development of nuclear energy seems "indispensable" in both countries.[34] A Franco-German agreement on the development of fast breeder technology was therefore signed on July 5, 1977, while President Carter announced on April 7 that construction of the American counterpart of the French Super Phoenix would be postponed. U.S. energy chief James Schlesinger commented as follows: "Other countries may make different decisions. But there are also cost effectiveness reasons why the Clinch River Project should not proceed. It is based on an already obsolete technology and would provide new insights neither for research nor for development. These are additional reasons for the President's veto which reinforce his reluctance to speed up the development of fast breeder reactor technology too much."[35]

And what if the United States wished to prevent the growth of European nuclear technology? In the spring of 1975, a not atypical, predominantly German-American conflict arose: without prior warning, the Nuclear Energy Regulatory Commission imposed an embargo on shipments of enriched uranium to Europe. The Bonn government vigorously protested this breach of contract, particularly because the Federal Republic obtained its atomic fuel exclusively from the United States. The embargo was lifted a few months later.[36] In France, the most significant event in the area of nuclear energy programs occurred in 1969. To become independent of the United States, the Office for Atomic Energy had decided to construct a type of reactor which turned out to be a technical success but a commercial failure since its installation was much too expensive, and this did not suit the only customer of the authority, the state-owned Electricité de France. There was thus no choice but to "buy American," i.e., to build with American know-how and to purchase enriched uranium from the United States.[37]

The inability to deal successfully with the financial and commercial aspects of ambitious technological decisions also characterizes the history of French computer technology and civil aviation. On May 12, 1975, when the government announced that the Compagnie Internationale pour l'Informatique—an association of several large French companies that had been founded with governmental help in 1966—would merge with the American Honeywell–Bull (which had been set up in 1970 when General Electric sold the firm which it had acquired in 1964 to Honeywell), Le Monde came out with the headline "Better the U.S. Than Europe!" A book of rare aggressivity with the polemical title French Ordinateurs[38] accused President Giscard d'Estaing and Industry Minister Michel d'Ornano (Prime Minister Jacques Chirac got off a little easier) of having betrayed de Gaulle's striving for independence by "murdering" the "Plan Calcul" of July 1964 by turning French computer technology over to the United States. The other decision through which the French computer industry was meant to become more profitable would have consisted in creating a European combine—Unidata—to be sponsored by Bull, Dutch Philips, and German Siemens. But it seems that here the same fear of German dominance was involved as before when President

Pompidou had decided for the dollar and against the mark. The Düsseldorf *Handelsblatt* commented: "Every time the interests of France are at stake in industrial policy decisions, Paris sermonizes its EEC partners to think and act as Europeans, i.e., as Frenchmen. But when the French themselves have to choose between Europe and the U.S., they all too readily forget the rules they impose on others."[39]

But whether it was the agreement with Honeywell or the Unidata project, wasn't the aim always the same, i.e., to keep giant IBM from achieving a monopoly? And wasn't the newly founded C.I.I.–H.B. 53 percent French, with the controlling interest held by the French government, which was largely financing the enterprise? When a thousand French-built type-64 computers had been sold by the end of 1977, eight hundred of them in the United States, the Minister of Industry had every reason to congratulate the managing director of the new company, Jean-Pierre Brule, the very man who had aroused such hatred because he had been behind the 1975 merger.[40]

Computers are too arcane to arouse the passions of non-initiates, but a beautiful plane is something altogether different. Begun as an Anglo-French project in 1962, the prototype of the Concorde made its first flight on March 2, 1969. Orders came in slowly. In March 1971, the U.S. Senate voted against the development of a supersonic plane. In January 1973, the two largest American companies, Pan Am and TWA, canceled their options. In September, the Concorde made its first flight from Paris to Washington. Regular flights between the two capitals began in May 1976. After a long legal battle with residents near New York's Kennedy Airport, the Concordes of Air France and British Overseas Airways could finally establish regularly scheduled flights to and from New York on November 23, 1977, the only problem being that each flight further increased the enormous deficit the plane had already caused both companies.

It might have been better for the French government if the Concorde had never been permitted to land in New York, for then the overwhelming majority of the French could have stuck to their conviction that only American malice was to blame for the fact that the technically very successful superjet failed as a financial venture. American airlines ordered no Concordes because they were in trouble at that time and had no desire to increase their deficit. And that Lufthansa continued buying from Boeing was not a matter of submission to the United States but due in part to the fact that the Concorde could not provide service between Frankfurt and New York. It was also because the state-owned SNIAS in Toulouse, which made the plane, had refused earlier to produce the Super-Caravelle, which Lufthansa needed when the Caravelle had become too small. The Super-

Caravelle, whose market would have been assured, was sacrificed to the Concorde for reasons of prestige. And reasons of prestige cost the French government and Air France dearly, but they profoundly satisfy national pride on both the Right and the Left. And the affront to this pride revives anti-Americanism.

But the Caravelle would have been an even greater success if McDonnell Douglas had not reneged on its promise to promote the French plane and launched its DC-9 instead. McDonnell Douglas and Boeing (the latter is to the aircraft industry what IBM is to computers) tried to conquer the market by treating possible European competitors as they were used to dealing with each other. And in 1977, McDonnell Douglas began playing the same game with the Mercure of Breguet-Dassault as they had earlier played with the Caravelle—they cooperated at first, then dropped the plane (and the Mercure had no commercial success in Europe).

The decision of the French government on July 27, 1976, to push through the not particularly advantageous collaboration between SNIAS, Dassault, and McDonnell Douglas was experienced as a catastrophe if not as treason by the German aircraft industry. Wasn't it a fact that the Franco-German Airbus had proved a first-rate plane even though it had come on the market relatively late because priority had been given the Concorde?

In 1977, European collaboration (France, Great Britain, the Federal Republic) seemed to be back on the agenda. Now, it was a matter of profiting from clear technological advances by looking for non-European markets.[41] But it was not a particularly encouraging sign when it became known in late December that the Dutch-German firm VWF Fokker had been obliged to suspend construction of the VWF model 614, especially since the German goverment had already invested 1.5 billion marks in the project.

The remorseless competition of American airplane manufacturers now appears as a direct threat to some 400,000 workers in the Western European aircraft industry, although orders placed with French firms, especially for military aircraft, helicopters, and missiles, increased from 9.7 billion francs in 1976 to 23 billion in 1977.[42] The only remaining question is what a European airplane really is. A third of the sales price for every Airbus goes to the United States, since the jet engines and much of the equipment are made there. One thus gets back to the national character of products and profits and to the general problem of multinationals, and yet it has become no easier to give clear answers to the question about the relations between transnational powers and national goals.[43] It is possible to simplify, of course, and to say that every national firm with foreign subsidiaries is an evil if it is privately owned and part of the world capitalist system. Public ownership then seems the only solution, yet no one can say to what extent expropriation of Péchiney-Ugine-Kuhlman by the French government,[44] for example, would change the situation in countries where the firm has branches, nor how the fundamental economic and social problem can be solved: during times of unemployment, it is especially deplorable when production is shifted to other countries, yet the economy of the country in which the parent company (including multinationals) is located profits significantly from the earnings of its foreign subsidiaries.

The protests of French unions against the international strategy of Michelin or Saint Gobain are as well or as poorly founded as the protests of American unions against the subsidiaries of large American firms outside the United States. It is not enough to put the multinationals into the "wake of the Yalta accords" and say: "The external development of French enterprises such as PUK, Saint Gobain, Pont-à-Mousson, Air Liquide or Renault testifies to a French imperialism which—though submissive to the dominant American imperialism—looks for its place in the sun of capitalism."[45] But it is equally a simplification to say: "The United States, for security reasons, tolerated European regionalism, discrimination against American exports, and export drives by Japan and Europe into the American economy," and thus carried "the financial burden of hegemony." Profits, which have been higher than capital expenditures since 1971, reflect technology transfers so that, if the United States continues in this direction, it will convert itself "into the type of rentier economy, i.e., one which lives off investment income, that Great Britain became in the latter part of the nineteenth century." For there is an impairment which corresponds to the growth of American wealth: "The U.S. has strengthened its industrial competitors and paid a high price in terms of real resources and productive capacity."[46] One would therefore have to stop exporting capital and to invest in the United States, if only to be able to export more.

In monetary terms, such a change in strategy could be expressed as follows: "A fixed, overvalued dollar or the conquest of the world by multinational U.S. concerns. . . . A floating, undervalued dollar or the reconquest of the world by American exports."[47] Has this change occurred? Is it correct that "American capital stays away from Europe" and that "one must look forward to a reduction in the creation of new enterprises in Europe and expect that American firms already on the old continent will increasingly finance their investments there from local revenues"?[48]

The figures fluctuate. At times, there are spectacular new ventures such as the enormous Ford plant in Spain which went into operation in October 1972 and will make the giant American company the most important exporter in Spanish industry. American investments in the Federal Republic, where "they are no longer considered a threat but rather a contribution to the West German economy," remain significant but are already being overtaken by those of the other EEC countries.[49] France seemed somewhat less attractive as the 1978 elections approached, but its share of American assets in Europe remained stable (14.3 percent in 1974 as compared to 8.1 percent in Italy, 23.4 percent in the Federal Republic, and 36.4 percent in Great Britain).[50] The most significant new element is probably the increased export of European capital. In both 1975 and 1976, the Federal Republic invested more abroad (5.1 billion marks, 23 percent of it in the United States) than was invested in it (3 billion marks, 25 percent of which came from the United States).

In spite of their different situation in terms of the flow of investment, the European countries continued to negotiate as a unit in the Tokyo Round, which was apparently especially difficult to get started because more than four years had passed between the Tokyo declaration in December 1973 and the beginning of what it is hoped will become the decisive phase of negotiations in Geneva in January 1978. In spite of the great number of participating countries—almost one hundred—official and unofficial debates are dominated by disputes between the United States, Japan, and the European Community.

A principal obstacle during the protracted preparations was the implications and applications of the new U.S. Trade Act which was to define the possibilities and limits of American negotiators. This act, which President Ford finally signed on January 3, 1975, had caused the Congress very difficult preparatory work and produced occasional heated debates, especially over relations with the Soviet Union. The text which was finally passed gives the President and therefore his representatives to GATT less authority than the Trade Expansion Act had on the eve of the Kennedy Round and certainly puts rather narrow limits on possible American concessions.

Tariff restrictions in international trade are once again a source of conflict. Once again, the American desire for a uniform reduction (this time, they demand a 40 percent reduction in tariffs) collides with that of the Europeans (represented by the vice-president of the European Community Commission, the German unionist Wilhelm Haferkamp, who has been a member of the commission since 1976) for special reductions on goods carrying high American import duties. Once again, trade restrictions not related to customs—i.e., hidden restrictive practices—occupy an almost equal space. In this area, complaints by either side are generally founded, for everyone tries to further his own exports by subtle tactics. "The group of experts has observed that there is reason to believe that advantages to which other contracting parties are entitled according to the overall agreement have been annulled or abolished": four GATT reports, published on the same day, concluded with this formula. Three of them criticized the principles according to which France, Belgium, and the Netherlands proceed in income tax matters, and the fourth criticized American tax law for American exporters.[51]

The idea that one would have to try to further liberalize trade in spite of the crisis is not something that can be taken for granted. Yet new protectionist tendencies are being fought on both sides of the Atlantic. In the United States, the traditional champions of free trade, the unions, are now demanding ever higher protective tariffs because there is increasing unemployment, and in France the debate prior to the 1977—78 elections produced a veritable torrent of endorsements of free trade, whereas one would rather have expected traditional protectionist sentiment, be it in the name of the nation or in that of French socialism in a capitalist world. For since the mid-1960s, economic conditions have undergone significant change. The French economy has become thoroughly international, and this has produced spectacular growth which was clearly greater during the ten-year period from 1965 to 1975 than that in the Federal Republic or the United States. At the same time, the awareness of this new reality has constantly increased on both the Left and the Right, though this process is hardly irreversible.

The competition for markets both within Europe and between Europe and America naturally also extends to trade with the Eastern European countries and the Third World. Trade with the USSR and the other Socialist republics can only develop through credits: the indebtedness of Socialist countries is constantly increasing. This constitutes a controversial point in the politics of détente and strengthens the interdependence of the two superpowers, and for that very reason perhaps their common power.[52]

But whether it be Western Europe, the USSR, or the Third World, the problems arising from American economic power are certainly not confined to trade in industrial products. American agriculture is becoming an increasingly important element in the political game. Its weight is of relatively recent date, the earlier confrontations arising from the Common Market notwithstanding. From less than $6 billion in 1971, U.S. agricultural exports rose to more than $22 billion in 1976 so that wheat, corn, and soy now contribute significantly to financing the import of oil. In the name of the international division of labor, the United States is strongly urging European agriculture to switch to cattle raising as quickly as possible and to use American feed. Vis-à-vis their European allies as vis-à-vis the USSR and the Third World, the United States, whose power had been largely industrial and military heretofore, now also wields power through food.[53] It is true, of course, that this power does not suffice as yet to "turn the Common Market into a mere element of the American economy," though in the view of an analyst of French agriculture, such is the trend.[54]

The developed countries are competitors, but they can also ally themselves against the underdeveloped ones. In July 1977, for example, during the Geneva negotiations, the United States and Japan supported the restrictive positions of the European Community on a renewal of the agreement on synthetic fibers. They were anxious to protect their textile industries from competition from Africa and especially Asia. No industrial country, in fact, has managed to deal with the contradictions of a two-track policy, and the attitude of France toward Morocco may serve as an example: to give effective development aid, the modernization and expansion of the Moroccan textile industry was furthered. But the moment it was able to produce, imports of its products into France were made difficult so as to avoid exacerbating the crisis in the French textile industry.

Yet the solidarity of the rich is not total. In the problem of regulating raw-material prices, the European Community countries show more sympathy for the needs of the Third World than does the United States. In this regard, the Lomé (Togo) convention, which was signed on February 28, 1975, between the Nine—both as individual states and as the European Community—and forty states in Africa, the Caribbean, and the Pacific, constitutes a very solid basis and, more important, a symbol of a desirable new international economic order. But already in May of that same year, during the fourth session of the U.N. conference on trade and development (UNCTAD) in Nairobi, it became clear that the Europeans were not a genuine unity. In its insistence on the principle of a free market economy, the German delegation was much closer to the American than to the French, which was more interested in a structured organization of raw-material markets, at one in this respect with the most important concern of the seventy-seven underdeveloped countries represented in Nairobi.[55]

The idea of a new international economic order is at the center of Giscard d'Estaing's foreign policy. Since his meeting with Gerald Ford in Martinique in December 1974, he had been urging the convocation of an energy conference and been concerned with currency questions and a settlement of the Franco-American dispute over the military bases that were evacuated in 1967. (The United States finally accepted a settlement of $100 million.*) Since France is not a member of the International Energy Agency (nor, of course, of OPEC), it chaired this conference, which failed in 1975 because the International Energy Agency was unwilling to extend negotiations on oil to other raw materials. And after numerous talks, meetings, and speeches, the even more ambitious enterprise of a general North-South meeting also failed in May 1977, at least for the time being.

But the French-American conference in Martinique was devoted primarily to currency problems. Hardly a year later, between November 15 and 17, 1975, a rather unusual meeting took place in Rambouillet, near Paris. It was attended by the heads of state or government of France, Germany, Italy, Great Britain, and the United States, while Canada and the five "small" countries of the EEC were deliberately excluded. At that time, the franc had again been part of the currency snake for four months. In principle, the French President was still fighting the American President for a return to fixed exchange rates. But by speaking more and more of "stable" rates, he had already initiated a reorientation. The upshot of the meeting was not presented in France as it was in the rest of the world. The final communiqué declared: "We have noted with satisfaction that at the urgings of numerous other countries, there has been a rapprochement between the views of the United States and France regarding the necessity of stability which is to be furthered by a reform of the world monetary system."

Though a peripheral event of the conference, a Franco-American accord was in fact reached. According to Le Monde, "it contains undeniable American concessions, for the U.S. is now ready to intervene on a regular basis to prevent 'erratic fluctuations' of its currency and this constitutes a 'significant success' for the French President." But in an ironic comment on this alleged concession, Die Zeit had this to say: "How the president of the Bundesbank Klasen and his American colleague Burns must have smiled when they heard of this text." For the two had been coordinating their interventions on the foreign currency markets for a long time. The American President had been clever enough to offer his French interlocutor a compensation which had merely prestige value as the latter took an important step toward recognizing reality, i.e., the system of floating exchange rates the Americans wanted.[56]

Some weeks later, the French change of mind became apparent. But

---

* About 450 million francs, a compromise between the initially rather widely divergent estimates of 200 million and 3.6 billion francs.

hardly two years thereafter, German-American coordination was to appear even less significant than the content of the Franco-American agreement at Rambouillet, for the conference of the twenty finance ministers of the interim committee of the IMF which convened in Kingston, Jamaica, from January 7 to 9, 1976, approved a reform of the IMF which actually legalized current practices. The communiqué expressly stated that the ministers "welcomed the agreement that has been reached on provisions concerning the important problem of exchange rates. In this respect, it has endorsed a new Article IV of the Articles of Agreement which establishes a system of exchange arrangements [i.e., effectively legalizing floating]. The new system recognizes an objective of stability and relates it to achievement of greater underlying stability in economic and financial factors." It was also agreed that Special Drawing Rights would constitute the most important reserve asset in the international monetary system, but these rights were defined neither in terms of gold nor of the dollar but on the basis of a "basket" of sixteen major currencies. No mention was made of an official gold price. The goal continued to be a system of stable but adjustable currencies, but the fluctuating standard of reference allowed all currencies to float freely.

The French government was in no position to plead for fixed rates, for two months later, on March 15, 1976, it was compelled to withdraw the franc from the "snake" since now the free float of the currency seemed the best response to speculative pressure. Although this change in the official French position had already begun to emerge during the general meeting of the IMF in September 1973, the fight against ratification of the Jamaica agreements in 1977 became one of the important elements in the political game of the "Anti-Giscardians," i.e., the Gaullists under Chirac who won in the sense that they got the Barre government not to place the debate on the agenda of the National Assembly before the end of the last session of the 1973–78 legislative period.

That France takes part in international decisions nonetheless, it owes in part to the caliber of its high functionaries: while René Larre has been director of the Bank for International Settlements in Basel since 1971, another Inspector of Finances, Jacques de Larosière, was nominated in early 1978 to succeed the Dutchman Johannes Witteven as director of the International Monetary Fund (a position which had been held by another Frenchman, Pierre-Paul Schweitzer, from 1963 to 1973). He is to devote his attention to a system that is in a state of total disrepair.

The fact that Europe participates in it less and less as an organized unit is both a cause and a consequence of the general debasement of currencies. Even if the French government stopped assuming what is no longer a dramatic but nonetheless persistent sort of protocolary anti-European stance (by resisting the participation of the president of the Brussels Commission in the May 1977 conference in London, for example), the economic and monetary union would be in serious trouble.[57] This is due particularly to the very dissimilar internal political developments of the 1960s. Italy finds itself in ever greater need of international financial aid, which is being granted by the IMF in exchange for monitored commitments in tax and economic policy. The United States and the Federal Republic also contribute because they want to prevent a success of the Italian Communist Party. As a result, the leaders of the Christian Democrats take recourse to those tactics of pressure through weakness by which they did so well in the early 1950s.[58] Initially, Great Britain found itself in a similar situation, but thanks to the North Sea oil, and thanks above all to the policy Harold Wilson and, after his surprising resignation on March 16, 1976, his successor, James Callaghan, made palatable to the unions, it finally managed to arrest the decline of the pound. But this recovery did not benefit Europe, since the British leaders seem to have taken it into their heads to justify all of de Gaulle's prophecies by acting in the least community-minded fashion in all European questions, and this in spite of their success in the June 5, 1975, referendum which confirmed British ties to continental Europe.

Of course, their attitude has less dramatic consequences for Europe than that of the American leaders, at whom both French and German papers display the same annoyance. "Irresponsibility," wrote *Le Monde* in capital letters. "American roulette, seven rules of a cynical game," the *Frankfurter Allgemeine* went so far as to say, and the director of the Swiss National Bank commented: "The economic policy of the United States is not on a par with its world-wide responsibility."[59] European criticism is all the less accepted in America as the great liberal press in New York and Washington, which normally takes the government severely to task, surprisingly adopts the changing attitudes of governmental policy in monetary questions.[60] But this policy, however profoundly and justifiably it may have shocked Europeans in 1977–78, is based on principles which are not always clearly understood in Europe, though they have been stated with the utmost clarity by one of the most highly reputed American experts.[61] The fundamental idea is simple: only U.S. national interests are taken account of, and that means favoring that international monetary policy which is most advantageous to it. To bring this about, the currency must be divorced from political power. For a long time, and often at the price of monetary difficulties, the international role of the dollar had been an instrument of political action. If the dollar is to continue in its function as a transaction and intervention currency, it can now share it with other currencies—which is even desirable, for one can only wish that it lose its politically all-too-dominant position. To the extent that the veto right of the united Europeans in the IMF makes possible a reduction of American responsibilities, the Special Drawing Rights tend in precisely this direction. But the new international system would have to deal with a contradiction: while every country tries to act in its national interest, there is at the same time a significantly larger need for concerted international management.

Of course, the dollar cannot simply be one currency among many. And it is also true that a policy which favors monetary and economic self-interest will unavoidably lead to irresponsibility if it acts as if the dollar were no more than just that. This is especially so when the U.S. government uses its currency to force other governments through pressure on theirs to change their economic policy because it wants to improve its balance of trade and deal with the crisis.

In 1974, it was still possible to believe that "for the immediate future, Germany as the home of the world's second currency might have to play a special leadership role alongside the United States."[62] But since the spring of 1977, the policy of U.S. Secretary of the Treasury Michael Blumenthal, who had already proven himself an unyielding negotiator during the Kennedy Round, has been to treat the German mark as an adversary. In the German press, this provokes such unusual headlines as "Stop Blumenthal Now!"[63] It also constantly forces the German leadership—the Chancellor or the new president of the Bundesbank, Otmar Emminger—to defend the financial and economic policy they maintain in the face of American pressure.[64]

Although in spite of his earlier reputation, Helmut Schmidt now speaks with a much softer voice than General de Gaulle once did, his disputes with the United States are no less burdensome. And while there is a much stronger interest in transatlantic harmony, the substance of these disputes is also much more important for all of the European countries.

"Imperialism is based on a special type of class alliance within the countries, on the social democratic alliance which overarches the division of the working class, a division which reduces its revolutionary potential by attributing greater importance to the struggles along the periphery. That is also the reason factions of the exploiting classes can make tactical moves along the periphery from the camp of the allies of imperialism to that of its enemies as the concrete conditions of the struggle and 'substages' of imperialism demand":[65] only on this supposition does the reversal which has been emerging in German-American currency disputes since 1968 accord with the thesis of a joint German-American predominance over the rest of the European countries, specifically France. If one does not share this view which makes it possible to explain everything according to an identical basic pattern, one will ask further questions about the political reality of transatlantic relationships during the crisis.

POLITICAL UNCERTAINTIES

In February 1978, the dollar fell to 2 marks (after having been worth 4.20 from 1949 to 1961, and 4.00 from then until 1969). At the same time, the German Chancellor refused to take the support measures the American government demanded. The situation of the Federal Republic vis-à-vis the United States had indeed changed. But on May 9, 1977, a "Declaration on Berlin" was published in London. It states:

The collective security ensured by the Alliance, in addition to enhancing global stability, provides the strength and confidence that enable the member-countries to persevere in their efforts to lessen the tensions between East and West and to increase progressively the areas of co-operation. . . . Improvement in East-West relations will depend on the extent to which all concerned show moderation and self-restraint both in Europe and in other parts of the world. With regard to Berlin and Germany as a whole, the other Allies fully associated themselves with the views expressed by the heads of state and government of the United States, the United Kingdom, France and the Federal Republic of Germany in their statement of May 9, 1977, and noted in particular that the strict observance and full implementation of the quadripartite agreement of September 3, 1971, are essential to the strengthening of détente, the maintenance of security and the development of co-operation throughout Europe. . . . The three powers will continue to reject all attempts to put in question the rights and responsibilities which France, the United States, the United Kingdom and the Soviet Union retain relating to Germany as a whole and to all of the four sectors of Berlin. . . .

Strict adherence to existing agreements on Berlin is "indispensable to the continued improvement of the situation and essential to the strengthening of détente, the maintenance of security and the development of co-operation throughout Europe."

The diminished position of the German Federal Republic has thus not changed, even though it has not so far found full understanding of its special concerns among its allies on both sides of the Atlantic. An Italian Communist had to be shot by error along the border between the two German states by East German border guards in August 1977 before Italy really grasped the bloody nature of DDR practices.

The violation of human rights in Eastern Europe is now a reality which no one in the West disputes—not even in those sectors of the public which were still rather hesitant during the late 1960s. But these practices do not result in any clear governmental policy toward the Soviet Union. There are no efforts, for example, to obtain its adherence to the Helsinki agreement. In February 1977, two conflicting tendencies emerged in Paris and Washington: President Giscard d'Estaing refused to receive the Soviet dissident Andrei Amalrik, while President Carter wrote a letter to the persecuted scientist and champion of the persecuted, Andrej Sakarov, to assure him of his support. Later, American and French policies coincided once again in their indecisiveness: Can one pressure the USSR without jeopardizing the desired détente? Can one remain silent and yet invoke the universal defense of universally acknowledged human rights?

Official silence has not prevented the image of the USSR from deteriorating. In his *Gulag Archipelago*, Alexander Solzhenitsyn revealed or, rather, confirmed the dimensions of that reign of terror whose nature was known or could have been known since before the war or at least since 1948. But the debate on "Stalinism" that now started did little to change the U.S. image among those who had persistently presented the Soviet Union as the incarnation of all virtues. In part, undoubtedly, because people refused to seriously rewrite history. The discovery that Stalin had been a mass murderer had no effect whatever on the French Yalta myth. General agreement on how Czechoslovakia had become Communist in 1948 or on the murderous trials between 1949 and 1953 did not prevent the French authors of an introduction to a book by the sons of the Rosenberg couple from asserting in 1975 that the only U.S. worry at that time had been "to stop the spreading oil slick of socialism."[66]

No condemnation of the United States was revised. It is unquestionably true that the bombing of Vietnam was atrocious, and to remember this in a country which tends to speak only of "red" criminals is useful.[67] But the portrayal of the Vietnam War as a confrontation between an America that supports tyrannical governments and the power of the people in its struggle for freedom has only been questioned very hesitantly and discreetly since April 1975, the brutality of the North Vietnamese attack on South Vietnam and the violation of all signed agreements notwithstanding, and notwithstanding the horrors of the regime which imposed the Khmer Rouge on its countrymen in Cambodia. The naïveté of the American negotiators and the cynicism of the Americans when they finally, when chaos was greatest, abandoned those Vietnamese who had helped them and whom they had promised their protection (an even greater cynicism than the French had shown in Indochina in 1954 and in Algeria in 1962) do not justify the retention of earlier conceptions of unilateral guilt. And though the uncovering of the total fiasco of the CIA in Saigon proves its presence,[68] it is precisely the failure of these efforts that should have prevented its activity from being judged a kind of moral equivalent of the brainwashing and massacres which have since been practiced by the victors in Cambodia and Vietnam.

The major revelations about the CIA which had their start in 1974 and were speeded up by the Senate investigating committee under Frank Church should similarly have provoked a twofold reaction in Europe, even though it is true that they brought to light an almost unbelievable number of coups and interventions of all kinds in nearly every corner of the globe. Condemnation of the CIA should have been coupled with admiration for the political mechanisms which allow revelations that are inconceivable in all other countries, including those of Europe. But the former aspect clearly predominated over the latter. There is no doubt that the explanation of world politics by the activities of secret services and hidden forces exerts a strong attraction on minds.

Rather than attempt to understand the new facts of the international system, such as the rise of European and Japanese economic strength, for example, it is very seductive to impute a mysterious power to the "Trilateral Commission." Established in 1973 at the initiative of David Rockefeller, president of the Chase Manhattan Bank, it includes influential American, European, and Japanese personalities. Up to 1977 when he became President Carter's adviser, Zbigniew Brzezinski had been its driving force. The group deals with problems of common interest. Its studies, which are not confidential and certainly not kept secret, occasionally set forth concrete proposals, such as doubling rice production in Southeast Asia. At other times, they contain scholarly analyses. The caricatural presentation of its character and work undoubtedly confirms the image of a world that is ruled by the cooperation of a central imperialism and several sub-imperialisms.[69]

But one may ask if the kind of equality the concept "trilateral" suggests exists at all. A diametrically opposite conception is also possible: "Economic giant, political dwarf: this was the definition of the Federal Republic that diplomats advanced 15 years ago. Today, all of Europe deserves that designation."[70] In the field of world politics, this observation sometimes seems correct, and exaggerated at others. Whenever the Soviet Union intervenes in Africa, be it directly or by Cuban proxy as in Angola in 1977 or in Ethiopia in 1978, Europeans count for little and are always ready to reproach the United States for its nonintervention only to complain later when it does intervene. The constant desire of France to act on its own changes nothing: that it recognized the People's Republic of Angola in February 1976, shortly before the other European states, has so far brought it neither material nor prestige benefits which might have made up for the annoyance the action provoked among its partners. But it is also true that the initiatives of the French government in Zaïre and Mauritania represent a real African presence whose value in the game of the superpowers is difficult to gauge.

As regards the Middle East, the Federal Republic has always maintained good relations with both sides, though without playing a significant role in the difficult, practically unattainable settlement of the conflict, and this perhaps precisely because it has no role in it. In spite of the predictions during the presidential election campaign in 1974, the French position from Pompidou to Giscard d'Estaing has remained unchanged. One need only remember the handshake of Foreign Minister Jean Sauvagnargues and Yasir Arafat in October 1974 and the permission given the Palestine Liberation Organization in October 1975 to open an office in Paris. Even more important, there is the support the French gave Egypt when its relations with the United States were not particularly good ("Egypt will always find France at its side," Giscard d'Estaing stated when he received Sadat in Paris in January 1975), and the sullen silence over the trip to Jerusalem of that same Sadat in December 1977, a time the United States played a central role by urging both adversaries to make meaningful concessions.

Yet the French government can also maintain that the United States had drawn increasingly closer to its theses, both as regards the areas occupied by Israel in 1967 and also concerning recognition of the special rights of the Palestinian people. The declaration on the Mideast situation which the nine European Community countries issued on June 29, 1977, does represent acceptance of the American point of view, but its text, which is based on the famous Security Council Resolution 242 of November 22, 1967, speaks principally of the "legitimate right of the Palestinian people to effective expression of its national identity" and of the "necessity for Israel to end the territorial occupation it has maintained since the 1967 conflict," and also states that the Arab side would have to be willing to "recognize the right of Israel to live in peace within secure and recognized borders." It thus resembles earlier French positions much more closely than those of the United States.

The statement of the Council of the European Community reflects the desire James Callaghan—in the Foreign Office at the time—expressed during the election fight on the British referendum in 1975:

"The Community in devising its procedures and its common positions must always try to work with America whenever it can."[71] Since 1974, the Labour government has made collaboration with the United States the guideline of its foreign policy, though no longer by way of the "special relationship" but as a mediator between the United States and the European Community, and that in a way which *The New Yorker* called "slipping into sycophancy" in September 1977. Domestically, this position involves no risk, for "neither the political parties nor public opinion wants to add to the effects of the crisis the consequences of a difference with the U.S. or to deprive themselves of its support in the solution of their difficulties."[72]

The European Community, in any event, appears less and less an acting unit. The smaller countries, Belgium, the Netherlands, and Denmark, react irritably to the free and easy manner with which the big ones, especially France, ignore them whenever negotiations about important currency questions are being conducted with the United States and Japan. And the internal conflicts—reasons for repeated ministerial crises in The Hague and Brussels—divert attention even more from global politics, to which one has no access in any event.

And what will become of the European Community if it becomes even larger (and thus more disparate) as those three Mediterranean countries which almost simultaneously rid themselves of their dictatorial regimes join it? But won't they have to be admitted so that their leadership, strengthened by becoming part of the community of nine pluralist countries, can buttress their still fragile democracies? Particularly as regards American attitudes and attitudes toward the United States, the changes in Greece, Portugal, and Spain differ. Born under the sign of anti-Americanism, the new regime in Greece has consolidated itself in part with the help of other Western countries, including the United States. But this has not lessened resentment. On the contrary, the election result of November 1977 seemed an American defeat, since the rise of an opposition party which invokes socialism and displays a vehement anti-Americanism sharply reduced Prime Minister Karamanlis' majority. Paradoxically, its spokesman is Andreas Papandreou, a man who had been an American citizen until the mid-1960s and taught at American universities for a long time. But the very fact that hostility toward the United States is expressed through this man signals the failure of American policy in Greece, and this is the reason one already hears American voices suggest that others, namely Willy Brandt and the SPD, should mediate the conflicts in Greece and on Cyprus, for they maintain good relations with the two most important adversaries on the Greek political stage.[73]

Actively supported by the government of the Social Democrat Helmut Schmidt and by François Mitterrand in the name of a noticeably different kind of socialism, the Socialist Mario Soares proved in Portugal in 1975 that Henry Kissinger's total pessimism was unjustified and that no CIA intervention was needed to prevent the Communist Party, which operated according to the Stalinist methods of the late 1940s, from seizing power.[74]

In Spain, the situation is different. Though this was provocative for the anti-Franco people who are in power in the Scandinavian countries and in the opposition in France, the American and French governments, acting in concert for once, had given their support to Franco when he tried to break out of his isolation and allowed a profound transformation of the Spanish economy and society to occur.[75] It is precisely this transformation, the changed role of the Catholic Church in Spanish public life during the 1960s, and the general fear of a new civil war which largely explain the surprisingly rapid and peaceful transition to pluralism which King Juan Carlos, though he had been brought up to succeed the dictator, could carry out within a few months when he became the provisional head of state on October 30, 1975, after Franco's long agony began.

For Greece, Portugal, and Spain, the period 1974–75 defines a clear break. In Italy, internal change proceeds slowly while foreign policy continues to be "a projection of domestic policy, a means to perfect society and consolidate the state." During the 1960s, it was a question of "consolidating the center-left by creating a large national consensus on a few international themes." During the 1970s, it was a matter of creating a balance between the Christian Democrats and the Communist Party by taking account of both the weight of American influence and the "sentiments of hurt pride which 30 years of Italian-American relations have caused among large sections of the population."[76] Against the background of a deteriorating currency, terrorism, and general unrest, the political life of Italy is increasingly dominated by the confrontation and its tacit understandings or the quarrelsome cooperation of the two great parties, particularly since the election of June 20, 1976, which confirmed the strength of the one and increased the power of the other. With 38.7 percent and 34.4 percent of the vote, respectively, and 263 and 227 of 630 parliamentary seats, the Christian Democrats and the Communist Party are driven toward that "historical compromise" which Enrico Berlinguer, secretary-general of the Communist Party since March 1972, has called for so tirelessly since the fall of 1973. The new government which Andreotti formed in August 1977 after prior consultation with the Communists has undoubtedly ushered in an important stage in their relations.

As a result, the foreign policy Berlinguer demanded and already practices is becoming very important. Like his appeals which call for economic austerity, it is based on a sense for realities and a wish for a transformation of Italy which will take the crisis into account.[77] American imperialism and American interventions are denounced as before, but contact with the United States is being sought and the card of European unity is being played. In this respect, the case of Altiero Spinelli is quite typical: a founder of the European federalist movement in the 1950s and a former resistance fighter like the French anti-Communist Henry Frenay and the German leftist Catholic Eugen Kogon, he became a member of the Brussels Commission, from which he resigned in 1976 to seek a parliamentary seat in the June elections as an independent candidate of the Left on the Communist ticket. He became head of the Left independents in the Chamber and a member of the Communist group in the European Parliament at Strasbourg, where he advocates a Europe which will be less dependent on the United States, more democratic, and continue to be part of the Atlantic Alliance.[78] This position reflects a twofold caution: Italy must not become a second Chile; and contact with the U.S. government must therefore not be broken off. More important, the Communist leadership must not suffer Alexander Dubček's fate. In other words, the "Euro-Communism"—a Communism based on pluralist principles—only has a chance if American protection preserves it from the application of the Brezhnev Doctrine. Without the Atlantic Alliance, Italy would be treated like Czechoslovakia in 1968 the moment it is governed with the cooperation of the Communist Party or, even worse, by that party alone.

The Americans meanwhile are afraid that the party will cause Italy to suffer the fate of Czechoslovakia in 1948. How can this be prevented? By constantly warning of this danger, as Henry Kissinger did, and as the Carter Administration continued to do after it had been somewhat more open or more cautious for a few months? Won't this strengthen the party one supposedly combats, since it makes it the symbol of national independence? But doesn't silence mean approval, which would ease its rise to power?

For the French Communist Party, the problem is both similar and different. Similar because the Italian and the French Communist parties agree on many things. Their joint declaration of November 17, 1975, states that the two "emphasize the necessity of the struggle against the arrogance of U.S. imperialism which intervenes in the affairs of nations and takes a stand against all foreign intervention." Both declare in favor of a "democratic, peaceful and independent Europe."[79] The two also differ because Georges Marchais' party is more afraid of Europe, for its ally and adversary François Mitterrand believes that the weight of the German Social Democrats supports him. Enrico Berlinguer, on the other hand, has no reason to worry about the rivalry of the small Socialist Party of Italy. A more important difference is that due to its tradition and national situation, the French Communist Party is much more thoroughly anti-Atlantic and anti-American than its Italian counterpart. "Independence" has become the magic word in French political life, and its meaning is essentially anti-American.

In the spring of 1974, new heads of government presented themselves to the parliaments in Bonn and Paris. Franco-German relations were good, and disagreements minor. Yet despite the apparent similarity in themes, the two statements revealed differences in the attitudes of the two countries:

Chancellor Helmut Schmidt declared on May 17: "In partnership with the United States, we advocate the political unification of Europe. . . . The Atlantic Alliance remains the fundamental base of our security and the necessary political framework for our efforts toward global détente. On the firm foundation of our alliance in the North Atlantic Pact, we maintain good relations with the Soviet Union and the states of the Warsaw Pact."

The speech of Jacques Chirac, whom the new President Valéry Giscard d'Estaing had appointed Prime Minister, sounded a little different: "National independence remains the inviolable goal of our policy. Independence means the ability to make those decisions on which our fate depends freely and on our own. . . . On the basis of strict equality and mutual respect, France intends to indefatigably enlarge its trade and expand its relations with other nations, including the United States, to which it is tied by two centuries of friendship and common struggles, the countries of the East . . . and China."

Independence and good relations with all countries and no special place for the great Atlantic ally. In its positive meaning, this theme could be endorsed by any French head of government in the name of any coalition. If taken negatively, opposing French parties could also agree to a considerable extent, as they did during the debate on June 15, 1977, on the ratification of the project for an election by universal suffrage to the Parliament of Europe. In his 1974 declaration, Jacques Chirac had also said: "European policy is no longer part of our foreign policy. It is something different that can no longer be separated from the fundamental project we have worked out for ourselves." Now, he reproached the government, which he criticized in the name of the party he heads within the majority: "I denounce the fact that every time the interests of a united and independent Europe and the preservation of the ties that unite this or that of our partners with the United

States are weighed against each other, the pendulum always swings in the latter direction. . . . What we must struggle against is the ambiguity that exists between the ambition of those—and that means all of us here—who want a truly independent Europe, and the ambition of several of our partners who actually favor a German-American Europe."

Speaking for the Socialist Party, Jean-Pierre Cot gave the following answer: "The President of the Rassemblement pour la République has just delivered a rousing eulogy on the creation of Europe and assured us that it is necessary to resist the hegemony of the United States. Who among us would not agree with him on these two points. . . . And yet I felt a certain malaise as I listened to him. For finally, M. Chirac, you still were Prime Minister a year ago. . . . Do I have to remind you, ladies and gentlemen, what head of government it was who, after assuming office, bowed to American demands in Ottawa? Do I have to remind you who ran the government when, a few months later, the Jamaica agreement was signed which put an end to Bretton Woods, established the hegemony of the dollar, and created international currency chaos? Must I remind you who was Prime Minister when the government decided to turn our computer industry over to Honeywell? Must I remind you who was Prime Minister when the government continued to sell out the nation? That M. Chirac should appear here after all that and give us lessons on resisting the U.S. seems singular to me, to say the least."[80]

General agreement on the conception of Europe and the necessary distance from the United States? But things aren't that simple because, to begin with, the most important front lines that emerge do not coincide with those of French domestic policy. Each of the two opposing camps is internally divided. The pressure Georges Marchais brings to bear on François Mitterrand has been paralleled since 1976 by Jacques Chirac's pressure on Valéry Giscard d'Estaing. And the pressure of both derives from the fact that both the Right and the Left make independence the highest value. What is meant here is a national independence which must primarily be won or asserted vis-à-vis the United States. Second, because the idea of a Europe independent of the United States, however widespread, also evidences considerable variations.[81] Third and above all, because it is not easy to distinguish between ritualistic affirmation and genuine political intentions. Reflection on conceptions such as dependence, hegemony, domination, and compulsion has certainly not been pushed very far, generally speaking (see Concluding Comments). The ambiguities of interdependence[82] have barely been examined, not even in serious analyses which use the concept of dominance with caution.[83] The result is a mixture of genuine problems and mythologies that is difficult to clarify. As one reads the relevant speeches, proposals, and manifestos, one often feels tempted to agree with that ironic definition which says: "Independence is basically the refusal to put oneself in another's place."[84]

Concerning the dominance of the United States or the necessity of a defense of economic and cultural independence, there exists an abundance of grotesque, caricatural statements. While the law of December 31, 1975, on the use of the French language may still be justifiable though it is impossible to apply,* the denunciation of "Gallo-Americanisms" by the so-called *analyse tétraglossique* has aspects of unintentional humor.[85] The fashion has become so widespread that wits are mounting a counterattack and now present us with "anti-American French."[86] When journalists wish to show benevolence toward the United States, they make this kind of comment on cultural TV programs: "Even in the United States, television can be considered a public service and not as a machine designed to stultify and promote sales," or "Not all of America lives under the rule of Business. Young Americans try to live differently—right now!"[87] This is the old saw once again: France is a country of culture, and America is not.

It is difficult to investigate the attitudes of those Frenchmen who are not part of the political and intellectual milieu. First of all, because one does not know how influential French television and the most widely read newspapers—especially *Le Monde*, which usually offer its readers only the most negative aspects of the American past and present—really are with their one-sided presentations. Secondly, and more important, because the questionnaires of opinion research institutes are also often very one-sided. This may be unintentional but is typical for that very reason. A poll of the opinion research institute SOFRES on views concerning the development of world politics, for example, gave only a choice between communism and capitalism and nowhere mentioned the word "freedom." The list of "significant" events named "the American defeat in Vietnam" and "the student rebellions in numerous Western countries," while repression (by whom?) in Hungary and Czechoslovakia was simply listed under "events" without additional characterization. When the opinion research institute IFOP presented a list of products which had come

---

* Article I of this law states: "In the designation, offer, presentation, in printed advertisements or commercials, in instructions for use or guarantees of a product or service, and on bills and receipts, the use of the French language is obligatory. All use of foreign terms or expressions is forbidden if there are terms or expressions which are admitted by decree no. 72/19 of January 7, 1972, on the enrichment of the French language."

from the United States where "the four most typically American" were to be identified by a cross, it enumerated chewing gum, the T shirt, the motel, and the snack bar but not a single scientific discovery, not a single cultural achievement.[88]

French anti-Americanism, like the recent anti-German feeling with which it has combined since the Federal Republic has become an economic and financial power, betrays a certain insecurity, among other things: one takes a stand against something because one doubts one's ability to maintain oneself by one's own strength. The crowing of the Gallic cock may be the expression of repressed anxiety or of unreflected vanity. As regards culture, insecurity often derives from ignorance of one's own riches. Like self-glorification, self-denigration also leads to the rejection of others. If French experiences in pedagogy were better known to the French, it would be more readily conceivable for the administration of a large French city to publish a brochure on American models in elementary, secondary, and adult education and public libraries (as the Senate of West Berlin did, for example).[89]

Conceivable, but not likely. France's relationship with the United States is too different from that of the Federal Republic, where one finds another kind of insecurity with different consequences. Many Frenchmen tend to overestimate the international prestige of their country and to underestimate the positive aspects of the political regime and the society in which they live. A threat to the status of France in the world is therefore felt more strongly than the possible breakdown of an always precarious achievement. And this threat is perceived as coming from America.

Many Germans, on the other hand, tend to underestimate the possible influence their country could exert in international affairs, particularly since they feel no need for major-power status. Conversely, they readily overestimate the excellence of their political regime and social system. The result is a feeling of insecurity that generates intolerance whenever the stability of this regime and this society seems threatened. Threatened by a danger which, for the moment, is expected from within rather than without. The sense of a danger coming from the Soviet Union is decreasing, although there is the impression that over the long term Soviet power will exceed that of the Americans.[90] The espionage cases, which are certainly more serious for NATO than the students on the extreme Left or even the existence of some Communist ministers in France—a possibility in 1977—don't disconcert the German parties and their voters as much as a few terrorists and groups that systematically criticize German society and, through it, capitalist society as such. While political ties with the

United States have become weaker, ideological solidarity has grown. The fact that German critics of the system are often directly influenced by their American colleagues—and influenced so directly that they frequently take over their vocabulary[91]—only strengthens the transnational aspect of the need for security.

In contrast to the early 1950s, today's unrest has no transatlantic dimensions. The Federal Republic is the only Western country that expresses its sense of insecurity in laws and decrees that limit freedom in its very name. Partly, because during a time of détente, it is the only Western country that feels threatened by subversive infiltration—though it is mistaken in so doing. And partly, and principally because, being unable to incarnate the nation, it has replaced the concept of the fatherland that must be protected and honored by that of the "free and democratic *Grundordnung.*" In France, unity is based on the idea of national independence. And it is America that serves as a threat in whose defense unity can crystallize. In the Federal Republic, it is domestic critics, and that produces a coalition between the defenders of the order as "free and democratic" and those who defend it quite simply because it is the order which implies the preservation of the existing social system. In this process, the United States is less necessary, less close, and less present than in those times when the pressure comes from the East. Yet transatlantic solidarity which is liberal and conservative at one and the same time is strengtened as a result of that fact.

CONCLUDING COMMENTS

This book tells a story. The report can have no conclusion since the history of the relations between the Western European countries and the United States continues. The second half of the 1970s may constitute a profound break in the economic development of all the countries concerned, but certainly no profound change in transatlantic relations—and certainly no clearly defined end of the period examined here.

This book raises questions. Insistent questions of many sorts. Questions of reality under both of its aspects: the facts which were uncovered through analysis, and the way the actors perceive those facts (or fail to perceive them). Implicit questions addressed to the reader: To what extent does he agree or disagree with the author's analysis of reality? And questions addressed to the author as to the nature of his questions: Why does he select this factor, why does he consider this event or that structure significant? In this respect, a concluding comment in the form of a backward glance is always possible—a backward glance which permits one once again to obtain distance from the report. To look back means to inquire if the way one raised questions and asked oneself was fruitful, and thus means justifying one's manner of carving up reality into portions and presenting them.

The question that recurs most frequently, that recurs practically every time a new period begins in this report, concerns the definition of constancy and change. But it cannot be answered so easily, since no change is radical and no constancy complete, particularly since continuity and discontinuity can exist simultaneously when they are considered on various levels or in various spheres. In retrospect, it becomes possible to get a more precise hold on difficulties and to uncover some fundamental trends.

One change emerges clearly: during the years from 1947 to 1949, the two archfoes of the United States in Europe, Germany (at least its large western part) and Italy, became its partners even before they took their place among its allies, while the great wartime Ally, the Soviet Union, revealed itself as the common enemy of the United

States and the European countries. Nothing so far has refuted the idea that none of the later changes compares to this one.

Our story comprises two very unequal periods: the second half of the 1940s more or less, and the succeeding three decades. During those thirty years, change has been profound. China has become a major power. Japan and West Germany have attained an importance their politicians could hardly imagine in 1949. Dozens of new states have come into existence on continents to which any expression of political autonomy was once denied. Societies have changed. Technologies have been revolutionized. But some essential characteristics have remained the same.

In a military sense, the 1947—49 malaise has persisted, all changes in arms and strategy notwithstanding. It does not have its origin in the United States but in the twofold nature of the Soviet Union, which is both a European country and a superpower, the only one on European soil. The reality is thus as simple as it is unpleasant: there can be no European security system. One either remains among Europeans, and in that case the Soviet Union has such preponderance that it need not even threaten to impose its political will on the Western European countries. Or the USSR sees its power kept at bay by the only Western country which is also a true superpower, and then European security is reduced to the condition of a subsystem of the Soviet-American system. Every Western European statesman experiences two contradictory feelings: satisfaction that the United States exists, and annoyance that the life and the death of his fellow citizens depend in large measure on the decisions of a foreign and distant President. Which of the two feelings dominates depends on time and country. In Germany, the former is usually more marked, in France it is the latter. But the objective fact which explains and justifies both has remained unchanged.

Politically speaking, this unchanged fundamental feature also has a connection with the nature of the Soviet Union. During both the Cold War and in times of détente, the Soviet Union has always invoked an ideology of political monolithism. The Western European countries, including the Communist voters in France and Italy, find themselves placed in the same category as the United States, i.e., the category of pluralistic regimes. At the moment one imputes importance to this criterion, belonging to the same category always also means being part of one and the same camp, however acute the conflicts within this camp may be.

Economically, the shifts in the distribution of power or prosperity have not touched the double reality that emerged in 1948. On the one hand, there is the special interdependence between the United States and the Western European countries, i.e., the fact that the correlations between the shifts on both sides of the Atlantic are more pronounced than those between the shifts of each of these two economic complexes and those of any other economic ensemble. There is, on the one hand, the asymmetry of this interdependence which has both its cause and its consequence in the weak or strong situation of the dollar. But there are also fundamental aspects which do not fit into the 1947–49 picture, the most important of which extends to the entire period examined here. For it turns out that none of the four most important Western European countries has solved the identity problem which arose after the war.

It is a problem faced by each of them but which in all four cases implies a particular kind of relation to the United States. The problem of international identity was least serious for Italy when it asked itself without excessive concern what its possible global role might be and felt neither the need to assert itself vis-à-vis the United States nor to exert any particular influence on its policy. But as a society, Italy has less homogeneity than the other three countries. Social change within its borders corresponds much more to a genuine national interest than it does in France, Great Britain, or the Federal Republic. And between 1947 and 1978, the United States has almost uninterruptedly acted as both accelerator and brake on this change. It accelerated it by economic aid, which contributed decisively to the modernization of Italian industry. It put a brake on it by its heretofore loyal political support of the ruling Christian Democrats, who are increasingly less willing or less able to change this society—and this support can be partly explained by, and partly explains—the rise of the Communist Party.

The most severe identity crisis was undergone by the Federal Republic. Whatever its past, whatever its present problems, Italy was and always remains Italy. France was always France, the number of its Republics doesn't matter. But the state that was born in 1949 was not Germany, though it would have liked to be. In its hour of birth, it had stated its willingness to end its existence to make room for a complete Germany as soon as all Germans were in a position to freely decide their fate. But it could not forever remain a provisional entity, and thus the Federal Republic became a community like all the others and even attained a rare institutional and social stability. But though this may have been because of just one peculiarity which has been mentioned time and again in this book, uncertainty as to its identity persisted. While the Federal Republic represents something like the symbol and the reincarnation of the international system of 1949, which is the system of a divided world and a divided Europe, it is at the same time the only Western European country which still lives within the international system of 1945, the system of victors and vanquished. The idea of German sovereignty as adopted by the Four Powers still confines the Federal Republic to a subordinate position, and it alone guarantees it the continued existence of the German nation, the existence of *Gesamtdeutschland*. Yet in spite of the presence of France and Great Britain at the side of the United States, it is primarily American power which confronts the desire and occasionally the will of the Soviets to extinguish the last traces of a national identity common to both German states. And the ideological and moral identity is also tied to the existence of the transatlantic reality, as we saw at the end of the last chapter.

Great Britain and France were the only countries that from the very beginning had to deal with a question to which there may perhaps be no answer: How does one continue exerting world-wide influence when one knows that one has stopped being a world power? In fact, this question was raised only hesitantly for a long time, since it was preferred to maintain the illusion that one was still a world power. Surprisingly at first glance, this illusion maintained itself in France in spite of its defeat in 1940 and even though it was not exactly powerful in 1945, and did so longer than in Great Britain, which had been so heroic and influential during the war and so certain of its role down to the 1960s. Both countries had to maintain themselves vis-à-vis the United States—Great Britain more frequently and under more humiliating conditions than the French with their myth of the "Anglo-Saxons" generally believe. The core of truth in this myth lies in the answer Great Britain would give if it were asked about its identity as an influential power: "It is by exerting a special influence on one of the two superpowers that I shall win or recover influence." France would give this answer: "It is better for me to promote a Europe in which I will be the only country to exert world-wide influence. This will permit me to speak with the weight of a European economic power," particularly to the United States.

Certainly, but what if the American ally no longer accords any privilege to the British? Certainly, but what if German economic power becomes so considerable that the Federal Republic exerts a great deal of influence, even without wanting to? Neither the British nor the French road has led to a new identity as a power with a special status. For Great Britain, the end seems to be resignation and concentration on internal problems. For France, the European question remains open: perhaps power will some day come from a European identity, but solitude is preferred to any idea of Europe which does not satisfy France's twofold striving for national self-assertion vis-à-vis the other Europeans and collective self-assertion vis-à-vis the United States.

This twofold striving for self-assertion combines with the conviction of a special mission which does not express itself through material power, which is indeed even opposed by a material power such as the United States represents. "Our actions are directed toward goals which are connected and which precisely because they are French are in accord with the interests of all mankind." "The indefinable genius which permits France to lay hold of and express the deep needs of the human spirit." Be it de Gaulle on television in 1967 or François Mitterrand in the National Assembly in 1975: the formulas are almost identical. And that high aim would be nobler still, were it not for the fact that it has for decades—or rather, as we saw in the first chapter, for more than a century—been nourished by a caricature of the United States. The persistence of stereotypes here seems like an act of defiance in the face of changes in regime and society.

Compared to all this, there appears a clear break in continuity around the middle of the period under investigation, the early 1960s. With the end of the colonial period of the European countries, the tone of the transatlantic dialogue changes. It is true that the moment is not the same in all cases. The Netherlands had already weathered the worst conflict of its decolonization when Portugal had not even entered into its. But the direct power of France, Belgium, and Great Britain fades in Africa at about the time the U.S. military presence in Vietnam takes shape. The accusation of colonialism which the United States had leveled against its European allies since Roosevelt at least loses its justification as the Europeans distance themselves from what the new countries will from now on combat as the central if not the only imperialism.

There are many definitions of imperialism. None of them is satisfactory if it means that disparate phenomena are put on the same plane. The political and economic domination of the United States over a small Central American country or the relationships between the oil companies and the Arab countries during the 1950s have little in common with American predominance over Western European countries or with the relations between IBM and European governments. And if one is going to maintain seriously that Great Britain, France, and the Federal Republic are part of an American empire, the formula has value only if one first makes clear that this kind of imperialism has hardly anything to do with what the Soviet Union practices toward Poland, Czechoslovakia, and the DDR.

Imperialism implies domination and exploitation. However one may feel about these, it should be said that the enormous development of the European economy, which was at least accelerated by Marshall Aid, does not testify to exploitation, even though the United States derived economic and political benefits from European growth. It is advisable here to draw on two very simple concepts from game theory. If the gain of one player equals the loss of another, one speaks of a zero-sum game. If the totality of gains (or losses) is higher than the totality of losses (or gains), one speaks of a non-zero-sum game. From our temporal perspective, the First World War looks like a game of the second category: France won, Germany lost, but the sum of gains or losses yields a clear total loss. Be it the reconstruction of Europe or transatlantic relations, often it is only a kind of cynical pessimism— especially in France—that stands in the way of the thought that the result of even an unequal exchange, negotiation, or even conflict may be advantageous to all participants.

Similarly, the mere fact of the dollar's privileged position is not tantamount to exploitation unless one maintains that growth during the 1960s would have been greater still if even then, as in the late 1970s, other currencies had been in equilibrium with it. On the other hand, Chapters 8 and 9 have shown us that the acquisition of foreign enterprises without a corresponding flow of capital from the United States and with the massive repatriation of profits does have something to do with exploitation. The same applies to the brain drain, since the cost of training was borne by European countries. But then one would also have to take account of the training of any number of European scientists and technicians in the United States and of the contribution multinationals have made to the development of national economies.

Domination presupposes the constant exercise of power. The various situations we encountered in the course of this book prompt an amplification of the initial question concerning the definition of power: Who can make whom do what and when? And if he can, does he do it or not? And if he does, was it because he so intended, or does the action of the other result from an unintended influence? The United States could have demanded even more of the Europeans, for the difference in power was significant enough for that. One would have to reexamine every single situation to determine whether the United States did not want it or whether it was afraid of the consequences—which would mean that the difference in power was not as great as it appeared.

Differences in attitude, in any event, did not necessarily lead to submission by those that were dominated, and similarities in attitude were not always the result of domination. The Fourth Republic began the Indochina war when the United States considered it a dangerous adventure. It ended it when the United States wanted to continue what had meanwhile come to appear to it—in part because of the influence of French theses—as an anti-Communist struggle. The European Defense Community was invented in Paris to put obstacles in the path of an American wish. It was buried in Paris, although then the Americans wanted to revive it. Conversely, it was not submission to the United States that prompted de Gaulle as the first French head of government to conduct an Algerian policy which reflected the desire of the American leadership. And is it necessary to remind the reader that the Atlantic Alliance did not result from American domination but from a European desire for security?

Yet domination was a reality, at times as an oppressive burden, at others as a specific action, the most humiliating of which was surely the punishment imposed on Great Britain and France for their Suez adventure. Domination refers to having and doing but also to being, which is so closely tied to seeming. The weak may desire what the strong considers good for him. Perhaps the strong takes nothing from the weak. But when the strong does not respect the dignity of the weak, what he has and what he does nourish resentment of his domination. From Roosevelt to Johnson, only a few American leaders have understood in their confrontation with de Gaulle that prestige can be as tangible, as respectable a goal of policy, as power or wealth. They were a little like the employer who sees in the workers' movement only the desire for prosperity, not that for recognition or dignity.

Domination is based on realities. To some extent, these can be modified by the will. To what extent? There is no certain answer. It seems that de Gaulle overestimated the capacity of the will to change reality—at least in his public addresses. In their dealings with the United States, the German politicians almost always believed that the reality of their need for protection forbade them the expression of will. A refusal to adapt may result in a better situation but also in defeat and humiliation. "Realism" sometimes leads to a confusion between adaptation and submission, and sometimes to the most skillful exploitation of a bad situation. And will can be expressed in a great variety of ways. One can attempt to reduce domination by confronting the dominant party or by trying to influence it so that it contributes to its own weakening by acquiescing in more equitable relations: General de Gaulle and Jean Monnet had an equal measure of will.

A balance sheet of the various attitudes is all the more difficult to draw up, since the most important values are not the same for all. In Germany, democracy and prosperity have greater priority than the nation. In the France of the Fifth Republic, independence is almost a mythical value, as we indicated before. It often takes on the meaning of a sort of noninvolvement. One must have one's hands free, be able to decide on the spur of the moment what one will do next—as if every tie, every commitment, the shouldering of any responsibility whatever, did not demand decisions over time. A person that always has his hands free may easily become the victim of his moods. Genuine will presupposes duration, and duration always ties one's hands to some extent, and that is true in party politics, in marriage, in an alliance, in the creation of a community of nations. The French desire not to be tied down has been considered a creative attitude neither by its allies in Europe nor by its American partner.

But how to differentiate between humiliating dependence and the realistic acceptance of the constraints a situation imposes? The same Michel Jobert who saw himself as the strict defender of French freedom of action declared in his very first speech as Foreign Minister before the National Assembly: "Every government, this like any other, is confronted with the same necessities, the same obstacles, and driven to the same solutions as it defines and implements its policy. In my eyes, a specific foreign policy for this government does not exist, and no other government has had one." There are times when it seems that the mere existence of American power is perceived as a constraint on French independence. At others, the necessity of a dependable supply of oil or uranium is so compelling that the French refusal to criticize the Arab states or the silent forbearance with the whims of a Bokassa cannot be understood as signs of dependence. In practice, compulsion is largely a question of choice between varying costs. When John Foster Dulles affronted his allies in 1956 and endeavored not to put Nasser in bad humor, we saw that he was free to do so because at the time, neither the British nor the French government could afford to resist American pressure and pay for it by a loss of their domestic prosperity, while for Egypt, which was poor in any event, a change in alignment was possible.

Power has its price, and our report ends at the very moment the Europeans reproach the Americans for no longer being willing to accept the constraints which their political power, their world-wide presence, entails for their internal development. Those same Europeans would be less dependent on the United States if they shouldered the cost of a European defense, which would mean a very noticeable reduction in their standard of living. In the Soviet Union, the leaders are not in the habit of first consulting the people when they burden them with the domestic cost of external power.

No political force in Western Europe, including the Communist parties, is ready in view of the cost of such an operation to do away with the restraints of transatlantic interdependence. All that is conceivable are acts which would make this interdependence somewhat less asymmetrical, and this takes us back to the old quarrel over European unification as a path toward greater dependence or more balanced interdependence.

Europe could have become one of the principal actors in our report and European solidarity a privileged solidarity, but that did not happen. The Community of Six and later of Nine only temporarily emerged as an acting unit, as in the Kennedy Round, the preparations for the Helsinki conference, the Lomé Convention. The reasons and the responsibility for this failure are complex, but its reality can hardly be disputed. The Community has no body, nor does it speak with a single voice. It is neither a subordinate configuration in a bloc under American leadership nor a second pillar of the Atlantic structure nor a new superpower between the two giants.

In a certain sense, the disunity is even greater than the abolition of barriers within the Common Market or the regular consultations between political leaders within the European Community might lead one to think. Internal problems preoccupy Holland and Italy more and more, the former because of its many political divisions, the latter because of its growing anarchy. In Great Britain, the old separatist conflicts have taken a tragic turn in Northern Ireland and threaten British unity in Scotland. Belgium is so wholly absorbed by the danger of a genuine disintegration of the nation that it cannot pursue much of a foreign policy. And the common Franco-German aim which was affirmed in 1950 and then with growing vehemence up to 1963, and after that date with a persistence of varying but dependable intensity, does not prevent a kind of drifting apart of the two countries, less in their relations than in the differing evolution of their internal political climate.

Yet it is not contradictory if one also notes growing convergences which are anchored in reality rather than fully perceived. Economic interdependence has become markedly stronger. The transformation of French society, which is less and less one of farmers, let alone rural, and increasingly industrial, ever more open to the outside world, makes it more and more similar to German society, which has recovered psychological normalcy through a process of rejuvenation. Twelve years of barbarism are no longer an experience undergone; they have become historical. The country has also accepted the permanence of the eastern borders. In spite of ideological disputes and differences in political culture, the most difficult problems for both countries (energy, unemployment, training) present themselves in similar terms.

And in spite of a turning inward, the transnational actors and currents are becoming more important. This is especially true of social democracy, in spite of everything that separates the Socialist Party of France and most of the other European members of an International which, though powerless, is stronger than at any other time during the last half-century. It is equally true of Catholicism, notwithstanding the distinct evolution of the German church, which, in contrast to the Church in France, Spain, the Netherlands, and even Italy, has once again drawn closer to pre-conciliar forms. And finally, it also holds true of organized Communists, though the differences in situation and inspiration between the parties of Italy, France, Spain, and Portugal are many.

To what extent do all these similarities or convergences constitute a specifically European whole? The answer is all the more difficult since it cannot be separated from the relations between this whole and the other, more permanent, more tightly structured but hardly less nuanced whole which the United States represents. It seems that there are at least three possible interpretations of the same reality.

To begin with, one may emphasize differences and disputes. Differences in power, presence in the world, and wealth, and disputes over trade and currency issues which are all the more vehement because, since the middle 1960s, the United States has been increasingly playing the game of the strong who exploits all available advantages over the weak without bothering too much with any proclaimed solidarity—a game which is quite similar to French practice, especially in matters of defense.

But while the presentation of differences, disputes, and divergences is the principal content of this book, the second interpretation shows a profound similarity. For the central political problem is the same on both sides of the Atlantic and can be set forth simply: What will turn out as more important over the long term? The orderly, rational character of organized and institutionalized political life which ultimately gives rise to few political conflicts, or the confused and even anarchic aspect of society as it expresses itself in increased violence, a questioning of all legitimacy, or the growing consciousness of the apparent impossibility of resolving such fundamental problems as the realization of equality in freedom? Profound crisis or temporary trouble? The answer is uncertain.

All that uncertainty is hardly less marked in the United States than in the Western European countries. Even if interdependence and mutual influence did not exist, the similarity in the situations would suffice to define a transatlantic totality. This second interpretation is all the more justified since the fundamental inequality of our prosperous societies is gradually becoming apparent on both sides of the

Atlantic. It is an inequality which is characterized less by differences among wage and salary earners than by the existence of millions of outsiders who, together with their offspring, are condemned to permanent exclusion.

The third interpretation of reality concerns the situations and attitudes toward the rest of the world. Convergence of attitudes toward the Soviet Union and the other Eastern European countries is greater than divergence: the rejection of and desire for détente, the desire for an internal change in the East and the inability to bring it about, are the same in spite of all differences in role and political culture. But this convergence may perhaps be less important in the future than that vis-à-vis three-fourths of mankind compared to which the differences in prosperity between Western countries (and even between the Western countries and the Communist Eastern European ones) appear altogether insignificant. How are the internal struggles for prosperity and equality to be reconciled with reducing the most terrible of all inequalities? How are the domestic economies to be adapted to the consequences of economic aid if that aid is really going to be meaningful?

Of course, politicians in both Europe and the United States only rarely present the problem in this manner. And that is understandable, for if they did, their election or reelection would become improbable. Yet it cannot be denied that the United States and Western Europe constitute a whole which is characterized by prosperity, political stability, and decreasing population and that it faces continents or subcontinents of growing population, misery, and political unrest. Compared to the central theme of tomorrow's history, and in spite of its scope, the subject of this book may thus perhaps be altogether secondary.

NOTES

[The figures in square brackets refer to chapter and note where the work in question is mentioned for the first time.]

CHAPTER 1

1. See especially Henry Pelling, *America and the British Left* (London: Black, 1956).

2. Quotations by René Remond in *Les Etats-Unis devant l'opinion française, 1815−1852* (Paris: A. Colin, 1962), pp. 764, 769.

3. Figures and analysis in Jean-Baptiste Duroselle, *La France et les Etats-Unis: Des origines à nos jours* (Paris: Ed. du Seuil, 1976), pp. 30-40.

4. Quotations in Denise Artaud, "La querelle franco-américaine des dettes de guerre," in *France-Amerique,* numero spécial du bicentenaire, 1976, pp. 55, 58.

5. Jean Monnet, *Memoirs* (Garden City, N.Y.: Doubleday, 1978), p. 58.

6. Quoted in André Kaspi, *Les Temps des Américains: Le concours américain à la France, 1917−1918* (Paris: Publication de la Sorbonne, 1976), p. 333.

7. See especially Michael Λ. Guhin, *John Foster Dulles: A Statesman and His Times* (New York: Columbia University Press, 1972), pp. 27-36.

8. See the demonstration in the recent thesis by Jacques Bariety, *Les Relations franco-allemandes après le Première Guerre mondiale, 10 Nov. 1918−10 Jan. 1925* (Paris: Pedone, 1977), pp. 723-56.

9. See especially Manfred Henningsen, *Der Fall Amerika: Zur Sozial- und Bewusstseinsgeschichte einer Verdrängung: Das Amerika der Europäer* (Munich: List, 1974), pp. 167-68.

10. Complete text in Jean-Louis Loubet del Bayle, *Les Non-Conformistes des années 30* (Paris: Ed. du Seuil, 1969), pp. 442-44.

11. Robert Aron and Arnaud Dandieu, *Le Cancer américain* (Paris: Edition Rieder, 1931), pp. 162, 149.

12. Complete text in Michael Wincock, *Histoire politique de la revue Esprit, 1930−1950* (Paris: Ed. du Seuil, 1975), pp. 381-87.

13. Quoted in Alan Bullock, *The Life and Times of Ernest Bevin* (London: Heinemann, 1960), Vol. I, p. 360.

14. See *Roosevelt and Churchill: Their Secret Wartime Correspondence,* ed. by F. L. Loewenheim (New York: Saturday Review Press, 1975).

15. Quoted as motto to the introduction of the essential book by Richard Gardner, *Sterling−Dollar Diplomacy: The Origins and the Prospects of Our*

International Economic Order, new expanded edition (New York: McGraw-Hill, 1969). The idea is also stressed by Elisabeth Barker, *Britain in a Divided Europe* (London: Weidenfeld & Nicolson, 1971), pp. 33-34.

16. Sketch of a balance sheet in Phyllis Auty and Richard Clogg, *British Policy Toward Wartime Resistance in Yugoslavia and Greece* (London: Macmillan, 1975).

17. Detailed chronology 1934—62 in appendix of report of one of the members of the French team, Bernard Goldschmidt, *L'aventure atomique. Ses aspects politiques et techniques* (Paris: Fayard, 1962), pp. 281-87.

18. The report by Paul-Henri Spaak, *Combats inachevés* (Paris: Fayard, 1969), Vol. I, pp. 173-78, is quite unconstrained.

19. Text in the best documented but not most objective book on the atomic problem, Martin J. Sherwin, *A World Destroyed: The Atomic Bomb and the Great Alliance* (New York: Knopf, 1975), pp. 85-86.

20. This is the general orientation of Gardner [I, 15]. See the clear presentation by Robert Triffin in the Preface, p. xiv.

21. "Summary of the Interim Report of the Special Committee on Relaxation of Trade Barriers" dated December 18, 1943, quoted in Gardner [I, 15], pp. 101-2.

22. *Ibid.,* p. 65.

23. Document from the correspondence of the Foreign Office, quoted on pp. 273-74 of the new study by J. E. Willaims, "The Joint Declaration on the Colonies: An Issue in Anglo-American Relations, 1942—1944," *British Journal on International Studies,* 2, 1976, pp. 267-92.

24. See Amry Vandenbosch, *Dutch Foreign Policy Since 1815: A Study in Small Power Politics* (The Hague: M. Nijhoff, 1959), pp. 200-4.

25. Pieter S. Gerbrandy, *Indonesia* (London: Hutchinson, 1950), p. 38.

26. Note by Acheson in *Foreign Relations of the United States* (further references to this series will be given as FRUS), *Diplomatic Papers 1945* (Washington, D.C.: U.S. Government Printing Office), Vol. VI (1969), p. 1163.

27. Telegram from Caffery to the Secretary of State, *ibid.,* p. 300.

28. Quoted by Philippe Devillers, *Histoire du Viet-Nam de 1940—1952* (Paris: Ed. du Seuil, 1952), p. 110.

29. FRUS, *1944* [I, 26], Vol. III (1965), p. 773.

30. Dean Acheson, *Present at the Creation: My Years in the State Department* (New York: W. W. Norton, 1969), p. 59. Pages 50-59 are filled with sarcastic comments.

31. Unfortunately, the solid and nuanced dissertation by E. Ramon Arango, *Leopold III and the Belgian Royal Question* (Baltimore: Johns Hopkins University Press, 1961), has not been translated into French. It might destroy a good many legends.

32. I have attempted to provide a more thorough analysis of the legitimacy conflict, especially in France, in Chapters 2 and 3 of my book *Au nom de qui? Fondements d'une morale politique* (Paris: Ed. du Seuil, 1969).

33. Famous passage from the *Mémoires de guerre,* quoted in the precise and vigorous testimony by René Brouillet, "Le Général de Gaulle et la Libération de la France," pp. 55-63 in Comité d'Histoire de la 2ème guerre mondiale: *La Libération de la France* (Editions du C.N.R.S., 1976).

34. Charles de Gaulle, *The War Memoirs* (New York: Simon & Schuster, 1955), Vol. I, p. 243.

35. Quoted by Brouillet [I, 33], p. 63.

36. Monnet [I, 5], p. 220.

37. Message dated November 19, 1942, in *Roosevelt and Churchill* [I, 14], p. 282.

38. Quoted on p. 250 of what is probably the most balanced and thorough book on events in Algeria, Arthur L. Funk, *The Politics of Torch: The Allied Landings and the Algiers "Putsch" 1942* (Lawrence, Kan.: University of Kansas Press, 1974).

39. FRUS, *1944* [I, 26], Vol. III, pp. 735-36.

40. *War Memoirs* [I, 34], Vol. III, p. 50.

41. The sharpest words are undoubtedly to be found in the message to Churchill of June 17, 1943, in *Roosevelt and Churchill* [I, 14], pp. 344-45. The nonemotional aspects of the quarrel are presented better in the short report by Martin Blumenson, "La place de la France dans la stratégie et la politique des Alliés," pp. 191-206 in *La Libération de la France,* than in the somewhat dated and/or too one-sided books by Dorothy S. White, *Seeds of Discord: De Gaulle, Free France and the Allies* (Syracuse, N.Y.: Syracuse University Press, 1964); Milton Viorst, *Hostile Allies: F.D.R. and Charles de Gaulle* (New York: Macmillan, 1965); or Maurice Ferro, *De Gaulle et l'Amérique* (Paris: Plon, 1973).

42. *War Memoirs* [I, 34], Vol. I, p. 209.

43. Ambassador Duff Cooper in *Old Men Forget* (London: Rubert Hart-Davis, 1953), p. 317.

44. Monnet [I, 5], p. 220.

45. *Discours fondamental* of April 1 to the National Defense Public Interest Committee in *Mémoires de guerre* (Paris: Plon, 1954), Vol. I, pp. 529-33.

46. Some characteristic extracts, pp. 33-36 from the book by Charles Foulon, *Le Pouvoir en province à la Libération. Les Commissaires de la République 1943–1946* (Paris: Presses de la Fondation Nationale de Sciences Politiques, 1976). An important work for an understanding of Franco-American disputes in 1944.

47. An analysis especially of juridical and political conditions including France in F. S. V. Donnison, *Civil Affairs and Military Government: North-West Europe, 1944–1946* (London: Her Majesty's Stationery Service, 1961). The text of the agreement between the United States and the Belgian government-in-exile of May 16, 1944, in FRUS, *1944* [I, 26], Vol. III, pp. 195-97.

48. Facsimile in Foulon [I, 46], p. 104.

49. Map in Donnison [I, 47], pp. 102-3.

50. Dwight D. Eisenhower, *Crusade in Europe* (Garden City, N.Y.: Doubleday, 1948), p. 363.

51. "La rete americana," especially partisan first chapter of the very well documented and interesting work by Roberto Faenza and Marco Fini, *Gli Americani in Italia* (Milan: Feltrinelli, 1976).

52. FRUS, *1944* [I, 26], Vol. III, p. 1114. See also the later presentation of the situation by the mediator in the Algiers 1942–43 conflict and later politi-

cal adviser of the military governor of the U.S. occupation zone in Germany, Robert Murphy, *Diplomat Among Warriors* (Garden City, N.Y.: Doubleday, 1964).

53. See for example the diametrically opposite interpretations by Antonio Gambino, *Storia del dopoguerra dalla liberazione al potere DC* (Rome: G. Laterza, 1975), and Giorgio Bocca, *Palmiro Togliatti* (Bari: Laterza, 1973).

54. Quoted from p. 208 of the first-rate work by Marlis Steinert, *Hitler's War and the Germans: Public Mood and Attitude During the Second World War* (Athens, Ohio: Ohio University Press, 1977).

CHAPTER 2

1. Illuminating analysis in Werner Abelshauser, *Wirtschaft in Westdeutschland 1945–1948* (Stuttgart: Deutsche Verlagsanstalt, 1975).

2. Quoted on p. 34 in William C. Mallalieu, *British Reconstruction and American Policy 1945–1955* (New York: Scarecrow Press, 1956).

3. See Acheson [I, 30], p. 122, and Harry S Truman, *Year of Decision* (Garden City, N.Y.: Doubleday, 1955), p. 476.

4. Details in Gardner [I, 15], pp. 208-35, and especially in Leon D. Epstein, *Britain, Uneasy Ally* (Chicago: University of Chicago Press, 1954), pp. 36-42.

5. Figures in Shepard B. Clough, *The Economic History of Modern Italy* (New York: Columbia University Press, 1964), pp. 298-99.

6. Quoted in *L'Année Politique 1944–1945* (Paris: Ed. du Grand Siècle, 1964), p. 390. To avoid an excessive number of footnotes, I will quote this important reference tool only sparingly. The same applies to my *La Quatrième République et sa politique extérieure* (Paris: A. Colin, 1961; 3rd ed. 1972).

7. Note of the French Embassy on the conversation of December 2, in the appendix to *Mémoires de guerre*, Vol. III [I, 45], p. 366.

8. Conversation of December 6, *ibid.*, p. 368. The following quotations can be found on pp. 369, 370, 375, 378.

9. Memorandum Stettinius of January 4, 1945; FRUS [I, 26], *The Conferences at Malta and Yalta*, 1955, pp. 293-94.

10. Arthur Conte, *Yalta ou le partage du monde* (Paris: Laffont, 1964).

11. See especially Athan G. Theoharis, *The Yalta Myth. An Issue in U.S. Politics 1945–1955* (Columbia, Mo.: University of Missouri Press, 1970). It should be noted that this is a work which sides with the good Roosevelt against the bad Truman.

12. Vol. III [I, 34], p. 99.

13. See Sherwin [I, 19], pp. 132-36, and documents in appendix, pp. 289-91 (quotation p. 291).

14. Texts of the manifestos in F. W. S. Craig, *British General Elections Manifestos* (Chichester: Pol. Ref. Books, 1970). Quotes on pp. 87, 104.

15. It is evidently impossible to present the global quarrel on the origins of the Cold War here. We simply would like to point out that after a first period where all blame was put on the USSR, and a second "revisionist" period with precisely the opposite prejudice, American historical research has now

yielded significant results and come out with solid and balanced studies, especially John L. Gaddis, *The United States and the Cold War 1941–1947* (New York: Columbia University Press, 1972); Lynn E. Davis, *The Cold War Begins: Soviet-American Conflict on Eastern Europe* (Princeton, N.J.: Princeton University Press, 1974); and Sherwin [I, 19], with a bibliographic appendix which includes all sources available in 1974. Presentation of the conflict in collections: Lloyd Gardner, Arthur J. Schlesinger, and Hans J. Morgenthau, *The Origins of the Cold War* (Waltham, Mass.: Ginn, 1970), and principally Richard S. Kirkendall, ed., *The Truman Period as a Research Field* (Columbia, Mo.: University of Missouri Press, 1974).

16. *Roosevelt and Churchill* [I, 14], p. 689.

17. Quotations in the excellent analysis by André Fontaine, *Histoire de la guerre froide* (Paris: Fayard, 1965), Vol. I, pp. 285, 325.

18. Title of an oddly optimistic Canadian book on the equality that was maintained in spite of a perceptible decline: Lionel Gerber, *America in Britain's Place: The Leadership of the West and Anglo-American Unity* (New York: Praeger, 1961).

19. The intelligently written, well-documented, and balanced book by John O. Iatrides, *Revolt in Athens: The Greek Communist "Second Round" 1944–1945* (Princeton, N.J.: Princeton University Press, 1972), seems especially illuminating, particularly when supplemented by Elisabeth Barker, *British Policy in South-East Europe in the Second World War* (London: Macmillan, 1976), and the somewhat colorless and rather tendentious general presentation by Stephen G. Xydis, *Greece and the Great Powers 1944–1947: Prelude to the "Truman Doctrine"* (Thessaloniki: Institute for Balkan Studies, 1963).

20. Text in Bickham Sweet-Escott, *Greece: A Political and Economic Survey* (London: Royal Institute of International Affairs, 1956), p. 38.

21. Quotes in Barker [II, 19], p. 146.

22. A very comprehensive analysis which also includes Italian-American relations on this problem in Jean-Baptiste Duroselle, *Le conflit de Trieste 1943–1954* (Brussels: Institut de Sociologie de l'Université libre, 1966).

23. "Als Emigrant in Amerika" in E. Schwarz and M. Wegner, eds., *Verbannung. Aufzeichnungen deutscher Schriftsteller im Exil* (Hamburg, 1964), quoted in Henningsen [I, 9], p. 176. A critical bibliography on the American occupation can be found in my updated *Geschichte Deutschlands seit 1945* [I, 54], 6th ed., 1977, pp. 488-90.

24. A comprehensive analysis does not exist. As regards Bavaria, see Lutz Niethammer, *Entnazifizierung in Bayern. Säuberung und Rehabilitierung unter amerikanischer Besatzung* (Frankfurt: Fischer, 1972).

25. The text and an abundance of other English-language documents on American policy in the appendix of Karl-Ernst Bungenstab, *Umerziehung zur Demokratie? Re-educationspolitik im Bildungswesen der U.S.-Zone 1945–1949* (Düsseldorf: Bertelsmann, 1970), pp. 171-201.

26. Reinhold Maier, *Ein Grundstein wird gelegt. Die Jahre 1945–1947* (Tübingen: Rainer Wunderlich, 1964), especially pp. 350-56.

27. Quoted in Pascal Ory, *La France allemande. Paroles du collaborationnisme français* (Paris: Gallimard, 1977), p. 166.

28. Henry W. Ehrmann, *La politique du patronat français 1936–1955* (Paris: A. Colin, 1955), p. 99.

29. See especially Jacques Duquesne, *Les catholiques français sous l'occupation* (Paris: Grasset, 1966).

30. Pierre Bauchet, *L'expérience française de planification* (Paris: Ed. du Seuil, 1958), p. 38.

31. A remarkable analysis by Reinhard Blum, *Soziale Marktwirtschaft* (Tübingen: J. C. B. Mohr, 1969).

32. Jacques Dumaine, *Quai d'Orsay* (Paris: Juillard, 1955), p. 87.

33. Merleau-Ponty, *Humanism and Terror* (Boston: Beacon Press, 1969), pp. *xxi, xv.*

34. The best presentation of the internal political debate on Germany is still Hans-Peter Schwarz, *Vom Reich zur Bundesrepublik. Deutschland im Widerstreit der aussenpolitischen Konzeptionen in den Jahren der Besatzungsherrschaft* (Neuwied: Luchterhand, 1966), and this in spite of the fact that in the meantime, the impressive though arrogant rather than searching book by Ernst Nolte, *Deutschland und der Kalte Krieg* (Munich: Piper, 1974), has appeared.

35. See the analysis of election themes in R. B. McCallum and A. Readman, *The British General Election of 1945* (London: Oxford University Press, 1947), p. 97ff.

36. This formulation of Michael Foot on p. 34 in his handsome, astonishingly nonpartisan book *Aneurin Bevan. A Biography. Vol. II, 1945–1960* (London: Davis-Poynter, 1973). Opposing points of view on the foreign policy of the Labour government and domestic political conflict concerning attitudes toward the United States in the following works: Michael R. Gordon, *Conflict and Consensus in Labour's Foreign Policy 1914–1965* (Stanford, Calif.: Stanford University Press, 1969) (an excellent analysis in spite of systematic belittling of the Left); Eugene J. Meehan, *The British Left Wing and Foreign Policy. A Study of the Influence of Ideology* (New Brunswick, N.J.: Rutgers University Press, 1960), and D. N. Pritt, *The Labour Government 1945–1951* (London: Lawrence & Wishart, 1963). In Meehan: Harold Laski: traitor; Bevin: hero. In Pritt: Attlee and Bevin: traitors; the USSR: innocent victim.

CHAPTER 3

1. FRUS, *1947* [I, 26], Vol. III, p. 689.

2. See Ruggiero Orfei, *Andreotti* (Milan: Feltrinelli, 1975), p. 46. (A report which was justifiably included in the account of the U.S. trip of Gasperi.)

3. See especially Gambino [I, 53], pp. 262-68.

4. Quoted in Meehan [II, 36], p. 99.

5. Protocol in appendix pp. 673-76 of Vincent Auriol, *Journal du Septennat*, Vol. I, 1947; edited with an introduction and notes by P. Nora (Paris: A. Colin, 1970).

6. In addition to my 1961 *La Quatrième République* [II, 6], see especially Georgette Elgey, *La République des Illusions 1945–1951* (Paris: Fayard, 1965), pp. 274-75, 282.

7. FRUS, *1947* [I, 26], Vol. III, pp. 923-24.

8. *Ibid.*, pp. 976-80.

9. See the third chapter "La rottura della coalizione antifascista e la svolta atlantica nel paese e nelle Forze armate (maggio 1947–april 1948)" in the tendentious but fundamental study by Enea Cerquetti, *Le Forze Armate Italiane dal 1945 al 1975. Strutture et dottrine* (Milan: Feltrinelli, 1975).

10. On the origins of the Marshall Plan, see the very lively presentation by Joseph M. Jones, *The Fifteen Weeks: February 21–June 5, 1947* (New York: Viking Press, 1955), which has meanwhile been rendered outdated by the comprehensive though not always wholly persuasive dissertation by Pierre Melandri, *Les Etats-Unis face à l'unification de l'Europe 1945–1954* (Montpellier, 1977), Vol. I (mimeographed), and the convincing proof of a "German" origin in John Gimbel, *The Origins of the Marshall Plan* (Stanford, Calif.: Stanford University Press, 1976), a work which already contains the seeds of his *The American Occupation of Germany: Politics and the Military 1945–1949* (Stanford, Calif.: Stanford University Press, 1968).

11. FRUS, *1947* [I, 26], Vol. III, p. 712.

12. This brilliant document should really be quoted in its entirety. It can be found on pp. 934-36 of *The Papers of General Lucius D. Clay: Germany 1945–1949*, ed. by J. E. Smith (Bloomington, Ind.: Indiana University Press, 1974). 2 vols.

13. See especially Lilly Marcou, *Le Kominform* (Paris: Presses de la Fondation Nationale des Sciences Politiques, 1977). Her presentation of the founding convention does not invalidate Eugenio Reale, *Avec Jacques Duclos sur le banc des accusés* (Paris: Plon, 1958), from which our quotations are taken.

14. A lively account of these days in Jacques Fauvet, *Histoire du Parti communiste français 1920–1976*, expanded edition (Paris: Fayard, 1977), pp. 393-400.

15. R. Neumeyer in the weekly *Force ouvrière* of October 30, quoted in Alain Bergougnoux, *Force ouvrière* (Paris: Ed. du Seuil, 1975), pp. 81-82.

16. *Ibid.*, p. 92.

17. For example George Morris, *CIA and American Labor: The Subversion of the AFL-CIO's Foreign Policy* (New York: International Publishers, 1967). Assertions rather than analyses.

18. U.S., Congress, Senate, Select Committee to Study Governmental Operations with Respect to Intelligence Activities, *Final Report of the Select Committee to Study Governmental Operations with Respect to Intelligence Activities* (Washington, D.C.: U.S. Government Printing Office, 1976). See note 40, Chap. 4.

19. This distinction is not made in most of the books on this subject. See especially Richard M. Freeland, *The Truman Doctrine and the Origins of McCarthyism: Foreign Policy, Domestic Politics and Internal Security 1946–1948* (New York: Knopf, 1972); Athan Theoharis, *Seeds of Repression: Harry S. Truman and the Origins of McCarthyism* (Chicago: Quadrangle Books, 1971); and the volume of essays by R. Griffith and A. Theoharis, *The Specter: Original Essays on the Cold War and the Origins of McCarthyism* (New York: Franklin Watts, 1974). See also note 36, Chap. 4.

20. Interview in Rodolfo Brancoli, *Gli U.S.A. e il P.C.I.—La personalità della politica e della cultura americana di fronte al "rischio Italia" dopo il 15 giugno* (Milan: Garzanti, 1976), p. 10. Examples for the joint action taken by the U.S. embassy and the American unions, etc.

21. FRUS, *1948* [I, 26], Vol. III, p. 737.

22. *Ibid.*, p. 632.

23. A very critical presentation of the power of Congress in Melandri, [III, 10], p. 349-91, though that author neglects somewhat the contribution of Hardley Arkes, *Bureaucracy, the Marshall Plan and the National Interest* (Princeton, N.J.: Princeton University Press, 1972). As regards overall development, meaning, and results of U.S. foreign aid, the two fundamental books continue to be William A. Brown and Redvers Opie, *American Foreign Assistance* (Washington, D.C.: Brookings Institution, 1953), and Harry B. Price, *The Marshall Plan and Its Meaning* (Ithaca, N.Y.: Cornell University Press, 1955). This should be supplemented by the remarkable study of the negotiations from a Dutch participant, Ernst B. Van der Beugel, *From Marshall Aid to Atlantic Partnership* (Amsterdam: Elsevier, 1966). Further information in Richard Mayne, *The Recovery of Europe: From Devastation to Unity* (London: Weidenfeld & Nicolson, 1970).

24. Detailed and illuminating presentation of currency problems in William Diebold, Jr., *Trade and Payments in Western Europe: A Study in Economic Cooperation 1947–1951* (New York: Harper, 1952), and especially in the witty and searching book by Robert Triffin, *Europe and the Money Muddle: From Bilateralism to Near-Convertibility* (London: Oxford University Press, 1957). Triffin's long introduction to Gardner [I, 15] is a good supplement.

25. A table in Brown and Opie [III, 23], p. 244.

26. A list in Price [III, 23], p. 59. Valuable source material in the Library of Congress, European Affairs Division. *The United States and Postwar Europe: A Bibliographical Examination of Thought Expressed in American Publications During 1948* (plus 1949–1950–1951–1952).

27. FRUS, *1948* [I, 26], Vol. III, pp. 1113-17.

28. According to information received from Val Lorwin, Professor at Oregon State University.

29. Quoted in Gordon [II, 36], p. 171. On public opinion, see Epstein [II, 4], pp. 44-50.

30. A balance sheet of national reactions in Price, pp. 261-76. On the atmosphere of the period, Halvan Koht, *The American Spirit in Europe: A Survey of Transatlantic Influence* (Philadelphia: University of Pennsylvania Press, 1949), is recommended supplementary reading. It is particularly interesting on the Scandinavian countries. See also Vera M. Dean, *Europe and the United States* (New York: Knopf, 1950) (useful interpretation of Europe for the American reader). The extensive comparative tables in Henry L. Munson, ed., *European Beliefs Regarding the United States 1949* (New York: Common Council for American Unity, 1949), are unfortunately based on technically questionable polls and investigations.

31. Pietro Nenni, *I nodi della politica estera italiana*, ed. by D. Zucaro

(Milan: Sugar, 1974), p. 74. The rehabilitation of finances which began in 1947 is described at the end of Enzo Piscitelli, *Da Pari à de Gasperi. Storia del dopoguerra 1945–1948* (Milan: Feltrinelli, 1975). General data on domestic political attitudes toward other countries in Norman Kogan, *The Politics of Italian Foreign Policy* (New York: Praeger, 1963).

32. The results of an international *enquête* of July 1947 are reprinted in the journal *Sondages* of January 9, 1947. The following figures are taken from the March 16 and April 16, 1948, issues and from the November 1949 issue.

33. Quotations from Henri Claude, *Le Plan Marshall* (Paris: Ed. Sociales, 1948), a book which gives a systematic presentation of all anti–Marshall Plan arguments. See also Georges Soria, *La France deviendra-t-elle une colonie américaine?* (Paris: Ed. du Pavillon, 1948).

34. See the series of articles in *Le Figaro* of August 1948 and other positive contributions reprinted in the brochure *Mission spéciale de l'ECA en France: La presse française et le plan Marshall* (Paris, 1949).

35. Francois Perroux, *Le Plan Marshall ou l'Europe nécessaire au monde* (Libr. de Médicis, 1948), pp. 46-47.

36. Paul Fraisse, "Les Français face à leurs responsabilités," *Esprit*, April 1948, pp. 623-31.

37. The precise wording in Wincock [I, 12], pp. 388-90.

38. See the report of the Ministerial Council and its demand for modifications in Vincent Auriol, *Le Journal du Septennat*, Vol. II, 1948, edited and introduced by J. P. Azema (Paris: A. Colin, 1974), pp. 281, 285-87.

39. Details in Melandri [III, 10], pp. 187-88, 276-77.

40. Quoted in Arkes [III, 23], pp. 313-15.

41. Paul Hoffman, *Peace Can Be Won* (Garden City, N.Y.: Doubleday, 1951), pp. 99-103.

42. Page 33 of the very one-sided but extremely informed book by Alexandre Kirsanov, *Les Etats-Unis et l'Europe occidentale: Les relations économiques après la seconde guerre mondiale* (Moscow: Ed. du Progrès, 1972).

43. Table in Brown and Opie [III, 23], p. 249.

44. Tables in Triffin [III, 24], p. 331.

45. Table, *ibid.*, p. 324.

46. For Italy, there are especially illuminating tables on pp. 333-37 of *Dieci anni tra Roma e Washington* (Milan: Mondadori, 1955) by Ambassador Alberto Tarchiani, a book which is pro-American in every respect. An overall balance sheet from a Dutch perspective (with an analysis by J. Tinbergen, "The Significance of the Marshall Plan for the Netherland Economy") in the official government publication, *Road to Recovery: The Marshall Plan* (The Hague, 1954).

47. See p. 328 in Présidence du Conseil. Commissariat général du Plan de modernisation et d'équipement: *Cinq ans d'exécution du plan de modernisation et d'équipement,* 1952.

48. See George von Csernatony, *Le Plan Marshall et le redressement économique de l'Allemagne* (Lausanne: Imprimerie Vaudoise, 1973), pp. 159-60.

49. See the brutal intervention of General Clay on July 16, 1948, in *Der Parlamentarische Rat 1948–1949. Akten und Protokolle.* Vol. I, *Vorgeschichte* (Boppard: H. Boldt, 1975), pp. 151-56. On the entire development of relations of dependence, see the condensed presentation by Ernst-Otto Czempiel, "Die Bundesrepublik und Amerika. Von der Okkupation zur Kooperation," on pp. 554-79 of *Die Zweite Republik,* ed. by R. Löwenthal and H. P. Schwarz (Stuttgart: Seewald, 1974).

50. See the speeches on the thirtieth anniversary of the Harvard address and on the fifth anniversary of the *Stiftung* of the German Marshall Fund in *Bulletin des Presse- und Informationsamtes der Bundesregierung* (will be cited as Bulletin) of June 7, 1977.

51. George Kennan's hypothesis as quoted by Francois Fejto in his balanced and comprehensive examination *Le Coup de Prague 1948* (Paris: Ed. du Seuil, 1976), p. 225. Complete text of the PCF on p. 225.

52. Table of results of poll 1949–61 on p. 89 in Eric S. Einhorn, *National Security and Domestic Politics in Post-War Denmark 1945–1961* (Odense U.P., 1975), a book we continue to follow here.

53. P. H. Spaak [I, 18], p. 217.

54. Text of the speech on pp. 13-14 in Samuel Van Campen, *The Quest for Security: Some Aspects of the Netherlands Foreign Policy 1945–1959* (The Hague: M. Nijhoff, 1958).

55. FRUS, *1948* [I, 26], Vol. III, p. 766.

56. Cf. especially Gianni Baget-Bozzo, *Il partito cristiano al potere. La DC di de Gasperi et di Dossetti 1945–1954* (Firenze: Vallechi, 1974), pp. 267-76, and the excellent presentation on the entire discussion in Italy by Giovanni di Capua, *Come l'Italia aderì al Patto Atlantico* (Rome: Ebbe, 1971). Supplementary reading should be Severino Galante, *La politica del PCI e il Patto Atlantico. 'Rinascita' 1946–1949* (Padova: Marsilio, 1973), a work which gives a wholly different evaluation of the Communist Party's opposition to the Marshall Plan and the Atlantic Treaty. Concerning the totality of the reciprocal influences between domestic politics and foreign policy since 1948, see Primo Vanicelli, *Italy, NATO and the European Community* (Cambridge, Mass.: Harvard University Center for International Affairs, 1974).

57. Report of the Ministerial Council in Vincent Auriol, *Mon Septennat 1947–1954;* journal entries published by P. Nora and J. Ozouf (Paris: Gallimard, 1970), pp. 198-201.

58. Reprinted in Hubert Beuve-Méry, *Réflexions politiques 1932–1952* (Paris: Ed. du Seuil, 1951), pp. 213-14.

59. Truman, *Years of Trial and Hope* (Garden City, N.Y.: Doubleday, 1956), p. 144.

60. Cf. the study by David Lazar, *L'opinion française et la naissance de l'Etat d'Israël 1945–1949* (Paris: Calmann-Lévy, 1972).

61. History and quotation in Henri Grimal, *La Décolonisation 1919–1963* (Paris: A. Colin, 1965), pp. 183-207. Documents on pp. 248-56.

62. Presentation of the problem in Arkes [III, 23], p. 326.

63. Argument from Dutch perspective in Van Campen [III, 54], pp. 81, 87, 110-12.

64. The extended, tragicomic report should really be quoted in full. It is among the documents which Jacques Tronchon gathered in his *L'Insurrection malgache de 1947* (Paris: Maspero, 1975), pp. 268-70.

65. FRUS, *1948* [I, 26], Vol. III, pp. 682-89.

66. "Policy Statement of the Department of State," September 20, 1948. *Ibid.,* p. 654.

INTRODUCTION TO PART II AND CHAPTER 4

1. See the first-rate report for the Council on Foreign Relations (New York) and the Royal Institute of International Affairs (London) by Henry L. Roberts and Paul A. Wilson, *Britain and the United States: Problems in Cooperation* (London: Royal Inst. of Int. Aff., 1953). On American foreign policy during the 1950s and 1960s generally, see the standard works by Raymond Aron, *République Impériale: Les Etats-Unis dans le monde, 1945–1972* (Paris: Calmann-Levy, 1973), and Stanley Hoffmann, *Gulliver's Troubles, or the Setting of American Foreign Policy* (New York: McGraw-Hill, 1968).

2. This is the course taken by the authors of the rich collection *United States–Western Europe Relationships as Viewed Within the Present Worldwide International Environment. A Compilation of Research Reports, Documents and Other Pertinent Information to Be Used as a Background for Discussion* (New York: Columbia University Press, the American Assembly–Graduate School of Business, August 1951).

3. Complete text in appendix, Monnet [I, 5], p. 525.

4. Quoted in Edmond Jouve, *Le général de Gaulle et la construction de l'Europe, 1940–1966* (Paris, 1967), Vol. II, p. 197.

5. Cf. Melandri [III, 10], passim.

6. Van der Beugel [III, 23], p. 246.

7. Monnet [I, 5], pp. 304-5.

8. Spaak [I, 18], Vol. II, p. 72.

9. George W. Ball, *Discipline of Power* (Boston: Little, Brown, 1968), p. 40. Following quote same page.

10. Nora Beloff, *The General Says No* (Baltimore: Penguin), p. 106. Quoted in a comprehensive presentation of Monnet's influence on Kennedy in Pascal Fontaine, *Le Comité d'action pour les Etats-Unis d'Europe de Jean Monnet* (Lausanne: Centre de Recherches Européennes, 1974), p. 128.

11. See especially Monnet, *Mémoires* (Paris: Fayard, 1976), pp. 319-20, 443-44.

12. Acheson [I, 30], p. 272.

13. R. Drummond and G. Coblentz, *Duel at the Brink: John Foster Dulles' Command of American Power* (Garden City, N.Y.: Doubleday, 1960), p. 37. Analysis of relations with Adenauer, pp. 40-52; with Monnet, pp. 52-60.

14. Georgette Elgey, *Histoire de la IVème République*. Vol. II, *La République des contradictions 1951–1954* (Paris: Fayard, 1968), p. 234. Concerning American participation in the formulation of the treaty, see Melandri [III, 10], pp. 624-25.

15. Monnet [I, 5], p. 468 (English translation).

16. Auriol, *Journal du Septennat*, Vol. VII, p. 708 (cited in Melandri [III, 10], p. 809).

17. See especially Drummond and Coblentz [IV, 13], p. 38; and p. 438 of the interesting and courageous book by Peter Lyon, *Eisenhower: Portrait of the Hero* (Boston: Little, Brown, 1974).

18. Extracts from the mimeographed document. On the committee up to 1972, see the analysis and documentation of P. Fontaine [IV, 10].

19. Auriol, *Journal du septennat*, Vol. V, pp. 65, 473, 587.

20. Acheson [I, 30], p. 341.

21. See, for example, the almost caricatural analyses of the "German expert" James K. Pollock, who was shortly to become president of the American Association of Political Science, in *German Democracy at Work* (Ann Arbor, Mich.: University of Michigan Press, 1955), which he edited.

22. Excellent presentation and explanation of the two ideas in Lewis J. Edinger, *Kurt Schumacher: A Study in Personality and Political Behavior* (Stanford, Calif.: Stanford University Press, 1965).

23. See especially Vol. I of the monumental work by Hartmut Söll, *Fritz Erler. Eine politische Biographie*. 2 vols. (Berlin and Bonn: J. H. W. Dietz, 1976).

24. See A. Grosser, "Die Rolle Konrad Adenauers in der jüngsten deutschen und europäischen Geschichte," Introduction to *Konrad Adenauer 1876–1976*, edited by Helmut Kohl (Stuttgart: Belser, 1976), reprinted in A. Grosser, *Wider den Strom* (Munich: Dtv, 1976).

25. Quoted on p. 75 of the authoritative work by Arnulf Baring, *Aussenpolitik in Adenauers Kanzlerdemokratie. Bonns Beitrag zur Europäischen Verteidigungsgemeinschaft* (Munich: R. Oldenbourg, 1969).

26. Konrad Adenauer, *Erinnerungen, 1945–1953*, 5th ed. (Stuttgart: Deutsche Verlagsanstalt, 1970), p. 559 ff. *Memoirs 1945–53* (Chicago: Henry Regnery, 1965).

27. Complete text of these two speeches in *Konrad Adenauer: Reden 1917–1967. Eine Auswahl*, edited by Hans-Peter Schwarz (Stuttgart: DVA, 1975), pp. 291-98, 316-24.

28. See Kurt Birrenbach, "In politischer Mission für Konrad Adenauer in den USA" in Kohl [IV, 24], pp. 53-56.

29. *Sehr verehrter Herr Bundeskanzler! Heinrich von Brentano im Briefwechsel mit Konrad Adenauer 1949–1964*, ed. by Arnulf Baring (Hamburg: Hoffmann & Campe, 1974), p. 206.

30. Quoted in Drummond and Coblentz [IV, 13], pp. 41-43; to be supplemented in some details by the essay of Dieter Oberndörfer, "John Foster Dulles und Konrad Adenauer" in *Konrad Adenauer und seine Zeit*. Vol. II, *Beiträge der Wissenschaft* (Stuttgart: DVA, 1976), pp. 229-48.

31. See the report of the most directly interested witness, Sherman Adams, *Firsthand Report: The Inside Story of the Eisenhower Administration* (London: Hutchinson, 1963), pp. 80-83.

32. Excellent overall presentation of the politics of the period in André Fontaine [II, 17], Vol. 2, 1950–1967.

33. Quoted in Lyon [IV, 17], p. 567.

34. See Goldschmidt [I, 17], pp. 84-85.

35. Dwight D. Eisenhower, *The White House Years*. Vol. I, *Mandate for Change 1953–1956* (Garden City, N.Y.: Doubleday, 1963), p. 224. Text of his explanatory letters, p. 225. A persuasive analysis of his attitude in the Rosenberg affair in Lyon, pp. 493-94.

36. On Eisenhower before McCarthy, see Lyon [IV, 17], pp. 521-25. On McCarthy's activities and character, see the good, many-sided collection by Earl Latham, ed., *The Meaning of McCarthyism* (Boston: D. C. Heath, 1965), and especially the first-rate study by Fred J. Cook, *The Nightmare Decade: The Life and Times of Senator Joe McCarthy* (New York: Random House, 1971). See also note 19, Chap. 3.

37. Quoted in Lyon [IV, 17], p. 598.

38. Complete text in Eisenhower [IV, 35], p. 599.

39. Quoted in Cook [IV, 36], p. 288.

40. See the excellent dissertation by Jack Kantrowitz, *Le rôle des syndicats américains dans le monde syndical international libre* (University de Paris-X, Nanterre, October 1977), and a book that pulls no punches, Joseph C. Goulden, *Meany: The Unchallenged Strong Man of American Labor* (New York: Athenaeum, 1972), and the rich but rather uncritical study by Carl Gershman, *The Foreign Policy of American Labor* (Beverly Hills and London: Sage Publications, 1973) ("The Washington Papers No. III").

41. Complete text in Peter Frisch, *Extremisten-Beschluss*, 4th ed. (Leverkusen, 1977). A kind of handbook to justify all measures from 1971 to 1977.

42. See A. Grosser, *Deutschlandbilanz. Geschichte Deutschlands seit 1945* [I, 54], pp. 202-5.

43. See for example Norman Kogan, *The Political History of Post-War Italy* (New York: Praeger, 1966), pp. 76-77, 90-91.

44. See the chapter "Un cas particulier: les catholiques," pp. 179-85 of my book *La Quatrième République et sa politique extérieure* [II, 6].

45. Pierre Courtade in *L'Humanité* of October 19, 1948, quoted in Jean-Pierre Plantier, *La vision de l'Amérique à travers la presse et la littérature communistes françaises de 1945–1953*, memoire a l'IEP de Paris, 1972, p. 50 (typescript). The following quotes *ibid.*, pp. 68, 69.

46. See especially David Caute, *Les Communistes et les intellectuels français 1914–1966* (Paris: Gallimard, 1967), pp. 225-26.

47. Pierre Daix, *J'ai cru au matin* (Paris: Laffont, 1976), p. 290. On the history of the staged accusation for bacteriological warfare, see P. Fontaine [IV, 10], pp. 63-64.

48. See Eisenhower [IV, 35], p. 139.

49. See the report of the participant at the time (who has meanwhile become a critic), Dominique Desanti, *Les Staliniens. Une expérience politique 1944–1956* (Paris: Fayard, 1975), pp. 212-13.

50. Joanny Berlioz in the monthly *Démocratie nouvelle*, quoted by Plantier [IV, 45], p. 55.

51. Analysis in Caute [IV, 46], pp. 404-5.

52. Quotations in M. A. Burnier, *Les existentialistes et la politique* (Paris: Gallimard, 1966), pp. 106-7.

53. The anti-American component of that "fellow-travelership" is analyzed in David Caute, *The Fellow-Travellers* (London: Weidenfeld & Nicolson, 1973), especially pp. 291-93, 302, 349.

54. *New Fabian Essays*, ed. by R. H. S. Crossman (new edition of the text of 1952) (London: J. M. Dent, 1970), pp. 31-32.

55. Remarkable analysis of the two trends in John T. Marcus, *Neutralism and Nationalism in France* (New York: Bookman, 1958), p. 207.

56. See the chapters "L'anti-américanisme du R.P.F." and "L'apparition du neutralisme" in Philippe Manin, *Le Rassemblement du Peuple Francais et les problèmes européens* (Paris: P.U.F., 1966), pp. 47-48.

57. "Européens et Americains" (Lecture in Rome, May 1951) in H. Beuve-Méry [III, 58], pp. 248-54.

58. Appeared in 1955; new edition, Gallimard (Paris), 1968. Also see the various, sometimes crude, sometimes acute analyses of the European attitude in the collection *America and the Mind of Europe*, introduction by Lewis Galantiere (London: H. Hamilton, 1951), especially the contributions by R. Aron, Stephen Spender, Melvin Lasky.

59. "L'opinion française et l'union de l'Europe 1947—1972, *Sondages*, 1972, I. II, p. 126.

60. FRUS, *1949* [I, 26], p. 470.

61. See for example the list of aid measures of the American Committee on United Europe in Max Beloff, *The United States and the Unity of Europe* (Washington, D.C.: Brookings Institution, 1963), p. 74.

62. Quoted in Lord Moran, *Mémoires 1940—1965* (Paris: Laffont, 1966), pp. 333, 306; also in Melandri [III, 10], p. 690.

63. See Epstein [II, 4], pp. 204-21.

64. Kogan [III, 31], p. 23.

65. Quoted in my book *La Quatrième Republique* [II, 6], to which I should like to refer here for the entire struggle over German rearmament and the European Defense Community. Also see the bibliography of the third revised edition. For readers of German, there is especially Paul Noack, *Das Scheitern der Europäischen Verteidigungsgemeinschaft* (Düsseldorf: Droste, 1977).

66. A remarkable balance sheet in Hans-Adolf Jacobsen, "Zur Rolle der öffentlichen Meinung bei der Debatte um die Wiederbewaffnung 1950—1955," in *Aspekte der deutschen Wiederbewaffnung bis 1955*, Militärgeschichtliches Forschungsamt (Boppard: H. Boldt, 1975), pp. 61-117.

67. Most recent study is Udo F. Löwke, *Die SPD und die Wehrfrage. 1949 bis 1955* (Bonn: Verlag Neue Gesellschaft, 1976).

68. Gustav W. Heinemann, *Verfehlte Deutschlandpolitik. Irreführung und Selbsttäuschung* (Frankfurt: Stimme-Verlag, 1966; new edition 1969), pp. 50-51. On the absence of this kind of consideration on the American side, see Robert McGeehan, *The German Rearmament Question: American Diplomacy and European Defense After World War II* (Urbana, Ill.: University of Illinois Press, 1971).

CHAPTER 5

1. Eisenhower [IV, 35], p. 337.
2. Auriol [III, 57], p. 295.
3. *Ibid.*, p. 444.
4. Complete text of the answer given in the course of a press conference in Lyon [IV, 17], p. 601.
5. Complete text in *L'Année Politique 1952* [II, 6], pp. 574-76.
6. Complete text of this important document in *The Pentagon Papers* (New York: Bantam Books, 1971), pp. 27-32; quotations on pp. 29, 31. The following quote, *ibid.*, p. 2.
7. Quoted in the chapter "L'oncle Ho et l'oncle Sam" of the biography by Jean Lacouture, *Ho Chi Minh* (Paris: Seuil, 1977), p. 222.
8. *Congressional Record*. Senate. February 21, 1966, quoted in Elgey [IV, 14], p. 440. (In her indispensable book, Elgey also uses numerous internal documents of the French Government.)
9. General Ely, *Mémoires*. Vol. I, *L'Indochine dans le tourmente* (Paris: Plon, 1964), p. 32. A significant and exceptionally valuable eyewitness account.
10. See especially the account on pp. 84-102 in Philippe Devillers and Jean Lacouture, *Vietnam: de la guerre française à la guerre américaine* (Paris: Seuil, 1969), the best analysis of the Geneva Conference and the period following it. Also Elgey [V, 8], pp. 511-32; Ely [V, 9], especially pp. 68-74 and 85-87; and Bernard B. Fall, *Hell in a Very Small Place: The Siege of Dien Bien Phu* (New York: J. B. Lippincott, 1967), pp. 301-14.
11. Complete text of these instructions in *Pentagon Papers* [V, 6], pp. 42-44.
12. See Devillers and Lacouture [V, 10], pp. 286-88.
13. *Ibid.*, p. 293.
14. *Ibid.*, p. 344.
15. Anthony Eden, *Full Circle* (Boston: Houghton Mifflin, 1960), p. 151; following quotation p. 155.
16. See for example, Lyon [IV, 17], pp. 589-614.
17. Analysis and quotations in Goulden [IV, 40], pp. 223-25.
18. Auriol [III, 57], p. 444.
19. Quotations in A. Grosser, *La Quatrième Republique* [II, 6], pp. 147-48.
20. Goulden, [IV, 40], p. 221.
21. See Marie-Claude Smouts, *La Politique extérieure Française et l'O.N.U.* (Paris: Presses de la Fondation Nationale des Sciences Politiques, 1978). I thank the author for having sent me the manuscript.
22. Harold Macmillan, "The Anglo-American Schism," pp. 89-179 of *Riding the Storm* (London: Macmillan, 1971). Except for the collusion between Israel and France where Macmillan hides the truth just as Anthony Eden does, this is an extremely interesting and illuminating account.
23. See especially the thesis of Jean Houbert, *Suez et la politique d'Anthony Eden au Moyen-Orient*, Thèse de 3e cycle (Paris: Presses de la Fondation Nationale des Sciences Politiques, 1967), typescript.

24. A remarkable though rather malicious analysis and a great deal of documentation on American policy in 1965 in Herman Finer, *Dulles over Suez: The Theory and Practice of His Diplomacy* (London: Heinemann, 1964).

25. See Randolph Churchill, *The Rise and Fall of Sir Anthony Eden* (London: Macgibbon & Kee, 1959), p. 231.

26. Macmillan [V, 22], p. 104. Account of the mission in London and Paris in Murphy [I, 52], pp. 398-404.

27. Enumeration of Dulles' mistakes in Finer [V, 24], pp. 492-95.

28. See Macmillan [V, 22], pp. 117, 125, and Churchill [V, 25], p. 259.

29. Quotations from Russel Braddon, *Suez: Splitting of a Nation* (London: Collins, 1972), p. 10.

30. A first account of the secret meeting (in hypothetical form since sources could not be revealed) in Michel Bar-Zohar, *Suez ultra-secret* (Paris: Fayard, 1964). A solid dissertation which became a bestseller. Lively recollections of the meeting also in the otherwise rather disappointing book by Christian Pineau, *1956: Suez* (Paris: Laffont, 1976), pp. 127-37. A good chronology of the entire affair in Georges Assima, *La crise de Suez 1956* (Lausanne: L'Age d'Homme, 1970), pp. 213-16.

31. Churchill [V, 25], p. 294. Significantly, the notebooks of the ambassador, though published more than twenty years later, contain no entries covering the period August 1956 to July 1958 (Hervé Alphand, *L'etonnement d'être. Journal 1939–1973* [Paris: Fayard, 1977]).

32. Texts of the confidential messages (which Eden and Macmillan do not mention in their memoirs) in Dwight D. Eisenhower, *The White House Years*. Vol. II, *Waging Peace* (Garden City, N.Y.: Doubleday, 1965), pp. 664-79.

33. Macmillan [V, 22], p. 164.

34. Finer [V, 24], p. 454; Braddon [V, 29], p. 132.

35. "La politique étrangère de la France et l'opinion publique 1954–1957," *Sondages*, 1958, No. 1-2, p. 179.

36. A. Grosser, "Faut-il se résigner à la loi de la jungle?" editorial in *La Croix*, November 13, 1956. For examples of the anti-Americanism prevalent in political circles in France in November 1956, see Herbert Luethy and David Rodnick, *French Motivations in the Suez Crisis* (Princeton, N.J.: Princeton Institute for International Social Research, 1956), especially pp. 66-68 and 95-97.

37. Quoted in Foot [II, 36], p. 540. (See the remarkable chapter "Suez," pp. 516-43.)

38. Detailed investigation by Leon D. Epstein, *British Politics in the Suez Crisis* (Urbana, Ill.: University of Illinois Press, 1964), pp. 139-72.

39. Quotations and figures, *ibid.*, pp. 56-57.

40. Macmillan [V, 22], p. 512.

41. *Times* (London) of October 26, 1957. Quoted on p. 141 of the fundamental work by Andrew J. Pierre, *Nuclear Politics: The British Experience with an Independent Strategic Force, 1939–1970* (Oxford University Press, 1972).

42. Acheson [I, 30], pp. 648-49.

43. Article reprinted in R. Duchet, *Pour le salut public. Les indépendants devant les grands problèmes nationaux* (Paris: Plon, 1958), p. 95.

44. *Sondages,* 1958, No. 1-2, p. 43.

45. General Ely, *Mémoires.* Vol. II, "Suez . . . Le 13 mai" (Paris: Plon, 1969).

46. *Ibid.,* p. 229.

47. Eisenhower [V, 32], pp. 417, 429-30. In the account he gives of these conversations, pp. 222-27 of his *Mémoires d'espoir* (Vol. I, "Le Renouveau 1958–1962" [Paris: Plon, 1970]), General de Gaulle does not mention these talks about Algeria.

48. C. L. Sulzberger, *The Last of the Giants* (New York: Macmillan, 1970), p. 20.

49. Quoted in Spaak [I, 18], Vol. II, p. 90.

50. *Ibid.,* p. 221.

51. See especially the chapter "L'intervention au Congo" (with bibliography) in Marie-Claude Smouts, *Le Secrétaire général des Nations unies* (Paris: A. Colin, 1971).

CHAPTER 6

1. Henry Kissinger, *Nuclear Weapons and Foreign Policy* (New York: Harper, 1957), p. 299.

2. R. Merritt and D. Puchala, eds., *Western European Perspectives on International Affairs: Public Opinion Studies and Evaluations* (New York: Praeger, 1968).

3. Acheson [I, 30], p. 552, also in Melandri [III, 10], p. 606.

4. Detailed table of organization of NATO in September 1958, pp. 53-65 of the comprehensive account of Margret M. Ball, *N.A.T.O. and the European Movement* (London: Stevenson, 1959).

5. General Valluy, *Se défendre? Contre qui? Pour qui? Et comment?* (Paris: Plon, 1960), pp. 182-86.

6. See especially Lyon [IV, 17], p. 424.

7. Jean Planchais, *Le malaise de l'armée* (Paris: Plon, 1958), p. 53.

8. Page 106 of the fundamental work by Robert E. Osgood, *NATO: The Entangling Alliance* (Chicago: University of Chicago Press, 1962).

9. See Kogan [III, 31], p. 117.

10. Quoted in Duroselle [II, 22], whose remarkable analysis we follow.

11. Figures in Kogan [III, 31], p. 27.

12. Especially because an eyewitness account, Adstans, *Alcide de Gasperi nella politica estera italiana 1944–1953* (Verona: Mondadori, 1953), pp. 188-89.

13. Eisenhower [V, 32], pp. 490-91.

14. Aneurin Bevan, *In Place of Fear* (New York: Monthly Review Press, 1964), p. 153.

15. Quoted (along with other texts of similar tenor) in Epstein [II, 4], p. 55.

16. Quoted in Gordon [II, 36], p. 175.

17. Especially vivid account in Leslie Hunter, *The Road to Brighton Pier* (London: A. Barker, 1959).

18. Arthur Schlesinger, Jr., "Attitudes Toward America" in *Hugh Gaitskell, 1906–1963*, ed. by W. T. Rodgers (London: Thames and Hudson, 1964), p. 146.

19. Complete text in *L'Année Politique, 1950* [II, 6], pp. 353-55.

20. Text of the long and very important memorandum of the French to the American government of August 5, 1950, *ibid.*, pp. 364-65.

21. Osgood [VI, 8], p. 109.

22. *Ibid.*, p. 126 (with bibliographic references).

23. Konrad Adenauer, *Erinnerungen, 1955–1959* (Stuttgart: DVA, 1967), p. 196. Extracts from Erler's speech, pp. 201-2; letter from John Foster Dulles, pp. 207-11. On the ideas and activities of Erler, see Soell [IV, 23]. Better account of the Bonn-Washington crisis with a precise analysis of American uncertainties in Hans-Geret Pöttering, *Adenauers Sicherheitspolitik 1955–1963. Ein Beitrag zum deutsch-amerikanischen Verhältnis* (Düsseldorf: Droste, 1975), pp. 62-90. See also the account of the personal conflict in Drummond and Coblentz [IV, 13], pp. 45-48 (and note 13, Chap. 8).

24. Quoted in Pöttering [VI, 23], p. 81.

25. Brief but very accurate analysis of the problem for the entire postwar period in the chapter "The Advanced Weapon Relationship" in Cora Bell, *The Debatable Alliance* (New York: Oxford University Press, 1964). My account is especially indebted to two works: the book by A. Pierre, *Nuclear Politics* [V, 41], and the earlier but by no means outdated *The Politics of British Defense Policy 1945–1962* by William P. Snyder (Columbus, Ohio: Ohio State University Press, 1964). The context is clearly defined in "The Special Relationship" by F. S. Northedge, in *Descent from Power: British Foreign Policy 1945–1973* (London: Allen & Unwin, 1974).

26. Figures in Pierre [VI, 25], p. 110.

27. Speech of March 1, 1955, quoted in Pierre [VI, 25], p. 93.

28. The three quotations in Snyder [VI, 25], p. 233.

29. French researchers are clearly uninterested in this subject. The only comprehensive study continues to be the excellent book by Lawrence Scheinman, *Atomic Energy Policy under the Fourth Republic* (Princeton, N.J.: Princeton University Press, 1965). This must be complemented by the lively report by General Charles Ailleret, *L'Aventure atomique française. Comment naquit la force de frappe* (Paris: Grasset, 1968).

30. Ailleret [VI, 29], pp. 130-31.

31. Quoted by George Lichtheim, *Europe and America: The Future of the Atlantic Community* (London: Thames & Hudson, 1963), p. 32.

32. The distinction between "trade creating" and "trade diverting impact," which was of decisive importance during the 1950s, in Triffin [III, 24], pp. 261-65.

33. Unpublished extracts from this letter in Elgey, *La République des contradictions* [IV, 14], p. 312. (Numerous details on the actions of employers, pp. 311-14.)

34. Murphy [I, 52], p. 329.

35. See Kogan [IV, 43], p. 107, whose comments on the activities of the U.S. ambassador probably come closer to the truth than Dow Votan in his very useful though one-sided (hostile to Mattei) book, *The Six-legged Dog. Mattei and E.N.I.: A Study in Power* (Berkeley: University of California Press, 1964).

36. Overview in Votan [VI, 35], p. 71.

37. Robert Marjolin, *Europe and the U.S. in the World Economy* (Durham, N.C.: Duke University Press, 1953), p. 89.

38. On this support, see especially Van der Beugel [III, 23], pp. 320-24, and pp. 78-82 and 171-79 of the thorough study by Pierre Melandri, *Les Etats-Unis et le "defi" européen 1955–1958* (Paris: P.U.F., 1975).

39. See Melandri [III, 10], pp. 158-61.

40. The fundamental book on these negotiations continues to be Myriam Camps, *Britain and the European Community 1955–1963* (Princeton, N.J.: Princeton University Press, 1964).

41. See Einhorn [III, 52], pp. 39-57.

42. Easily readable tables in Kirsanov [III, 42], pp. 98, 117.

43. Tables and analyses in Melandri [III, 10], pp. 191-93.

44. See the very illuminating study by Lloyd A. Free, *Six Allies and a Neutral: A Study of the International Outlook of Political Leaders in the United States, Britain, France, West Germany, Italy, Japan and India* (New York: Free Press, 1959).

CHAPTER 7

1. For this quotation and the entire analysis I refer to my book *La Politique Extérieure de la Vème République* (Paris: Ed. du Seuil, 1965). The best overall presentation of this policy is probably by Edward A. Kolodzie, *French International Policy Under de Gaulle and Pompidou: The Politics of Grandeur* (Ithaca, N.Y.: Cornell University Press, 1974). On relations with the United States, see the report by Maurice Couve De Murville, *Une politique étrangère 1958–1969* (Paris: Plon, 1971), an impassive book that is totally devoid of any self-criticism. The best-founded defense of de Gaulle's position in the Franco-American disputes can be found in the section "La France dans le monde," pp. 315-463 of Stanley Hoffmann, *Essais sur la France* (Paris: Ed. du Seuil, 1974). The severest and occasionally also the most sarcastic criticism, a mixture of interesting information and arbitrary interpretation, is in John Newhouse, *De Gaulle and the Anglo-Saxons* (London: A. Deutsch, 1970).

2. Vol. III, *Salvation*, p. 245.

3. *Ibid.*, p. 235.

4. Arthur M. Schlesinger, Jr., *A Thousand Days* (Boston: Houghton Mifflin, 1965), p. 815.

5. Italics in Eisenhower [V, 32], p. 556.

6. Macmillan, *Pointing the Way* (London: Macmillan, 1972), p. 180.

7. Charles de Gaulle, *Memoirs of Hope, Renewal and Endeavor* (New York: Simon & Schuster, 1971), p. 168.

8. Couve de Murville [VII, 1], pp. 90-91 and 23.

9. Text (and all of de Gaulle's letters to Eisenhower from 1958 to 1961 though not the latter's answers) in *Espoir*, Revue de l'Institut Charles de Gaulle, No. 15, June 1976.

10. *Atlantic Community Quarterly*, No. 3 (Fall 1966), pp. 457-58, and also reprinted in the appendix of the excellent book by Lois Pattison de Menil, *Who Speaks for Europe? The Vision of Charles de Gaulle* (London: Weidenfeld & Nicolson, 1977).

11. On Franco-German relations under the Fifth Republic, I refer to my writings and the occasionally excessively severe analysis of Gilbert Ziebura, *Die deutsch-französischen Beziehungen seit 1945. Mythen und Realitäten* (Pfullingen: Neske, 1970). (On relations with the United States, see especially the chapter "De Gaulle und Adenauer: der verschleierte Konflikt," pp. 94-108.) On the continuities and discontinuities of Franco-German contacts on other levels, see John E. Farquharson and Stephen C. Holt, *Europe from Below: An Assessment of Franco-German Popular Contacts* (London: Allen & Unwin, 1975).

12. *Memoirs of Hope* [VII, 8], pp. 180-81.

13. Except in general works such as Waldemar Besson, *Aussenpolitik der Bundesrepublik* (Munich: Piper, 1970) (a very good analysis of the effects of Camp David, pp. 235-37), or my *Deutschland-bilanz* [I, 54], material on German-American relations during the 1960s can be found in the first-rate research report by Manfred Knapp, "Zum Stand der Forschung über deutsch-amerikanische Nachkriegsbeziehungen," pp. 7-85 and 255-66 of *Die deutsch-amerikanischen Beziehungen nach 1945*, ed. by M. Knapp (Frankfurt: Campus Verlag, 1975), and in the lucid but somewhat dry study by Roger Morgan, *The United States and West Germany 1945–1973: A Study in Alliance Politics* (New York: Oxford University Press, 1977). On the 1958–62 crisis, the best work on Adenauer is *Konrad Adenauer und seine Zeit*. Vol. II, *Beiträge der Wissenschaft*, ed. by D. Blumenwitz et al. (Stuttgart: DVA, 1976). The final volume of memoirs of Konrad Adenauer, *Erinnerungen 1959–1963* (Stuttgart: DVA, 1968), must also be mentioned. This is the best part of the memoirs since the author's death prevented him from retouching the text and because the editors of the volume supplied remarkable chronologies. There is also the detailed though somewhat partial (very anti-Adenauer) study by Walter Stützle, *Kennedy und Adenauer in der Berlin-Krise 1961–1962* (Bonn: Verlag Neue Gesellschaft, 1973). Recommended supplementary reading on Soviet policy: Robert M. Slusser, *The Berlin Crisis of 1961: Soviet-American Relations and the Struggle for Power in the Kremlin, June-November 1961* (Baltimore, Md.: Johns Hopkins University Press, 1973).

14. See the terrible accusation that is the fascinating book by David Halberstam, *The Best and the Brightest* (New York: Random House, 1972). The author deals principally with Vietnam but really describes a specific milieu.

15. Helmut Schmidt, *Strategie des Gleichgewichts. Deutsche Friedenspolitik und die Weltmächte* (Stuttgart: Seewald, 1969).

16. Schlesinger [VIII, 4], pp. 291-92.

17. See Raymond Aron and Alfred Grosser, "A European Perspective," pp.

141-57 in *Cuba and the United States,* ed. by John Plank (Washington, D.C.: Brookings Institute, 1967).

18. Text in *Sehr verehrter Herr Bundeskanzler!* [IV, 29], pp. 315-16. The selection and commentary by Arnulf Baring are particularly illuminating in this section.

19. *Ibid.,* pp. 310-13.

20. *Erinnerungen 1959–1963* [VII, 13], pp. 93-96.

21. The literature on Berlin is enormous. On the crisis during the summer of 1961 and its German-American aspects, see particularly the book by Stützle [VII, 13] and the especially rich (though not always verifiable) documentation in three long articles in *Der Spiegel* (No. 34-36, 1966), "Koniew liess aufmarschieren. *Spiegel*-Report über den Bau der Berliner Mauer."

22. See the survey of opinion polls 1950–76, p. 553 of Elisabeth Noelle-Neumann, "Die Verklärung: Adenauer und die öffentliche Meinung 1949 bis 1976" in *Konrad Adenauer und seine Zeit* [VII, 13], pp. 523-54. Also there, the 1976 listing which indicates that Adenauer and Kennedy rank above Brandt and de Gaulle as the first politicians of the postwar era.

23. Quoted in Stützle [VII, 13], p. 15.

24. *L'Express* of December 5, 1977.

25. Quoted on p. 37 of the very lucid study by George Lichtheim, *Europe and America: The Future of the Atlantic Community* (London: Thames & Hudson, 1963). On the entire debate in England, see Myriam Camps [VI, 40].

26. Joseph Kraft, *The Grand Design: From Common Market to Atlantic Partnership* (New York: Harper, 1962), pp. 115-16.

27. Quoted in Beloff [IV, 61], p. 114.

28. Complete text in *Recueil des communiqués et déclarations du Comité d'action pour les Etats-Unis d'Europe 1955–1965* (Lausanne: Centre de recherches européennes, 1965).

29. Sulzberger [V, 48], p. 876.

30. An exceptionally calm analysis of de Gaulle's conception from the perspective of an American "Atlanticist": Harold Van B. Cleveland, *The Atlantic Idea and Its European Rivals* (New York: McGraw-Hill, 1966), pp. 142-44.

31. This formulation in Ben T. Moore, *N.A.T.O. and the Future of Europe* (New York: Harper, 1958), p. 232.

32. See the remarkable study (with a good deal of information, intelligent analysis, and scope) by Robert Bloes, *Le "Plan Fouchet" et le problème de l'Europe politique* (Bruges: Collège de l'Europe, 1970).

33. Thorough analyses of Dutch foreign policy in its relation to domestic trends in the very detailed dissertation by Robert de Bruin, *Les Pays-Bas et l'intégration européenne 1957–1967* (Paris: Institut d'études politiques de Paris, 1977), mimeographed.

34. Paul-Marie de La Gorce, *De Gaulle entre deux mondes: une vie et une époque* (Paris: Fayard, 1964). The best account of the affair from de Gaulle's perspective.

35. "Contre l'Europe des Patries," *Réalités,* May 1962; quoted in Bloes [VII, 32], p. 427).

36. Bloes [VII, 32], p. 398.

37. Harold Macmillan, *At the End of the Day* (Vol. VI of the memoirs) (London: Macmillan, 1973), p. 335.

38. Sulzberger [V, 48], p. 873.

39. On British policy and the Anglo-American conflict of 1962, see especially A. Pierre [V, 41], pp. 216–43, and Richard E. Neustadt, *Alliance Politics* (New York: Columbia University Press, 1970) (where the chapter on the Skybolt crisis came out of a report for Kennedy, who wanted to know how such a crisis could have developed).

40. Macmillan, [VII, 37], p. 339.

41. The content of the talks remained in dispute for some time, but there are hardly any differences between Macmillan's detailed report, *ibid.*, pp. 345-54, and what de Gaulle told the Chancellor in January 1963 as reported by Adenauer [VII, 13], pp. 204-5.

42. Complete text in appendix, Macmillan [VII, 37], pp. 553-55.

43. Couve De Murville [VII, 1], pp. 410-11.

44. Adenauer [VII, 13], p. 205. On the preparation of the treaty, see especially the report by Thomas Jansen, "Die Entstehung des deutsch-französischen Vertrages" in *Konrad Adenauer und seine Zeit* [VII, 13], pp. 249-74, which is based on the documents of the author's father.

45. A lively, intelligent, but also bitter analysis of the entire final phase of the negotiations on British candidacy for the EEC is provided by Nora Beloff [IV, 10]. The best account of the military situation in the early 1960s is A. Buchanan and P. Windsor, *Arms and Stability in Europe* (London: Chatto & Windus, 1963).

CHAPTER 8

1. A. Grosser, "L'obsession américaine," *Le Monde,* July 19, 1967.

2. Alphand [V, 31], p. 407.

3. See Charles E. Bohlen, *Witness to History: 1919–1969* (New York: Norton, 1973), p. 517. The memoirs of the American ambassador to France are not much more intelligent or inspiring than those of his French colleague in Washington.

4. *Memoirs of Hope* [VII, 7], p. 242. See also special issue "Vive le Québec libre! Une intuition ou une politique?" *Espoir,* No. 20, 1977.

5. See especially Samy Cohen, *De Gaulle, les Gaullistes et Israël* (Paris: A. Moreau, 1974), pp. 152-54, to be supplemented by Sylvia Crosbie, *A Tacit Alliance: France and Israel from Suez to the Six Day War* (Princeton, N.J.: Princeton University Press, 1974).

6. Paul Balta and Claudine Rulleau, *La politique arabe de la France de De Gaulle à Pompidou* (Paris: Sindbad, 1974), p. 58.

7. See Nils Orvik and Niels Haagerup, *The Scandinavian Members of NATO* (London: ISS "Adelphi Papers," No. 23, 1965), pp. 6-7.

8. The best analysis of these contradictions is probably still Henry Kissinger, *The Troubled Partnership* (New York: McGraw-Hill, 1965). The most complete account from the American perspective which places all of the

blame for the disintegration of the Atlantic Community on de Gaulle is Eliot R. Goudman, *The Fate of the Atlantic Community* (New York: Praeger, 1975), pp. 50-134, 241-96.

9. This term in Harold Wilson, *The Labour Government, 1964–1970: A Personal Record* (London: Weidenfeld & Nicolson, 1971), p. 836.

10. Excellent presentation in Morgan [VII, 13], pp. 146-51.

11. Raymond Aron, *The Great Debate* (Garden City, N.Y.: Doubleday, 1965), pp. 91-92.

12. See especially Pöttering [VI, 23], pp. 148-228, and the concise and thorough analysis in the large study by Helga Haftendorn, *Abrüstungs- und Entspannungspolitik zwischen Sicherheitsbefriedigung und Friedenssicherung. Zur Aussenpolitik der BRD 1955–1973* (Düsseldorf: Bertelsmann, 1974). Helmut Schmidt, *Verteidigung oder Vergeltung* (Stuttgart: Seewald, expanded edition 1965), is of course, from today's perspective, of considerable interest among the publications of that period.

13. The two best-documented and most thoughtful works on French policy are by authors that are not French: Wilfrid L. Kohl, *French Nuclear Diplomacy* (Princeton, N.J.: Princeton University Press, 1971), and Lothar Ruehl, *La politique militaire de la Vème République* (Paris: Presses de la Fondation Nationale des Sciences Politiques, 1976).

14. Excellent plan in K. Hunt, *NATO Without France* (London: ISS "Adelphi Papers," December 1966), p. 8.

15. Lyndon Johnson, *The Vantage Point, 1963–1969* (New York: Holt, Rinehart and Winston, 1971), p. 305.

16. Table in Duroselle [I, 3], p. 239.

17. For a comparison of French and German attitudes toward the United States, see Karl Deutsch, Lewis Edinger, et al., *France, Germany and the Western Alliance: A Study on Elite Attitudes* (New York: Scribner's, 1967), and A. Grosser, "France and Germany in the Atlantic Community," in *The Atlantic Community*, ed. by F. Wilcox and H. F. Haviland (New York: Praeger, 1963), pp. 32-56; "France and Germany: The Divergent Outlook," *Foreign Affairs*, October 1965; "France and Germany: Less Divergent Outlooks?" *ibid.*, January 1970.

18. Wilson [VIII, 9], p. 408.

19. *Ibid.*, p. 93.

20. In this spirit, Pierre Uri wrote the substantial report *Dialogue des Continents. Un programme économique* (Paris: Plon, 1963) (the English title is clearly less neutral: *Partnership for Progress: A Program for Transatlantic Action.* [New York: Harper, 1963]), a synthesis of studies of the International Committees of the Atlantic Institute. Same tenor in what is probably the most remarkable analysis written during the period under discussion here: Richard N. Cooper, *The Economics of Interdependence: Economic Policy in the Atlantic Community* (New York: McGraw-Hill, 1968).

21. A. Lancelot and P. Weill, "Les Français et l'unification politique de l'Europe d'après un sondage de la SOFRES," *Revue française de Science Politique*, I, 1969, p. 152.

22. Quoted in the intelligently critical book of the American Robert Gilpin,

La science et l'Etat en France (Paris: Gallimard, 1970), an expanded edition of *France in the Age of the Scientific State* (Princeton, N.J.: Princeton University Press, 1968), which is fundamental to our subject.

23. Gilpin [VIII, 22], French text, pp. 15-16.

24. Gilpin, *ibid.*, English text, p. 40.

25. See especially the recollections of André Turcat, *Concorde. Essais et Batailles* (Paris: Stock, 1977), pp. 25-27.

26. Quoted in the very polemical but useful book by James McMillan and Bernard Harpis, *The American Take-over of Britain* (London: L. Frewin, 1968), p. 164. Balance sheet and bibliography of the phenomenon in the article by Alessandro Sils, "L'Europe devrait-elle rappeler ses savants?" *30 Jours d'Europe,* January 1970.

27. Etiemble, *Parlez-vous franglais?* (Paris: Gallimard, 1964). Quotations on pp. 333, 291-92, 329-330.

28. Régine Pernoud, *Pour en finir avec le Moyen Age* (Paris: Seuil, 1977), p. 42.

29. Examples of the confusion: the revised French edition of the excellent book by Rainer Hellmann, *Weltunternehmen nur amerikanisch?* (Baden-Baden: Nomos, 1970), is entitled *Puissance et limites des multinationales* (Paris: Mame, 1974). Among the works I selected from the huge literature on this topic, this work and Raymond Vernon, *Les entreprises multinationales. La souveraineté nationale en péril* (Paris: Calmann-Lévy, 1973), were the most useful. (Same phenomenon in the "deamericanized" title for the original one reads: *Sovereignty at Bay: The Multinational Spread of U.S. Enterprises.*) See also note 6, Chap. 9.

30. On the destruction of the myth of the unity of these actors, one should read the exceptionally clear and thorough analysis by R. A. Bauer, I. de Sola Pool, and L. A. Dexter, *American Business and Public Policy: The Politics of Foreign Trade* (New York: Atherton Press, 1963). One can learn much about the concept of power from Charles P. Kindleberger, *Power and Money: The Politics of International Economics and the Economics of International Politics* (New York: Basic Books, 1970), and from the many studies by François Perroux.

31. Hellmann [VIII, 29], p. 277 (figures after 1969 from the French edition, p. 219).

32. J. J. Servan-Schreiber, *The American Challenge* (New York: Atheneum, 1968), pp. 3, 26.

33. These are the claims that provide the point of departure in Leo Gundy, *Le vilain businessman américain en Europe* (Brussels: Elsevier, 1976).

34. Solid study which expresses and provokes contradictory judgments in Edward A. McCreary, *The Americanization of Europe: Americans and American Companies in the Uncommon Market* (Garden City, N.Y.: Doubleday, 1964).

35. A positive yet moderately critical balance sheet is drawn up by John H. Dunning, "Technology, United States Investment and European Economic Growth" in Charles P. Kindleberger, ed., *The International Corporation* (Cambridge, Mass.: MIT, 1970), pp. 141-78.

36. Balanced presentation of the convergences and divergences in the economic area in Leon Gorny, *Les politiques européennes face aux Etats-Unis* (Paris: Emile Paul, 1976), pp. 145-260.

37. "It is not a matter of closing Europe to this or that investment, which are most often highly profitable to our countries, but simply of avoiding excesses." Quoted as motto to the appendix (with the German text of the Commission draft of October 27, 1965, for a directive of the Ministerial Council on investments abroad) in Rainer Hellmann, *Amerika auf dem Europamarkt. US-Direktinvestitionen im Gemeinsamen Markt* (Baden-Baden: Nomos, 1966).

38. Quoted in Hellmann, *Weltunternehmen* [VIII, 29], p. 129 (in the course of a concise but excellent presentation of the economic-political conceptions in the various countries).

39. Unpublished texts in the intelligent study by Allan W. Johnstone, *United States Direct Investment in France: An Investigation of the French Charge* (Cambridge, Mass.: MIT, 1965), pp. 27-28.

40. Complete text in the appendix of Charles P. Kindleberger, *Les investissements américains dans le monde,* enlarged French edition (Paris: Calmann-Lévy, 1971), pp. 253-55.

41. All aspects of French policy (preparation, implementation, substance) are presented in the monumental collaborative study ed. by Joel Rideau, Pierre Gerbet, M. Torrelli, and R. M. Chevallier, *La France et les Communautés européennes* (Paris: L.G.D., 1975). I omit the ample and ultimately disappointing literature on the theory of European integration. See the very clear balance sheet by Ilan Greilsammer, "Theorizing European Integration in Its Four Periods," *The Jerusalem Journal of International Relations,* II, 1 (Fall 1976), pp. 129-56.

42. See especially John Newhouse, *30 juin 1965: Crise à Bruxelles* (Fond. Nat. des Sc. Pol., 1968); and Myriam Camps, *European Unification in the Sixties: From the Veto to the Crisis* (Oxford University Press, 1967).

43. A text which is remarkable in all respects in *Le Monde,* February 26, 1964.

44. Club Jean Moulin, *Pour une politique étrangère de l'Europe* (Paris: Ed. du Seuil, 1966), p. 40. Otherwise, the study is intelligent and balanced.

45. Merritt and Puchala [VI, 2], p. 259.

46. On the development of Italian policy, see especially Istituto Affari Internazionali, *La Politica estera della Repubblica Italiana* (Milan: Ed. di Communità, 1967) 3 vols. (especially Umberto Segre, "Atlantismo e neutralismo nella politica estera italiana," pp. 559-589; Nenni [III, 31]; and Mario M. Ferrara, *La politica estera dell'Italia libera* 1945-1971 (Milan: Pan, 1972).

47. Texts in the appendix of the clear and balanced though rather optimistic report by one of the American negotiators, Ernest H. Preeg, *Traders and Diplomats: An Analysis of the Kennedy Round of Negotiations under the General Agreement on Tariffs and Trade* (Brookings Institute, 1970); which should be supplemented with the analysis by Gordon L. Weil, *A Foreign Policy for Europe? The External Relations of the European Community* (Bruges: Collège d'Europe, 1970); and, above all, by the two middle sections

of vol. I of the exceptionally ample and substantial collection by Andrew Schonfield (with a brilliant introduction pp. 1-142 where he shows the reciprocal relations between economics and politics) for the Royal Institute of International Affairs, *International Economic Relations of the Western World 1959–1971*, 2 vols. (Oxford University Press, 1976): Part II by G. and V. Curzon, "The Management of Trade Relations in the GATT," pp. 143-286; and Part III by T. K. Warley, "Western Trade in Agricultural Products," pp. 287-404.

48. Quoted in Weil, p. 237.

49. Lawrence B. Krause, *European Economic Integration and the United States* (Brookings Institute, 1968).

50. Good comments on p. 49 of the exemplary study by Susan Strange, "International Monetary Relations" in *International Economic Relations of the Western World*, Vol. II, pp. 18-359 (probably the best section of this excellent collection for its exemplary clarity and objectivity and an equally exemplary sense for the relationships between politics and economics). The good survey of the 1966 and 1967 crises in Morgan [VII, 13], pp. 147-148, should be supplemented by the data provided in Horst Mendershausen, *Troop Stationing in Germany: Value and Cost* (Santa Monica: Rand, 1968); and, most importantly, the solid presentation by Monika Medick, "Burdensharing und Devisenausgleich als Problem der deutsch-amerikanischen Beziehungen" in M. Knapp [VII, 13], pp. 188-227. On the 1966 confrontation, see also the very simplified version of the facts by President Johnson [VIII, 15], pp. 306-307.

51. To better understand and explain the connections, I referred especially to Susan Strange [VIII, 50]; to Paul Einzig, *The Euro-Dollar System*, 5th ed. (New York: St. Martin, 1973); and to two French works which are remarkable for their clarity, the one pedagogic and "pro-floating," the other strongly "anti-floating": Jean Carrière, *L'or noir et l'or jaune* (Paris: Ed. du Seuil, 1976) and Jean Denizet, *La grande inflation: Salaire, intérêt et change* (Paris: P.U.F., 1977).

52. Wilson [VIII, 9], p. 439.

53. Denizet, pp. 110-12.

54. Robert Triffin, *Gold and the Dollar Crisis* (addendum to the paperback edition, "The Twilight of the Gold Exchange Standard"), p. 163, quoted by S. Strange [VIII, 50], p. 287.

55. Jacques Rueff, *Le Péché monétaire de l'Occident* (Paris: Plon, 1971), p. 24.

56. Quoted in Carrière [VIII, 51], p. 127.

57. Johnson [VIII, 15], p. 316.

58. Detailed table on p. 352 of a book that is probably overestimated in the United States: Herbert Y. Schandler, *The Unmaking of a President: Lyndon Johnson and Vietnam* (Princeton, N.J.: Princeton University Press, 1977). Compact analysis of the decisions of the President in which the other countries and governments are not mentioned at all.

59. Very detailed chronology in the appendix of the rather exciting report by an actor and eyewitness: Chester Cooper, *The Lost Crusade: America in Vietnam* (New York: Dodd Mead, 1970), pp. 473-523.

60. Quotations and analysis in Soell [IV, 23], Vol. II, pp. 478-83.

61. Besson, *Die Aussenpolitik der Bundesrepublik* [VII, 13], p. 446.

62. Nenni [III, 31], p. 163.

63. Giorgio Galli, *Fanfani* (Milan: Feltrinelli, 1975), pp. 103-7.

64. Wilson [VIII, 9], p. 80.

65. The episode reported in Cooper [VIII, 59], pp. 352-368.

66. Couve de Murville [VII, 1], p. 127.

67. *Ibid.*, p. 129.

68. Both letters in the official French documentation, *Articles et documents. Textes officiels, 23 février 1968*. (This is a one-time reference to this constantly used source.)

69. Text of both letters in *Le Monde*, July 22, 1966.

70. *Le Monde*, September 6, 1969. The encounter is described in the moving but very uncritical book by Jean Sainteny, *Face à Ho-Chi-Minh* (Paris: Seghers, 1970), pp. 187-90.

72. Text of both letters in *Le Monde*, April 25, 1967.

73. Couve de Murville [VII, 1], p. 140.

74. A. Grosser, "La comparaison algérienne," *Le Monde*, September 4, 1966, supplemented by the article "Les Etats Unis, leurs Alliés et le Vietnam," *Le Monde*, March 11, 1967.

CHAPTER 9

1. *Mater et Magistra* (Glen Rock, N.J.: Paulist Press, 1961), p. 53.

2. *The Gospel of Peace and Justice: Catholic Teaching Since Pope John* (Maryknoll, N.Y.: Orbis Books, 1976), p. 220.

3. *The Sixteen Documents of Vatican II* (Boston: Daughters of St. Paul, n.d.), pp. 581, 587, 589.

4. *The Gospel of Peace and Justice*, pp. 394-95.

5. "Pour une pratique chrétienne de la politique." Report submitted by the plenary assembly of the French episcopate in 1972 in Msgr. Gabriel Matagrin, *Politique Eglise et Foi* (Paris: Le Centurion, 1972), pp. 83-84.

6. See especially the bestseller (with controversial analyses) by Claude Julien, *L'empire américain* (Paris: Grasset, 1968); the presentation of the problem of the multinationals as a "taux de racket" (an international racket) by Christian Goux and J. F. Landeau, *Le Peril américain. Le capital américain à l'étranger* (Paris: Calmann-Lévy, 1971); and the economic theory most often referred to in accusations of the United States: Samir Amin, *Le développement inégal. Essais sur les formes sociales du capitalism périphérique* (Paris: Ed. de Minuit, 1973), and other works by that author.

7. Pierre Moussa, *Les Etats-unis et les nations prolétaires* (Paris: Ed. du Seuil, 1965), p. 37.

8. Institut für Demoskopie Allensbach, *Jahrbuch der öffentlichen Meinung 1968–1973* (Allensbach: Verlag für Demoskopie, 1974), p. 556.

9. See Department of the Army, *Report of the Department of Army Review of the Preliminary Investigations into the My Lai Incident*. Vol. I, *The Report of the Investigation 14 March 1970* (Washington, D.C., 1974). Further volumes were not published. The most comprehensive and most one-sided ac-

cusations are raised in the texts of the "Russell Tribunal," 1st and 2nd session
1966–67. See Bertrand Russell and Jean-Paul Sartre, *Das Vietnam-Tribunal I
oder Amerika vor Gericht. Das Vietnam-Tribunal II oder Die Verurteilung
Amerikas* (Reinbek: Rowohlt rororo No. 1091 and 1213, 1968).

10. Subtitle in Tilman Fichter and S. Lönnendonker, *Kleine Geschichte des
SDS* (Berlin: Rotbuch Verlag, 1977), p. 123.

11. See the reprints in Ulrike Meinhof, *Dokumente einer Rebellion. 10
Jahre "konkret"-Kolumnen,* ed. by K. R. Röhl (Hamburg: Konkret Verlag,
1972), pp. 52, 59, 76. On the nexus between Vietnam protest, anti-
Americanism, and German extremism, see for example Gerd Langguth, *Die
Protestbewegung in der Bundesrepublik Deutschland 1968–1976* (Bonn:
Bundeszentrale für politische Bildung, 1976), pp. 33-34.

12. Detailed international chronology (but very partisan and sometimes
caricatural) in Peter Moser, *Was wir wollten. Was wir wurden. Studenten-
revolte zehn Jahre danach* (Reinbek: Rowohlt, 1977), pp. 249-95.

13. Noam Chomsky, *American Power and the New Mandarins,* quoted on
p. 10 of Robert Tucker, *The Radical Left and American Foreign Policy* (Baltimore: Johns Hopkins University Press, 1971), a remarkable work whose critical but calm analysis makes it almost unnecessary to read such aggressive
books as Harry Magdoff, *The Age of Imperialism. The Economy of U.S.
Foreign Policy* (New York: Monthly Review, 1969).

14. This is the beginning of the clearest, most balanced (and least revolutionary) presentation of the crisis in France: Adrien Dansette, *Mai 1968* (Paris:
Plon, 1971). A survey of possible explanations in the by no means outdated
article by Jean Touchard and Philippe Beneton, "Les interprétations de la
crise de mai-juin 1968" in *Revue française de Science politique* (June 1970).

15. This is emphasized by all the contributors to a collection of essays
edited by Anthony Smith which will shortly be published in London and is
devoted to television in the political life of the countries of Western Europe.
But above all, one should read the excellent chapters on the Netherlands,
Germany (K. Shell), France (Marianne Debouzy), and Great Britain in A. N. N.
Den Hollander, ed., *Contagious Conflict: The Impact of American Dissent on
European Life* (Leiden: Brill, 1973).

16. "Yalta ou le mythe du péché originel" by Raymond Aron, *Figaro,* August 28, 1968.

17. Couve de Murville [VII, 1], pp. 282-3.

18. On the conflicts of German-American relations as regards *Ostpolitik,* a
remarkable, abundantly documented dissertation by Rüdiger Löwe (University of Munich) will soon be published.

19. See the analysis in the revised edition of my *Deutschlandbilanz* [I, 54].

20. Michel Jobert, *Memoirs d'Avenir* (Paris: Grasset, 1974), p. 164.

21. *Ibid.,* p. 202.

22. Susan Strange [VIII, 50], p. 301.

23. Paul Einzig [VIII, 51], pp. 152-53, 159.

24. Denizet [VIII, 51], pp. 68, 54.

25. Text and brief critique of the communique in S. Strange, pp. 292-95. A
readily accessible chronological and analytical presentation of the monetary

crisis 1968–1974 in Jean Marchal, *Le système monétaire international: De Bretton Woods aux changes flottants 1944–1975* (Paris: Cujas, 1975), pp. 24-118.

26. Table 1960-1970 for the most important countries in Strange, p. 296.

27. *Memoirs of Hope, Renewal and Endeavor* [VII, 7], p. 244. An extreme economic interpretation of the constraints on de Gaulle's policy in Edward L. Morse, *Foreign Policy and Interdependence in Gaullist France* (Princeton, N.J.: Princeton University Press, 1973).

28. Address before the American Bankers Association in Munich, quoted by Strange, p. 334.

29. Precise and credible report on this decisive negotiation in the lively and clear book by Rainer Hellmann, *Dollar, Gold und Schlange: Die letzten Jahre von Bretton Woods* (Baden-Baden: Nomos, 1976). A report which makes even the presentation of S. Strange, let alone that of J. Denizet, appear inaccurate.

CHAPTER 10

1. Until further studies with more perspective appear, Rainer Hellmann [IV, 29], with a great deal of precise information, should be mentioned. His report extends to 1977.

2. Synthesis of a very illuminating series of articles "L'action de Georges Pompidou" by Jean-René Bernard (adviser to the Prime Minister and then the Premier, finally as deputy secretary-general of the Office of the Presidency from 1962 to 1974 and, as of 1967, secretary-general of the important Inter-ministerial Commission for questions of economic cooperation in Europe) in *Le Monde*, April 1-4, 1975.

3. All texts on the trip in *La politique étrangère de la France: Textes et documents*, First Semester 1970, September 1970, pp. 56-91. (This is a fundamental biannual publication of the *Documentation française*.)

4. Jobert [IX, 20], p. 170.

5. Philippe de Saint Robert, *Les septennats interrompus* (Paris: Laffont, 1977), p. 138.

6. Usable, detailed chronologies on pp. 75-146 and 151-97, respectively, of the two quite non-analytical books by François Visine, *Trente ans d'Europe 1945–1975* (Paris: Ed. Techniques et Economiques, 1975), and Pierre Cousté and François Visine, *Pompidou et l'Europe* (Paris: Librairie Technique, 1974).

7. See especially David Brent Smith, *The Opposition to Ostpolitik: Foreign Policy as an Issue in West German Politics 1969–1972*. Unpublished dissertation, Harvard University, 1976.

8. Taken from p. 39 of the fundamental book by Uwe Kitzinger, *Diplomatie et persuasion. Comment la Grande-Bretagne est entrée dans le Marché commun* (Paris: A. Moreau, 1974; English version 1973). Also the very personal and lively presentation by Nora Beloff, *Transit of Britain: A Report on Britain's Changing Role in the Post-War World* (London: Collins, 1973).

9. Pages 17-18 of the short, exceptionally dense, and clear study by Alastair

Buchan, *L'Europe et l'Amérique. De l'Alliance à la Coalition* (Paris: Institut atlantique, 1974). On the thinking of the new team and its effects, see Benjamin J. Cohen, "The Revolution in Atlantic Economic Relations: A Bargain Comes Unstuck," pp. 106-13 in Wolfram F. Hanrieder, ed., *The United States and Western Europe: Political, Economic and Strategic Perspectives* (Cambridge, Mass.: Winthrop, 1974). An excellent reader. See especially the contribution by Stanley Hoffmann, pp. 79-105, with a good *compte rendu* of transatlantic relations at the time of the 1973 turn. A more systematic account which is based on collaborative preliminary work by several research institutes: Karl Kaiser, *Die europäische Herausforderung und die USA. Das atlantische Verhältnis im Zeitalter weltpolitischer Strukturveränderungen* (Munich: Piper, 1973). This should be supplemented by the chapter "Europe and America: The Uneven Dumb-Bell" of the solid study by Roger P. Morgan, *High Politics, Low Politics: Toward a Foreign Policy for Western Europe* (Beverly Hills and London: Sage Publications, 1973).

10. André Fontaine, *Le dernier quart de siècle* (Paris: Fayard, 1976), p. 23.

11. Cohen [X, 9], p. 112.

12. On this missed contact, see Marvin and Bernard Kalb, *Kissinger* (Boston: Little, Brown, 1974). Characteristically, this book, which extends to January 1974, hardly mentions Europe at all.

13. Complete text of the "European" part of the report in the appendix to Hanrieder [X, 9], pp. 293-311.

14. Cohen [X, 9], p. 127.

15. Marc Perrin de Brichambaut, "La crise économique occidentale depuis 1971," in *Les politiques extérieures européennes dans la crise,* ed. by Alfred Grosser (Paris: Presses de la Fondation Nationale des Sciences Politiques, 1976), pp. 42-43.

16. Quoted in P. M. Doutrelant, "'L'inimaginable' affaire du soja," *Le Monde,* August 3, 1973.

17. Quotations in *L'Année Politique 1973* [II, 6], p. 249.

18. Anthony Sampson, *The Sovereign State of ITT* (New York: Stein & Day, 1973), p. 265.

19. Good presentation of transatlantic tensions in Maurice Ferro, *Kissinger, diplomate de l'impossible* (Paris: Ed. France-Empire, 1976), pp. 316-17. On the problem of missile bases in Italy, see John Earle, *Italy in the 70's* (London: David & Charles, 1975), p. 172.

20. Good chronology of the affair before the Yom Kippur War in *Le Monde,* April 25, 1972. Completed chronology in *L'Express,* August 12, 1974.

21. Text in *Le Monde,* December 18, 1973. See also A. Grosser, "Deux Grands sur le même plan," *ibid.,* December 4, 1973.

22. Tables pp. 6 and 9 in Robert J. Lieber, *Oil and the Middle East War: Europe in the Energy Crisis* (Center of International Affairs, Harvard University, 1976), a short, especially illuminating book on all aspects of the crisis (based principally on the excellent account of Françoise de la Serre, "L'Europe des neuf et le conflit israélo-arabe," *Revue française de science politique,* August 1974). On the earlier energy policy of the Federal Republic and its consequences, see the solid analyses in Manfred Horn, *Die Ener-*

*giepolitik der Bundesregierung von 1958 bis 1972. Zur Bedeutung der Pene-
tration ausländischer Ölkonzerne in die Energiewirtschaft der BRD für die
Abhängigkeit innerer Strukturen und Entwicklungen* (Berlin: Duncker &
Humbolt, 1977). On Italian and French oil policy up to the crisis, see Henri
Madelin, *Pétrole et politique en Méditérannée occidentale* (Paris: A. Colin,
1973). General survey of the problems from 1970 to 1972 in Jean-Marie
Chevalier, *Le nouvel enjeu pétrolier* (Paris: Calmann-Lévy, 1973).

23. Philippe de Saint Robert [X, 5], p. 128.

24. This aspect omitted in the otherwise detailed report of the parliamentary investigating commission, *Sur les sociétés pétrolières opérant en France*
(Paris: Union gén. d'éd., 10/18, 1974).

25. Detailed table in Marchal [IX, 25], p. 103.

26. Nicolas Sarkis, *Le pétrole à l'heure arabe* (Paris: Stock, 1975), p. 60,
quoted by Guy de Carmoy, "Les Etats-Unis face au défi de l'énergie,"
Politique étrangère, 5, 1977, p. 501.

27. See *Le Monde,* January 31, 1974.

28. Complete text in *Politique étrangère de la France. Textes et documents,*
First Semester 1974, pp. 70-73.

29. *Ibid.,* p. 100.

30. See for example an article which created a considerable stir, "Fearing
French Domination, U.S. Halts Push for United Europe," *International
Herald Tribune,* April 9, 1974.

31. French text in *Le Monde,* March 28, 1974.

32. List of themes in David Butler and Dennis Kavanagh, *The British General Elections of October 1974* (London: Macmillan, 1975).

CHAPTER 11

1. Complete text in the clear and courageous book by François de Rose
(permanent French representative in the NATO Council from 1970 to 1975),
La France et la défense de l'Europe (Paris: Le Seuil, 1976), pp. 117-21.

2. On the nature and scope of the 1974 crisis, see especially Lothar Ruehl,
"Die atlantische Allianz und die politische Stabilität in Südeuropa," pp. 3-49
in *Sicherheitspolitik vor neuen Aufgaben,* ed. by Karl Kaiser and Karl Markus
Kreis (Frankfurt: Metzner, 1976). See also the contributions in favor of the
Greek position and very critical of the United States in a colloquium on "Défense et sécurité dans l'Europe des contradictions," *Politique étrangère,* 3-4,
1977, pp. 241-430 (G. Tenekides, pp. 322-42, and Ch. M. Woodhouse, pp.
348-53). On the bases of the conflict, see the excellent study by François
Crouzet, *Le conflit de Chypre 1946 –1959* (Brussels: E. Bruylant, 1973), 2 vols.

3. See the chapter by Marie-Claude Smouts, "Du Gaullisme au néo-
atlantisme: les incertitudes françaises," in *Les Politiques extérieures dans la
crise* [X, 15], especially p. 98.

4. See Richard Woyke, *Die NATO in den siebziger Jahren. Eine Bes-
tandsaufnahme* (Opladen: Leske, 1977), pp. 68-70.

5. F. de Rose [XI, 1], p. 52.

6. Good analysis by Stanley Hoffmann in Hanrieder [X, 9], p. 99.

7. Indian proverb, quoted by Pierre Hassner in his especially illuminating contribution "Europe and the Contradictions in American Policy," in *America as an Ordinary Country: U.S. Foreign Policy and the Future,* ed. by Richard Rosecrance (Ithaca, N.Y.: Cornell University Press, 1976), p. 72. On the whole complex of the problems addressed here, see especially the detailed and well-documented if somewhat dry book by Dieter Dettke, *Allianz im Wandel. Amerikanisch-europäische Sicherheitsbeziehungen im Zeichen des Bilateralismus der Supermächte* (Frankfurt: Metzner, 1976), especially in reference to the conflict of interest between the United States and the European states, pp. 120-76). See also the chapter by Hans-Peter Schwarz, "Das atlantische Sicherheitssystem in einer Ära ohne grosse Alternative," in *Amerika und Westeuropa. Gegenwarts- und Zukunftsprobleme,* ed. by Karl Kaiser and H.-P. Schwarz (Stuttgart: Belser, 1977), pp. 165-203.

8. See pp. 334-38 of the new study by Jan Höhn, *Aussenpolitik der EG-Staaten: im Fall der KSZE. Geschichte, Struktur, Entscheidungsprozess* (Munich: Tudurg, 1978), which, however, neglects the last phase, which is better expounded in Pierre Hassner, "Les politiques envers l'Est. Rivalités et convergences," in *Les politiques extérieures européennes dans la crise* [X, 15], pp. 57-80.

9. Quoted in Jean-Pierre Brulé, *L'Arsenal mondial* (Paris: Le Centurion, 1975), pp. 141-42.

10. Good analysis of this situation by the director of the London Institute for Strategic Studies before the CDU Congress on security questions: Ch. Bertram, "Europa darf nicht mehr Zaungast sein," *Deutsche Allgemeine Sonntagszeitung,* January 29, 1978. A preliminary survey of the extensive discussion on the neutron bomb in Manfred Opel, "Zur Diskussion um die Neutronenwaffe" in *Aus Politik und Zeitgeschehen,* Beilage zu *Das Parlament* (February 25, 1978).

11. Complete text in *Revue de défense nationale,* May 1975, pp. 11-15.

12. Text, *ibid,* August/September 1977, pp. 7-19. On the objections to the doctrine which either insist even more strongly on a purely French defensive strategy or demand a completely egoistic recourse to the Allied defense system, see the very controversial study by Commandant Guy Brossolet, *Essai sur la non-bataille* (Berlin, 1975), or the book by Admiral Antoine Sanguinetti, *Le fracas des armes* (Paris: Hachette, 1975), pp. 55, 70. A very "European" interpretation of Gaullism in the concluding chapter of Commandant Guy Doly, *Stratégie France-Europe. Sécurité de la France et Union européenne* (Paris: Ed. Média, 1977).

13. See the sober and matter-of-fact survey by Lothar Ruehl [VIII, 13], pp. 413-30.

14. This expression derives from the title of an article by General Ailleret, "Défense 'dirigée' ou défense 'tous azimuts,' " *Revue de défense nationale,* December 1967.

15. Table of military expenditures of NATO countries since 1960 on pp. 204-5 of the very pessimistic book by General R. Close, *L'Europe sans défense? 48 heures qui pourraient changer la face du monde* (Brussels: Ed. Arts et voyages [sic!], 1976).

16. Graphic presentation on p. 67 in *Rüstung und Abrüstung im Atomzeitalter*, ed. by the Stockholm International Peace Research Institute (SIPRI) (Hamburg: Rowohlt, 1977).

17. Table in James Digby, *Precision-guided Weapons* (London: Adelphi Papers, 1975).

18. Yearly tabulations in *Rüstung und Abrüstung* [XI, 16], p. 61.

19. See the balance sheet of Walter Schütze, "La République Fédérale d'Allemagne et le marché international des armements," in *Documents*, March 1976, pp. 34-55.

20. Figures in *La Croix*, August 26, 1977.

21. On the entire complex of these disputes, see the very lively book with comprehensive but occasionally inaccurate data by Anthony Sampson, *The Arms Bazaar from Lebanon to Lockheed* (New York: Viking, 1977).

22. Good presentation of the affair which took its course against the background of Franco-American rivalry, *ibid.*, pp. 132-62. The account utilizes the report of the investigative commission.

23. Complete text of the letter to the President and the note in the appendix of the book which was written on the spot: Paul Stehlin, *La France désarmée* (Paris: Calmann-Lévy, 1974), pp. 159-81. See also Sampson [XI, 21].

24. Firmly held viewpoint of Norman Gall, "Atoms for Brazil: Dangers for All," *Foreign Policy* (Summer 1976), pp. 155-201. See also Andrew Pierre, *Nuclear Proliferation: A Strategy for Control* (New York: Foreign Policy Association, Headline Series, October 1976).

25. Text in "Dokumente zur Unterzeichnung des Kernwaffen-Sperrvertrages durch die Bundesrepublik Deutschland" in the regular documentation of the journal *Europa-Archiv*, XXV, I, January 10, 1970, D 1 to D 24; among other places.

26. Complete German text in *Bulletin des Presse-und Informationsamtes der Bundesregierung*, January 17, 1978.

27. See Dennis L. Meadows, et al., *The Limits of Growth: A Report for the Club of Rome Project on the Predicament of Mankind* (New York: University Books, 1972). On the entire complex of economic problems, see the six contributions of the section "Handling the Economy," E. O. Czempiel and D. A. Rustow, eds., *The Euro-American System* (Frankfurt: Campus, 1976), pp. 31-140.

28. We follow the excellent study by Henri Rieben, *L'Europe sidérurgique au défi.* I: *La bataille de l'acier* (Lausanne: Centre de Recherches européennes, 1977).

29. Very stimulating table in *Newsweek*, May 2, 1977.

30. G. de Carmoy [X, 26], p. 505-6.

31. More detailed table in the article by Shell director Geoffrey Chandler, "The Innocence of Oil Companies," *Foreign Policy* (Summer 1977), p. 60; see also the contribution of Senator Frank Church in the same issue, "The Impotence of Oil Companies."

32. See especially the severe survey by François David, *Autopsie de la Grande-Bretagne* (Paris: Hachette, 1976), pp. 91-112.

33. On the significance of the energy problem in Great Britain's total situa-

tion, see the analysis by Françoise de la Serre, "Les ambiguités de la politique britannique," *Les Politiques extérieures dans la crise* [X, 15], pp. 137-61.

34. "Le nucléaire inéluctable," a solid article by J. Fontaine and M. Herblay in *L'Expansion*, November 1977. "Für unser Land unverzichtbar," report of the research minister of the Federal Republic, *Die Zeit,* September 16, 1977.

35. *L'Express*, December 5, 1977.

36. Gundy [VIII, 33], p. 260.

37. Analysis of the institutional aspects of the French failure in Gilpin [VIII, 22], pp. 392-93.

38. Jacques Jublin and Jean-Michel Quatrepoint, *French ordinateurs. De l'affaire Bull à l'assassinat du Plan Calcul* (Paris: A. Moreau, 1976). Intensely interesting and passionate but one-sided report which is important for knowledge of the case itself and for a knowledge of the power relationships in the highest echelons of French political life and the image people there have of the United States.

39. Quoted *ibid.*, pp. 244-45.

40. Ch. Guéry, "Une experience réussie: du Plan Calcul à Honeywell-Bull," *Le Figaro,* January 28, 1978.

41. See H. Michaels, "Ernüchtert über die Zusammenarbeit mit den Amerikanern suchen deutsche, französische und britische Flugzeugbauer nach einer europäischen Lösung," *Die Zeit,* June 3, 1977.

42. *Le Monde,* January 21, 1978.

43. "Transnational Powers and National Goals," title of a synthesizing chapter (pp. 176-90) of the combative and stimulating book by Raymond Vernon, *Storm over the Multinationals: The Real Issues* (Cambridge, Mass.: Harvard University Press, 1977).

44. See M. Beaud, P. Danjou, and J. David, *Une multinationale française. Péchiney Ugine Kuhlmann* (Paris: Le Seuil, 1975).

45. *Socialisme et multinationales.* Colloquium of the Federation of the Socialist Party (Paris: Flammarion, Coll. "La Rose au Poing," 1976), pp. 21, 27. Very simplistic reports and contributions. The preface to the book by François Mitterrand is rather distanced. An informed, thoughtful, and critical account in Michel Delapierre and Ch. A. Michalet, *Les implantations étrangères en France: Stratégies et structures* (Paris: Calmann-Lévy, 1976).

46. Robert Gilpin, *U.S. Power and the Multinational Corporation: The Political Economy of Foreign Direct Investment* (New York: Basic Books, 1975), pp. 150, 199, 188, 189. An occasionally brutal book, much more systematic and closer to political realities than Vernon's. His analyses apply anywhere.

47. Pierre Pescallon, "Un nouveau leadership américain," *Projet* (May 1976), pp. 542, 544.

48. *Le Monde,* January 4, 1977.

49. Numerous tables, figures, and ideas in the two excellent informational notes of the financial adviser at the French embassy in Bonn, "Investissements allemands à l'étranger et investissements étrangers en République fédéral," and "Prises de participation des firmes nord-américaines en République fédéral d'Allemagne," June 3 and 22, 1977 (No. 12 and 14, 1977, a

regularly appearing, semi-confidential series which is one of the best sources for information on the German economy).

50. Graphic presentation of the development 1957–74 in *Expansion* (July-August 1976) in an interesting study, "Des Français en Amerique."

51. *Accord Général sur les Tarifs Douaniers et le Commerce.* Documents L/4422, L/4423, L/4425 of November 2, 1976.

52. This thesis is advocated with an equally marked anti-Communist and anti-capitalist emphasis, though not always convincingly, by the American unionist Charles Levinson. See his book *Vodka-Cola* (Paris: Stock, 1977).

53. See for example the very aggressive presentation of the problem in *Weizen als Waffe. Die neue Getreidestrategie der amerikanischen Aussenpolitik.* A study of the North American Congress on Latin America (Hamburg: Rowohlt, 1976). Also the incisive but balanced analysis by Henri de Farcy, "L'arme alimentaire des Etats-Unis," *Projet* (November 1976).

54. Yves Tavernier, *La fin de la France paysanne de 1914 à nos jours* (Vol. IV of *Histoire de la France rurale* by G. Duby and A. Wallon) (Paris: Le Seuil, 1976), p. 617.

55. For the German point of view, see Bundesministerium für wirtschaftliche Zusammenarbeit, *IV. Welthandelskonferenz in Nairobi* (Materialien Nr. 53), Bonn, June 1976. The brochure contains the parliamentary debate on UNCTAD IV.

56. "L'esprit de Rambouillet," *Le Monde,* November 19, 1975; "Ein Trostpflaster für Giscard," *Die Zeit,* November 29, 1975.

57. See what is in spite of the forced optimism of its concluding comments a resigned analysis by Pierre Werner, *L'Europe monétaire reconsidérée* (Lausanne: Centre de recherches européennes, 1977). Werner originated the plan that was never implemented.

58. On Italy's growing dependence, see especially the analysis by Geneviève Bibes, "Les antinomies de la politique extérieure italienne," in *Les politiques extérieures dans la crise* [X, 15], pp. 163-86.

59. Title of the articles by Paul Fabra, *Le Monde,* July 23, 1977, by Hans Jürgenien, *FAZ,* December 16, 1977, and of an interview, *La Croix,* on the same date.

60. Acute comments by Raymond Aron, p. 39 of his "The Relations Between Europeans and Americans," in the collection *Western Europe: The Trials of Partnership,* ed. by David S. Landes (Lexington, Mass.: Lexington Books, 1977).

61. C. Fred Bergsten, *The Dilemmas of the Dollar: The Economics and Politics of United States International Monetary Policy,* published under the auspices of the Council on Foreign Relations (New York: New York University Press, 1975), seemed especially illuminating to me. See also the less comprehensive, more recent study by Michael J. Brenner, *The Politics of International Monetary Reform: The Exchange Crisis* (Cambridge, Mass.: Ballinger, 1976). Compared to this, J. Antoine Kosciusko-Morizet and Jean Peyrelevade, *La mort du dollar* (Paris: Le Seuil, 1975), seems quite superficial in its simplistic aggressiveness.

62. Bersten [XI, 61], p. 557.

63. *Die Zeit*, July 29, 1977.

64. See for example the highly analytical but very firm speech, "Die internationale Bedeutung der deutschen Stabilitätspolitik," reprinted in *Europa-Archiv*, August 10, 1977.

65. "Toile de fond de toute analyse de la crise," in Samir Amin, *La crise de l'imperialisme* (Paris: Ed. de Minuit, 1975), p. 8

66. M. and R. Meeropol, *Nous sommes vos fils*, preface by Martine Monod and Stellio Lorenzi (Paris: Ed. Sociales, 1975), p. 9. Original ed.: *We Are Your Sons* (New York: Houghton Mifflin, 1975).

67. See for example the account in *Der Spiegel*, February 6, 1978.

68. Frightening report by Frank Snepp, *Decent Interval: An Insider's Account of Saigon's Indecent End, Told by the CIA's Chief Strategy Analyst in Vietnam* (New York: Random House, 1977).

69. The "Triangle Papers" appear regularly in English in New York, Paris, and Tokyo. No. 14, ed. by Richard Cooper, Karl Kaiser, and M. Kosaka, *Toward a Renovated International System* (1977), discussed by the commission in January 1977, does not propose a revolutionary solution to the problems of interdependence, though the co-author subsequently became Undersecretary of State for economic affairs. For the charges leveled against the Trilateral Commission, see the caricatural book by Maurice Goldring, *Démocratie croissance zéro* (Paris: Ed. Sociales, 1978), and the series of articles in *Le Monde Diplomatique*. A more balanced presentation is in *Die Zeit*, October 28, 1977.

70. This is one of the conclusions in Raymond Aron, *Plaidoyer pour l'Europe décadente* (Paris: Laffont, 1977), in which he vehemently criticizes the "self-destruction of the liberal democracies"—a self-destruction which results especially from exaggerated self-criticism as a response to charges of being imperialist.

71. Quoted in David Butler and Uwe Kitzinger, eds., *The 1975 Referendum* (London: Macmillan, 1976), p. 33. (Relations with the United States were not an important topic in this election campaign.)

72. F. de la Serre in *Les politiques extérieures dans la crise* [X, 15], p. 153. The quote from *The New Yorker* in her "L'Europe avec les Anglais," *Le Monde Diplomatique*, March 1978.

73. C. L. Sulzberger, "U.S. Is 'Loser' in Greek Vote," *International Herald Tribune*, November 26, 1977.

74. Lively analysis which is very hostile to Kissinger by Tad Szulc, "Lisbon and Washington: Behind the Portuguese Revolution," *Foreign Policy* (Winter 1975/76), pp. 3-62. See also the contribution by Juan J. Linz, "Spain and Portugal: Critical Choices," in *Western Europe* [XI, 60], pp. 237-96.

75. See the excellent analysis by Guy Hermet, *L'Espagne de Franco* (Paris: A. Colin, 1974).

76. Conclusions of Sergio Romano in his lively *Histoire de l'Italie du Risorgimento à nos jours* (Paris: Le Seuil, 1977), pp. 272-73. Interesting developments in the reports and discussions of the Instituto Affari Internazionali, *La politica estera italiana. Autonomia, interdependenza, integrazione e sicurezza* (Milan: Ed. di Communità, 1977); see there especially W. Galli, "Il

sistema politico italiano e la politica estera," pp. 89-102; E. di Nolfo, "Dieci anni di politica estera italiana," pp. 103-18; and F. Gozzano, "La Nato e i rapporti euroamericani nell'ultimo decennio," pp. 225-36. Some pointers in the summary presentation of the conference, *Italy and the Changing European Relationship*, ed. by Wilfrid L. Kohl and Gianfranco Pasquino (Bologna: Johns Hopkins University Center, 1977), and especially in the study by Michael H. Harrison, *Western Europe to the Extreme Left: Implications for Atlantic Relations* (*ibid.*, 1977).

77. Examples of such appeals in two 1977 speeches by Berlinguer, *Austerità, occasione per trasformare l'Italia* (Rome: Ed. Riuniti, 1977). Texts by Berlinguer put together by Antonio Tato: *La Questione Comunista, 1969-1975*, 2 vols. (*ibid.*, 1975); and *La politica internazionale dei comunisti italiani, 1975-1976* (*ibid.*, 1976). (These texts contain little on Italian-American relations.) Critical reply by Luigi Preti, *Il compromesso storico. Una problema che divide gli Italiani* (Milan: Rosconi, 1975); see especially pp. 101-3 on the import of the American decline and pp. 231-32 on the consequences of the foreign policy. Good retrospective in Donald L. M. Blackner, "Continuity and Change in Postwar Italian Communism" in *Communism in Italy and France*, ed. by D. Blackner and S. Tarrow (Princeton, N.J.: Princeton University Press, 1975), pp. 21-68.

78. See the explanation of his position in his articles, especially *Die Zeit*, May 21, 1976, and *Le Monde*, February 18, 1977.

79. Complete text in *Les P. C. espagnol, français et italien face au pouvoir*. Introduction, translation, and notes by Mariangela Bosi and Hugues Portelli (Paris: Ch. Bourgeois, 1976), pp. 30-36.

80. I quote, as always in the case of parliamentary debates, from the *Journal Officiel* (June 16, 1977, pp. 3807, 3809).

81. Most of the more recent publications deal very critically with relations with the United States. Claude Bourdet, *L'Europe truquée. Supranationalité. Pacte atlantique. Force de frappe* (Paris: Seghers, 1977), is at least tendentious (written in the name of a wholly Socialist, i.e., anti–Social Democratic, Europe); Jean-Marie Benoist, *Pavane pour une Europe défunte* (Paris: Hallier, 1976), is downright ridiculous (see the harsh but accurate critique by Raymond Aron, *Plaidoyer* . . . [XI, 70], pp. 450-54). The aggressiveness is more pronounced in the pamphlet by José Fralon, *L'Europe c'est fini* (Paris: Calmann-Lévy, 1975) (Chap. 8, "Les Etats-Unis, dixième 'européen' ") than in the important book of the former commission member and later ambassador and Secretary of State Jean-François Deniau, *L'Europe interdite* (Paris: Le Seuil, 1977) (Chap. 10, "Etats-Unis/Europe ou mésalliance"). The argument is more inconsistent in Yann de L'Ecotais, *L'Europe sabotée* (Brussels: Rossel, 1976) (Chap. 11, "L'hypothèque américaine") than in the positive, balanced, slightly utopian perspective of the Socialist historian Jacques Huntzinger, *Europes* (Paris: Ramsey, 1977) (Chap 5, "Le camp de la liberté").

82. Raymond Aron, "Les ambiguïtés de l'interdépendance," in *Le combat pour la solidarité alliée dans un monde interdépendant* (Paris: Assoc. du Traité Atlantique, 1977), pp. 5-20.

83. "Notre politique étrangère et le fait américain," *Exchanges et Projets*,

II, 1976. Theoretically more developed reflections in the studies by George Lichtheim, *De l'impérialisme* (Paris: Calmann-Lévy, 1972), and especially Benjamin J. Cohen, *The Question of Imperialism: The Political Economy of Dominance and Dependence* (New York: Basic Books, 1973). But one may disregard the not very original reflections by Gerhard Mally, *Interdependence: The European-American Connection in the Global Context* (Lexington, Mass.: D. C. Heath, 1976).

84. This was the answer of the economist Henri Guitton to a poll: "What does economic independence mean today?" *Le Figaro*, November 29, 1975. But see the very interesting collaborative study of the Institut Charles de Gaulle, *Les conditions de l'indépendance dans le monde moderne* (Paris: Cujas, 1977), especially the introductory remarks by Raymond Barre, pp. 317-20, and the study by Jean Charlot, "Les élites et les masses devant l'indépendance nationale d'après les enquêtes d'opinion," pp. 39-50.

85. Not everything is irrelevant in the outburst of Henri Gobard, *L'aliénation linguistique. Analyse tétraglossique*, preface by Gilles Deleuze (Paris: Flammarion, 1976).

86. Pierre Daninos, *Les nouveaux carnets du Major Thompson* (Paris: Livre de Poche, 1975), pp. 59-65. But see the attack by Jean-Francois Revel in his successful book which subscribes to other myths: *Neither Marx nor Jesus* (New York: Dell, 1974).

87. *Télérama*, April 16, 1977; *La Vie Catholique*, April 5, 1977.

88. SOFRES. *Les Français et les principaux changements survenus dans le monde depuis la fin de la deuxième guerre mondiale*, May 1975; IFOP poll in *Le Point*, May 17, 1976.

89. Presse- und Informationsamt des Landes Berlin: *Vorbild Amerika. Auf den Gebieten Schule, Erwachsenenbildung und Bibliothek* (Berliner Forum, 1976/6).

90. *Allensbacher Jahrbuch für Demoskopie*, ed. by E. Noelle-Neumann (Munich: Molden), pp. 280-81 (1976) and 134-35 (1977).

91. See the analysis by Betty Falkenberg, "Strohhalme im Wind," in *Verwöhnt in alle Ewigkeit? Kritischer Dialog über Gegenwart und Zukunft Amerikas und Deutschlands*, ed. by Werner Höfer (Düsseldorf: Econ, 1976), p. 142. The best political survey of German-American relations is probably Uwe Nerlich, "Entwicklungsstrukturen im deutsch-amerikanischen Verhältnis," in *Amerika und Westeuropa* [XI, 7], pp. 330-60.

INDEX OF NAMES

ABOUT THE AUTHOR

Alfred Grosser has been called an "acerbic and lucid analyst of French public life and diplomacy" (Stanley Hoffmann, Harvard University) and "the emperor of West German studies in Europe" (*The New York Review of Books*). Author of over a dozen books, political columnist for *Le Monde*, TV commentator, and contributor to *Foreign Affairs, Foreign Policy* and many anthologies, Dr. Grosser is professor of political science at the Institut d'études politiques and director of the graduate program at the Fondation nationale des sciences politiques, Paris. He has also lectured and taught at many American universities, including Harvard, Stanford, the University of Illinois, and Johns Hopkins. In 1975 he received the German Peace Prize for his mediating activities between the French and the Germans, and between Europeans and people of other continents.